Calm in the Face of the Storm

Spiritual Daily Practice for the Peacemaker

Nan Waller Burnett

Devenio Restituo Pacis Publishers

DRP Publishers

Devenio Restituo Pacis

Manufactured in the United States of America
Published by Devenio Restituo Pacis Publishers

For inquiries contact:
Devenio Restituo Pacis Publishers
DRP
1746 Cole Boulevard
Building 21, Suite 295
Golden, CO 80401
303-273-0459
www.calminthefaceofthestorm.com
info@calminthefaceofthestorm.com

Artwork by David Grojean www.grojeanstudio.com

Cover design and layout by Erin Zimmer www.designer-editor.com

Library of Congress Cataloging-in-Publication Data
    Calm in the face of the storm: spiritual daily practice for the peacemaker
        Burnett, Nan Waller. 1952-
           p. cm.
        CIP Number 2007934657
1. Spirituality – Meditations 2. Self-help 3. Psychology – Dispute Resolution - Law
             I. Title
        10 9 8 7 6 5 4 3 2 1
        ISBN 978-0-615-15533-3

To my children
Hilary, Austin, and Taylor

and

for Alan

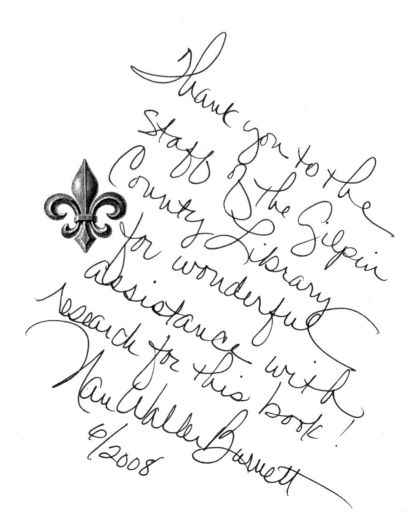

Thank you to the
Staff of the Gilpin
County Library
for wonderful
assistance with
research for this book!
Nan Waller Burnett
6/2008

There are some things learned best in calm, and some in storm.

Willa Cather

Contents

Daily Entries

Introduction

The most beautiful experience we can have is the mysterious. It is the
fundamental emotion which stands at the cradle of true art and true science.
He to whom this emotion is a stranger, who can no longer pause to wonder
and stand rapt in awe, is as good as dead: his eyes are closed.

Albert Einstein

The Mystery: A Daily Practice

Uncovering the mysterious is a daily quest for the peacemaker. The mission to discover the mystery requires the training of one's mind in order to see that which cannot be seen. Unfortunately, as a result of one's practice, a residual effect of standing within the vortex of the storm of conflict is the reduced capacity for living one's own life. I have written this book of meditations and reflections as a spiritual-path guidebook for daily use. Adherence to a daily path ensures commitment to one's mind, health, and spirit. Research shows that the practice of taking twenty minutes for oneself every day increases general health and productivity. I believe it also helps create inner peace, the ability to make a difference at work, and the opportunity to foster peace on the planet, one day at a time.

Each day sets forth a theme, a short discussion of the topic, an introduction to a meditation, and a suggestion for a journaling exercise. Meditation is a powerful tool to access your creative and spiritual energy. The meditation exercises offer a concept to ponder related to the day's theme, as an entry point to the stillness; but the goal of meditation is always to just "be" and to be willing to experience inner peace. The suggestions are simply a starting place to the inner journey. Journaling is a wonderful way to record your personal progress. On days when bearing the journey seems unattainable, you can leaf back through the pages of the recorded adventure to prove not only your success throughout the year, but also your important commitment to renewal and inner peace.

Working for inner peace, peace for the planet, and transformation in relationships has been my passion for many years. I have not, however, been able to sustain that level of peace personally, without intentionally making inner peace a priority. In the course of working with conflict every day, I found that I had chosen isolation. I felt trampled and deprived of energy on the weekends. I noticed my life becoming increasingly negative and pain-ridden. I was swimming in the problem-saturated ocean of my clients. In talking with other practitioners, I discovered that I was not alone.

This book is dedicated to my late business partner, Alan Levin, who, in 2002, lovingly but firmly insisted that I take good care of myself every day by connecting to my soul, my inner core, thereby providing solace for my wounded heart. We formed a spiritual-path group and chose a different daily spiritual-path book every year. We supported each other on the journey by taking personal retreats. Sharing the journey with a group was most helpful in making the commitment to keep growing and to share in support of one another. When I made this very important change in my life, my practice began to soar. Together, Alan and I undertook the development and facilitation of retreats for flight-crew members experiencing post trauma from 9/11. As a result of this journey of self-care, I experienced immediate and measurable differences in my practice. I noticed an increase in my ability to effect change and transformation in the relationships of those in conflict who were showing up at my table. Also evident was a boost in my daily energy and productivity. My perceptions of the world became more positive and hopeful. I sailed my ship back to the safe harbor of comfort every night and was unafraid to set sail in the morning to weather the storms of life before me. Alan's words still resonate with me: "Nan, you only need to be willing. Your willingness will be enough for you to receive whatever inspiration you need to be effective in your work and your life."

The Discovery: My Personal Path

As a mid-century baby at the tail end of the boom, I suspect that my life path has been similar to that of many of my colleagues. I do finally understand, however, that my particular set of qualities is rare. My strands of DNA are woven from the lineage of powerful matriarchs. I was fortunate enough to have three wonderful, strong, Southern grande dames for models while growing up in the French-Catholic South of Baton Rouge, Louisiana. Witnessing them through youthful eyes cultivated the permission I needed for my own growth and for that of the progeny of the future. I learned how to provide a warm, loving, aromatic home and other maternal wizardries from my mother, Mary Nell. I learned from my regal Aunt Hilda (no one ever told her she was not royalty) how to host a dinner party for eighteen and how to embody style, class, and grace while wearing a simple black dress from the Sears catalogue with a fur—don't forget the pearls! Brilliant Aunt Corinne, my chief sage, was an exceptional woman of many talents. An engineer in mind, an artist with heart, a Bohemian, and a lifelong learner, she has been an inspiration to me my entire life. Born a century before her time, she served as my mentor and told me often and without hesitation that I could do anything I wanted to do. I have a cherished photograph of her in the field at Standard Oil's Baton Rouge Refinery, holding a clipboard, wearing pants, a hard hat, and jack boots. The year was 1943. What an inspiration! Having said that, I also felt I was born in an unfamiliar "cabbage patch." My high school years in the 1960s were spent witnessing the turbulent times of integration in the South, and it was not pretty. Thankfully, the South did continue to evolve; but I had known early on that I did not want to raise my children to know a line of color and migrated to Colorado by 1970.

Although I was always in search of meaning and purpose in my life, I languished as a rudderless ship in the formidable decades of my development until my professional mentor and valued friend, Verna Salmon, grabbed me by the collar and shook me until I woke up. My mid-30s ahead of me, I decided that I had wasted enough time. This journey into conflict resolution has not been of my choosing, but one of simply taking the next step that lay in front of me. I now recognize that I was answering an appeal from a higher source and that I knew that the fearlessness present in my personality would be useful—and necessary—as a conflict practitioner. This work is not for the faint of heart!

Great books have sung to my soul along the way. I am inspired by the classical philosophers, Epictetus, Aristotle, Plato, Plotinus, Heraclitus, and my personal favorite, Marcus Aurelius. Lao-Tzu, Thich Nhat Hanh, Thomas Moore, Joseph Campbell, James Hillman, and Ralph Waldo

Emerson provide resonance to my weary ears when I am down. I am charmed and feel hopefulness when I read the words of the Dalai Lama and enthralled by Ken Wilber's unbelievable brain. Scientists Albert Einstein, Max Planck, Danah Zohar, and Fritjof Capra provided my foray into the physical sciences after forty years of education. I am fascinated by the intersection of quantum physics and spiritual energy as it informs human evolution. Although I was a devotee of the "recovery from codependency movement" in the 1980s, a personal, authentic, daily excavation path of my interior began in earnest during the 1990s with Sarah Ban Breathnach's *Simple Abundance*, followed by all the work, every volume, of the prolific Wayne Dyer, Marianne Williamson, and Joan Borysenko. I found the simplicity of *The Work* of Byron Katie, in *Loving What Is*, to be immediately applicable to brief interventions in my own life as well as in the lives of clients. Julia Cameron's *The Artist's Way* was such a delight of hilarity and reality, it allowed me to remember deep in my bones that God has a sense of humor and to also know that being artistic was actually possible for me!

I am an unlikely author of this subject; neither piety nor outward displays of reverence are behaviors of mine. If I had to choose a word to describe my involvement in religion or things of a spiritual nature, I would say "irreverent" is much closer to the truth. I have found kindred souls in all faiths. I was introduced to *A Course in Miracles* at the turn of this century. The musings that follow on these pages are rooted in that tolerant, open philosophy of acceptance, redirection of negativity in thought, and the choice for inner peace.

I began thinking more deeply about the future of the field of conflict resolution as seminal works by some of the masters of our discipline, Kenneth Cloke, John Paul Lederach, Daniel Bowling, David Hoffman, Bernard Mayer, Michelle LeBaron among them, began to find their way to the bookshelves and into my soul. I so honor these authors for having the courage to write them. In reading Cloke's, *Mediating Dangerously*, I felt validated, that there was at least one other soul traveling the same road. I became more encouraged about the direction of the field as I read the unification theories of conflict resolution coming together in the minds of these great teachers. This was important to me because my particular learning path is through conceptual analysis and theoretical foundation. I have strong opinions about the practice of training peacemakers and conflict professionals to be "step-followers." We need to be training the practitioner to be reflective, to understand theory and to bring a more personal holistic force to the table.

I felt the need to design a daily ritual of practice for the care of the valiant soul who agrees to sit at the table of resolution and peacemaking—a template to form a ritual of daily introspection for the working life. I feel that passion and compassion are common denominators among those who are called to this work. As this eclectic mixture of philosophy, psychology, science, and spirituality poured onto the pages, I was moved by a force greater than I to press forward regardless of the road blocks I encountered, such as scarcity of time, or how inept I felt as a scribe of such work. This book is meant to provide a platform for daily mindfulness: a chance for you to question how you live and how you practice, a chance to care for your soul, and most important, a reason to sit quietly and just be still.

A deeper level of understanding in the engagement of conflict is a welcomed place for the weary conflict practitioner. The topical selections in this book are not simply focused on the positive. Conflict engagement and denial go hand in hand, both in the client and in the practitioner. We need to feel more comfortable with extreme emotion. Toward that end, in addition to uplifting entries, I have brought forth some painful subjects for review. As Jung noted, "the shadow self" follows the human condition and must be explored.

Lately, I have witnessed conflict professionals, regardless of discipline; move in droves toward the center of transformation of peace and conflict and away from the dialogue of yesterday, which usually involved arguing positions of polarity on how the field should be practiced and who should be allowed to practice. Perhaps you will not find new information between the pages of this daily book of reflections. What you will find, however, is intention and a selection of inspirations that is my own concoction. I have also noticed that many of my colleagues are moving in the same direction of personal renewal and spirituality. That is *no* mistake. I recognize them when I meet them. I have developed deep and rich friendships with these fellow travelers since this odyssey began. In reading about this journey of *my* personal discoveries, you may recognize that it mirrors your own, or maybe reading these thoughts of mine will spark a new adventure for you. One thing is certain: if you adhere to the ritual regularity of putting yourself first every morning, your life, as well as your practice, will be changed. It will become your unique journey and not mine.

This book is meant to live on the bedside table and to be read only one topic at a time. It is a touchstone, a reminder to reflect, to invite stillness and mindfulness, to feel your feelings, to prompt you to schedule fun, to laugh, and to bolster your boundaries each and every day. When I first undertook the assignment of maintaining my own daily path, I expected the task to be laborious. It proved to be the most important fifteen minutes I spent every day. Since then, I have been able to maintain sanity and strength. My hope is that it will provide the same for you.

A few words about the term "spirituality." I welcome all people on their path to their source, the inner journey, whatever that means for them. Some think that spirituality is synonymous with religion, but one's spirit has nothing to do with religion. Religion is a collective choice, while spirit is the essence of each person, as well as an individual relationship with your higher power. For me, the simple definition of spirituality is the experience I feel when connected to my higher power or my inner core. In that awareness, I find love and the support of a power greater than I. Throughout the ages, man has tried to apply human opinion and influence on heavenly things, and I don't purport to have any special information for anyone other than myself. My opinions are my own. Each soul finds its own way and, for me, that is the beauty of it. I have tried to teach my children to be tolerant and respectful of others and their beliefs. In the text of this book, I may use the term God, Heavenly Father, Source, or Higher Power, while you, the reader, may prefer Jesus, Buddha, Mohammed, Yahweh, Zoroaster, She, or Ethos. My intention is to provide a welcoming dialogue for all seekers, with no exclusions. If your work is in human relationships, peace, conflict, or conciliation, with patients, employees, or citizens—or you simply want peace on the planet—this book is meant for you.

> *May all who agree to enter this daily ritual*
> *Find joy, freedom, safety*
> *A realization of their true nature and peace.*
> *And let it begin with me.*
>
> Adapted from a Unity prayer

Meditation

Your first step…Don't make it a big deal. You can't get this wrong. Just do it!

*Thinking you are unable to meditate is a little like thinking you
are unable to breathe, or to concentrate or relax.*

Jon Kabat-Zinn

In his book *Wherever You Go There You Are,* Jon Kabat-Zinn noted that often people do not think they can meditate, that somehow they are not doing it right. He suggested that meditation is neither a "special state" nor a certain feeling, but an "emptying of the mind." A starting place is to simply agree to meet your mind where it is and observe your thoughts floating across the logical brain. You cannot meditate incorrectly. There is no "place" to go. It only involves the intention to practice it every day, the promise to yourself to capture those few moments of timelessness every morning. Similar to the process in mediation, the process in meditation will take care of the rest.

Mark Thornton, in *Meditation in a New York Minute,* asks the listener to drop the expectation that meditation should look a certain way. You need no paraphernalia, no special room, no bells, no candles; you don't even have to be sitting. The choice of those accouterments may enhance your experience but are not necessary. You can meditate in your chair at the office before clients arrive, take a walk around the building, or listen to soothing music in the car on the way to work. Just remember to breathe deeply and with fullness. I have noticed that it is easier for me to train my thoughts if I begin meditation with a certain theme of concentration and then let my mind fall away into silence. In my work leading groups in therapy, I found that the first step through the door of change was commitment to oneself. This is much harder to do than it sounds, and I found that, once self-permission was given, the journey was 50% complete.

Here is one suggestion for structured meditation adapted from Tibetan Buddhism:

1. Choose a quiet place.
2. Create a sacred space.
3. Sit comfortably, your posture straight but not rigid.
4. Rest your hands on your lap in an open position.
5. Gaze down with your eyelids half-closed, or if you prefer, fully closed.
6. In the stillness, hear the sounds, feel your body, notice your breathing.
7. Focus your attention on the incoming and outgoing breath.
8. When your mind begins to wander, simply notice where it takes you.
9. With gentle respect for your process, refocus your attention on your breath.
10. In the present moment, allow your mind to flow and observe.
11. Refocus on your breath.

Start with ten minutes every day. You should try to work up to twenty minutes if you have the time. Remember that meditation can be practiced anywhere, anytime.

Journaling

Journaling can seem too time-consuming. Yet, everyone can write two lines of free-flowing internal dialogue in a journal. You may find that you "purge the poison" of the brain and discover your artistry through those pages of prose. Even if you only record two lines of linear logic, it is immeasurably helpful in the end. Journaling will serve as the evidence of your success in self-care for the coming year. Here is one suggestion for journaling adapted from *The Artist's Way*, by Julia Cameron:

1. After meditation, take your pen in hand and let the words pour onto the sheet.

2. Write whatever your mind presents to you. No one else will read it.

3. Don't think about how it is coming onto the paper. Just flow, just be, and just write.

4. Write two lines if that is all you can do or have the time to do.

5. When the page is full, stop writing.

6. Do this daily for the journey throughout the year. The journal will serve as your personal history. Your life and your practice will be transformed.

Thank You

Without the devotion and professionalism of my book angels, I would never have taken this to press. Thanks to: Erin Zimmer for her talented design, clarity of thought on presentation, and being a gifted creative editor who turned this streaming book into an understandable text; Marj Hahne, editor, for her talent and clarity in the first half of the book; Melinda Eskridge and Claire Beland for supporting me emotionally and technically with their assistance in ordering and editing the edits; Arlene Brownell and Joan McWilliams for their willingness to share their journeys with me; and, Laurie Mulhouser and Dana Miller for supporting me in listening to the voice inside that wanted to be heard.

I would like to give a special note of thanks to artistic genius and my dear friend, David Grojean (www.GrojeanStudio.com). David shares my values and was willing to share his talent on this project. His vision in capturing the essence of this work was astounding and I am blessed to have him on my path.

I want to give thanks and appreciation to those kindred souls who have been trailblazers in the field, those who have traveled my path, and those who have been in my thoughts while writing this book. Thanks for your words, your support, your encouragement, and your tireless work on my behalf and your willingness to be present:

In memoriam, Alan Levin and Corinne Voorhies Smith.

Bob Burnett, Judy Kersch, Suzy Nystrom, Verna Salmon, Charlie Turnbo, Miles Davies, Joe McMahon, Lili Zohar, Robin Amadei, Sally Ortner, Michael Aloi, Louise Phipps Senft, Cristina Cullens, Joe Gillick, Kristin Thompson, Terri Harrington, Jeannie Hallett, Marilyn MacDonald, Tammy Long, Alexis Namaste, Louise Wildee, Lois Tilley, Diana Ward Collins, Ken Sullivan, Mary Margaret Golten, Christine Coates, Michael Spangle, Nanette Winston, Ken Cloke, Joan Goldsmith, Erica Ariel Fox, Daniel Bowling, and John Paul Lederach. I have a very maternal nature and I understood early on that my children were extraordinary individuals. Everything I have accomplished, I have done with intention, to trailblaze for Hilary, Austin, and Taylor.

> *Out beyond ideas of wrongdoing and rightdoing,*
> *there is a field. I'll meet you there.*
> *When the soul lies down in that grass,*
> *the world is too full to talk about.*
>
> Rumi

    Together we can change the world. We can teach the citizens of the planet the skills to respectfully engage in conflict. Together we can support practitioners to become fully present at tables across the world. Together we can be the peace, one conflict at a time. Thank you for sharing this work with me.

Nan Waller Burnett
September 2006
Golden, CO

The Journey

Our life's journey of self-discovery is not a straight-line rise from one level of consciousness to another. Instead, it is a series of steep climbs and flat plateaus, then further climbs. Even though we all approach the journey from different directions, certain of the journey's characteristics are common to all of us.

Stuart Wilde

As we begin to open up to new awareness and ponder concepts greater than our own ego, we enter a realm of understanding, a collective pool of untapped energy. Our journey down this positive path exceeds mere observation and elevates us to the post of transformer in situations of conflict. You already possess all that is needed for this journey. You only need to honor your path and give yourself permission to take the trip. This journey is about locating those inner resources that are already present. It is about embracing the not-knowing of it all. You drop the need to be an expert on anything other than the willingness to stand in the energy of the universe and drink from the well of possibilities. The universe will expand your awareness and you will have a grateful heart. Offer possibilities for your clients' lives and also for your own life.

A journey of a thousand miles begins with one step.

Lao Tzu, *Tao Te Ching*

Meditate today on the word "adventure." Sit in the quiet of the dawn and allow your breath to gently escape, to course from the depth of the abdomen through the blood vessels—the channels of life—and easily slip from the nostrils. Just breathe the breath of peace. Allow your thoughts to center on the adventure you are about to embark on.

Write in your journal about what the journey means to you in the coming year. Do you feel anxious, excited, apprehensive, joyful? What do you intend to bring with you on your journey?

Self-Care

In God's hand is the soul of every living thing and the breath of all humankind.

Job 12:10

The first step toward a new tomorrow is to stay in the present moment. This is where the opportunity for personal peace and happiness resides. We cannot work with the history of yesterday. We cannot find joy in the planning of tomorrow. For me, care of the self begins with care of the soul. Permission can only be granted by me for the intention of caring for me. The threat of depletion of my resources and spirit looms large against my soul each day that I agree to stand in the face of negative energy. I have found that if I do not honor my spirit first, I cannot continue in the work to assist others with their personal peace. I have discovered that I must hold self-care as a top priority for the successful continuation of my passionate work.

Meditate today on the word "energy." As you agree to become silent this morning and listen to your spirit, agree to give yourself permission to put your energy and your needs first in the day, so that you may be strengthened in your ability to be present for the parties in mediation.

Write in your journal about your plan for care of the self. List the things that you can commit to today that will embrace, uplift, and care for you. What are three commitments you can make to yourself today and for the rest of the year? Design a path for the New Year.

Perception

If the doors of perception were cleansed every thing would appear to man as it is: infinite.
For man has closed himself up, till he sees all things thro' narrow chinks of his cavern.
William Blake, "The Marriage of Heaven and Hell"

It is important for us, in our role as practitioners, to educate our clients about the realities of perception. Through gentle questioning, it is often possible to demonstrate to clients that the truth is *their* truth, allowing the possibility of a shift from positions to opportunities. It is also important to remember that we make subjective interpretations about our own reality. Perception is choosing what we want to see, who we want ourselves to be, and the world we paint with our story. Knowing that we can change what we believe helps others change what they believe.

Meditate today on the word "perception." What are your unchanging truths? What are the truths you are unsure of? As you settle into your breath, fill the synapses of your brain with the breath of fresh air that will cleanse the lenses of perception.

Write about one issue in your life that you want to view with new eyes.

Peace

*Many who work for peace are not at peace... To preserve peace, our hearts
must be at peace with the world, with our brothers and our sisters. When
we try to overcome evil with evil, we are not working for peace.*

Thich Nhat Hanh, *Love in Action*

As peacemakers and the engagers of conflict dialogue, we must be conscious of how our unsettled energy can affect the parties at the table. In the preparation of the day, review the areas of your life that are not peaceful. Each day try to make peace with yourself. Forgive yourself for harboring unmerciful thoughts for others, and if others are not peaceful with you, send them love and light. Tapping into the vastness of universal energy, you can create personal peace and peace in your practice.

*Peace comes within the souls of men
When they realize their oneness with the universe.*

Black Elk, Medicine Man, Ogallala Sioux Nation

Meditate upon this topic, beginning with "As I float in the warm light of comfort, I send inner peace and comfort to all those who have a need.

Write about any thoughts about peace that arise in meditation. What does peace feel like to you? How do you know you are peaceful?

Authenticity

The most exhausting thing you can do is to be inauthentic.

Anne Morrow Lindbergh, *Gift from the Sea*

Genuineness is a quality I am always seeking in others. Authenticity is an acceptance of personal humanness, a willingness to share, a realization that all beings have value, a thirst for discovery, and comfort in who they are. I have noticed that I have an alarm that sounds a warning when I perceive in-authenticity approaching. My reaction comes from the fact that *was* inauthentic in my early years. Looking back, I was a *human acting*, rather than a human being and I found myself looking to others to see how I should behave. I have since forgiven myself, as I now realize that it is part and parcel of normal early adult development. As Lindbergh notes in the quote above, it was exhausting working to keep the mask in place. As I go forward into the second part of my life, I notice that I no longer judge others for in-authenticity; I just move on. I continue my personal trajectory, looking for members of my particular tribe who are looking for me. I reached a point in my life when it was simply too exhausting to be inauthentic. Are there remnants of a mask across your persona? Is your ego still camouflaged with pretense? Drop the façade of pretense and feel the freedom in authenticity.

Meditation today should begin with the word "inauthentic." Quietly agree to look into the corners of your mind for evidence of the pretense. Breathe deeply in release of those disguises and reveal the beauty of the authentic you.

Write down one area of denial that you may still hold in the darkness away from your awareness. Go beyond the disguise and lift the veil to the authentic you. What is one way that you can be more authentic today?

Practice

It is a fundamental error to assume that moving into higher states of spiritual development is easy.... Only through long-term disciplines can you make the experiences stable, permanent structures of consciousness. It is very hard work. The truth is that transforming oneself is a long, laborious, painful process.

Ken Wilber, *What Really Matters*

When I first read Ken Wilber, I was completely in awe of his clarity and ability to impart the vast depth of his studied knowledge to his readers. Ken Wilber is the true philosopher of our time. His focus has been much the same as Aristotle's - a general categorization of thought, though on a much deeper level. He has an uncanny way of quickly drawing a line from the collective query to an answer. While an extreme pragmatist, he operates from a deep spiritual perspective in his view of the world. I think this is why I am drawn to his work. He recognizes that reaching the plane of inner peace is no different from climbing a mountain. It is through the journey that peace becomes the new operating system. We transit the highway of opportunity to replace thinking with being, doing with simple connection, and "getting there" with finding joy on the path. How can one develop spiritual intelligence? For me, adherence to the daily practice is the only way to invite existence in the present moment.

Begin your meditation today with practiced breathing. Breathe in the lifeline of sustenance, and breathe out the impatience of the quest. Breathe in the anticipation of finding gifts on the journey; breathe out the deep tension of apprehension.

How can you enhance your personal practice of self-care? In what ways have you already begun to change your habits of the day?

Artistry

Inside you there's an artist you don't know about. Say yes quickly, if you
know, if you've known it from before the beginning of the universe.

Rumi, "Say Yes Quickly"

The reason you were drawn to this work was to leave your own mark. Each time you agree to become receptive to inspiration, to trust your instincts, or to respect your inner voice, you are "in spirit" and "inspired." We are all unique in our expression of humanness. In a workshop with Michael Lang and Allison Taylor about artistry in practice, I felt overwhelming relief at the suggestion to reward ourselves with the permission to be creative and artistic in our practice of conflict engagement. This was at a time when the powers presiding over the field were in dialogue about the "proper" way to practice as a practitioner. I am grateful for that experience and now each day, I look for ways in which I can exercise artistry in my practice. Today, give yourself permission to be creative in life.

Meditate today on the word "artistry." Breathe in the creative air of promise, and breathe out the stale air of yesterday's inventory or failures. Breathe in the ease of connection to creativity, and breathe out the fear of getting it wrong.

Write a few lines today about artistry. What evidence do you already have of artistry in your practice? How are you artistic in your daily life? Affirm your creative nature.

Role of the Practitioner of Peace

The purpose of poetry is to remind us
how difficult it is to remain just one person,
for our house is open, there are no keys in the doors,
and invisible guests come in and out at will.

Czeslaw Milosz, "Ars Poetica?"

In our daily practice, we wear many hats. It takes an artist to change them so quickly that no one notices. How fluid a practitioner must remain to be able to flow with the needs of the client. When Dr. John Paul Lederach spoke to a group of practitioners I once hosted on retreat, he shared the poetry of his heart: haiku. A simple and powerful form of poetry, haiku allows him to share much more with much less. He uses haiku as a metaphor for the conflict, stringing together phrases woven from intakes with various groups in his work. In this way, his artistry as a peacebuilder is infused with a more powerful message.

Begin your meditation with "In the many rooms of my mind sit the characters of my practice, and as I become still, I see myself floating through the doors. I notice my comforter, my expert, my creative intelligence, my listener, and my passion. Today, I embrace all my characters and value them for their contribution to the whole of my practice."

Ponder for a moment how many characters you house in your mind. Journal today about the many roles you must assume during the course of working with your clients; see if you can identify them by character.

Solace in Nature

Every spirit builds itself a house, and beyond its house a world, and
beyond its world a heaven. Know then that world exists for you.

Ralph Waldo Emerson, *Nature*

What is more pleasing to the soul than to walk in the clear, crisp air of the mountains, through a solitary grove of aspen on the edge of a lapping glacial lake; or to meditate upon violet-blue dragonflies as they skim the surface of the water? This week, allow yourself to be in the spirit of nature.

For today's meditation, imagine your hair flowing with a gentle alpine breeze, cool on your face as the sun warms your bones. Even if you cannot physically be there, you will be there in spirit. In the stillness, enjoy this verse from Japanese Zen philosophy:

Zazen on the Mountain
The birds have vanished down the sky.
Now the last cloud drains away.
We sit together, the mountains and me,
Until only the mountain remains.

Li Po

Journal about the sensations you experienced in your meditation.

Gratitude

*Gratitude unlocks the fullness of life. It turns what we have into enough, and more.
It turns denial into acceptance, chaos to order, confusion to clarity. It can turn a
meal into a feast, a house into a home, a stranger into a friend. Gratitude makes
sense of our past, brings peace for today, and creates a vision for tomorrow.*
                                                                    Melody Beattie

In my experience, I know that there is no surer path out of depression than keeping a record of the things I am grateful for. There are days when I can only manage to scribble down "I am grateful that I didn't yell at the children." But then there are those days when just directing my attention toward gratitude allows me to see the wonder of the blessings of my life. "I am grateful that I am healthy" or "I am grateful that my children are healthy" suddenly takes on a whole new light, and I can easily fill the page with gratitude. In a matter of seconds, my day becomes transformed, my clarity returns, and I am able to be present for my clients.

Meditate today on the word "gratitude." As you allow your body, tense from the apprehension of the day, to feel the ground beneath you, and as you release your breath from lungs constricted with tension, now focus instead on the gratitude you feel for the blessings in your life.

Write in your journal about the joyful reasons for gratitude that you discovered today in your meditation.

Creating a Sacred Space

You must have a room or a certain hour of the day...where you do not know what was in the morning paper...a place where you can simply experience and bring forth what you are, and what you might be...At first you may find nothing...But if you have a sacred place and use it, take advantage of it, something will happen.

Joseph Campbell, *The Power of Myth*

Carving out a corner of your house for the creation of a sacred connection is an empowering act. Claiming the stillness of the morning as your own initiates the quest for discovery. Embarked on before the business of your day begins, at a quiet time when you know you will not be disturbed, your journey toward the center allows a peaceful presence to enter the soul. By retreating to that personal sacred space, you generate the opportunity for connection. As Joseph Campbell suggested, to withdraw from the world for a few moments allows you to "bring forth what you are." To permit this period of sacred communion and to await creation of an idea allows discovery of the self. This space, carved out of the day, is essential to remaining whole. Though you do not know what will be brought forth, the circle of creation has been opened, and a channel for flowing genius has the opportunity to open up. Create your sacred space today and await its mystery.

Meditation today should begin with the phrase "create a sacred space." Breathe deeply into an image of creation; breathe out the not-knowing. Settle into the cadence of the creative breath.

Record in your journal the images you saw in your meditative state. List all the possible areas for the sacred space to be built in your world.

My bounty is as boundless as the sea,
My love as deep;
The more I give thee,
The more I have
For both are infinite.

William Shakespeare, *Romeo and Juliet*

When we love without fear and give freely of our heart, we are blessed beyond measure. When we choose to take the high road in life and offer our love and good wishes with abundance, without the thought of return, we are rewarded with limitless blessings. Both the giver of love and the receiver of love experience love more abundantly because that process invites the multiplication of good will all around. In his book *Beyond Neutrality: Confronting the Crisis in Conflict Resolution*, Bernie Mayer asks practitioners to explore ways to impact the engagement of conflict for good. How can we individually move peace forward on the planet? To love freely takes courage, intention, and action.

And though I have the gift of prophecy, and understand all mysteries, and all knowledge; and though I have faith, so that I could remove mountains, and not love, I am nothing.

Corinthians 13:4

Meditate today on the phrase "love freely." As you go to that place of peace in your mind, breathe in the warmth of the thought "I will love freely"; breathe out the fear of rejection.

Write in your journal about having the courage to love freely, without thought of return.

The Tao that can be told is not the eternal Tao.
The name that can be named is not the eternal name.
The nameless is the beginning of heaven and earth.
The named is the mother of ten thousand things.
Ever desireless, one can see the mystery.
Ever desiring, one can see the manifestations.
These two spring from the same source but differ in name; this appears as darkness.
Darkness within darkness.
The gate to all mystery.

Lao Tzu, *Tao Te Ching*

There are some mysteries of life that we will never understand—and perhaps it is not really necessary to understand them. However, there are certain mysteries that need to be unraveled, and the mystery of a journey may bring an excavation of the soul that creates clarity in life. The mystery is a vision that is truly your own. Embracing the mystery of it all can assist you in staying on your path throughout the year.

You could never arrive at the limits of your soul, no matter how
many roads you have traveled, so deep is its mystery.

Heraclitus

Today, meditate on "embracing the mystery." Bring to the forefront of your mind the mysterious path you have found yourself on. Breathe in the anticipation of the mystery, and breathe out the fear of not knowing. Settle into the comfort of a warm sun on your face, and release any tension that comes to your mind.

Write in your journal about your mystery today. Try to find words that paint a picture of your mystery so that you feel comfortable embracing it.

As our body is a part of the universe, so our soul is a part of the Soul of the universe....
Souls are responsive to one another because they all come from the same soul.

Plotinus

A sense of being at one with all has often come to me in the practice of meditation. Also, a great deal of healing has taken place in that act of trusting the stillness. The intimacy we crave with others, often elusive in the course of living, may be reconciled in the knowing of being one. As we come to terms with things as they are, we deepen our sense of compassion for ourselves and others.

For today's meditation, imagine yourself as a gently flowing stream pouring into a river of great energy. Breathe in the waters of oneness, and breathe out the merging of your waters with the source.

Journal about what images came to your mind during your meditation. What did tapping into the source of energy feel like? Could you feel that release? What came up for you when you read the phrase "being at one with all"?

There is only one journey. Going inside yourself.

Rainer Maria Rilke

Rilke identified the self as the next frontier of exploration for most of us at mid-life. After we have raised our young, after we have built our empire, after we have expended our energy swimming upstream through the rapids of life, a time for renewal is presented to us. It is our choice whether or not we take that journey. If we are critical of all that we have achieved or not achieved, the inner critic will rule the decision to renew or not. The quest for the Holy Grail is to find, at your core, that you are divine and to also understand that the quest ends in peace. I see empty souls wandering the planet all around me. They seem to either choose addiction or depression or both. I notice that many of them are ensnared in deeply conflicted relationships, and some show up at my table, at work and at home. With nothing to attach their bleeding parts to, no place feels like home and deep sadness and misery pervade their tortured souls. They live in regret, stuck in the past, or are wishing for a better 'thing' to fix their pain. These souls choose not to take the journey. If you are about to embark on the journey for the Holy Grail, know the quest quenches the thirst for inner peace. Embark on the journey with open eyes, listening ears, a loving heart, and forgiveness of your young spirit. We are all on this one journey together.

Meditation today should begin with the word "quest." Seek the quiet place. Agree to beckon the call of inquiry. Breathe deeply into the question and breathe out the fog of the misty journey through life.

Write down the questions that came to you in meditation. Can you find solutions in the inquiry?

> *To live in this world*
> *You must be able to do three things:*
> *To love what is mortal;*
> *To hold it*
> *Against your bones knowing*
> *Your own life depends on it;*
> *And, when the time comes to let it go,*
> *To let it go.*
>
> Mary Oliver, "In Blackwater Woods"

Mary Oliver is one of my new favorite poets. I was first introduced to her work in a seminar I took with Joan Borysenko and Oriah Mountain Dreamer in 2003. So profound are her words, and to me, so representative of reality. Letting go is the hardest part, I think. I believe one's happiness depends on the ability to let loved ones, familiar habits, a long-held job, or passages of life drift into memory and to embrace the new ones.

Meditate today on the phrase "living in this world." Sit in the calm of the morning, and breathe in the crisp air of a new day; breathe out the attachment to the history of yesterday. Observe your mind as you center on the word "impermanence."

Write in your journal about fear. What are you most afraid of losing? What are you most willing to let pass through the door? What images and thoughts came to your mind in your meditation as you contemplated the journey of living in this world?

Bravery

Make Me Brave for Life

God, make me brave for life: oh, braver than this.
Let me straighten after pain, as a tree straightens after the rain,
Shining and lovely again.
God, make me brave for life; much braver than this.
As the blown grass lifts, let me rise
From sorrow with quiet eyes,
Knowing Thy way is wise.
God, make me brave, life brings
Such blinding things.
Help me to keep my sight;
Help me to see aright
That out of dark comes light.

Grace Nowell Crowell

No one escapes the certain pain that comes with living. It takes courage to weather the storm. Just when we feel we have climbed the mountain, life has a way of showing us the new horizon. One thing that meditation allows is the connection to our higher power every day, the opportunity to tap into a collective re-energizing source that bolsters our courage and reinforces our ability to weather the storm of the day, to become brave each and every day. I truly believe that we are never alone. Today, consider the ways in which you feel afraid and perhaps alone. Reconsider those issues as opportunities for growth.

As you sink into your body and feel your breath deep in your lungs, focus on the word "bravery." When does the mountain seem too high? Feel courage in your inhale and release fear in your exhale.

Journal about bravery. List all the ways that you feel that you are brave. Take an inventory of those positive attributes that make one resilient.

Instead of imposing your will on every situation…focus on including everyone else, and just that little adjustment of attitude gives you the space to understand where and who you are.

Wynton Marsalis

A musician perfects the fine art of listening to notes with a sense of mystery, the tone of the instrument, the anticipation of the entry, the promise of crescendo. As peacemakers, we become the maestros of the orchestra as the parties dance the conflict at our table. Listening is our highway to solutions, our treasure hunt for answers to the validation of their souls. A practitioner who can tap into the language, the underlying cries for help of one to another, has the best capability to assist them on their path out of pain and into understanding. If we are unable to be attentive enough to truly hear their message, are we imposing our own will onto a conflict? As we listen with concentrated attention to every word we are told, we allow the revelation to be understood by others. Uncovered treasures are able to rise to the surface of the conflict before the heart of the attentive listener.

Meditate today on "listening", with heart, ears, eyes, and soul. Breathe in the attentive inquiry, and breathe out the confusion in your mind. Breathe in the willingness to hear your own wisdom this morning in preparation for a day of intentional listening; breathe out the clutter of the hurried mind. Become still and find the guidance you need to become truly present.

Write in your journal about listening with new ears. In the past, when did you notice that you had become inattentive in mediation sessions? When did you notice complete attention in sessions? Have you noticed that when you are focused, you are more effective? In what ways can you become a better, deeper listener?

*Many of us today experience creative silence. Not the hush of the heart necessary
to bring forth the unexpressed from Spirit, but the creative silence brought about
by circumstances we feel are beyond our control: lack of time, and/or lack
of space or a place to create. Perhaps we also suffer from a lack of clarity, a
failure to realize how necessary it is to nurture our sacred creativity daily.*

Sarah Ban Breathnach, *Simple Abundance*

Sarah Ban Breathnach fostered my first commitment to a spiritual path in her work *Simple Abundance*. A beautiful writer and poet, she warmed my heart with her words and gave me the confidence to stay connected to my heart throughout the year. Excavation of the soul, treasure hunts, and nurturing the self were all concepts that were new to me in the late 1980s as I read her book. In the end, I left that journey determined to live my life differently. Clarity is such a simple concept, and yet, how often do we set out on a new day with no clarity of intention, desire, or need? Today, think of your path to commitment. First think of how you can truly nurture yourself each day. In creative silence, ponder for a moment how nurturing your body, your soul, and your mind can improve your life and your practice. A nurtured and refreshed practitioner is much more available to their clients.

In your meditation today, breathe in the nourishing warmth of the soul, and breathe out the tired air deep within your lungs. Meditate on nurturing your mind, and bring clarity to your thoughts. Meditate on nurturing your energy, and bring peace to your body. Meditate on nurturing your soul, and give thanks in gratitude for the gifts you already have that make you a willing transformer of conflict into peace between the parties.

Today, list all the paths to nurturing yourself in this day, this week, this year. Focus on immediate goals, ongoing goals, and long-term goals of the nurturing heart.

Innocence

*True innocence is an achievement that comes through a thorough acknowledgment
of our own moral shadow, by taking neither the moral high ground, but struggling
with the lifelong attempt to ever deepen our ethical vision and responses.*

Thomas Moore, *Education of the Heart*

Thomas Moore is an author who writes with impeccable clarity and wisdom. He suggests that, through innocence, we become open, willing participants in the journey of inquiry. His writings raise ethical questions that ask us to examine our approach to living. Each day we are constantly evaluating, in some measure, ethical dilemmas that arise, not only in our response to situations that we are working in, but that our clients may unwittingly thrust upon us. To remain in a place of innocence, the not-knowing, the retrieval of powerful information can then be revealed to those who need to see it, maybe for the first time.

Meditate today on the word "innocence." Breathe in the vulnerability of innocence, and breathe out the fear that may rise in response to that suggestion. Breathe in the willingness to remain open and not know; breathe out the constriction of the heart.

In your journal, examine how you may appear innocent to the parties in ways that constructively support inquiry in them.

Frustration

Ask, and it shall be given to you; seek, and ye shall find;
knock, and it shall be opened unto you.

Matthew 7:7

In performing the daily tasks of work in our practice, frustration can come to visit so easily. Ticking off the items on the list takes us away from the urgency of what is really important: being present in each moment. When you find yourself behind the eight ball, the clock racing through the day, and you are caught up in a 'to-do' list, simply ask for peace. Take thirty seconds, breathe deeply, and ask to choose again in regard to your dilemma of the moment. The answer will always be given to you—for the peace of the day is only found in the intending to be peaceful and present. Ask for inner peace and a release of frustration today.

Meditate today on creating peace rather than frustration in the present moment. Breathe in the gentle breeze of peace, and force out the frustration of the list, the day, the present conflict. Breathe in a peaceful wave, and breathe out the tightness of your frustrated lungs.

Write about frustration. What came to the surface in your thoughts of frustrations about your life or practice? In what ways can you intend to have this day be more peaceful?

Balance

*Balanced living implies an innate inner harmony and
order to moving one along in creative ways.*

Margaret Stortz

One of my most important processes is finding the balance of living. I notice myself seeking that equilibrium for inner peace, and when I don't have it, my soul suffers. I have a tendency to hone in on the project in front of me, grab it for all that its worth, and neglect the rest of my life. I lose sleep, forget to eat, drop out of friendships, refrain from exercise, or let fall through the cracks other tasks that need attending to. I have discovered that I need to set the intention every day to find that balance by setting time limits around the daily commitments of my life. I have learned over the years to accomplish the must-do's first. I must set aside thirty minutes in the morning for spiritual practice. I must do thirty minutes of exercise every day. I must schedule downtime on the weekend for hiking or some form of entertainment. I must give myself permission to have fun on the weekend and actually schedule it. When I do these tough tasks by setting a certain amount of time for them, the mountain is chipped away day by day, and I don't feel so overwhelmed.

Meditate today about "balance." Breathe in the flow of balance, and breathe out the tension of imbalance. Imagine the river flowing gently through your life. Feel the cool water coursing over your arms as you float along with buoyancy and balance.

In your journal, list all the areas in your life in which you are currently experiencing balance. Where have you had success in balance, and which areas need more attention?

The afternoon knows what the morning never suspected.

Swedish proverb

When we expect the unexpected, we become open to the creativity of the universe. When we guide clients through the mud of perceived limitations to the clarity of the flowing stream, we have transformed part of the conflict. We can then assist them in creating a new story within their conflict and teach them to expect the unexpected. Always asking for more information creates an atmosphere of possibility. In our own lives, when we find ourselves looking toward a new day with anticipation and promise, it is a good indication that we are exercising our possibility thinking. Learning to enjoy the ride on the highway of unforeseen left turns and hard rights is a precursor to possibility thinking. The practitioner who enters a problem-saturated story can shine light on the avenue out of the conflict and into the land of solutions. Carry the torch for possibility in your own life, and you will carry it into the negotiating room.

Meditate today about promise and the word "possibility." Breathe in the newness of an opportunity-filled day, and breathe out the murky haze of the morning. Breathe in the comfort of being supported by the universe, and breathe out the limitation of the mind.

List every new possibility that flowed into your life this week. What are the signposts present in your life that indicate an unexpected left or a right turn of events?

What we speak becomes the house we live in.

Hafiz, Sufi poet

Choice of words is an expression of choice of thought. If we choose our thoughts intentionally, not only do we have immeasurable power in creating a day filled with joy, but what we speak creates a house filled with esteem and the promise of a new day. Self-talk is both constructive and destructive, and our mind is constantly filled with the cacophony of thoughts pouring through from different centers of the brain. If you discover that your self-talk is negative this morning, you have the power to choose again. Today, choose words of possibility and promise, words of hope and encouragement. Begin the day with one positive affirmation that you can carry throughout the day to uplift your day. It will become the foundation of a workday filled with success that you can easily translate to your clients.

Meditate today beginning with the word "self-talk". Say "I am making a difference in the world." Breathe in the empowerment of that phrase; breathe out the tension of not being good enough. Breathe in soothing reassurance, and breathe out the negative self-talk of the morning.

Write in your journal about self-talk. In what way are you choosing again? Write examples of ways you have redirected the committee of critics that reside in your thoughts. Write one positive affirmation that you can carry with you throughout this day.

Finding the Path

*Meditation is simply about being yourself and knowing about who
that is. It is about coming to realize that you are on a path whether
you like it or not, namely the path that is your life.*

Jon Kabat-Zinn, *Wherever You Go, There You Are*

Finding the right path to unlock your life mission is of utmost importance to peacemakers and conflict practitioners. Many of us feel that we are working in the trenches for transformation of the planet, one case at a time. To move the mountain before us, it is imperative that we realize that peace begins with us. Consider the necessity of daily meditation. We allow our own inner peace to have time to unfold; we become clear about our personal intentions for the day; we reconnect with vital collective energy that recharges our soul and makes us ready for the new day. You create your path each and every day, and if you do it mindfully, with intention, the day unfolds in a way that is always for your highest good. You then become an agent of solutions.

Meditate today about finding your personal path. Breathe in the mystery of not knowing, and breathe out the fear of the unknown. Breathe in the sense of wonder, and breathe out the need to know.

Write about what rises to the surface in your meditation. How can you discover the path that feels right to you, the one that uplifts you, and supports your journey.

There is only the fight to recover what has been lost
And found and lost again and again:
For us there is only the trying.
The rest is not our business.

T.S. Eliot, "East Coker," *Four Quartets*

When we decide to view our life as a puzzle to be solved, progress can actually begin. When things are not proceeding the way we want, we have the choice to ask one of two questions: "Why is this happening to me?" or "Things happen for me. What is the lesson I need to learn?" When the choice is the latter, we are moved toward clarity. To recover from the lessons in life that knock us flat, we need to be able to choose again. We need to be able to let it go and trust that what is presenting itself in our life at that moment is for our highest good. The rest is none of our business. When we are willing to recover, we can then be a model of resiliency and recovery for our clients. When we recover, we allow peace to sit within us at the table.

Meditate today about the word "recovery." Breathe in the peace of permission to sail on smooth water; breathe out the pain of feeling taken down by occurrences in our life. Breathe in acceptance of "what is," and breathe out the resistance to reality.

Write about an event from your life that you have successfully traversed to follow a smoother path. What is the major lesson that you can remember learning? Give yourself an intentional thought of recovery that will bolster your day.

Fear

Our deepest fear is not that we are inadequate. Our deepest fear is that we are
powerful beyond measure. It is our light, not our darkness, that most frightens
us.... You are a child of God. Your playing small does not serve the world.

Marianne Williamson, *A Return to Love*

Follow the fear. In former retreats, my co-facilitator, Alan, would have the participants answer two questions: "What is the worst thing that can happen to you?" and the follow-up question, "And then what would happen?" The goal, of course, was to face the fear and discover that
it exists only in our minds, thus acknowledging that we have power over the fear. When facing
our fear, we become fully conscious, and clarity lifts the fogginess from our mind. Allowing our
fear to follow us through the day gives credence to doubt and limitation. We create the thing we
are most afraid of. Release the thoughts of fear from your mind this day.

Always do what you are afraid to do.

Ralph Waldo Emerson

Meditate on the word "fear" today. Breathe in the peace of confidence; breathe out the
thoughts of doom and doubt. Breathe in the promise of self-assurance, and breathe out
the dread of failure.

Write in your journal about the most fearful thing that stops you from living your day to
the fullest. Ask yourself Alan's two questions.

Creativity

Life isn't about finding yourself. Life is about creating yourself.

George Bernard Shaw

We have access to all the creative inspiration we will ever need, when we agree to use mindfulness and intention to set it into motion. It is with this creativity that we share our gifts with the world. We have only one job: to have the courage to offer that creative expression to the universe. We are unique expressions of spirit in a common cause for common ground. We will make our mark on the world by sharing those gifts and knowing we are tapping into the creativity we already possess.

The faculty of creativity is never given to us all by itself. It always goes hand in hand with the gift of observation. And the true creator may be recognized by his ability always to find about him, in the commonest and humblest thing, items worthy of note.

Igor Stravinsky

Meditate today on the word "creativity." Breathe in the fluid nectar of genius, and breathe out the restriction of negative thought. Breathe in the brilliance of new ideas; breathe out limitation of the ego mind.

Recognize the ways in which you exercise the power of your personal genius. In what way can you make a creative difference today?

I truly believe that individuals can make a difference in society. Since periods of change such as the present one come so rarely in human history, it is up to each of us to make the best use of our time to help create a happier world.

His Holiness the Dalai Lama

During times when we are unsure of how to proceed in our life or in our practice, we need only remember that we are guided and directed by our higher power within. Others may be expecting proactivity on our part. In order to provide clarity of leadership, it is sometimes necessary to put aside personal issues that may be clouding our perceptions on how to proceed. Realizing that we are all part of a larger tapestry of global movement gives us the confidence that we have all the resources we need to act in a position of leadership. Conflict practitioners are in a period of transition in this field. You can make a difference one day at a time. Make the best use of your time today.

Spirituality, it seems to me, is about openness, about receptivity, about empathy, about the courage and faith to venture out into the unknown.... As I continue to understand more clearly the role that I need to play in leading this process of cultural change, I increasingly become aware that my primary task has a spiritual dimension to it.

Diane Chapman Walsh, Wellesley College

Meditate today on the phrase "leading them out of pain." Breathe in the awareness that the path is clear; breathe out the apprehension that may be locked deep within your body. Breathe in clarity of direction, and breathe out the feeling of insecurity.

Write about times when you feel called to leadership. List the occurrences when you performed successfully in that role.

The moment you take credit for anything that flows through you, you lose it. But if you permit "this that is within you" to flow, it will make you great in the eyes of the world.

Joel S. Goldsmith

Much has been written lately about finding the purpose of your life. Many conflict practitioners are drawn to this field for reasons of commerce, only to discover gifts of purpose, rich treasures of fulfillment, a feeling that they matter, a sense of a higher calling. Pride is a quality of ego that one cannot afford to feed in this field and hope to be successful in the long run. Pride is a construct of the ego mind. When consciousness is heightened with presence in living, it becomes easier to drop urges of the ego that cause a prideful stance. Taking credit for things that we should not, such as the solution to another's problems, may cause the identification with the ego. To intentionally focus on mindful consciousness provides an antidote to identifying with the ego through pride. A careful inventory of our personal life may find prideful thoughts restricting our life in some way. Know that a higher power is working in your own life as well as through those who come before you. Today, be an instrument for peace on the inside and on the outside. The opposite of pride is humility, and in the choice to become more humble, we embody love for one another.

Meditate today on the word "pride." Breathe in the present energy; breathe out the mightiness of pride. Breathe in the freedom of happiness, and breathe out the constriction of limitation.

Write a few lines in your journal about pride. List any changes you have noticed as a result of a conscious intention not to be prideful or to identify with the ego.

Nothing is more honorable than a grateful heart.

Seneca

Ken Cloke, in his book *Mediating Dangerously*, posits that one breakdown in the process for conflict professionals' is to miss the opening for the transformation of communications. When peacemakers follow a direct line of questioning about the substantive elements of the conflict over the heart felt elements, the window of opportunity may be shut forever. Then escalation of the conflict can be worsened by the professionals' involvement. A profound level of caring about the heart felt elements of the dispute encourages the line of questioning to follow a different path. When conflict professionals bring their humanity to the table and head for the heart of the issue, then the process will take a very different path. The path leaves *the adversarial contest* and marches toward collaboration which seeks first to dissipate the reason of origin for the conflict. The rest is a matter of process. Ken Cloke is transforming this field with his innovative brilliance. How can you transform your practice? If the first question becomes "What do they really care about?" your preparation and development of hypothesis will take a very different direction. It seems like it is such a simple concept to think about. What do you care deeply about in your practice and what do you profoundly care about in your life? How does caring deeply about something have an insightful impact on your journey?

Meditation today should begin with the word "caring." Breathe the question into your lungs, breathe out the fogginess of yesterday...breathe deeply into trying a different path today...even if you do place caring above all else, how can you more deeply care about the story today?

Record the elements of caring about your own life that were presented to you in your meditation. Choose one person to move toward in a deep way today.

No longer forward nor behind
I look in hope or fear;
But, grateful, take the good I find,
The best of now and here.

John Greenleaf Whittier, "My Psalm"

History no longer exists in this moment. It is only a construct of the mind. Happiness cannot occur in history unless it is remembered. Proactivity does not exist in the past. Active possibilities reside only in this moment. We must keep our attention focused in the present moment throughout every day. This moment holds the space to find what we need for our lives. This moment is where the options for our clients present themselves to us. If we remain focused in the past, we are not present for the day. Since the past is no longer here, we must refrain from seeking to lay blame for events that do not exist anymore. When we engage in blame, a cycle of shame is activated. We then stay stuck in expectation and miss the answer, which is found only in the present. If we can successfully accomplish a new perception of this reality in our personal life, we can teach our clients to let go of the past. The solution resides right here, right now.

Meditate today on the phrase "let go." Breathe in the willingness to become as light as air; breathe out the retribution of the past. Breathe in the promise of the moment, and breathe out the sadness of yesterday.

Write in your journal about your ability to let go. What are you holding on to that you cannot seem to let fall away? How can you stay focused in the present today?

Playing the Hand Dealt

The problem is…basically: how to remain whole in the midst of the distractions
of life; how to remain balanced, no matter what centrifugal forces tend
to pull one off the center; how to remain strong, no matter what shocks
come up in the periphery and tend to crack the hub of the wheel.

Anne Morrow Lindbergh, *Gift from the Sea*

In her beautifully reflective book, *Gift from the Sea,* Anne Morrow Lindbergh writes of the days and nights of annual solitude she granted herself at the edge of the sea. Using seashells as metaphors to describe the chapters of a life, she leaves the reader with a clear perception of reality and with a benevolent hope for the future. The book was written in the 1950s in a style that is poetically honest, with an acceptance of life and a personal presence that are remarkable. Like the work of other great writers—Marcus Aurelius in the first century and St. John of the Cross in medieval times—her musings on the page are applicable to any life in this millennium. In the most widely reported story of the early part of the last century, Lindbergh's beautiful baby boy was taken from his crib in the darkness of night and never returned to her. Such an unimaginable loss produced decades of deep melancholy, which forced her to make choices for living and push her grief and anguish through the eye of the needle toward creativity. She wanted to make a difference in her world.

Her husband, Charles Lindbergh, did not handle the loss as well and was prone to dark depression in his later years. They suffered together in silence, yet separated in their sorrow. Despite all the trials she endured in her life, Anne Morrow Lindbergh was resilient, as evidenced by the quote above: she was strong in the hub of the wheel, regardless of the cracks forced into the center. Her tenacity for remaining centered and balanced is extraordinary. By the end of her life, she discovered how to play the hand she was dealt with grace and authenticity. No one reaches the final chapter without adversity; some of life's lessons are more painful than others, and the price that some must pay for the experience of living is heartbreaking. How does your journey look to you? Are you succeeding in remaining whole? Or does the centrifuge of existence succeed in pulling your spirit off-center? How can you remain whole today as the distractions of life enter your realm?

I've never quite believed that one chance is all I get.

Anne Tyler

....

Meditate today on the phrase "strength in the storm." Relax into the posture of open listening. Breathe a cleansing breath of clarity and watch for images to appear.

In your journal, list the trials that you are currently experiencing. Choose one of these trials to perceive differently today. What strategy can you invent to play the hand well today?

Dreams

Dreaming is a nightly dip, a skinny dip into the pool of images and feelings.

James Hillman

What are dreams but the mind continuing to think? As lungs breathe, minds think. Perhaps it is another form of our reality, just another plane on which our conscious mind is not centered during the waking day. Jung said that we choose our dreams from a subconscious mind. If this theory is true, this means that we have the choice for happy dreams. The neuroscientists believe that we dream from the creative center of our brain. Nothing in the dream state exists without the hope of change and betterment. Today, set a positive intention on creating peaceful dreams.

Meditation today should begin with the word "dreams." Reflect today on dreams you can remember from your recent past. Feel your breath slow and as the flowing of your breath allows you to enter a deep peace, meditate upon the image that comes to your mind. Settle there and discover other images that follow.

Write in your journal about the images that came up for you in your meditation.

Anger

Do not use your anger to conceal a radiance that should not be hidden.

Rumi

As a society, it seems that we do not handle anger well. Evidence of road rage is apparent everywhere as the evidence of societal courtesy and consideration have degenerated over the last several decades. Carl Jung thought that repressed anger could be found in all cultures. He was of the opinion that anger is not an undesirable emotion, rather it was the bearer of information, an indicator of a crimson rage buried under the surface that simply reflected rejection of the shadow self. I love to read Carl Jung's writings; doing so allows me to hear the message that my humanity is normal. I teach divorcing parents a high conflict class every month. I have a segment in my lecture that suggests that students welcome their anger and then give them tools to deal with the rage. Usually, anger arises due to a perceived violation and exposes a lack of skill in handling emotion. I think anger in men covers frustration, and in women, it is displayed to conceal tears, to connote power unable to be expressed and generally felt as low power. My sweet mother arrived in the 1920s and was raised during a nationwide crisis of hunger and financial unsurety. Mary Nell was well-born, the youngest of her siblings, and a gentile woman who had no permission. She believed the message of her development: "you will be cared for." She was a product of her culture and was ill-equipped to deal with the adversity of the 1940s much less my dad's alcoholism which began on the battlefields, a Sergeant Major in Patton's Third Army. She could not say "no" to any request, and thus became the Madonna of a slew of cousins as well as the four of us. She would have never cursed; she considered that "common," and dealt with the feeling of impotence of power by denying her anger and aiming it inward. In her early 70s, her repressed anger finally exploded in a quick series of mini-strokes, and she chose to check out of the misery. Her radiance was never owned, never explored, never realized. As social scientists, I think we have not done enough to teach that anger, like conflict and power are not negative behaviors. We do not teach skills for understanding rage and violence, only how to repress it. Repression with no outlet for expression, leads to continuing conflict everywhere on the planet. How do you deal with anger? How do you handle it professionally?

Anger is your spirit flashing out of you.
It is your presence on earth insisting upon itself.

Thomas Moore

Meditation today to release your anger and should begin with the quest for inner peace, to welcome the alchemy of peace with its "yang", anger, rage, and conflict. As you consent to settle into breath, invite your anger home, to become a part of you and to love the shadows of yourself.

Write one thing that you can do today to own the messages of anger and rage and make a different choice born out of its embrace.

We make the leap not with our minds alone but with our total selves—our words,
our stories and our life engagement—and wager that we are on the way, that
the metaphor sees in a glass darkly what we do not see and cannot know.

Sallie McFargue Teselle

We can only "know" through the eyes of Spirit. Being willing to stand in the face of the client's fear, we trust that what needs to be said today will be said at a higher table, driven by higher power. Think of your own experience. How often have you peered into the darkness of the abyss? This is a frightening experience, especially for those who are locked in conflict. As practitioners, we can provide a sacred space of safety for our clients when life forces them to leap without the surety of a safe landing. Often, our clients are swirling in the middle of a massive life transition. Help them by asking, "If I risk, what will happen?" Ask yourself, "What is the thing I fear the most when I agree to mediate on the edge?

Meditate today on the fear that a "leap of faith" may create for you. Breathe in the freedom of being supported, and breathe out the fear of falling. Breathe in the trust of being lovingly caught by spirit; breathe out the feeling of not finding your safety net of love.

Journal about falling. What image comes forth in your mind when you think about the leap of faith? When have you let yourself leap successfully? On what area of your life can you shine a light of faith?

I make the effort to maintain a ground of oceanic silence
Out of which arises the multitude of phenomena of daily life.
I make the effort to see and to passionately open in love
To the spirit that infuses all things.
I make the effort to see the Beloved in everyone
And to serve the Beloved through everyone (including the earth).
I often fail in these aspirations because I lose the balance
Between separateness and unity, get lost in my separateness,
And feel afraid.
But I make the effort.

Ram Dass

There are situations in our life that often do not seem worthy of the effort of investment. We may be triggered into flight or into erecting a wall of safety. When we perceive that others are attacking us personally or finding fault with us in some way, the easy fork in the road is toward protection. The more difficult path is the one of investment in the effort. It requires a deposit of trust: the act assigns value where none is warranted; it requires an extension of faith in the person as a human being; and it comes with the risk of our feeling trampled upon. I think one can cultivate the habit of making the effort, a choice of natural action that follows a questioning of the effort, an extension of trust as a matter of course. In review of the situations in our life when the natural response is to recoil, how much easier would life be if we would simply choose again?

Meditate today on the phrase "making the effort." Breathe in the willingness to make the effort, and breathe out the bands of protection over your heart. Breathe in the peace that comes from seeing the Beloved in all; breathe out the walls of safety.

Inventory the relationships in which you may need to make the effort. List the people toward whom you can build the bridge of peace.

You will go out in joy and be led forth in peace; the mountains and the hills before you will burst into song, and all the trees of the field will clap their hands. Instead of the thorn will grow the cypress, and instead of briars will come up the myrtle. This will be for the glory of the Lord, for an everlasting sign which will not be destroyed.

Isaiah 55:12–13

How do we recognize joy in life? We often grind through life unable to see the miracles around us. If a joyful nature is not projected forth, a joyful world cannot be seen. But how do we project joy at the office while engaging those in conflict who project painful energy? My colleague Lexy taught me that we must create a metaphoric bubble of joy around us through intentional visualization of joy. Then, others are not able to penetrate and poison our joyful nature with toxic energy. Meditation is an intentional tool that should be in every practitioner's toolkit. When practiced daily, meditation provides protection from a toxic field of energy. Make a choice to see joy, peace, and beauty in nature today. Begin with meditation, and symptoms of joy will rise to the top of your mind this day.

Meditate upon the phrase "joyful nature." Breathe in the light of joy, and breathe out the inner judge. Breathe in the expansion of the universal energy; breathe out the thickets and thorns around your heart.

Write about the things that have increased joy in your world this year. Identify areas in your life that need a creative visualization adjustment.

Mind the Gap

The gap is the space between thoughts. Releasing thoughts in the gap is like fertile ground for your thoughts to manifest themselves into fulfilled desires.

Bill Roper

If you have ever been to London and ridden the Tube, or the underground train, you know the phrase "Mind the Gap." A very pleasant female voice echoes through the area to caution travelers to be careful of the space between the platform and the train. It seems that when we are young and being socialized, we live in a world of caution and fear of falling through "the gap." "Watch out!" "Be careful!" "Draw within the lines!" "Follow the rules!"—all are messages that loving mothers give to their children for protection. As we get older and know to look both ways before we cross the street (also a necessary precaution in London), we must unlearn the fear that is a natural by-product of protection from caring parents. Allow your mind to welcome "the gap," the not-knowing, the promise, the possibility of life. Embrace the adventure of being along for the ride. Searching for "the gap" in your thoughts, your energy, and your theories of practice will lead you to the discovery of unfulfilled desires. Change your mind about "minding the gap" to "finding the gap." Embrace the unknown, for in that space, you may also find peace.

Meditate today on the phrase "mind the gap." Breathe in the space between your thoughts; breathe out the apprehension of taking the wrong step. Breathe in the freedom to explore, and breathe out the restrictions of fear.

Journal about minding the gap and finding expansion in thought. When have you allowed yourself the freedom to expand? List areas in which you can focus your mind on finding the creative gap? List the ways you can redirect your thoughts from ones of defeat to thoughts of personal triumph.

Addiction

There is pain – so utter –
It swallows substance up –
Then covers the Abyss with Trance –
So Memory can step
Around – across – upon it –
As one within a Swoon –
Goes safely – where an open eye –
Would drop Him – Bone by Bone.

Emily Dickinson

We are creative in our addictions; we will do anything not to feel pain. I often have clients say, "I drink because my dad drank." "I got addicted to painkillers because I am not healthy." "I was abused as a child, so I eat everything that I see." It has been said that addiction is evidence of a disconnected heart. We check ourselves into the addiction facility on the corner and slap a bandage on the oozing soul. We often emerge free from physical dependency but with no recovery, shifting from physical addiction to emotional addiction. The soul is searching, and depression permeates the soul. Avoidance of pain is the goal. Thomas Moore wrote in *Dark Nights of the Soul* that if one chooses not to traverse the dark nights of life but rather takes a path of diversion, some form of compulsive behavior enters and substitutes for the soul. We encounter addiction everywhere: in our own soul, in the community, and in the clients before us at work. As a child of an alcoholic, I share certain hallmarks of behavior of the system from which I was flung into a rather chaotic orbit. I learned early that I was on my own, set apart from the mother ship. Tethered to a robotic, codependent shell of a mother in denial and to a family filled with rage, I carried a heavy cross my entire life, always locked in "the striving" to bear the pain and in "the will" to somehow thrive. My addiction took the form of control, and to calm the chaos in my stomach, I became an outstanding project manager and a productive overachiever. Leaving no box unchecked, I excelled in running my world. One never recovers fully from the ingrained reactivity of addiction. I have found that I must arise each day and will the intention to choose again. I now awake every morning with "thy will, not my will." "Don't throw the baby out with the bathwater" was a familiar phrase I heard in recovery from this craziness. I still am amazingly productive, am a lifelong learner, and strive to leave no box unchecked. But when it comes to control of the environment or my life, I have learned to just "pedal" and let go of steering the journey. On many days, I succeed.

Meditate today the word, "addiction" with a focus on letting go. Be comfortable in your body and release the tension. Breathe in freedom from addictive behavior, and breathe out the fear that begins the marathon into aversion. Breathe in the comfort that you are never alone in the climb; breathe out the frantic energy surrounding your soul.

Journal about addiction present in your life. Can you let go? Can you choose again? What behaviors do you see in reaction to anxiety? What can you do to soothe your soul?

Calm in the Face of the Storm

*Our true home is in the present moment. To live in the present moment is a
miracle. The miracle is not to walk on water. The miracle is to walk on the
green Earth in the present moment, to appreciate the peace and beauty that is
available now. Peace is all around us—in the world and in nature—and within
us—in our bodies and our spirits. Once we learn to touch this peace, we will be
healed and transformed. It is not a matter of faith; it is a matter of practice.*

Thich Nhat Hanh, *Touching Peace*

When I was growing up, a miracle was a divine act that only nuns, popes, and saints experienced. I was a lowly human with no chance of that happening to me. Not to mention the fact that I was convinced I was flawed, with many sins already on my scorecard. By the third grade, I figured that I had racked up enough sin to never see the pearly gates. I think that was the moment I headed for the exit, made my personal exodus from the world of religion, and along with it went any possibility for an early miracle. Today, I have recovered from my fear-based thinking, especially about a higher power and my relationship with myself. Today, I know that every morning brings the opportunity for new miracles, and it is hard for me to miss that reality. I awake every morning with the majesty of the Rocky Mountains before me. The greatest connection I make to my higher power is not within the sanctuary of church; it is through choosing stillness, sitting in awe of the beauty of nature around me. Hiking has become a spiritual experience for me. None of this was possible before I made a conscious effort to stay in the present moment. I found that this is the only time when I feel alive. I have also found that, once I made that commitment, my life began to transform. The key to connection is to consciously set that intention and practice peace every day. Then I sit back and watch the miracles of each day unfold. As I choose love over fear each moment, I recognize the simple miracle.

*There are only two ways to live your life. One is as though nothing
is a miracle. The other is as though everything is a miracle.*

Albert Einstein

Today, meditate on the word "miracles." Breathe in the potential miracles that choice brings to experience today; breathe out the tunnel vision that comes from living your life looking downward. Breathe in the sweet air of the morning, and breathe out last night's stale air of unawareness that is lingering. As the choice is made to love more and fear less each moment, the miracle is realized.

List in your journal all the miracles that happened to you last week. Who showed up on your path at just the right time? Tonight, list the miracles you experienced today. When were you able to change your perception about something and see it differently?

A story of real importance is not an argument so much as it is a presentation and an invitation. It presents a realm of experience accessible through the imagination and invites participation in imaginative responses to reality, indeed to respond to reality as imaginative. The temptation is always to stop listening—to stop listening, to stop responding, to stop storying—but premature death…is always to be mourned.

James Wiggins

We are story-bound creatures. Our reality is constructed from our perception, experience, and desires. Our clients come before us with problem-saturated stories that they cannot see, much less change. We are able to harvest solid clues for solutions from the stories told by clients. The gift of realizing that reality is contrived leads to the door of possibility. The ground is fertile for the creation of a new story. That notion is exciting to me! The successful direction of a new play on our personal stage allows us to impart that possibility to the client. We light the torch that leads them out of the darkness of the box into the light of the circle of conversation. The key is to listen very carefully, and keep listening; all the questions of the story are contained within the conversation. Listen for the narrative that holds the key to the door out of a self-constructed hell. Today, listen to your heart for the clues of your own story. Is it also inundated with problems or maybe in need of a few new thespians? You are the director! Write a new script today. It is possible to begin anew each day!

Meditate today on the word "narratives." Breathe in the promise of new script, and breathe out the old story of fear, sadness, lack, depression, or a broken heart. Breathe in the excitement of the new day, and breathe out the fables of old.

In your journal, write down the narrative in which you live. List the players and the stories that you have already let go. Make a list of experiences and people that can be on the stage of your new story.

Incline us, oh God! to think humbly of ourselves, to be severe only in the examination of our own conduct, to consider our fellow-creatures with kindness, and to judge of all they say and do with that charity which we would desire from them ourselves.

Jane Austen, Evening Prayer, *The Works of Jane Austen*

Humble pie is a staple not originally stocked in my behavioral kitchen. I escaped the task of examining my shortage of humility by learning not to care what others thought of me. Not caring that I lacked humility was easier than being humble—or so it seemed at the time. I never believed the nonesense about "the meek inheriting the earth." Yet, I always abhorred arrogance, the antithesis of humility, and, as with most things in my life, I sought the balance between them.

Despite some youthful worries that I might never enter the pearly gates, I believe God doesn't keep a scorecard for entrance to heaven. What I have always known and followed is the deep inner prompting that I should treat everyone with kindness and charity. I moved laboriously through awareness building and personal development in my 30s and 40s, and finally, in my middle years, I have discovered that ego is the driver of arrogance, and a healthy self-image is the origin of humility. Today, I embrace the humility that I denied in my youth.

Meditate today on the word "humility." Breathe deeply, let you mind be still, and with charity, examine your thoughts.

Write down examples of humility in your life. In your journal, write down situations when your arrogance backfired and humility would have more likely guaranteed your desired outcome. Write down instances when your humility was the quality that ensured, or helped ensure, your success."

Let me remember that each life must follow its own course, and that what happens to other people has absolutely nothing to do with what happens to me.

Marjorie Holmes

I have spent my life comparing myself with others. I didn't realize until my forties that there is no comparison. We are all so unique in the expression of soul and self. No one moves along my exact passageway; no one has my exact experiences. I have been fortunate to meet kindred souls whom I recognize as fellow journeymen, but the comparison ends there. I believe that we are teachers and angels for each other, an agreement of prior existence. The act of comparing ourselves with others has been destructive in our culture and in our field. Because there is no practitioner who can meet the needs of all clients, there is no peacemaker who is capable of assisting in the solution of all conflicts. Much of the disagreement among clients at our table comes from comparing the behavior of others. They are assuming that their truth is *the* truth. As the opportunity presents itself, the practitioner can illuminate the consequences in perception, and out of the differences, common ground can be revealed to the clients. I take the position that if clients have shown up at my table, they need to be there. I take comfort in the fact that there is no need to worry; if I am still and mindful and willing to clear my own agenda, they will receive the messages and questions that are meant for them. Drop any comparisons you make with others in your work and in your life.

Meditation today should focus on the word "comparison." Breathe in the freedom from the ego mind, and breathe out the harsh comparisons with others. Breathe in the knowledge that we all carry gifts of information for one another, and breathe out any competitive thoughts that arise in the mind.

List all your unique qualities. Embrace those qualities. Look for evidence of those qualities this week.

We must be willing to get rid of the life we've planned,
so as to have the life that is waiting for us.

Joseph Campbell

Remodeling my life has been a favorite pastime of mine. While climbing the mountain of my particular journey, reaching Mt. Forty brought a new vision. Base Camp Reality was constructed during that time in my life. When I feel that my ego is in charge and is taking over, I stop, choose again, and refocus on the map for Nan. When my ego wins the daily battle—and this happens frequently—I have discovered that I can only fall as far as Base Camp. Base Camp Reality is where I do major remodeling. When I prepare to depart, I ask, "What should I do, where should I go, what should I say and to whom?" Then I do what is before me, what my higher power has planned for me, not what my ego constructs. The rest of the climb is spectacular. When I shut up and let the journey unfold, the view is amazing.

Begin meditation today with thoughts "remodeling" and finding the clearing. Breathe in the promise of new horizons, and breathe out the plans you have designed for your journey. Breathe in the opportunities that you will notice on the new adventure; breathe out the house of yesterday and the fear that accompanies it.

In your journal, write a few lines about exploring a time when remodeling opened your life to an opportunity that seemed serendipitous?

I say "Soul-Making" Soul as distinguished from an Intelligence. There may be intelligences or sparks of the divinity in millions—but they are not souls till they acquire identities, till each one is personally itself. Intelligences are atoms of perception—they know and they see and they are pure, in short they are God... As various as the Lives of Men are—so various become their souls, and thus does God make individual beings, Souls, Identical Souls of the sparks of his own essence.

John Keats, *The Letters of John Keats* (edited by Hyder Edward Rollins)

In the nineteenth century, John Keats wrote about atoms of intelligence, connection to the spirit, and sparks of essence. How remarkable that these are the very thoughts reaching critical mass in our twenty-first-century society. The planetary consciousness is changing. The cultivation of individuality as a bridge to spirituality is so necessary for the development of a holistic path. Honoring the uniqueness of each spirit not only allows admission to universal energy that is our birthright, it allows the grace of tolerance for individuals with gifts for us. Some of these gifts are painful, raising tender wounds for us to explore. Some gifts are angels with torches of light to assist us on our journey. It may be the client who is willing to go on a path out of pain and choose peace instead, or the child who has struggled but suddenly begins to blossom into his own. Perhaps it is the relationship that changes directions on the journey—all bring us signposts along our own road of richness.

When you meditate today, honor your, "individuality." Breathe in the spirit, and accept the golden keys to the universe. Breathe out the holding patterns of life, and breathe in the wondrous nature of limitlessness. Breathe out the dark anteroom of the critical heart, and float in the unique individuality of you.

Write a few lines today about your individuality. In what ways have you already owned your individuality? List three ways you can embrace your true nature today.

Genius

When Nature has work to be done, she creates a genius to do it.
Ralph Waldo Emerson, "The Method of Nature"

Seeing the genius within is not an easy task. Why is it so difficult for us to honor the genius that flows through spirit? Is it because embracing our genius is considered conceited or arrogant? Have we been socialized to believe it is not acceptable to recognize our own efforts of creativity? When it comes to genius, I think the inner critic works overtime. When an inventory is taken of our professional practice, we find that we spend the day helping our clients find creative solutions out of conflict. Stop to think about it: the helping professions are filled with individuals demonstrating genius every day. We can more easily find the genius in others. Why not honor your own genius today?

Meditate on the word "genius." Breathe in the genius from creative intelligence, and breathe out self-doubt and criticism. Breathe in permission to express genius every day; breathe out that which is stopping you.

Write a list of creative acts that you can recognize as genius in your life. Write down the intention to honor the genius in you every day this week.

Love One Another

If I speak in the tongues of men and angels, but have not love, then I am a noisy gong or clanging cymbal. And if I have prophetic powers, and understand all mysteries and all knowledge, and I have faith, so as to remove mountains, but have not love, I am nothing. If I give away all I have, and if I deliver my body to be burned, but have not love, I gain nothing…so faith, hope, love abide, these three; but the greatest of these is love.

I Corinthians 13:3-13

As I love myself, I can love others. But what does it really mean to love one another? When we think of loving another, we often reduce it to, "love me first, then I will love you"; or "I need something from you"; in other words, romantic love. In the desire to feel that romance and to be loved by others, we often hold them in bondage, a hostage to the oneness of us. To the rational mind, the act of 'loving one another' means we are extending that which we think others do not yet deserve. The message of Jesus Christ to Christians was "as I have loved you, love one another"; or "act as I act and you will be saved." But saved from what? To me Christ's admonishment means saved from a life of misery and heartache, attachment to ego, and an insatiable thirst for gain: gain of love, gain of possessions, gain of power, and owning love. As I love another, I am loving myself. As I am never alone, I do not need others. I choose others and the difference is stark. Meeting others on your path exactly as they are and where they appear is the way to 'love one another'. Am I loving others when I do not honor their choices or the essence of who they are? To me loving others can mean being willing to trust their process. I trust that every adult has the ability to know what is best for them in the current moment; even those whom I perceived to injure me or who continue on their perilous journey without me, have their own process for life. On some level, if I judge am I not suggesting that I know what is best for them? They may believe they know what is best for me. On this topic, I am the only expert. I know of a few humans who have been able to truly embody "love one another." I am not one of them. I rise every morning and try to make "love one another" my mantra. Some days I am quite successful, on other days my ego rules. The next morning I rise and begin again. What about your life? What does "love one another" mean to you?

Meditation today should begin with the phrase "love one another." Today bring your consciousness to honoring the lives of others. Say, "I am willing to trust my higher power and love one another by honoring others."

Write down all the things you love about yourself. Extend that love to others today.

Happiness is not a possession to be prized. It is a quality of thought, a state of mind.

Daphne du Maurier

Imagine a child chasing a butterfly or her sheer joy of laughter when a puppy showers her in kisses. Carefree in nature, she is able to be completely present without worry of the next moment. We all aspire to attain that level of happiness, the holy grail of contentment, but where do we seek it? The only opportunity for happiness is in this moment, now. Wayne Dyer asks, in his book *The Power of Intention*, "Am I nowhere, or am I now here?" The difference is, of course, where we place our attention while acting with intention. It is incumbent upon on us to clean the lens of our perceptional awareness. When I become aware of the dawn, the first thing I decide upon is that happiness is a choice.

If you observe a really happy man, you will find him building a boat, writing a symphony, educating his son, growing double dahlias in his garden... He will not be searching for happiness as if it were a collar button that has rolled under the radiator.

W. Beran Wolfe

Meditate today on the word "happiness." Breathe in the joyful nature of a child, and breathe out the memory of yesterday. Breathe in the lightheartedness of the new morning; breathe out old patterns of thought.

In your journal, list all the ways you can choose happiness. What can you do differently today that will place you in the now here?

Peer Support

No man is an island, entire of itself;
every man is a piece of the continent,
a part of the main.

John Donne

Have you ever had that feeling that you knew someone before you could have possibly known them? I have felt an instant connection with many colleagues, as if we agreed somewhere in time to meet again and travel the same path. Many of them have shared wonderful gifts of knowledge, freely extended the gift of friendship, and warmly connected with me, a glow of understanding in their eyes, as if to say, "I know you—you are a kindred spirit!" As in the ancient words of Homer, the characteristics of intelligence, energy, and passion have been shared by my colleagues as they impart such passion about their work. A former litigator and judge once stated, "I never intended to be a conflict resolution evangelist. It surprises even me!" If you are in private practice, it is essential to connect with others who travel this path to peace, one case at a time. Working in isolation in the arena of discord is extremely taxing to the soul. Join with another or others in peer support. Offer your office for a gathering. Reach out to those whom you trust. Bring your "warm feelings of friendship."

For today's meditation, imagine that you are surrounded by earthly angels, those who support your soul. Breathe in the strength of many; breathe out the aloneness of the night. Breathe in the sustenance of the circle, healing and complete.

Make a list of those who are already in your circle of support. Whom could you enlist to bear witness to your journey? Whom could you reach out to?

It's not the load that breaks you, it's the way you carry it.

Lena Horne

One cannot traverse the human experiential mountain without understanding there are tribulations on the journey. No one can escape the lessons sent for us learn; nor can we relieve the burden of learning for our children, our loves, or our clients. What makes a person unable to carry the load? I think adaptability, perception, and acceptance have much to do with it. I have a dear friend of 30 years who has always astounded me with her ability to just get up, dust herself off, and continue on the path of *whatever.* An amazing ability of resiliency, she has moved across the bridge of life with grace and love for decades. A trusting soul and always a giver, she lived through two husbands, abuse both verbal and economic, a love with no hope of a happy ending, and severely advanced cancer at a time when she was the sole support of her precious 6 year old daughter. She is one of the most positive *'let's make the best of it'* women I know. Most people I know who have that much adversity in one lifetime select a course of denial as the method of choice for disaster; but my friend has a firm understanding of acceptance and, as life presents itself to her, she adapts. She reframes her perceptions of misery, puts one foot in front of the other, and continues forth on the road to joy. She creates new friends easily and shares her knowledge with others readily. She has raised a beautiful daughter and has enjoyed a full and rich life. Think of your own trials? Do you need to adjust the way you carry your load for the crossing?

Meditation today should begin with the word "trials." Agree to sit in the promise of this day and review the cross you bear ... feel the weighty load lifted from the shoulders of the divine in you. Breathe peacefully knowing that you can always choose again.

Make a list in your journal of the times in your life you have considered to be trials. How did you resurrect your soul from those tribulations? Will those methods work again? Choose one area of your life that you may consider a trial. Apply one of the proven methods from your past to your tribulations and see if you can carry it with more ease.

Positive Attitude

Love wholeheartedly, be surprised, give thanks and praise—
then you will discover the fullness of your life.

Brother David Steindl-Rast

Many of the great philosophers throughout the ages have taught that we become what we think we are. Many also teach that we create our tomorrow today, in the present. I have seen evidence of this truth in my own family and believe it to be true for my life. When we awake each morning, our first breath brings the first choice. What shall I create today? Often, the creations are choices of perception as to how to interpret the unfolding day. A positive attitude is contagious. When the choice is made to embrace a hopeful outlook for our own life, the opportunity exists for us to spread hope contagiously throughout the day, in every interaction of the day.

Meditation this morning should begin with the thought of creating a positive world. Breathe in the creation of good, and breathe out the old patterns of doom. Breathe in the choice of joy and breathe out the sadness of yesterday.

List the positive attitudes that you can embrace today. What positive beliefs do you already hold in your life?

For Spirit is first of all power, the power that drives the human spirit above
itself towards what it cannot attain by itself, the love that is greater than
all other gifts, the truth in which the depth of being opens itself to us,
the holy that is the manifestation of the presence of the ultimate.

Paul Tillich, *The Eternal Now*

Power is a subject that I have been interested in for a long time. As a teacher of conflict theory and mediation, I think a clear understanding of power dynamics is essential for students of conflict analysis. Understanding our own power in the dance of the client's conflict is also of great value. One who can effectively assist in the balance of power holds the keys to resolution. Power is sought after by all participants in disputes; how they manifest that power determines how engagement leads to solution. At the end of the day, the practitioner can feel depleted, drained, and spent, as though a transfusion of energy had taken place at the table. One of the great gifts of leading a mindful life and practicing meditation is that reserves of energy can be restored through attention to those paths. Power up with meditation first thing in the morning and after a high-conflict day, take time for reflection on your journey and spiritual connection.

When power leads man towards arrogance, poetry reminds him of his limitations.
When power narrows the areas of man's concern, poetry reminds him of the
richness and diversity of his existence. When power corrupts, poetry cleanses.

John F. Kennedy

Begin your meditation today with the thought of tapping into personal power. Breathe in the soothing energy of the source; breathe out the fog of confusion. Breathe in the bright illumination of your soul; and breathe out the labor of yesterday.

In your journal, write a few lines about your personal sources of power. Where do you feel power? When are you able to share your power without depleting your own source?

Abundance

*The mind is a powerful instrument. The choice is yours in maintaining a spiritual
awareness of what prosperity is to you. When you are positive, generous and upbeat,
you actually radiate feelings of trust, openness, and abundance—this is prosperity.*

Gary Quinn

Think of the times when your life is flowing beautifully. You feel complete, operating on all
cylinders. Attitude, love, and energy are easy to share during those times because they originate
from a place that does not begin with you. The source is limitless. Gifts of abundance come
from giving ourselves permission to become still, to become one with our nature, and to receive
unlimited love. Our ability to give freely and live in abundance originates in the mind. You have
the ability to change your mind about the reality of your life. Spiritual awareness is a conscious
choice that you can make. Prosperity follows naturally. When you stop worrying about your
practice, your practice will flow abundantly.

Meditate today on the word "abundance." Breathe in the gratitude of awareness, and
breathe out the fear of not having enough. Breathe in the feeling of being taken care of;
breathe out the negative thinking of limitation.

Write in your journal about abundance. List the abundance that naturally occurs in your
life. How can you create more abundance in your life?

The Zen of Mediation

Being as empathetic with both parties as possible, without losing ourselves...
Being as honest with both parties as possible, with being judgmental...
Being as committed as possible to revealing choices involving resolution and
transformation, without caring one bit what either party chooses.

Kenneth Cloke, *Mediating Dangerously*

It is easy in the course of living to become upset with those in your circle of concern and to judge the actions of others, whether they are at your table or in your home. But usually, we judge ourselves more harshly than we do others. We then can carry that judgmental behavior into our sacred circle of conflict engagement. In *The Power of Intention*, Wayne Dyer says that we need to "stop being offended." We can model non-judgment and teach our clients to hear the language from a different chair. Judgment and being offended go hand in hand. Embrace the neutral ground of observation, and behold the nuggets of truth that arise when the filters of judgment are released.

Meditate upon this topic, beginning with "As I feel my breath flow in and out of my body, I release any judgment I have of my thoughts, of others, and of myself. I embrace my loving spirit."

Write in your journal about judgment. Record any thoughts about judgment that came up in your meditation. Notice how your mind handled this topic in your meditation. Inventory the areas of you life in which you are being offended or are creating offense. Review the acts of judgment that have come up this week, and make a commitment today to choose again.

I think sages are the growing tip of the secret impulse of evolution. I think they are the leading edge of the self-transcending drive that always goes beyond what went before.... I think they disclose the face of tomorrow, they open us to the heart of our own destiny, which is also already right now in the timelessness of this very moment, and in that startling recognition the voice of the sage becomes your voice...

Ken Wilber, *A Brief History of Everything*

I recognize and honor the sages that have graced my life. Those extraordinary human beings held a torch above my path for me to find my way out of a dark forest, and helped illuminate a goal of completeness for me to seek. The sages that came to shake me out of the nightmare, or the dream, were those who moved me to shift my thought paradigms again and again. Even though many of my sages have made their transition, they have not left me, and I frequently see the signs of serendipitous communication along my journey. Those funny intelligent voices pop into my stream of consciousness all the time. In my advancing age, I answer.

For today's meditation, summon the "sages of wisdom" to your journey today. Breathe in the warmth of collective purpose, and breathe out the feeling of aloneness. Breathe in the wisdom of knowing the greater good, and breathe out the fear of the fork in the road. Embrace the sages of wisdom sent to you this day.

Who are your sages? List them in your journal, and invite them to sing at your table.

"Disappointment is the chariot to enlightenment" is an expression of the universe inviting
us to grow, to move beyond blaming others and judging ourselves. By our willingness to
expand our awareness, we are able to propel ourselves into higher states of consciousness.

A Zen Saying

When the landmarks of sorrow litter your highway of development, it might be time to
create new landmarks. Landmarks of limitation can be painful but provide the catalyst for the
creation of new perceptions. What is an appropriate motivation to build a bridge to new awareness? The painful process of uncoupling produces huge shifts in the trajectory of one's life. The
motivation for choosing a different course arises from the ashes of the fire of dissolution. When
the hurt is heavy on our heart, it is not normal to think positively, rather negative thought is
the standard. The motivation to choose again must be intentional. Where is your chariot carrying you? Are you intentionally choosing to build a new bridge or are you smoldering in the
aftermath of yesterday?

Begin meditation today with the thought of "motivation." Breathe in the possibilities
of the morning, and breathe out the sorrows of your heart. Breathe in the assurance of
awareness; breathe out the reluctance to change lanes.

What motivates you? When do you feel the most creative? How can you motivate yourself
to choose the light of joy and not the blues of depression?

The universe also distributes something of itself to its parts, both spontaneously
and because it feels the attraction of something else to part of itself which
is essential to its own parts, because they share the same nature. After all,
he who demands something from the universe is no stranger to it.

Plotinus, *The Enneads*

Is it possible that Plotinus, the sage of ancient Egypt and Rome from the third century, understood quantum theory seventeen centuries ahead of his time? His disciple, Porphyry, wrote that Plotinus "seemed to be ashamed of being in a body and thus refused to reveal his personal history." Upon hearing a speech by Ammonius Saccas, the self-reported "God-taught" philosopher said, "That is the man I have been seeking!" Clearly, he seemed to his fellow citizens to not be of this world. Plotinus was a man on a mission, with vision beyond his defined world. Have you been drawn to the mediation field by the current of a river that you do not fully comprehend? How can you work with the system to change the trajectory of conflict? Can you demand something of your universe as you understand it? I believe it is easier than we think to accomplish this. When I have agreed to meld with the system and hold the sacred space open for the possibility of resolution, a transformed orbit was created—one that was not possible before.

....

Begin meditation today with the thought of working with the quantum system of collective energy. Breathe in the power of becoming part of the whole, and breathe out the feeling of insignificance. Breathe in the opportunity of common ground; breathe out the restriction of control.

Write a line in your journal about the agreement to be part of a larger movement. Can you identify a way by which you already practice quantum thought in your practice?

Even if you are on the right track, you'll get run over if you just sit there.

Will Rogers

At times, I have felt paralyzing depression, resulting in a period of inactivity. I experienced a general malaise, a feeling of being overwhelmed or not fully connected to my path—off the right track. It seems that when the mountain is looming large on my horizon, it knocks me back into inactivity. One of the skills used by practitioners in conflict is fractionation. I have discovered that when I can divide the mountain into blocks of manageable issues, I can successfully traverse the terrain. I begin to feel that I can do anything if I just do a little of it each day. As negotiators, we can model this life skill for those we assist in the engagement of conflict. Put on those running shoes and "Just do it."

Begin meditation today with the word "proactivity." Breathe in the energy of movement, and breathe out the inertia of being overwhelmed. Breathe in a powerful breath to break the dam of inactivity; breathe out the depression of being stuck.

Write a line or two in your journal about inactivity and proactivity. In what areas of your life are you currently inactive? Proactive? Find clarity today. What action step can you take today to create a freer flow of movement?

*Learn to get in touch with the silence within yourself and
know that everything in this life has a purpose.*

Elisabeth Kübler-Ross

The purpose of life can only be uncovered in stillness. The Buddhist Sutra teaches that only in the stillness can the mind ascertain information with acceptance. Acceptance allows purpose and direction to be discovered. We are conditioned in our youth to be active and goal-directed, which, in and of itself, is not a bad life strategy; however, we become so caught up in the quest for more that we feel we have somehow been left alone and in control of our destiny. Life has a purpose for each one of us that is revealed slowly from the cloudy edges of awareness, a daunting venture into the unknown. The wild success of Rick Warren's bestseller, *The Purpose-Driven Life,* testifies to the millions in search of meaning. We all know souls who are the captains of empty ships in the harbor of life, empty themselves and searching for passengers to journey into the dark storm with them. Those who reach the middle years missing the true richness of life but with an abundance of material possessions and stature, are left to ask, "Is this all there is?" Rick Warren's message is clearly stated in the introduction to his book: we are all here for a reason; we each have a purpose to fulfill and a duty to discover the fullness of life. He entreats us to return to the spiritual path, and millions of people have embraced his message. The story of a young woman held hostage in her Atlanta home a few years ago speaks to the power of our knowing we are loved by a higher power and are endowed with a purpose. She sat in silence and, although terrified, she listened to that quiet, inner voice telling her to extend love and understanding to the soul before her—her captor—who was terrified in his own way. As she read to him for hours from Warren's book, his heart softened, and he eventually released her and surrendered to the police. Willing to listen to that still voice, she encouraged this tormented soul to consider that he, too, had a purpose: to be caught in order to evangelize to fellow prisoners. Epiphanies occur in silence. Agree to become silent today, and know that your purpose will become clear.

Meditate today on the phrase "sitting in silence." Breathe a cleansing breath of wonder as you look inward and behold the power of your maker from within.

In your journal, write down your purpose in life. Free-associate, and write the resultant words on the page. Does your list reveal new information? How can you assist another in their search for meaning and purpose?

*Difficult times have helped me to understand better than before how
infinitely rich and beautiful life is in every way and that so many things
that one goes worrying about are of no importance whatsoever.*

Isak Dinesen

No one escapes the trials of life. When we work with people in great pain, it can often trigger memories of our own misery. The great turning point in my life began with the still voice that whispered through my pain, "Choose again." I use the tool of choice to effectively model for clients who are entrenched in the conflict and in the task of finding solutions amid the wreckage of their relationships. What will the difference be in the end? We have the choice to focus on the position of our rights and on what is lacking, or on the teary path out of the forest. Strength is what is required to lay the bricks of the path out of darkness.

Meditate today on the word "strength." Breathe in the fortitude of collective energy, and breathe out the anger of the violation. Breathe in the ease of vision, and breathe out the patterned pain of unimportant things.

How many times in the recent past have you successfully chosen again? Today, look into your rich world: What can you see that enhances your ability to discern light from darkness?

Come to me; what I seek in vain
Bring thou; into my spirit send
Peace after care, balm after pain;
And be my friend.

Frederick Tennyson, adapted from Sappho

The truth is we have to be the kind of person we want to attract. We must be content in loving ourselves, where we are right now, before we can attract a mate more attuned to our dance. The work begins at home. Here is how I think it works: hold the desire for this kindred spirit in your heart, but without attachment to the manifestation of a particular person. Expect that someday one, who is more suited to you, will walk into your life, but let go of any expectations as to who this will be and how it will happen. Focus instead on bringing clarity to your own life and choose to be the kind of person you are seeking. Be happy now. Enjoy your life. Then you may see a new world unfold around you. Transform into one you were meant to be when you came to be!

Give thanks for nights spent in good company,
And take the gifts a tranquil mind may bring;
No heart is dark when the kind moon doth shine,
And grass-grown riverbanks are fair to see.

Hafiz, *Teachings of Hafiz*

Meditate today on the phrase "shared love." Breathe in the warmth of companionship; breathe out the fear that no one exists for you. Breathe in the silken air of a kindred understanding; breathe out the attachment to have that soul look a certain way.

List all the relationships you have that are already based in love and respect, regardless of whether it is a love, friend, or business relationship. What exact qualities of those relationships make you feel loved? Today, find a kindred spirit of companionship on your path.

I look back on my life like a good day's work—it was done and I am satisfied with it. I was happy and contented; I knew nothing better and made the best out of what life offered.

Grandma (Anna Mary) Moses

We usually have no problem taking an inventory of our flaws and mistakes made while traveling the path. When taking a personal history, however, it is more difficult to view with satisfaction the choices made along the way. If you live your life full out, making choices along the way that have no regrets attached to them, the chances are you can look in the rear view mirror and be pleased. My Aunt Corinne was a woman who lived well with her choices. Corinne was the mother of five, an engineer, an artist, and served the country during World War II as a "Rosie the Riveter" manning posts at the oil refinery left vacant by soldiers. She spent the long sweltering summers in Louisiana making dolls for poor children in Central America and the winters traveling through the Mexican and Guatemalan countryside giving them away to children she met on her journey. I learned a great deal from my Aunt. She was so deliberate in her life, that when she reached 80, a razor sharp mind encased in an ailing body, she called her children to her bedside in the hospital, revealed her decision to die, and asked their permission to move on. Her request, to ascend to the heavenly plane to the peace and comfort of release from her body, astounded all who witnessed this with a feeling of awe. "I remember her saying, I have lived long, I've done everything I wanted to do, I have no regrets, I am content. I am tired and I would like to die now." I was astonished. Her strength, her conviction, her courage, and her unyielding belief in God left me with a profound sense of my own faith. The family sat in reverent observation for two weeks with her as she left the planet. The gifts she left to me and my extended family were remarkable. The contentment was palpable, and like Grandma Moses, "she knew nothing better and made the best out of what life offered."

Mediation today should begin with the word "contentment." As your breathe rises to meet your heart, feel the peace of contentment.

Write a few lines in your journal about contentment in your life. What is one thing that you can do today to feel satisfaction with your work, your life, or your relationships of choice.

A good motivation is what is needed: compassion without dogmatism,
without complicated philosophy; just understanding that others are human
brothers and sisters and respecting their human rights and dignities. That we
humans can help each other is one of our unique human capacities.

His Holiness the Dalai Lama

When I ask clients to seek the higher road to communication in disputes, I am asking them to move a mountain. Emotions are so elevated that even recognizing that another way exists is difficult. Concrete examples of the higher road can only be understood by my modeling "being the higher road." If I can somehow help them see the need to drop the assumptions they hold about the other party, the road becomes clearer to them. My presence in their sacred space provides the opportunity to explore the unknown way out. Finding the road to compassion outside of the workplace is an intentional journey. I often feel immediate anger when I perceive a boundary to be broken by others in my life. I must force myself to seek compassion first, without judgment, and honor my unique human capacity to do so. Compassion provides the motivation to stay connected within the space of negative energy. I choose to see that others are just doing the best they can with what they have.

Meditate about "compassion" as a healing process. Breathe in the warmth of love and consideration, and breathe out the constriction of the heart. Breathe in the free air of acceptance, and breathe out the anger of violation.

Write down one act of compassion that you performed this week. Look for an opportunity to demonstrate compassion to be revealed today?

One [experience of centering prayer] is the affirmation of our
being at the deepest level, which comes through peace and spiritual
consolation and enables us to entrust to God our whole story.

Father Thomas Keating

To come to the center through prayer and meditation is to move toward inner peace through self-awareness. It is in the act of centering that we can build trust in a higher power and meld with an interior honesty that illuminates the soul. Father Thomas Keating wrote of the process of centering prayer. Fr. Keating noted that in the act of centering prayer, we build the trust in God necessary to confront our darker side. In our work with clients, particularly in relationship conflicts, clients can often arrive in a state of darker side identification while at the same time in denial about the actual source of their anger. Ego, possession, expectations, insufficiencies, distrust, rights violations, accusations, and rage are among the emotions presenting from the darker side of personalities in conflict. Fr. Keating noted the act of centering is not the prayer or meditation itself but the preparation for it. The act of centering prayer allows us to go within and release *what is* to the unconscious. Fr. Keating suggested that centering prayer is not an act of *attention* but rather *intention*. In the act of intention, we are stating our choice— the willingness to surrender. We are cultivating a spiritual center when we agree to become still and dedicate the morning thoughts to connection with the divine.

According to Fr. Keating, there are four steps to the process of centering prayer. One should first select a sacred word that serves as a mantra; a word or phrase that is representative of your intention, such as harmony, choose again, peace or "I am worthy." The second step is to sit quietly and repeat the sacred word over and over again until the interior connection is made. Thirdly, when you are aware that your thoughts are straying from the mantra words, simply return them to the centering word. At the end of your time of connection, you should sit with the word in solitude for a few moments to ritualize the experience. Fr. Keating noted this process will bring the intention of the focus to fruition. These steps are amazingly close to ones in eastern meditation. You will have effectively disarmed the stimulus response of the negative thoughts. As each session is completed, day-by-day, the result is an easily traveled path to your source every day. Center yourself this morning. In the agreement to go within, you are setting the intention to thrive in peace.

Meditation today should begin with the phrase "centering prayer." Softly speak your sacred sound. Breathe serenely and let your statement of intention connect to your soul.

Write down your sacred word. Try to center on this word, three times today for five minutes. Write down the differences you notice in your ability to focus and choose again.

Before, this mind went wandering
however it pleased,
wherever it wanted,
by whatever way that it liked.
Today I will hold it aptly in check—
as one wielding a goad, an elephant in rut.

The Dhammapada

Modern philosopher Ken Wilber posits that the Age of Reason in the eighteenth century launched a long course of developing the cognitive skills of logic and finite science and separating from knowledge derived from emotion and spirit. Humans began analyzing every bit of information. As a result of critical thinking, we ceased "being" and began "doing." Mindfulness meditation is a disciplined training that seeks to correct this error in the mind. Danah Zohar, in her book *Spiritual Intelligence*, observes that we are in the midst of an evolutionary cycle of development of the central brain and that new information can be accessed through training the mind to connect with one's spiritual self. Citing current brain research, she hypothesized that we can develop across the central brain processor an increase in brain activity, or a spiritual quotient of intelligence (SQ). I think that much of the depression rampant in this world is the result of the feeling that we are disconnected from our central core, our spirit. Meditation is a practice that is necessary for the training of the mind to not think but "to just be."

You want to be happy.
You want peace.
You do not have them now,
Because your mind is totally undisciplined...
You must learn to change your mind about your mind...
Try to identify with that part of your mind where stillness and peace reign forever.

A Course in Miracles

Meditate today on the word "discipline." Breathe in the willingness to be still, and breathe out the frantic raving of the mind. Breathe in the commitment to change your mind; breathe out the wandering thoughts.

In your journal, write down three ways you can add discipline in your life today.

When we live in accordance with our own nature, fulfilling our own characteristic function, we live also in accordance with the nature of the universe.

Marcus Aurelius

Marcus Aurelius was a man centuries ahead of his time. Or, could it be that a millennium of generations veered off the track of development? Over the course of history, did humankind take a wrong turn? This Roman Emperor, who was educated by the slave Epictetus, wrote volumes of meditations to reflect the seasons of his life. The teachings of Marcus Aurelius are amazingly applicable to our current world. He illustrates the conflict of beliefs that build character and inspires one to have patience and fortitude. He believed that all people should aspire to their higher good. He had a strong sense of duty. He shared his solitary musings on honesty, integrity, inner peace, and peace in his ancient world. He felt that happiness and inner peace rest solely with oneself. His optimistic belief was that the universe provides promise and prosperity, sameness and change, decay and transformation all at once. In his age of chaos, as well as in that of our own, his belief in the deeper reasoning—the reasoning of looking for the good in the universe—and his conviction in the spirit of man, and, ultimately, in a higher power come to comfort us in the knowledge that circularity defines the universe. Marcus Aurelius was a devotee of "The Now."

You are born with a character; it is given; a gift, as the old stories say, from the guardians upon your birth.

James Hillman, *The Soul's Code: In Search of Character and Calling*

Meditate today on the word "character." Breathe in the strength of honor, and breathe out the doubt of the unknown. Breathe in the patience of inner peace, and breathe out the chaos of the mind.

What characteristics do you possess that drew you to this field? What personal characteristics can you honor about yourself?

Integrity has no need of rules.

Albert Camus

The members of every professional practice have boundaries to guide them—ascribed rules that contain within them the potential to turn artists into professional robots by espousing predictability and standards of practice that remove individuality from that practice. I am an admitted rule buster. It seems that ethical dilemmas abound in our practice, but is it not more important to place a higher value on integrity and ethics than to perform in a manner that conforms to models designed by another? Conflict resolution is a profession of artistry, with many academic disciplines that meld together to form a mosaic in various permutations. I welcome the difference in opinion; I honor the many paths to the same outcome. When training mediators, I won't show a videotape of a mediation session. I have found that when I do, the student spends the simulation time in emulation, not in learning to listen to the inside track, not in taking an inventory of their own values, thereby missing the cues of their intuition and precluding their own, original creativity in the path of questioning. In the living of life, our creativity can also be constricted by "the rules": too much crayon outside the line there, not enough conformity to the uniform of the day here. I think peacemakers are, by nature, nonconformists. It seems to me that the tendency to want to make peace has much to do with tolerance. When you color outside the lines of your life, do you give yourself permission to be unique? When you bend the branches of the willow tree in the search for solutions, do you honor yourself as an artist?

Begin meditation today with the phrase "the rules." Where does the flow of thoughts take you? Breathe yourself out of that thought pattern and back into the present.

Write down the thoughts about "the rules" that came to you in meditation. List the qualities you possess that are not within the lines.

You can't teach a pig to sing. It's a waste of time and it annoys the pig.

Author Unknown

Absurdity is defined as something that is ridiculously unreasonable or unsound—perhaps something that is out of place or not applicable in a situation. How many of our clients are locked in conflict because they are trying to teach a pig to sing? In intractable conflict, often the only option for intervention comes in the directive stance of the mediator. How much time do *we* waste following the pig around the mediation table, trying to teach it to sing? How many of our own relationships are stuck in the same insanity? A common misperception in relationships is that the couple should sing the same song, should travel in the same car down the freeway of life. After all, isn't a shared vision of the future the reason we paired off with our mate? So when our individual paths diverge, we can waste countless hours trying to get our mate to sing a different song, to hop into our car and abandon their own on the side of the road. It not only "annoys the pig," but it is absurd to think that a partnership requires these stringent rules of engagement. In our search for commitment, we may misunderstand the intention of the word. Commitment in relationship needs to be an expandable quality, an agreement to hold the space open for growth and with honor for both individuals. When couples arrive at a fork in the road, uncoupling is not the only option. Is it not better to first consider allowing individual growth within the coupleship? I am not promoting that we stay locked in commitment in relationships that no longer serve either person; rather, I am suggesting that uncoupling should not be the quick and easy answer to dissimilar directions of growth. Think about your personal life. Are you trying to teach a pig to sing? Is the pig annoyed? Can you discard your expectations and choose acceptance?

Meditate today on the word "absurdity." Breathe deeply and release all actions of absurdity in your relationships.

Write about the impulses that came up in your meditation. What do you need to release in order to allow more space for growth in your relationships?

I am happy and content because I think I am.

Alain-Rene Lesage

The thinking mind holds the room we live in: a narrative, or story, as a snapshot of hope. We create a script for the drama of life, and often, disillusionment dispels our expectations for the happy photograph we struggle to recreate. We invite people onto our stage to play a part, not of their creation, but of ours. The motivation of our life becomes the search for the replacement of those actors who do not deliver the correct lines. We have the ability to choose another motivation. If we chose poorly each day, a shift in motivation for constructing a new narrative is required. One helpful tool is to help to identify the path out of the inaccurate story and replace it with a hopeful narrative, to begin each with the intention to set up success, rather than failure; to be happy because you think you are! The road to inner peace lies in the story becoming one of hope and acceptance moment by moment.

Begin meditation today with the thought of happiness and hope in thought. Breathe in deeply and clear your negative thoughts from your mind, breathe out the old mind and breathe in inner peace and the beginner's mind...just be still.

Write a few lines in your journal about your story of hope. What ideas float through your mind? How can you change the focus of your story today and be more hopeful? How can you choose again? Design this day to be different; create a new story just for today.

Healthy Thoughts

All that we are is the result of our thoughts; it is founded on our thoughts and made up of our thoughts. With our thoughts we make the world. If you speak or act with a harmonious thought, happiness will follow you as your own shadow, never leaving you.

The Dhammapada

Cultivating healthy thoughts rather than negative ones is more about choice than about being an innate personal behavior. I think we miss a step when we try to bypass processing the negative. This can lead us to denial rather than acceptance. As Byron Katie lectures in "The Work," the brain is an organ doing its job, like the beating heart or the lungs breathing, not a reflection of who we are. If, in our mistaken mind, we think that our thoughts are "who we are," we have no choice but to immerse ourselves in negativity. Attention to negative thoughts breeds negativity. We are judging machines, and in the end, the object of our judgment mirrors our thoughts of ourselves. To separate our essence from the brain doing its job is such a freeing concept! I notice, in my dealings with clients, that I can observe my thoughts of judgment about one of the parties, and I can choose to let those thoughts dance right off the stage without attachment to them. I choose to think that this person is in pain and has a counterproductive way of expression. This person has made the wrong choice. How can I assist him or her in choosing again? When judging ourselves, the task is more difficult. We are often the worst critics of our performance, our behavior, our choices, and our thoughts. Be kind to yourself, and you will be kind to others. Choose healthy thoughts.

Meditation today should begin with the phrase "healthy thoughts." As you relax into the calm morning, breathe in a deep, cleansing breath, and watch your mind produce thoughts, one after the other. Observe your thoughts, bring them back to the center, and choose the healthy ones.

Write about the subjects that floated across your mind in your meditation. Where does your mind want to go? Record those thoughts. How can you make a different choice in thought today?

Solitude

It is a difficult lesson to learn today to leave one's friends and family and deliberately practice the art of solitude for an hour or a day or a week.... It is not the desert island nor the stony wilderness that cuts you from the people you love.... It is the wilderness in the mind, the desert wastes in the heart through which one wanders lost and a stranger.

Anne Morrow Lindbergh, *Gift from the Sea*

There is a difference between solitude and isolation. Solitude is a chosen state of being, necessary for regeneration of the soul—an intentional break in the constant wave of activity that saturates one's life. Often, isolation is borne of shame or anxiety. The fine line that separates the two is often blurred, depending on the emotions of the day. If you are removed from your soul, you are removed from the love of your relationships, even if you are in their presence. I live in my head so much of the time. My thoughts drive my brain, my life, my work, and my interests. For me, the act of deliberate solitude is necessary for disconnection from my endless analyzing and for reconnection with my heart. I find that isolation is frequently the result of anger, hurt, embarrassment, or sadness. I also notice that isolation is not rejuvenating, but rather depressing. Is it that solitude removes us from the ones we love or is it chosen isolation? Today choose a peaceful solitude of exploration.

Ordinary men hate solitude.
But the master makes use of it,
embracing his aloneness, realizing
he is one with the whole universe.

Lao Tzu, *Tao Te Ching*

Meditation today should begin with the word "solitude". As you sink into the depth of your breath, feel the cadence of your heart beat. Envision a peaceful wilderness where the music of the animals can be heard in the stillness.

Draw two lines on your paper and on one side list the ways that you isolate and on the other list the ways that you re-energize with solitude.

Resistance

How far you go in life depends on you being tender with the young, compassionate with the aged, sympathetic with the striving and tolerant of the weak and the strong. Because someday in life you will have been all of these.

George Washington Carver

Resistant energy works to pull one back to a place of beginning. There can be no movement forward in resistance. With the feeling of resistance comes tension, fear, dread, worry, and avoidance. Stagnant behavior is circular; the dysfunctional dance from hell: "The Push Me, Pull Me Polka." In introspection, one takes a journey of discovery and asks: "Why?" "What makes me recoil?" "What is my fear?" "What is the worst thing that can happen to me?" Follow that query with ,"And *then* what will happen?" Relationship intimacy is the most common area of resistance. "What will happen if I just love that person?" We constantly compare ourselves to others. We sing the "I'm not good enough" song and claim loneliness rather than take a risk. I love Garth Brooks' song "The Dance." In a few stanzas, he drew a perfect picture of the dilemma of love and living. The song brilliantly sings a philosophy of living that encourages us to "just dance." Choose to risk your heart; you are meant for love. Our primary job on this planet is not making peace or engaging conflict; our job is to extend our love. And the next step in the dance requires that we then receive love. Go within, what are you resisting?

Meditation today should begin with the word "resistance." As you take your place at the altar of self-devotion, gift yourself the blessing of dance. Dance with the resistance of your mind, move your thinking forward into presence. Move forward into willingness and move forward into love.

Write down the thing to which you are most resistant. What can you do today to dance with the resistance…pull resistance close to you and shower it with your willingness to dance differently today?

Without an education, the heart presents itself as a cauldron of raw emotions, suspicious desires, and disconnected images. Dreams appear stupefying, longings inappropriate, and relationships confounding... Education of the proper kind brings into view the order and sense in matters of the heart that otherwise seem elusive, and position the heart to play a significant role in affairs of the mind.

Thomas Moore, *The Education of the Heart*

When clients agree to bring their conflict and pain before us, it is clear that imparting our knowledge becomes a necessary act. We educate them; we model a sense of presence and a genuine engagement in dialogue; and we provide clarity of communication, openness, respect, and awareness of another point of view. Although I consider myself transformative, I am quite an active participant in any sacred circle. I consider it my duty to promote peacemaking through education. Instructing clients on the power of choice proves to be monumental in creating positive movement out of disorder and chaos. This proactivity promotes the tearing down of boundaries erected from skewed perceptions, of the "us vs. them" mentality that pervades so much of the thinking in conflicted souls. Be an educator in your practice. Dare to be a leader at the table.

Meditate in stillness about "education." Breathe in the vast knowledge from the cosmos, and breathe out the uncertainty of the next step. Breathe in shared wisdom from your soul, and rest your mind.

Write a line or two in your journal about education. What do you value most about education? What can you impart to those around you?

Direction

Our plans miscarry when they have no aim. When a man does not know what harbor he is making for, no wind is the right wind.

Seneca

I imagine that Seneca never expected his words to be read over two thousand years after writing them. I am continually amazed how the great philosophers were so focused on the necessary elements for living a good life. They knew that mind training was crucial. Having goals and direction has been the struggle of humans throughout the ages. While I grapple with the paradoxical sensibility to plan one's life and stay fluid, I have come to know it is necessary to be comfortable enjoying the flow and not having a set agenda. I have unlimited sources of energy, at least during the day. My trial in life has been to stop long enough to truly experience that vertical moment of no activity. Alas, I find the same fork in the road realized by Seneca in ancient Rome: mind training versus incessant internal dialogue. I choose mind training. I now use the early morning meditation to force quietness. I make myself become still and just listen. While I admit to still being day-planner-driven, I have devised a way around that by planning twenty minutes for stillness: spiritual enrichment, uplifting reading, listening to soothing music. I have experienced that vertical moment with success! The funny thing is that when I protect those twenty minutes, I can recognize the present moment several times throughout the day—the moments when it is comfortable to not know where the harbor lies beyond the horizon.

Begin meditation this morning with the word "direction." Let your breath settle into your lungs, and breathe out that frantic impulse toward movement. Breathe in the luxurious stillness of a calm sea, and breathe out the need to leave your body.

Write a line or two in your journal about direction. Do you have a plan for the day? What would it feel like to not think ahead?

May there always be work for your hands to do.
May your purse always hold a coin or two.
May the sun always shine on your windowpane.
May a rainbow be certain to follow each rain.
May the hand of a friend always be near you.
May God fill your heart with gladness to cheer you.

Irish blessing

This Irish blessing rings in my soul. It is so positive in nature, a true representation of the phrase "be love." To offer one the Irish blessing speaks of honoring another's soul, an act I want to perform with regularity. But I have to intentionally make sure I do that every day. This world moves so quickly that blessing another with richness of life has to be intentional. Leading a rich life sounds so inviting to me. I am fortunate to be content in the comforts of my life. I am sure that age makes that possible (I am now in my mid-50s). But our society is a society of collection, a gathering of things our parents could never obtain. Having many possessions does not bring a rich life; it can bring emptiness and depression. Having wonderful friends does bring richness. Choosing joy and cheerfulness enriches the soul. Making sure that the "sun always shines on your windowpane" brings clear and positive perception. Having "work for your hands to do" keeps you engaged in fulfilling activity. And "a rainbow" promises possibility. To me, these things weave gold into the tapestry of one's life.

Bring the warmth of richness to your meditation today, and explore richness with each breath. Feel the sustenance of peace bless your soul.

Write a line or two in your journal about the images of richness that came to you in your meditation.

Pain

My soul is a broken field, plowed by pain.

Sara Teasdale

Pain in life can be unbearable from time to time, and pain escapes no one. The trick is what you do with pain. What helps, for me, is to try to discern what is under the particular pain of the day. As a psychotherapist, I know that pain is the first human response, but often, it is masked by anger or isolation. That realization represents a choice to express or suppress the feeling. I think it is important to feel your feelings when they arise. Many interpret the "correct" spiritual path to be one that short-circuits pain or goes straight for the "love thy neighbor" clause of faith. That only creates a spiritual bypass and, to me, smacks of robotic, often disingenuous, "I should" action. While I think it is extremely important to end up with the "love thy neighbor" creed, if we didn't first experience the real depth of our emotion, we would already *be* the higher power. Don't skip the steps of the process. Pain is your friend. When your body experiences pain, the pain gives you information: "I have a cut on my foot." When you experience emotional pain, your body gives you clues: "You have touched a nerve." Your throat may tighten, your chest may constrict, tears may well up in your eyes, or you forget to breathe. Move into the pain, feel it, accept it: it tells you that you are human—and it is your job to be human. Then the decision for what to do next will arise in clarity.

Many of us spend our whole lives running from feeling with the mistaken belief that you cannot bear the pain. But you have already borne the pain. What you have not done is feel all you are beyond that pain.

Kahlil Gibran

Meditate today beginning with the word "pain." Imagine that you are soaring through the pain, that you will reach that full breath of smooth air as you choose to ascend above the turbulence of the moment. Breathe in the peace of transcendence, and breathe out the needles in the heart. Breathe in the clarity of altitude, and breathe out the expectations.

In your journal, note one source of pain you experienced yesterday. What other choice can you make this week if you feel that pain coming back?

When I look into the future, it looks so bright it burns my eyes.

Oprah Winfrey

What an incredible inspiration Oprah is to the planet. She is so willing to share her good fortune, but more important, she is willing to share her knowledge and to provide new knowledge through her *O: The Oprah Magazine* and book-club selections. I think the reason for Oprah's success is that she chooses to see the future as bright. Her circumstances growing up were anything but bright, and yet, look what she has created with the opportunities that life has presented her. Many things have happened to me that required a conscious choice. Alcoholism in my family growing up, sudden deafness in one ear, a neck injury that must be holistically managed daily, and relationships that did not match my dream—all had to be dealt with in stages throughout my life. To escape the emotional and physical pain, I had to make a choice at every juncture, every day. Collectively, we have lost the hope that the future is bright. Depression is rampant in society. Billions of dollars are spent each year on mood elevators for millions of people, all so that we do not have to transcend that pain to get to the joy. Is it possible that millions of people in this country have organic brain dysfunction? Or is it the easy choice? I think that what is missing is the intestinal fortitude to process the pain and choose to see that the future can be so bright it will burn your eyes. I have to choose to look for the surprise every morning when I get up. When I can't get there, what's missing is connection with my soul.

Meditate today on the word "surprise." Breathe in the anticipation of the day, and breathe out the hopelessness on the heart. Breathe in the freshness of the morning; breathe out the inertia of depression.

Write down, in one sentence, one thing that happened today that was surprising. Is there a deliberate choice that you can make for tomorrow that could have surprising results?

Out of life comes death,
*   And out of death, life,*
Out of the young, the old,
*   And out of the old, the young,*
Out of waking, sleep,
*   And out of sleep, waking,*
The stream of creation and dissolution never stops.

Heraclitus

The process of the earth can be viewed by looking at the seasons and seeing the circularity. "Out of life comes death" in the autumn, "and out of death, life" can be seen in the spring. The sleeping can come to life during conflict, and those screaming in pain can choose silence . The theory of quantum physics is one of circularity, that all energy is conserved and continually takes new forms. Pain-ridden systems of conflict repeat until at least one member of that system chooses again. As a family-systems therapist, I was trained to look for the repetitive behaviors in systems of people. "One bad apple spoils the bushel" is one way to look at negativity in conflict. The other approach is to look at the system with hope: one person making a different step can change the trajectory of the chaos and move the system toward resolution. Studying the circularity of conflict provides the most valuable clues to the practitioner. All power dynamics can be understood by examining repetitive behaviors. Studying the circularity of one's own life can provide clues to creating a new orbit. The circle has been a metaphor for philosophers and great writers for centuries. Rituals are performed in circles; peace is found in circles.

Meditate today on the circle. Envision the comfort of a circle of peace, and breathe out the fear of unending pain. Embrace the newness of life, and breathe out the reluctance to fully participate in your life today.

In your journal, draw the circles in your life. Study them. Are they circles of people? Are they circles of repetitive behavior? Are they circles of thought? Are they peaceful circles or are they painful circles? What needs to change in your thinking that will make a change in your circles?

Aloneness

*Until you make peace with who you are, you'll never
be content with what you have become.*

Doris Mortman

Until I turned fifty, aloneness was a state of being that I spent my entire lifetime dreading. I have conquered my worst fear, and now I welcome being alone. I find myself guarding my time viciously. Perhaps to balance out my efforts, I have once again run to the negative extreme, on the opposite end of the spectrum. One day soon, I will get the balance right, for I am resolute. I am on a mission to make peace with who I am, looking for contentment in the very place I was sure it could not exist. Although I'm still in doubt of who I've become, one thing is certain: I will continually transform. I am unwavering in my conscious pursuit of personal transformation—a soul intentionally seeking self-actualization. The problem is that when we resolutely pursue a course of action, we might miss the turn in the road. In my single-mindedness, I tend to tune out the signposts along the path of my life. For now, I am exploring new rooms in the house of solitude, creating my sanctuary of peace, and remembering to look out the window from time to time so that I can see the right turn when it becomes visible on the horizon.

Begin meditation today with the word "alone." Breathe in and out the comfort of turning inward, allowing all things human to commune with the divine.

Write a line or two in your journal about aloneness. What images do you see in your mind's eye?

The definition of insanity is doing the same thing over and
over again and expecting a different result.

Albert Einstein

Most people, have minor eccentricities that others would view as neurotic. I am sure that my incessant bargain shopping is driven by a need for security and a lack of abundant thinking. In personal relationships, neuroses take on a whole new dimension. Often the term "insanity" is a matter of perception, and different shades of presumed insanity show up daily in conflicted relationships. Often, our clients get hung up expecting the same response in a bad relationship to produce a different result. Some forms of insanity are worse than others. I am a systemic thinker; I have observed that every relationship operates within a system, and I guide the mediation process within that framework. One useful tool for resolution when working with a neurotic relationship is to educate the saner individual on ways to strengthen boundaries. Another tool is the structured sharing of information that allows the person another perspective. It is in the expectation of a different result that question the opportunity for disengagement. Sometimes, all you can do is to suggest that the less neurotic person, the one who is continually stepping on the hoe handle, make another choice. Often, in the caring professions, our personal relationships are the ones that really suffer the trials of personal and perceived insanities. Occasionally those differences are merely 'dis-ease' of the mind, in need of introspection. Examine your own life. Is there evidence of a little neurosis here and there? Which hoe handle are you trouncing on? Can you successfully redirect that energy with another choice?

The diseases of the mind are more destructive than those of the body.

Cicero

In meditation today, review the perceived insanities in your relationships. Do you recognize behavior that drains your energy? With clarity of thought, get in touch with old patterns of behavior and explore new paths to change. Breathe in a freshness of mind and breathe out familiar behaviors that do not bring you inner peace.

Journal about thinking that brings you back to old problems, the ones you can never seem to resolve. What is one thing that you can do differently today that can place you on a new trajectory?

Your pain is the breaking of the shell that encloses your understanding. Even as the stone of the fruit must break, that its heart may stand in the sun, so you must know pain. And could you keep your heart in wonder at the daily miracles of your life, your pain would not seem less wondrous than your joy; And you would accept the seasons of your heart, even as you have always accepted the seasons that pass over your fields. And you would watch with serenity through the winters of your grief.

Kahlil Gibran, *The Prophet*

The length of the grieving process is hard to gauge. There is no set timetable for the grief train to arrive at the station of joy, and no one escapes grief when loss permeates our cocoon of safety. Avoidance seems to be the first step in my personal process of grief, and it generally looks like a dive from the high board into work or some mental activity. However, grieving is a passage, a transition from a dark night to the rainbow at the end of the storm. Gibran's metaphor of the passage of grief as a winter, as one of "the seasons of your heart," is so beautiful and hopeful. The choice becomes one of process versus denial. Denial feeds grief and extends its season. Grief is not a door we willingly enter; it is easier to dull the throb with a glass of wine, or the training regimen for a marathon, or the exhilaration of a new romantic interest. The death of a loved one, divorce, the leaving home by children, the decay of an ideal, an unmet expectation—all are events of loss that can evoke grief. If we attempt to shortcut the grieving process, to medicate the pain with work, substances, or any other compulsive behavior—or if we languish in the grief interminably—grief will follow us until we deal with it. We all know people who live in the sarcasm of grief—"Life's a bitch and then you die."—and it is easy to stay there, a victim of life, waiting to die. It is challenging to get it right. When I am swimming in a sea of grief, I am fairly tough on myself. "Snap out of it!" is a message my internal committee yells from the cheap seats. I never know when it is acceptable to sit with the grief and let a spiritual healing occur, or when I should start cracking the whip. Since patience is something that was issued while I was primping in heaven, it seems to be my ongoing lesson, appearing daily for me to practice until I get it right. Recognizing grief when it presents itself is a large part of the successful transition through the grief.

Meditation today should begin with the word "grief." Let your mind rest on grief. Is there grief that needs processing and healing? Breathe in the permission to grieve, and breathe out the sorrow that surrounds it. Breathe in the peace that waits beyond the season of winter, and welcome the season of spring.

Write in your journal about grief. If you don't have time to fully explore this topic before your day begins, take your journal with you and excavate this area of pain during the day. Bring it to the light, and give yourself permission to bring closure to the grief still lurking in sorrow.

You must remember the value that you add to others and not just
what others have added to you. That's how we build self-worth,
which, in my opinion, is just as important as net worth.

Suze Orman, *O: The Oprah Magazine*, September 2003

Suze Orman is a financial expert and dynamic motivational speaker. She makes her living as the town crier for the necessity of a financial education. She educates people holistically, treating the client and their relationship with money as one. Let's face it: we all need money. We may as well have a healthy relationship with abundance. Focusing on the acquisition of money, hoarding money and possessions, miserly greed, living on nothing without any comforts—all are extreme behaviors that result from an unhealthy relationship with money. As with any other area of our life, finding the balance becomes a daily task. Suze Orman's mantra is that we should understand our personal value in all areas of our life. If the life we choose to live is one in which we honor our own self-worth and handle our finances in a healthy way, abundance will follow. In the helping professions, it is easy to devalue the work we do, the money we earn, and the contributions we make to our relationships. We become so good at helping fix the problems and ease the pain of other people that we neglect our self-worth in the process. Today, remember the value you bring to your own life.

Meditate today on the word "value." What images of value float through your awareness? Do you value your journey? Do you value your worth?

In your journal, record the images of value that came up in your meditation.

Fork in the Road

In the middle of our life journey
I found myself in a dark wood.
I had wandered from the straight path.
It isn't easy to talk about it:
it was such a thick, wild, rough forest
that when I think of it my fear returns.

Dante Alighieri, *The Divine Comedy*, "Inferno: Canto I"

No one escapes the fork in the road. Choices must be made at each juncture. Sometimes we are wrought with ambivalence, seeking another choice, not knowing why, regretting or questioning every step. Other times, we choose to just go with it and refuse to look back. As I move into the "middle of my life journey," I find that times of stillness and introspection provide me the information I need to sort through ambivalence or indecision. In my younger years, fear usually meant, "Forget everything and run!" Running down the wrong path was my customary choice back then. After decades of conditioning myself to obey the fear, the diversion can still loom ahead of me. Overcoming my reactivity has been a daily assignment. Are you approaching a fork in your road?

For your meditation today, visualize a fork in your journey's path. Breathe in the warm welcoming and excitement of the new turn ahead; breathe out the fear of making the wrong choice. Breathe in the air of comfort in your coming choice; breathe out the reluctance to approach it.

Write a few lines in your journal about the road you envisioned in your meditation. What did it look like? What do you need to explore today to provide more clarity in making the choice?

Dark Nights of the Soul

In the dark night something of your makeup comes to an end—your ego, your self, your creativeness, your meaning. You may find in that darkness a key to your source, the larger soul that makes you who you are and holds the secrets of your existence....You have to give yourself receptively to the transforming natural powers that remain mysteriously dark.

Thomas Moore, *Dark Nights of the Soul*

Thomas Moore's *Dark Nights of the Soul* validated for me that I was not slipping into a dark place for the rest of my life. During a phase of darkness, I felt depressed, hopeless, and anxiety-ridden about what was happening on my journey. Moore notes that one should not fear a dark night, that "it's a time of waiting and trusting," and one must be comfortable sitting in discomfort and wait for the right course to unfold. Many souls, searching for a purpose to their life, experience sudden periods of sadness, turmoil, pain, and disconnection, but out of the shadows, a new course is always revealed. Perhaps it cannot be seen without walking through the dark. Moore maintains that dark nights are not necessarily bad or uncommon occurrences, that, in fact, they are a natural part of life and revisit us many times during the span of our life. He further claims that sometimes this period of transformation is for the benefit of others and not for your own clarity. Have you recently experienced a dark night?

Meditation today should begin with the word "dark." What image is summoned to your senses? What can you see along the edges of the path? Embrace your reality in this moment.

Write in your journal about the dark nights of your soul. What lessons did you learn? What gifts did you receive as a result of the transformations?

*Whether we listen with aloof amusement to the dreamlike mumbo jumbo of
some red-eyed witch doctor of the Congo, or read with cultivated rapture thin
translations from the sonnets of the mystic Lao-tse; now and again crack the hard
nutshell of an argument of Aquinas, or catch suddenly the shining meaning of a
bizarre Eskimo fairy tale: it will always be the one, shape-shifting yet marvelously
constant story that we find, together with a challengingly persistent suggestion
of more remaining to be experienced than will ever be known or told.*

Joseph Campbell, *The Hero With a Thousand Faces*

Each of us was meant to be the hero of our own journey. In her book *Sacred Contracts*, Caroline Myss posits that we all arrive with very specific contracts lived through archetypes, and the hero is one such powerful archetype. A cultural anthropologist, Joseph Campbell wrote many books about myth and religion throughout his lifetime. Much of his youth was spent trotting the globe for information about the rituals, myths, beliefs, and religions of different cultures. He lived among various peoples and studied their cultures, not for the purpose of defining the differences, but rather for discovering similarities. How are we all alike? How are we connected in our themes and narratives for nurturing our soul? Recognizing the oneness of purpose we share with those who appear before us to engage in conflict—and in resolution—makes it easier to assist them in finding their hero within. But first we must look for the hero residing in our own soul, the contract we made to be the peace we want to see in the world.

Meditate today on the word "hero." Watch your mind as it floats, and breathe toward this word. What images come to mind? In the stillness, give form to the images.

In your journal, write down or draw the images that came to you in your meditation.

The most immutable barrier in nature is between one man's thoughts and another's.
William James

Often, in the making of peace, we try to fashion a resolution while working with problem saturated language. Thoughts are reduced to speech that can sound impervious to change, and present a barrier to resolution. This communication of doom expresses a hopelessness that will be realized if the barrier-ridden thoughts are not reframed. For true understanding to occur, perception must be shifted through the revealing of deep personal experience that resides below the surface of the stated problem. Yet our clients come to us in caught in a terrible struggle, fixed in a positional stance and their backs against the rope with their dukes up. It is imperative that, as agents of change, we use our power of intervention to move into the tension through our choice of questions, to be comfortable with moving towards the center of the ring where the unspoken sources of conflict are waiting to be uncovered. While we search for the opening, we should elicit answers that draw a concrete picture of the opposing party's reality. This allows the other client to refocus their lens, see beyond the barrier, and envision the possibility that a different outcome will emerge. In our personal lives, we also have barriers that keep us from peace. Today, take an inventory of barriers that you recognize in your life. What can you do to restructure the barriers of thought that prevent you from being authentically present?

Meditate today on the word "barrier." Breathe in the limitless horizon, and breathe out the dark shadow cast by the wall before you. Breathe in the promise of the peaceful view and breathe out the overwhelming climb that will enable you to see over the barrier that you have placed between your thoughts and the thoughts of another.

Note in your journal the areas of your life in need of reconstruction. What barriers are impeding your attainment of peace? What can you do today to remove that barrier?

Self-Acceptance

To love one's self is the beginning of a lifelong romance.

Oscar Wilde

Self-acceptance arrives in the misty morning of mid-life and rarely before then. The striving for self-acceptance is a hazardous endeavor and can be a lifelong trial for everyone. Sometimes "the striving" is a club we use to bludgeon ourselves into a submissive, "less than" state of limitation. No one else can grant us self-acceptance. That task is reserved for the enlightened, the willing, and the brave. My road leading to self-acceptance was lengthened by decades of self-rejection. The clearing that appeared as I neared the road's end, allowed a view of majestic mountains that brought peace and clarity—those final miles traversable only after I extended to myself the tolerance I had for others. If you don't feel accepted, imagine that you do. What you intentionally focus on will become your reality, if you allow it. It will begin a lifelong romance with you.

You are accepted, *accepted by that which is greater than you and the name of which you do not know. Do not ask for the name now; perhaps you will find it later. Do not try to do anything now; perhaps later you will do much. Do not seek for anything; do not perform anything; do not intend anything.* Simply accept the fact that you are accepted*!*

Paul Tillich, *The Shaking of the Foundations*

Meditate on the term "self-acceptance." Breathe in the comforting cloud of self-appreciation, and breathe out the doubting darkness of the ego. Breathe in the peace that comes with sufficiency, and breathe out the pain of not measuring up.

Which of your qualities can you readily embrace today? How can you chart out and focus on a passage to self-acceptance?

Honesty

Only one thing is more frightening than speaking your truth. And that is not speaking.

Naomi Wolf

I am not certain exactly why I *have to* speak my truth—perhaps it has something to do with my sweet mother, who was never empowered to do so—but, for me, not speaking my truth is frightening, unethical, and mendacious. It nevertheless took years to be able to see my honesty, though often brutal, as a positive quality and not just chancing to hurt another's feelings. Hurting another's feelings was the greatest sin a Southern woman could commit. I'm over it. When colleagues ask me why I continue to choose to work with highly conflicted clients, I reply that I have no fear—these are my people! Conflict resolution is the puzzle for which my particular brand of tactlessness is appropriate and the tools for success include a two-by-four and a mirror. Because I do not fear the emotion of my clients, they do not feel judged, and if they do, they can see it coming, no surprises. So I travel my road of "calling a spade a spade," and I never look back. Examine your perception of honesty. It will likely not match mine, but can you welcome your honesty? Can you use it to "mediate dangerously," as Ken Cloke says? Honesty can be loving, empowering, compassionate, or very scary. What does speaking your truth look like to you?

Meditate today on the word "honesty." Breathe in questioning stillness. Feel your truth rising with your breath.

Write a few lines in your journal about honesty. How comfortable are you with speaking your truth?

Perfect valor is to do unwitnessed what we should be capable of doing before all the world.

Francois Duc de La Rochefoucauld

Peacemakers and those willing to stand in the face of conflict are truly valiant people. We welcome hurting hearts into our cocoon of magic. The magic is in our willingness to be present and work within the system of conflict to create a different course for the healing to unfold. We hope that the butterfly within them will stretch its wings and fly, shedding the cumbersome trappings of conflict. We are willing to hold a higher honor, an ethical standard, a position of valor, unwitnessed, with no chance of anyone else knowing how we performed—no kudos calling from the distance, no praise from the gallery. But we know when we have performed with valor. That is enough.

Begin meditation today with the word "valor." Breathe in a higher course to follow; breathe out your sense of insignificance. Breathe in the willingness to stand in the face of the storm, and breathe out the concern that you can't make a difference.

In your journal, attest to the evidence of your valiant performance in your work.

In this bland, flowing atmosphere, I regain, one by one, my faculties, my organs; life returns to a finger, a hand, a foot. A new nimbleness,—almost wings, unfold at my side,—and I see my right to the heaven as well as to the farthest fields of the earth. The effect of the conversation resembles the effect of a beautiful voice in a church choir…which insinuates itself as water into all the chinks and cracks and presently floats the whole discordant choir and holds it in solution in its melody.

Ralph Waldo Emerson, *Journals of Ralph Waldo Emerson, 1820–1872*

With the renewal of the spring season every year, the life cycle affords the opportunity to experience a personal renewal. In the stillness of the winter, we are introspective, contemplative, and orderly. But as each spring is born, a more luminous feature to the landscape arises, and our life wants to renew itself as well. Emerson paints a beautiful unfolding of essence and spirit that builds to a melodious crescendo. Thusly, our fruitful thoughts flow in spring, first in a trickle and then in a waterfall of potential through intention. How can we bring that promise and intention forth in our relationships, in our responsibilities to life? I believe that we need only to appreciate the blessings of our life. Gratitude brings the permission for appreciation to flow into new awareness.

Meditate today on the word "appreciation." Breathe in the blessings of your life, and breathe out the stale history of the winter. Breathe in the creation of spring, and breathe out the cocoon of stillness.

Write a few lines about the things you appreciate in your life. List three new thoughts that you will embrace today. How can you come to appreciate your essence?

The willingness to reach inside every part of yourself opens the door to total understanding. When you hold some part of yourself in reserve you deny it exposure to life; you repress its energy and keep it from understanding what it needs to know.

Deepak Chopra, *The Book of Secrets*

Deepak Chopra believes that deciding to experience our passion releases all the energy we possess, even the fear, negativity, and doubt of success of the passionate creation. He notes that these emotions discourage so many people from bearing the fruit of their passion. If we dislike the negative parts of ourselves so much, we will hold our passion in check, hoping that life will be made safe. Tapping into our passion needs to be an adventure! Examining the things we are passionate about is a way of owning our creativity, our power, our zeal. Many of us entered the field of peace and conflict engagement because of our passion for making a difference in the world. Many of us are actively searching for a better way. Owning our reasoning for choosing to be a practitioner can make us more effective in that practice. Practice your passion.

Meditate today on the word "passion." Breathe in the intensity of passion, and breathe out the anxiety of expressing passion. Breathe in the peace of the day, and breathe out the panic of producing your dream work.

List the passionate ideas you have in your creative mind this morning. Intend to act on one of these passions today.

I would like to beg you...to have patience with everything unresolved in your heart and to try to love the questions themselves... Don't search for the answers, which could not be given to you now, because you would not be able to live them. And the point is, to live everything. Live the questions now. Perhaps then, someday far in the future, you will gradually, without even noticing it, live your way into the answer.

Rainer Maria Rilke, *Letters to a Young Poet*

Depression is a growth industry in our world. Medications that were designed to be temporary are ordered in bulk. Billions of dollars are spent on medications to feel good, because we feel so bad. In my estimation, 90% of those who medicate their pain have no organic brain-chemistry problems or hormonal imbalances. Life can be depressing from time to time. If organic imbalance is your reality and you are in the other 10%, this does not apply to you. No life escapes depression. Depression asks, "Is this all there is?" It says, "I am nothing without somebody," or "I only see the sadness." I hear these feelings expressed on the negotiating field of human misery every day. So much of the dialogue of depression is the language of lack, and it avoids the pain of transition—to something better, to slough off the old skin, to leave the cocoon. Most philosophers and transpersonal psychologists say that we are not connected with ourselves, that we live inside our mind, seeing the world through the lens of the thinker, not through the heart of spirit and emotion. Theologians give as many reasons for depression as there are theologies: we are not living righteously, we are not devoting our lives to the Lord, we are not living the Word, and many other excuses. In the long run, it does not matter what others think; our search continues. What are we searching for? I think we are searching for ourselves through the resistance of the thinking mind: "I am what I think I am." The search cannot be successful, for the soul cannot be found in thought. Thomas Moore, Carl Jung, and Joseph Campbell affirm that we have lost our rituals as a society. We don't have milestones of transition that guide us through this life. Moore builds on the writings of the medieval mystic, John of the Cross, and suggests that depression is just a "dark night of the soul" that serves to force the spirit from one transformation to another. We should not try to escape it, but rather sit in the dark room, surrender to the process, and let the transformation take place: "Discover the very point of your personhood: the process of constant renewal." We are the world's most creative reframers of language. Rather than label depression a disease, why not reframe it into a process of transformation?

Today in your meditation, let your heart feel free of the heaviness of depressing thoughts. As the list of sad things sink in your mind choose again. Let joy guide your heart as you live in the moment of this day.

Write down in your journal the topics of turmoil that drive your mood. Intentionally let go of one of these topics today.

All mortals tend to turn into the thing they are pretending to be.

C.S. Lewis

In psychology, there is a term for this: *delusional*. Of course, I'm teasing! Still, I think I would rather reframe the adage *fake it until you make it* into an optimistic possibility. Faking it is not an image that lends itself to authenticity. This quotation is another way of saying, "Create your own reality by envisioning that you already possess that quality." If you *fake it until you make it*, that act is evidence of authentic intention. Delusional behavior is escaped when you are not in denial about the fact that you are faking it! Other ways to say 'fake it' are, "I intend to be loving and open even though my heart wants to protect and hide," or "I intend to forgive even though I'm having difficulty forgetting." Sometimes the 'faking it' requires the assistance of the divine. We may have an intention that cannot be exercised without higher power bridging the gap. As the Christian apologist C.S. Lewis inferred, pretense does not always result in failure, sometimes we actually get there. Clear intention marks the first step in designing a new life, creating a new narrative and is evidence of artistry. Think about areas of your life that you would redesign. We are always afforded mercy through the act of being willing to change. Turn into the intention today.

Meditation today should begin with the words "fake it." Agree to entertain a mantra this morning as a way of envisioning yourself going within…silently review in the stillness the act of transformation. As you go into the cocoon what do you see forming the wings of the butterfly?

Write in your journal what images came to you in meditation. Review your recent past. Do you see evidence of 'making it'? In what area of your life do you need to set forth a new intention?

Our world needs spiritual giants, and it takes not ego...but humility to sign up for the effort. Many of our problems arose because we chose to play small, thinking that we would find safety. But we were born with wings, and we are meant to spread them. Anything less will hurt us, will deny love to ourselves and others, and will mean that we end our lives not having flown the flight of spiritual glory.

Marianne Williamson, *A Return to Love*

Peacemaking and interpersonal engagement take great courage. We have such a significant role in the larger picture of global evolution. Many feel called to do this work. But whatever brought you to your work, do not deny the significance that making peace in the community is playing in your life at this moment. Yesterday is gone and tomorrow is not here, but in this moment, you are powerful, a change agent, a catalyst, a blessing, a warrior, and your role is one of great significance on the planet today. Do not take this role lightly, and honor yourself for your bravery in the face of the storm.

Meditate today on the significance of your life. Breathe in the calling in the wilderness, and breathe out the mindlessness of days past. Breathe in the magnitude of powerful influence, and breathe out the small ego's implication of playing small in the world.

In your journal, write about the evidence you have of the significant role you play in your work.

It is up to us to present our divine gifts by sharing and allowing them to become manifest, in all unique forms of expression they may take. None of us is alike and we can make our mark upon the world by expressing as only we can.

Ron Vernen, *Science of Mind Magazine*, February 2006

When I first thought of manifesting changes in my life, I felt ridiculous and powerless. Who am I to put my wishes above my ego, the committee member in my head who says, "Who the hell do you think you are? You can't do this! You are never going to get there. You can never be that good." In the 1980s, a valued friend and mentor told me, "Act as though you CAN do whatever your heart is telling you to do. Just do it for a week, for fun, and write about how it felt to play that part." As absurd as that sounded to me at the time, I followed her advice and have gone forth to sing her mantra to countless others. Amazingly, you can bridge to whatever future you are drawn to by setting the intention to manifest it, as long as you are ethical and authentic in your intention. For me, the last piece of that intention is to let go and allow the natural unfolding, moment by moment. Choosing not to slam the square peg into a round hole is a careful consideration when traveling the path. The path that appears in the clearing seldom looks as I would have imagined it. Imagine yourself as you wish to be. Imagine your life as you wish it to be. Imagine your work as you wish it to be. See that reality appearing in the clearing of your personal forest. We are powerful beyond earthly calculation. If you feel inconsequential, you will be. If you are a failure in your mind, you will fail.

Meditate beginning with the word "manifestation." Listen for the quiet information that arises as your breath takes you inward. Breathe in clarity and wisdom for your journey, and breathe out the dense fog of the ego mind. Breathe in the peace of a power greater than your own, and breathe out the fear that accompanies the choices before you. Intend to change your path.

What images came to you in your meditation? What situations do you wish to change? Name one thing you can do today to open the door to personal empowerment.

No one ever built a monument to a critic.

George Bernard Shaw

Performance in problem solving requires the carefully honed skills of decision making. Although we are trained to have a watchful eye for problems, this habit can become a real deterrent to living. We may feel the need to control our own environment, or have an air of superiority, or be corralled by our opinions and limitations of understanding. We are all equal in our humanness, and when we use our gifts incorrectly, we run the risk of sparking the flame of self-criticism. My friend Dana has given her inner critic a name, "Fanny the Fault Finder." Self-criticism triggers our emotional slide into personal hell. This ugly monster starts a downward spiral of circularity that impedes personal growth and happiness. Ego rears a dragon that is difficult to slay. Today, choose to see yourself in others with charity. Recognize your fears and vulnerabilities in those who are in front of you. Corral your inner critic; you will have not only patience for others, but acceptance of yourself.

Begin your mediation today with exploration of your "inner critic." Breathe from deep within your lungs and warm your heart. Breathe out the harshness of criticism, and breathe in the blessings of creative intelligence. Breathe out the self-imposed constraints of your actions and thoughts.

Write a few lines in your journal about your inner critic. Can you give your inner critic a name? How can you work today to quell your inner negative dialogue?

Today's main paradigm for understanding a human life, the interplay of genetics and environment, omits something essential—the particularity you feel to be you… [L]ift the pall of victim mentality from which individual people cannot recover until the theoretical paradigms that give rise to that mentality have been seen through and set aside.

James Hillman, *The Soul's Code: In Search of Character and Calling*

Hillman's thesis in *The Soul's Code* is that the victim archetype has ruled the planet for too long and we need to focus the individual on the flip side of that coin, the hero. He cites the Myth of Er from Plato's *Republic,* which spoke to finding your calling: that we come to this life with a purpose and a companion to guide our way, what the Ancient Greeks called "daimon," the Christians "The Holy Spirit," and the Romans "genius." Purpose can drive us to greatness, to radical change, to destiny, to ruin. It can possess us and force us to examine the depths of our being, our darkest thoughts. Hillman posits that if we excavate and discover our purpose, the driving force behind our work, our love, our being, we will find that spark of uniqueness. We will uncover the mission of our life, our reason for being here. Have you examined your purpose in life? Do you feel as though you have been called to this work? Are you in need of a paradigm shift?

Meditate today on the word "paradigm." Sit in silence listening for the call, and breathe in the misty air of discovery; breathe out the stale air of languishing ambiguity. Breathe in the clear air of invention, and break through to shift the paradigm and find a purpose for your life.

Write in your journal about the paradigms which operate in your life.. List the questions you have for yourself. What is one thing you can do today to understand more fully what shifts need to occur in your life?

Warm Hands, Warm Heart

Health, a light body, freedom from cravings, a glowing skin, sonorous voice,
fragrance of the body: these signs indicate progress in the practice of meditation.

Shvetashvatara Upanishads

One of the advantages of a daily practice of meditation is improvement of one's health. I began to notice this after my spiritual group began a regular morning ritual of meditation in 2001. Typically, I have cold hands, especially the right one due to a neck injury that causes muscle spasm and a reduction of blood flow to my hands. I was amazed when I began to meditate. I could feel my hands radiate heat. At the end of every meditation, my hands were actually hot, and the effect lasted throughout the morning. Through the act of meditation, it was as though all the parts of me were connected in a way the energy could actually be felt in my hands. Daily devotees of meditation will say, "Well of course!" But for me it was a revelation. The "force" was with me when I meditated. My vascular system was speaking to me! There is abundant research to show that mental alertness and calmness are increased when meditation is regularly practiced. Combining a yoga practice with meditation tones the body and strengthens the core. Consider your physical exercise regimen. Can you choose to warm your hands and warm your heart at the same time? Your life and your body will speak to you!

Meditation today should begin with the phrase "warm hands, warm heart." Settle into your breathing with the intention of a longer period of stillness. Feel the warmth of your heart extend to your extremities, feel the crown of your head...breathe out the balmy breath of the morning as you rejuvenate your energy for the day.

This week keep an entry in your journal specifically about meditation and the changes you notice in your body.

Intimacy means that we're safe enough to reveal the truth about ourselves in all its creative chaos. If a space is created in which two people are totally free to reveal their walls, then those walls, in time, will come down.

Marianne Williamson

Trust is something that has always been hard for me. I am so protective of my heart that, over the years, I shut out a significant amount of love in my life. When I was 23, very much in love, and a bride of just three years, I came home one evening to find my prince charming, charming the wife of his best friend right into my bed. I wanted to die; the wave of betrayal and grief drowning me. Ill-equipped to digest the horror of what my eyes were telling me, I got in the car and drove to another city, immediately divorced him, and cried for 18 months. That may have been the catalyst for my trust issues, or perhaps it was my present, though absent, father drowning the images of war in Patton's army with vodka. Regardless of the origin of my pain, trust was not in my repertoire for many years. I expended a great deal of energy trying to control the chaos in my life, creative or otherwise. Thankfully, as the years have passed, I have taken a few layers of bricks from the wall of sadness. Today, I can feel the fears of trusting arise, simply observe, and say "Yes there they are…I can choose again." To shut out love when it walks in the door is to never risk your heart. While in those years of protection, the emptiness of the walls surrounding me urged me to want to live a different kind of life. In my 30s, I began to seek relief from the repetitive patterns of my youth. By my 40s, determination intensified, and I chose a completely different course of action. Distrust was replaced by risking the heart. When you risk, you live. When you play it safe, you lose. I began to ask myself, "What is the worst thing that could happen to me if I reveal who I really am to someone close to me?" The answer is always, "Well you might experience pain." "And then what would happen?" becomes my next question. The answer is always the same, "I will choose again." How do you perceive trust in your world? Trust the process of life today.

Meditation should begin with the word "trust." Trust your lungs to drink the nectar of life from the energy around you and breathe out the fear of risk. Trust that a power greater than you is ready to hold you while you learn to fly.

Quickly write down all the people you trust. Why do you trust them? Find a new person to trust today.

I have heard of a man lost in the woods and dying of famine and exhaustion at the foot of the tree, whose loneliness was relieved by the grotesque visions with which, owning to bodily weakness, his diseased imagination surrounded him, and which he believed to be real. So also, owing to bodily and mental health and strength, we may be continually cheered by a like but more normal and natural society, and to come to know that we are never alone.

Henry David Thoreau

Henry David Thoreau is famous because of his intentional hermitage, where he wrote *Walden*. He spoke to no one; he meditated in the nature and the wilderness, finding his way out of the woods and back into life. Thomas Moore, in *Dark Nights of the Soul*, wrote extensively about embracing these periods when we seem to be retreating from life in confusion. He posited that the dark journey bears fruit of discovery that we cannot access in periods of joy and communion with others. No life escapes periods of bewilderment. When we are being led astray by strange urges to retreat, confusion, a feeling that we are adrift in a sea of mystery, the proper course of action is to surrender and become lost in the woods. The agreement lies in the willingness to be lost in order that we may find ourselves and return to society with enthusiasm. As Thoreau illuminated, we must "come to know that we are never alone."

Meditation today about being "lost in the woods" and go to the place of discovery. Notice the woods around you. Breathe in the solitude of the quiet morning, and breathe out the fear to enter the dark wood. Breathe in the treasures that lie in the stillness; breathe out the baggage of the restless night.

Write a line or two in your journal about being lost in the woods. What images of that trip come to mind? How can you welcome the next excursion into surrender?

*Everyone is a prisoner of his own experience. No one can
eliminate prejudices—just recognize them.*

Edward R. Murrow

When clients come to engage in conflict and to resolve issues, certain biases and prejudices may be driving their perceptions in negotiations. Uncovering deep prejudice may hold the keys to the release of discrimination or unfairness. I find prejudice to be growing rather than declining in our society. Before the turn of this last century, it seemed the planet was moving in a positive orbit, but lately, I worry that we are spinning in retrograde. I have made a commitment to be more aware of personal prejudices and judgments I may unknowingly harbor. Being really honest with myself about personal prejudice is only the first step for me. I am only human, and human's judge. It is merely the way the brain orders information, and I can make a different choice. Once I am aware of personal prejudices, the prison cell opens and I exercise the choice to leave the cell. Think about prejudice today. Do you harbor prejudices of which you are unaware?

*A great many people think they are thinking when they
are merely rearranging their prejudices.*

William James

Begin meditation today with the word "prejudice." Breathe in the full circle of life; breathe out all categories of judgment. Breathe in the tapestry of oneness humans represent; breathe out the differences we manifest in our humanness.

What prejudice do you hold that you can shine light on today? How can you let go of the feelings that prejudice brings to your heart?

Can you see the holiness in those things you take for granted—a paved road or a washing machine? If you concentrate on finding what is good in every situation, you will discover that your life will suddenly be filled with gratitude, a feeling that nurtures the soul.

Rabbi Harold Kushner

We all take life for granted at certain times. When on retreat in the mountains to prepare for a workshop, I received a call that my strapping, healthy 18-year-old had been taken from work to the hospital. When the doctor told me the evidence pointed to a stroke, my knees became noodles in disbelief. How quickly life can change, yet it was just another opportunity for a mother to witness the lessons that life presents to a child. This is not the first time the heavens opened for my Taylor; his calling keeps him tethered to life. He is still in the process of discovering what that calling is, but whatever it is will be extraordinary. As I sat in the waiting room while they repaired a tiny hole in his heart, the source of the stroke, I focused on the beauty of the mountains, the flowers blooming in the hospital gardens, and the blessing that the stroke only did minor damage, with no long-term effects for this child just beginning his extraordinary life. To find the beauty in small everyday things is the doorway to happiness. Finding the sacred in disaster is a gift of peace. To be in a situation from which you cannot escape and still find serenity in a sunset is a process of remembering where we came from. Can you find gratefulness in the everyday blessings of life?

Meditate today beginning with the word "gratefulness." Take in life-giving atmosphere; sit in the stillness of the morning and receive sustenance from the air surrounding this planet. Be grateful that you are here and experiencing the peace of the moment.

Make a list of things you take for granted. Today, find a way to express gratitude for each of the items on your list.

We must have…a place where children can have a whole group of adults they can trust.

Margaret Mead

To me, "dependence" is an ugly word, although the reality is that we are all interdependent in some way for community and relationship. I have spent much of my life seeking independence. But when it comes to children, "dependence" is a word of love, duty, and responsibility. Margaret Mead said over fifty years ago that children must be able to trust the adults that have been put in their lives, *all* the adults. We know that this is a great challenge. Our society has not done a good job in responding to responsibility for the sake of the community's children; well-meaning governmental agencies working with families may do more harm than good. I take the responsibility for children very seriously. Many children who are embroiled in the vortex of familial conflict have no voice. I feel an ethical responsibility to make sure that children are taken into account when assisting in the solutions for bi-nuclear families. Parents are often so confused and entangled in the pain of uncoupling that they cannot see the needs of the children. This doesn't mean they don't love them or don't want the best for their children. Asking the right questions often focuses the parents back on the reason for the conflict. Moving toward and making known the obvious fear drags the avoided emotion of loss to the surface. Effectively dealing with that inevitable reality shines light on the correct path out of dispute and into solution. Even if you may not work directly in the area of family issues, look at personal relationships with children. How can you better the life of any child by being that person who listens, is available and trustworthy?

Begin meditation today with the word "dependence." Sit with the images of childhood; look for the faces of those you could trust.

Write down the images that came to your mind in meditation.

That I've failed, others must succeed, because those who do not have
the power over the story that dominates their lives, power to retell it,
rethink it, deconstruct it, joke about it, and change it as times change,
truly are powerless, because they cannot think new thoughts.

Salman Rushdie

Every day we feel some small bit of failure. Could we have made a deeper difference in our day? Could our conversations with our loved ones could have been a little softer? Could our work could have been more effective? As Salman Rushdie noted, if we cannot think new thoughts, choose again about those feelings of failure, then we become powerless in our journey. As clients come to sit with us, to resolve seemingly unsolvable issues, their general state is powerlessness. They are entrenched in a story they are compelled to repeat again and again until they can find an ending and feel empowered to choose a new story. Let their perception of failure not discourage you but encourage you to climb into the saddle of solutions and ride again.

Meditation today should begin with the word "success." Let the perception of failure melt into the drain...let the feeling of success warm your heart...care enough about your soul to move to joy.

How about your own story of living? Can you reconstruct a painful part of your narrative? Can you turn a perceived failure into a succession of hope, inner peace, and vitality? What can you do today to move toward success in your story? Write a new narrative about your life for the day...live it.

When one has weighed the sun in the balance, and measured the steps
of the moon, and mapped out the seven heavens star by star, there still
remains one self. Who can calculate the orbit of his own soul?

Oscar Wilde, *De Profundis*

Oscar Wilde was imprisoned for homosexuality for a period of time in his life. In the solitude of his "dark night," he wrote with such creativity that he doubted that level of artistry could have been accessed without the pain. It seems that we have a choice on earth: to wrestle with the realities of our human experience or go through our life as if we are already dead. Often we cannot take flight and soar without a visit to the bottom of the pit. "Who can calculate the orbit of his own soul?" It is impossible to calculate your orbit, unless you are willing to be launched from the comfort of sameness to the terror of the unknown. How often do we avoid that journey? How painful is it to choose introspection? Who among us would rather circle the equator, safe and balanced, than inventory our level of living? At the end of the day, we came into this alone and we orbit the planet alone. Our soul is the heavenly engine powering our ship.

Meditation today should begin the with the word "soaring." Breathe in the ecstatic atmosphere rushing past your face. Feel the lift-off of excitement as it courses through your body; breathe out the heaviness of yesterday. Breathe in the freedom and the vantage point of orbiting the stars; breathe out the not-knowing of walking death.

Write in your journal about the images that came to you in meditation. What would it feel like to soar? What is one thing that is stopping you?

Carl Jung said that he thought that the major focus of the second half of life should be mortality and that anything that took away from that was in the direction of not being mentally healthy. I think in our society we see so much denial of aging and ways that people try to pretend to themselves that aging is not happening and I worry about that being a not-healthy direction. I think a common correlation we see as people become older is that they have greater interest in things spiritual or non-physical.

Andrew Weil, M.D.

The "boomers" approaching the golden years is very scary sight. An emphasis on youth in society has resulted in people being willing to undergo unspeakable pain in the form of face-sculpting, gut-sucking, butt-lifting, skin-torching, laser-burning and muscle-injecting horror. All are procedures that produce a generation of people looking as if they are in perpetual re-entry into the atmosphere after a lunar launch or are the monster in a Lon Chaney movie from the 1930s. We can take pills to feel younger at 80 than most 40-year-olds felt at mid-century. Most of the advances in medicine have improved our life; after all, what is wrong with enjoying activity long into the golden years? But what are we really in search of? Why is it so difficult to enter the door to wisdom and grace? Rather than throw out the baby with the bathwater, one need only realize that aging is a natural rite of passage that allows the mellow weaving of a life of experiences into a tapestry of beauty. Moving into the inevitable decline of the mortal body lays bare your authenticity in a way that youth cannot. Embrace the next frontier of development in life; open your eyes to see the next act of the play: it is sweet, it is wise, is it more peaceful, it is spiritual. And if you are young, enjoy the sweet innocence of taut skin and strong muscles. In these gifts, spirit is also found.

Begin meditation today with the word "aging." Pause quietly in the morning to honor every crease around those wise eyes. Envelop your soul with the wisdom of experience. Welcome the peace of knowing.

List one area in which you can refocus your critical view of yourself.

Mourning

When the ripe fruit falls
Its sweetness distills and trickles away
Into the veins of the earth.

When fulfilled people die
The essential oil of their experience enters
the veins of living space, and adds a glisten
to the atom, to the body of immortal chaos.

For space is alive
As it stirs like a swan
Whose feathers glisten
Silky with the oil of distilled experience.

D.H. Lawrence

The loss of a loved one leaves a hole for the surviving lover to fill. A gray winter of transition follows the empty conversations, the dreams together that had to be surrendered, the aloneness of late evening. A step into the unknown causes many of us to become trapped in perpetual fear. But a choice to change the focus of mourning to one of celebration and gratefulness for the experience of a life shared stops the decent into a hell of loneliness. To realize the essence of that soul was a blessing in our life by the lessons they agreed to teach us, the joy or pain we experienced agreeing to stand next to them, and the memories we cherish for the duration of our time here, make the "letting go" an easier task. All hearts are absorbed into the "veins of the earth," their "essential oil" distilling in the frozen furrow, and out of the gray winter comes the enriched soil ripe for spring to burst forth and awaken us from the mourning. If you are in mourning for a loss of someone or something, allow that mourning to pass and honor the gift of the process that encourages the emotion to shift.

Meditate today on the word "mourning." Allow the feeling of loss to bubble up into the still mind. Allow the alchemy of hope and promise to blend into reality. Sit with the intention of transition.

Write a few lines in your journal about mourning. What images came to you in meditation?

Calm in the Face of the Storm

When we live cautiously, we retreat from life's challenges, from doing
what is right, from authenticity and from relationships. Without danger,
there is only stasis, status quo, and anticipation of death.

Kenneth Cloke, *Mediating Dangerously*

A life well lived involves the risk of leaving the zone of comfort. The fear of making a wrong move, a mistake-ridden history, or living with the consequences of the erro, can stop any movement at all—even a good one. To risk forces me to the edge—but to what edge am I thrust? What is the worst thing that can happen if I risk? The path to logic becomes clearer, if I agree to take that chance. For I have learned in the decades preceding, the worst thing that happens is I need only choose again. Armed with the mantra of "Do No Harm," I allow myself to listen to internal signals and go for it. If I am wrong, I can move in another direction. I am more successful in the risks I take at work than in the ones involving my own heart. We become accustomed to hoarding the memories of the broken heart close to the surface for easy access. Rather than risk the possibility that the purity and bliss of a heart in love will break irreparably, as we age, we become fixed in our cocoon of safety, a dog of Pavlov laden with conditioned pain.

Those who come before us in the earnest attempt to engage effectively in conflict are drowning in fear and pain—no trust to be had, searching for the morning in the blackness of an endless night. Is it not worth the risk of pushing the dangerous envelope to lead them from the misery of the moment to release of buried rage? Safety is soothing; the willingness to venture into the unknown is petrifying. In what dangerous chance can you find safety?

I dip my pen in the blackest of ink, because I am not afraid of falling into my inkpot.

Ralph Waldo Emerson, *The Conduct of Life*

Meditate today on the word "chance." Breathe in the willingness to listen to intuition; breathe out the fear of falling. Breathe in the comfort of knowing that you are not alone; breathe out the reticence of yesterday.

Write a line or two in your journal about risk in your life. What is one way that you can risk today?

In my own experience, the period of greatest gain in knowledge and
experience is the most difficult period in one's life…Through a difficult
period, you can learn, you can develop inner strength, determination, and
courage to face the problem. Who gives you this chance? Your enemy.

His Holiness the Dalai Lama

The lessons that can be learned through the turbulence present in every life are invaluable. I have noticed in the times that are most painful to me, my prayer becomes, "Please open my eyes to the lesson buried within this pain so that I may quickly move through it." Once again, I head for the door of avoidance, rocketing through the muddle, in resistance to the process of darkness. Unearthing the reason for the painful lesson, reactive causality surely at its root, seems unlikely while in flight. If the "guts" to withstand turmoil can be summoned from deep in the vortex of experience, inner peace can be a likely outcome. Perhaps we can then pass "Go" and collect our $200, never having to repeat the lesson. Turmoil arrives at our hearth usually in the form of human relationship. If your rage rises from the deep, if the alarm of boundary breach is screaming to you, look closely: your angel stands before you. Your enemy, the one who agreed to help you learn that lesson, has reported for duty.

Begin meditation today with the word "turmoil." What feelings bubble to the surface of your heart on the mention of the word? Sit in stillness with turmoil for a moment or two. Follow the thoughts.

Write down the images that came to you in meditation. Who wears the face of turmoil in your life?

*Learn to get in touch with the silence within yourself and
know that everything in this life has a purpose.*

Elisabeth Kübler-Ross

If we do not choose to go within, we are looking for our wholeness from somewhere outside ourselves. To find your purpose in life is the holy grail of treasures. As in the Biblical metaphor, our society has become "a flock with no shepherd." We are sheep following the master of the commercial media: you need this to be beautiful; buy that to become attractive. Not to minimize the desire to take good care of ourselves, but what are trying to attract? We are captives of our addictions. When we choose instead to consciously connect to ourselves, we discover the field for spiritual energy that allows regeneration. We then become that beacon that our clients are looking for to hold the light over the path leading to peace. Connection to a spiritual path is a systematic way to ensure that we have success in the journey. Search for the presence of peace every day and you will be successful in discovering the sacred necessary to live a fulfilling joyous life and also to do a wonderful job. Without connection, we are busy machines. Without the intention to make time for connection each morning, our critical mind becomes our guide, using the thinking frontal lobe and not the central whole-brain processor, which allows us to connect with another source for sustenance. Agree to provide for yourself first this morning. Connect to your purpose.

Meditation today should begin with the word "connection." Imagine the feeling of connection to your source; with each breath, you are cared for and regenerated.

Write down the images that came to you when meditating. What does connection look like to you?

The supreme act of forgiveness is when you can forgive yourself for all the
wounds you've created in your own life. Forgiveness is an act of self-love.
When you forgive yourself, self-acceptance begins and self-love grows.

Don Miguel Ruiz

Don Miguel Ruiz, a medical doctor by vocation, is a descendant from a lineage of Toltec masters in Mexico known as "naguals" who passed down information from generation to generation. Thousands of years ago, the Toltecs were scientists and artists known as the people of knowledge in ancient Teotihuacan, the city of pyramids outside Mexico City. As with their counterparts in ancient Western civilization, the Greeks, the Toltecs were philosophers. In his book *The Four Agreements*, Ruiz delineates four doctrines of living. You will see that these principles of ancient knowledge outline reflective communication used in conflict engagement every day. The first is "Be impeccable with your word." He suggests that people should not only speak clearly and with integrity but they should use their word in the direction of truth and love. The second agreement is "Don't take anything personally"—to take offense makes one the object of needless suffering. The third is "Don't make assumptions." Instead, find the words to ask for what you want. Ruiz suggests that if you do this one thing, it will transform your life. The last personal agreement is "Always do your best," and he explains that the key to this practice is stopping "self-judgment, self-abuse, and regret." I agree that it is necessary to be able to forgive yourself before you can forgive others. To practice this daily means that you get to begin again each day, each moment. When you can successfully forgive yourself, you will embody forgiveness when working with clients. My analytical mind produces thoughts of personal criticism each day. As a top priority for beginning a new day, choose to rearrange the thinking brain and forgive as your first act of the morning.

Meditation today should focus on the word "forgiveness." Become still with the breath of forgiveness. Breathe in honor for your journey; breathe out the regrets of yesterday.

Write one thing in your journal that you can forgive yourself for today.

Let us be grateful to people who make us happy; they are the
charming gardeners who make our souls blossom.

Marcel Proust

A circle of support is essential for a life of purpose. We all have those treasured friends easily recognizable, the ones who have always been there, making us smile with enjoyment. There are also the new friends we have collected, the ones we cherish as angels of mercy, sent to us to overcome the loneliness sometimes found in the spiritual journey. And there are the soul mates, that circle of friends with common values and purpose whom we delight in meeting. If we live mindlessly, we can miss these angels of support—the charming gardeners who quietly till the soil in preparation for the blossoming of our soul. But through mindful awareness, we discover that all the angels have been with us for years, unnoticed by our frantic, searching soul. Take an inventory of your assembly of angels. Some may be mentors of joy. Gratitude for them comes easily. Some may be adversaries bringing messages that are rejected on sight. Be grateful anyway. Some may be providers of security, so that we can venture forth in the unearthing of our purpose. Today, be grateful for the charming gardeners who make your soul blossom.

Meditation today should begin with the word "support." When you dive into the waters of the unknown current, whom do you see? Sit with the support of the assembly of angels in meditation; breathe with them; unite in oneness—one soul transferring the light of tender sincerity to another.

Make a list of your assembly of angels. Whom do you need to express gratitude to today?

The power of decisions is all that is yours.
what you can decide between is fixed,
because there are no alternatives
except truth and illusion...
remember this: Every decision you make
stems from what you THINK you are,
and represents the value that
you put upon yourself.

A Course in Miracles

Personal discernment can be a difficult process. We alone have the power to decide which paths we travel, what work we choose, and whom we spend our time with. Truth is personal perception, and in the process of discovering our truth from illusion, we endlessly ruminate through selected historical data burned into our memory. One's illusions are truth for another. There is no black-and-white-only perception. The decisions we make drive our awareness. It seems people who choose optimism have an easier life. If they think they can do something, they actually do it, and people who dwell in lack and negativity seem to create the same. The powerlessness that comes from negativity is paralyzing.

Many entering our circle of concern ask for a more hopeful view. Assisting them in the climb to a new vantage point and cleansing the soot away from the lens of perception increases the possibility that they can continue on their trek with renewed encouragement. Understanding that their perception of violation may not have been the intention of the offender often provides enough room for translucence of thought to rise from opaque reasoning. The illusion of conflict can be removed. In reflecting upon your own experience, what do you think you are? What qualities describe you? Do you feel they are valuable? Is there a cleansing of illusion on your horizon?

Meditate today beginning with the word "decision-making." Settle into your soul and search for the veil of illusion; silently expect that the lifted veil will reveal a personal truth. Breathe in clarity of mind. Welcome a new vision.

Write a few lines in your journal about the illusions revealed to you in your meditation.

*There is no higher religion than human service. To work
for the common good is the greatest creed.*

Albert Schweitzer

I like teaching at a Jesuit university for two reasons. While the Jesuits are faith-based academics, they are also intellectuals, unafraid of controversy and welcome dialogue on all points of view. Although at times in church history they were considered heretics, they pressed forward in a constant search for knowledge. Second, they are always offering opportunities for students and faculty alike to learn through service to others and they lead the quest for empowerment of man, the search for the common good. Jesus, Mohammed, Buddha, Zoroaster, Plato, Epictetus, some of the greatest teachers of all time, lived lives of example through love and human service. The founder of the Jesuits, St. Ignatius Loyola, like Aristotle before him, asked the question "How ought we to live?" In pondering that question and by looking outside of our own needs, we focus on the common good. I often have people ask me why I work with high-conflict couples. This work is what I can do for the common good of the planet. I have neither the skills nor the opportunity to stop war in the Middle East, but I can work to create peace, no matter how fleeting, one case at a time. It represents a mission of many before me and will be a mission of many following. What do we leave behind, a monetary estate or the gift of giving back to others?

Meditate today on the term "common good." What thoughts does this phrase evoke in your mind?

Write one thing that you can do for the common good today.

I do not feel obliged to believe that the same God who has endowed us
with sense, reason, and intellect has intended us to forego their use.

Galileo Galilei

I love history. The study of the past brings to light the trials and tribulations of our ancestors, how far we have progressed in technology and understanding, and how little our problems have changed. Galileo had to think outside the box when every principle that the medieval culture tried to instill in him conflicted with his intelligence. His vision forced him to risk heresy, pressing forward to follow his creative soul until science found birth in the Renaissance. Endowed with brilliance by his Maker, he trusted that knowledge, choosing instead to believe in a higher power that wanted him to use his gifts. Moving from science to the field of human interaction, thinking outside the box is something that Kenneth Cloke, the author of *Mediating Dangerously*, does effortlessly. He urges practitioners to risk the rules and willingly travel to the edge of the chaos to discover the path out of the darkness. When I read his book, I was validated. Dancing with danger for years working with high-conflict couples, and fearless by nature, I welcome the families whom the judge has just excommunicated from the halls of justice. Secure in my ability to meet clients where they stand, I noticed that I could lead repeat conflict offenders to drop the tug of war with a certain degree of surety. Risk is the key word. Do I risk offending them when I ask, "What the hell are you thinking?" Absolutely. Do I risk that they won't feel fairness or impartiality? Yes. Do I get agreements? You bet. Adding spiritual preparation to my practice a few years ago exponentially improved results in my work. I am okay with not knowing how those words fly out of my mouth, confident in the comprehension that I am being used through my willingness to act with intelligence.

Meditate today on the phrase "thinking outside the box." Explore what information rises to the surface for you. Feel the permission in your bones to let your muscles relax. Breathe the clear air of knowing.

Write a few lines in your journal about your practice. What gifts do you have? What wonderful qualities do you bring to your methodology at work?

Always follow these two rules: first, act only on what your reasoning mind proposes for the good of humanity, and second, change your opinion if someone shows you that it is wrong.

Marcus Aurelius

Marcus Aurelius is one soul whom I relish meeting when I leave this earthly plane. Pragmatic and dependable in his reasoning, he emanates brilliance in simplicity of thought. His values ensured his life was well lived. When I think of brilliance in leadership, I think of Marcus Aurelius. Now in my middle years, I find that all my values are in question. Spinning at mach 5, not only am I in flux, but the earth is in transformation, as are relationships, and certainly the field of mediation. It seems the rule book I was raised with is out of print. One thing is certain: whether it's the first century or the twenty-first century, opinion is perception and perception can be changed. To hold your values to the highest honor and shift the paradigm is the mark of a forward thinker. Changing your opinion is the most powerful tool of a practitioner of conflict engagement, and as we model this, our clients can transform alongside us. To remain objective is to choose possibility. To be willing to see the other point of view as it opposes yours is a gift of discernment.

Meditate today on the word "objectivity." How does one remain objective? What images rise to your mind when you repeat the word "objective"? Listen for the door to opportunity.

Write a line or two in your journal about objectivity. How objective are you in your personal life and at work?

Inner Voice

Someday perhaps the inner light will shine forth from
us and then we shall need no other light.

Pierre-Simon de Laplace

The inner voice provides information from a place we do not fully understand. Meeting the mind in quiet resonance, the inner voice is what I call intuition. The inner voice appears in flashes, and many report that their "gut" does the talking. A presumption of emotional processing is usually present in the explanation of the intuitive, inner voice. In another point of view, Danah Zohar, coauthor of *Spiritual Intelligence*, believes that intuition comes from a central brain process, tapping a body of information that neither the logical brain nor the emotional brain can explain. In *The Soul's Code*, James Hillman defines intuition as "direct, unmediated knowledge." This knowledge is delivered in clear, quick immediacy, as though a revelation arrives, not from reflective thinking or cognitive function. Hillman categorizes perception as intuitive data. We are only now beginning to understand the brain and how it functions. How does one communicate with the inner voice? Mindfulness, prayer, meditative practices, a willingness to listen to the inner voice are all paths to understanding this data that arrives quickly and leaves us to wonder whether we should act upon it. Hillman, a Jungian psychologist, believes that the intuitive, inner voice is not the same for all. He believes that the inner voice can also have a dark side that leads us to make incorrect choices. One needs to process intuition using the whole brain: valuing feeling and historical or traditional data and evaluating intuition logically. How do you listen to your inner voice? Is your response always the same? Do you act or do you discount? I have had to learn to give much credence to inner voice. I seem to deny it first, then upon insistence, listen again.

Meditation today should begin with the phrase "inner voice." Observe the thoughts and images present in your mind as you agree to relax the body and breathe deeply into your mind. What is your inner voice saying to you? Out of the grayness, let the light arise.

What came to you this morning in your prayerful stillness? What is one way that your can listen more carefully to your inner voice?

None of us can help the things life has done to us. They're done before you realize it, and once they're done they make you do other things until at last everything comes between you and what you'd like to be, and you've lost your true self forever.

Eugene O'Neill, *Long Day's Journey into Night*

Losing your true self is not a bad thing. It depends on the way you view human metamorphosis. If you believe that living your life is an opportunity to grow and to learn from all experiences, then losing the layers of past perceptions takes on new, hopeful meaning. Eckhart Tolle encourages us to live in "the Now" because history no longer exists. The choice then becomes one between "Why is this happening to me?" and "This happens for me." O'Neill was a master at illuminating the human condition in his epic play. Many of our clients are drowning in human-conditional misery. Expectations and perceptions of violation saturate the narratives of the soul. When one searches for fulfillment though relationship, it is necessary to replace the despair of expectation, with the gift of optimism. Choosing an optimistic view renews anticipation and allows one to ascend up the ladder where new heights of hope can be realized. Have you lost your true self forever? What is between you and what you would like to be? Can you discover the newness of you upon the horizon of tomorrow? Getting in touch with that part of your lost self can also improve your performance at work.

Meditate today beginning with the word "climb." Agree to succumb to the need for flight of the body, inviting the soul to fuse with your heart in an alchemy of spirit. Breathe deeply and with freedom, feeling every pore of your skin cool with the breeze of diaphanous wings of angels. You are safe in your ascent to wholeness.

Write a few lines of permission in your journal. Give yourself the permission to climb with joy for and anticipation of whatever your heart desires.

We live in a Newtonian world of Einsteinian physics ruled by Frankenstein logic.

David Russell

Bruce Lipton, a biologist and author of *The Biology of Belief: Unleashing the Power of Consciousness, Matter & Miracles*, examines cellular structure and the regeneration of genes. Epigenetics is a scientific discovery, showing that the nucleus of a cell is not the life force of a cell; rather, the membrane of the cell is the component of life that responds to outside influences. The membrane is dynamic and open to transformation at all times. This theory challenges genetic determinism, which holds that, embedded in our DNA is the blueprint for living and reaction. Lipton posited that we are much more malleable than predisposition would allow. Transformations can and do take place at the cellular level continuously. Change being constant, we are only now beginning to discover consciousness and the intersection of brain functioning and consciousness. As thoughts permeate each cell, how do we have power over what we create in the world? That we have power at all is a threat to this rules-based world, finite and concrete. The metaphor of the glass half-full or half-empty is so representative of the optimism or misery of the mind. What logical pattern will you choose to follow today?

Meditate today on the word "logic." How has logic been your friend or your enemy? As you settle your breath into openness and begin the process of discovery, breathe in an awareness of emptiness and let your spirit guide your meditation. Breathe in the willingness to go to the source of logical energy.

Write a few lines in your journal about logic. What came to you while you meditated this morning?

Love all Creation,
The whole of it and every grain of sand.
Love every leaf,
Every ray of God's light.
Love the animals.
Love the plants.
Love everything.
If you love everything,
You will perceive
The divine mystery in things.
And once you have perceived it,
You will begin to comprehend it ceaselessly,
More and more every day.
And you will at last come to love the whole world
With an abiding universal love.

Fyodor Dostoyevsky, *The Brothers Karamazov*

In contemplating a universal reality, is it not true that it all comes down to the love in our heart? If we are constantly seeking love from outside the self, is it possible to truly find it? Imagine for a moment that if we could focus only on the universal reality in the present moment, right here and now, we could effect an immediate movement in the universe. If we are the embodiment of love in the present moment, the possibility for transformation increases exponentially.

Meditate today upon the phrase "universal reality." Breathe in the soothing air of oneness, and breathe out the emptiness of the search. Breathe in the possibility of melding with universal love; breathe out the restrictions in your mind of the ego.

Write a few lines in your journal about universal reality. What images come to your mind when you encounter this phrase? What do you want your universal reality to be? How can you tap into that energy today to increase your impact for good in the world?

As we begin to discover the power of ritual, we also increase our sense of community.
We come together in groups to share our rituals and to give them more power...
and slowly begin to affect the society, resulting in greater overall awareness.

Rachel Pollack

Rituals are so important in binding the experiences of life together. Joseph Campbell told Bill Moyers, in an interview in the PBS series *The Power of Myth,* that the societies of the planet have lost their rituals. Rituals are bookmarks that place in memory the significant stages of one's life. Clarissa Pinkola Estes' also writes extensively about the importance of ritual in our culture in *Women Who Run With the Wolves.* She affirms that traditions and stories about values and life lessons are passed from elder to child through stories in the family. Today, take note of the rituals in your life. Do you have rituals of spring? Rituals you perform every day or every week? If you feel as though you are sailing on a rudderless ship, review areas of life in which the creation of rituals might enhance your life or provide a new bookmark in your life. Taking time every morning in prayer or meditation is one ritual that provides sustenance for the day. In a workshop with Julia Cameron, she counseled us to write every morning in free association "to siphon off the poisonous sludge stuck in our brains from the night before." I love that! I faithfully followed her advice for a year, and it works!

Today, begin your meditation with the word "ritual." As your breathing becomes the focus of your mind, breathe in the comfort of your space, and breathe out the unnecessary thoughts. Breathe in the hope of fresh morning; breathe out the fear of the day before.

Journal about the rituals you have and the rituals you can create to enhance and support you in your journey.

*Passion is holy—a profound Mystery that transcends and transforms
thought rapture. We need to accept that a sacred fire burns within,
whether we are comfortable with this truth or not. Passion is part of real
life's package because we were created by love, for love, to love.*

Sarah Ban Breathnach, *Simple Abundance*

How many of us have let the fire die? A passionate life burns deeply within us and often rises to the surface, but in the daily work of dealing with conflict and anger, our protective shell allows little or no passion to burst through the dissonance of emotion. Numbed by the unceasing psychic pain of our clients, we unknowingly absorb much of the muddy water of conflict that extinguishes the flame within. To "keep the sacred fire" burning, we must intentionally provide the opportunity for clarity, growth, and cultivation of our passion for life and love for others. I have been asked how I can truly be impartial when faced with a personality who triggers me on sight. I go to that place of willingness that allows me to see the person as one who is full of fear, a cauldron of reactive causality, unable to stop the ship from sinking and prepared to drag those whom they use as life preservers down into the vortex of fear. Clients trigger me daily. I have reached a point where I can internally recognize, "Yes, there it is. Can't stand that. Oh well, poor soul," and as Bill Ury teaches, "go to the balcony of my mind". With compassion assist them in finding their way out of their self-imposed prison. It is within compassion that I can access my passionate soul and allow the work to transmit love for the client in a way that keeps me in touch with the mystery of process. Don't let your fire die. Intentionally give your heart time to reconnect and express your passion for what you love.

Meditate today on the phrase "fire of passion." Breathe in deeply the quiet search for that flame that burns within your soul; breathe out the stale air of the night. Breathe in the quest for a passionate place of renewal.

Write a few lines about your fire within. Give that passion form and concrete parameters. Draw that passion in your mind. List the things that draw passion forth from your heart.

My business is not to remake myself,
but [to uncover] the absolute best of what God made.

Robert Browning

The search for who we are, our purpose in life, and the happiness we all desire is a full-time quest. In pursuit of the holy grail of inner peace, we think excavation is required. Entire self-improvement libraries can be found in the homes of those in my generation, proof of the underlying question "Is this all there is?" playing as a broken record in the mind. We dig unceasingly. Meditation seeks to tame the racing mind riddled with anxiety. In search of peace, the stillness of daily prayer and meditation allows the opportunity for "the absolute best of what God made" to rise to the surface. If we can put down the pickaxe for just a few moments every day and agree to listen, our unique qualities and gifts can be revealed to us in the fog of the morning. In the agreement to cease the laborious task of personal remodeling, we realize that remaking the soul cannot be accomplished with human "hands".

Meditate today beginning with the word "uncover." Breathe in the willingness to be tranquil; breathe out the urgency of the search. Breathe in the clearing of the hushed meadow of mind; breathe out the need to remodel the soul. Allow your higher power to speak to you.

What images came to you in meditation today? List "the absolute best of what God made." Honor your worth.

To live in an enchanting world we also have to assume a receptive posture
rather than an exclusively active one. We can become skilled at allowing the
world in, taking its secrets to heart and finding power outside of ourselves.

Thomas Moore, *The Education of the Heart*

To live an enchanting life, one needs a sense of wonder and appreciation for the mystery of life. The questions that can't be answered require us to cultivate receptivity and remain open with an inquisitive mind while developing hypotheses. I am becoming accustomed to beginning the morning with a sense of excitement, awaiting the gifts laced through the fabric of mystery that will arrive throughout the day. Life wasn't always like that. Neither was my practice. In earlier decades, I lived in fear of making the wrong move, dreading choices not chosen, being in the wrong place, not having the information I needed, or failing to follow the rules set before me. Once I discovered that I was not operating in that car alone, I began to slip out of the front seat and be comfortable with just riding through the mystery, in life and at work. The view is different when you "get" that you are just doing your part; that you are not in control. In life I yield to my higher power; at work I yield to the process, the energy and direction of the client and, my higher power. My receptive posture allows me to hear the cues I need in order to know which direction to take in my questioning and orchestrate the path out of the chaos. My enchantment with the mystery of life allows me to love "what is" and know that I will understand "why" when I look in the rear-view mirror. Enchantment in my work allows me to appreciate that, mysteriously, words come out of my mouth that did not run through my logical brain. Do you have a sense of enchantment and mystery about your life? Can you cultivate the "receptive posture" in your work?

Begin meditation today with the word "enchantment." Become still and receptive. Wait with a sense of wonder as you watch your mind stream the thoughts of tranquil peace. Breathe in the fullness of an enchanting morning. Await the peace of the prayer.

In what ways can you cultivate a sense of enchantment in your life today?

What actions are most excellent?
To gladden the heart of a human being.
To feed the hungry.
To help the afflicted.
To lighten the sorrowful.
To remove the wrongs of the injured.
That person is the most beloved of God
Who does most good to God's creatures.

The Prophet Mohammad

The Prophet Mohammad wrote of the correct action of the enlightened soul. The message that Jesus brought to the world was the same message, "Love one another, as I have loved you." The Buddha taught the same lessons in a different part of the world. And yet, the majority of interactions currently displayed in the world do not match this teaching. In interacting with others, do we judge them for not adhering to this creed? We must not. To be successful in the work that we do, we must move to accept the humanness of our condition. We hold somewhere in our consciousness the same behavior. To greet each conflicted soul with respect provides a way to "lighten the sorrowful," as we are their angels of enlightenment. Coaching clients to the other side of conflict feeds the hungry of heart and helps the afflicted. As Marianne Williamson said, "We are powerful beyond measure."

Meditation today should begin with the word "interaction." Breathe deeply and feel the blending of your purpose and your soul. Sit in stillness with those whom you have not yet met and know that together you are one.

Write down the impressions that came to you today in your meditation.

Love and compassion are necessities, not luxuries. Without them humanity cannot survive.

His Holiness the Dalai Lama

In my experience, I find peace builders and conflict practitioners to be people of deep compassion. When I sit among souls on a common journey, I am filled with hope for tomorrow. Bernie Mayer in his book, *Beyond Neutrality: Confronting the Crisis in Conflict Resolution*, called upon practitioners in this field to be more involved in the state of affairs on the planet. He noted that not one conflict resolution practitioner had been called to an advisory position after the tragedy on September 11th. I sincerely believe that humanity will not survive unless we, as practitioners of conflict resolution and advocates of peace, pledge involvement in our future.

What will be the offering that we, as practitioners, leave to this earth? We are ambassadors for the engagement of conflict in constructive ways. Every one of us needs to work in our particular area to move this planet toward better solutions, and to help parties in conflict to discover another path: co-existence with those whose perceptions do not match their own.

Meditate today with the phrase "the offering." Sit quietly and contemplate the legacy of your soul and your soul's work. What will your offer be today? How can you best bring love and compassion to your table?

Write down the images that came to you in your meditation. What do want to leave in your wake? What does your soul impart to the world?

We have forgotten who we are,
We have lost our sense of wonder and connectedness,
We have degraded the Earth and our fellow creatures,
And we have nowhere else to go.
If we lose the sweetness of the waters,
We lose the life of the land,
If we lose the life of the land,
We lose the majesty of the forest,
If we lose the majesty of the forest,
We lose the purity of the air,
If we lose the purity of the air,
We lose the creatures of the Earth,
Not just for ourselves,
But for our children,
Both now and in the future.

Earth Charter

I think that we are being awakened to a distant but steady drumbeat. Either we can choose to ruin this beautiful place where humans thrive and come to learn, or we can save it for our progeny. In the 1970s and 80s, much was done to restore and protect the environment in this country. Industrial areas in the East were cleaned up and became beautiful places to live again, with clean air, clean rivers, and widespread urban renewal. Lately, it seems, a reversal has occurred and causes me to wonder if our values are not misplaced. Many decisions made in the 1920s and 30s gave rise to national parks and common areas that we all enjoy now, but what about the future for our grandchildren? The choices made of late about the environment are reflective of choices we make about ourselves. Are we really grounded? Do we no longer care about the preservation of our values, ethics, integrity, or honesty? What thoughts do you have about being grounded to yourself and to the planet? What is your personal charter for being grounded?

Meditation today should focus on the word "grounded." As the morning washes over you in stillness, breathe in the images arising from deep in your soul; breathe out the smallness of impotence in making a difference. Breathe in the power of your core. Explore the feeling of the ground beneath you and how connected you are.

Write down a few lines about being grounded as it was presented in your meditation and how you can become more grounded today. Do you notice your behavior when you are not grounded? Is there a way to remind yourself to reconnect?

The art of teaching is the art of assisting in discovery.

Henry Adams

When the light bulb comes on and acknowledgment registers on the face of a client, I see the process of discovery beginning. A large part of a peacemaker's job is assisting in that discovery. By digging under the stated issue and asking the right question at the right time, information unseen before becomes evident to all who are present. Conflict engagement and teaching can be artistry. My work ethic and value is to impart as much information to the client as they can understand. Book lists, referrals to other professionals, understanding power dynamics, and systemic reactive causality are resources one needs in the throes of conflict. I want parties to know that whatever they are embroiled in is normal, that no one is different than another in the dispute arena. There are some who would not agree with me: "not your job," they would say. There are some who would say that I was not operating according to standards of performance: "crossing the line," one might note. As we have the duty to report potential or current endangerment, I feel that it is also my duty to educate. If we peace-build through education one case at a time, can we not change our village, our nation? I have always believed that one person can make a difference. Teaching and sharing knowledge is one thing that we can all do for others. What about the self-taught? Introspection and mindfulness are ways to self-assist in the discovery; a personal archeology of your life unearths clues in ways that are empowering. Meditation allows the mind to be stilled long enough to discover the obvious. A new twist on the old adage, "When the teacher is ready, the student appears," accompanies my belief that we are all students and teachers to each other at the same time. Welcome the opportunity to engage in the act of discovery for yourself and for others!

Meditation today should begin with the word "discovery." As your breath settles into your muscles, release the stiffness in your joints and become fluid in motion. What can you discover in the stillness this morning?

Write a few lines in your journal about the images that came to you in your discovery. What can you learn from the new awareness?

Nan Waller Burnett

*The ultimate aim of the quest must be neither release nor ecstasy for
one's self, but the wisdom and the power to serve others.*

Joseph Campbell, *The Power of Myth*

As we ponder thoughts of purpose and ask why, we only need to remember the particular gifts we brought with us into this world. Through the veil of birth, we forget, and thus lose sight of, our purpose. Introspection marks the beginning of the quest for the curious mind. Through inquiry, our purpose can be revealed. Through meditation, our purpose can be clarified. Through journaling, our purpose can be seen as the words flow on the paper. At the end of the day, purpose is found in the willingness to leave something behind, to make a difference in the world. I am sure there are good reasons that I don't understand, but why does the yogi who only meditates, levitates, seeks astral projection, never interact with his fellow humans? Should we seek only our nirvana or seek to share our abundance with others? I have never understood why Thoreau needed to live his life in exile. I have never understood those who spend their life gathering resources and never share them. For me, the quest is in the gifting. Although I require a great deal of time alone, I believe that if we are endowed with a gift of intelligence, we should use that to share our knowledge with others. If we have the gift of a skill or we are a craftsman, we should use that to help those less fortunate. We have become such a money-driven society that we have forgotten about abundance. Jimmy Carter has done so much in retirement after his presidency to improve the planet. Habitat for Humanity and the peace building of the Carter Center are landmarks to his legacy. I recently read about a man in Arizona who has taken one community in a border town and raised money to fund twenty-six duplex homes for poverty-stricken Mexicans. He requires that the residents get a GED, attend vocational school, and run their own community government. He provides scholarships for homeless girls to go on to higher education and feeds the elderly who have been abandoned in the street. He does all of this with the labor of volunteers from the border states, who come down on their vacation and build roads, schools, and houses; one man on his ultimate quest, with a vision. Anita Roddick, the founder of the Body Shop, insists on purchasing her products from third-world countries. If they have natural resources and no way to access them, she will build a factory, employ them as future owners, and train them to be suppliers to first-world nations; one woman on her ultimate quest, with a vision. I think peace practitioners are on a quest, searching for a better way, in whatever their application of work, in whatever arena. There is a particular passion that is born in the heart of those who work with spirit. If they stumble into this field by chance, it seems they remain by choice. What are your particular gifts to share?

....

Meditate today on the word "quest." As you lean into the quiet morning, value the inaction; listen to your heartbeat. What voice is calling to you? Breathe in the welcoming quest.

Write in your journal about your gifts to share. How can you best share them?

All truths are easy to understand once they are discovered; the point is to discover them.

Galileo Galilei

Galileo, a Florentine scientist of the Renaissance, sought to quench his thirst for the truth. Unafraid of failure and intrigued by his world, he made one of the most important discoveries of any astronomer before him. He had the courage to stand by his assertion that the Earth was not the center of the universe despite seemingly blasphemous nature of the statement. In our work as practitioners of peace, we set out on the voyage of discovery every day. We set out to discover how we can increase the understanding of our clients. Through the dissection of conflict-ridden stories, we uncover the pieces to the puzzle, the key to unlocking the cell of the war-worn, and the validation that lies in the understanding. Another of Galileo's contemporaries, Leonardo da Vinci said, "All our knowledge has its origins in our perceptions." The artistry of questioning and reframing allows one to unlock the "box of Pandora," risking that the snakes of misunderstanding might slither through the story and spoil the process. Can we risk for the truth? We must. Do not be afraid to ask the question for which there is no foreseeable answer. The parties in conflict know the answer, and it is the question that has been avoided that has brought them to your table. The point is for us to discover it.

Meditation today should begin with the word "truth." Wait in the silence for the message of your truth to appear. What do you see in the cloudy morning? Breathe in the gathering message of significance which points to your voyage of discovery.

Write down your thoughts about truth.

The goal of the spiritual life is to allow the highest and
most divine qualities to flower in one's self.

Larry Dossey, M.D., *Recovering the Soul*

The spiritual life is not one we can sit and wait for. I think that one must set the goal of daily devotion to spirit and cultivate those seeds planted in our earliest memories. When my children were very young, they had a knowing, an innocent understanding of the soul, that I, as an adult, had forgotten. My daughter, who was three at the time, observed my worry as I tended to her baby brother with a high fever. She said, "Mommy, let's bless his head. I'm sure that will help!" I remember thinking how in tune to the divine she seemed to be. She had an intimate insight and awareness that I could only take on faith. The funny thing is that when I enthusiastically agreed that blessing his head was the perfect choice, she knelt down and put her sticky, warm little hands on his head and prayed from her soul, and as she completed her precious prayer, I suddenly felt the burden of worry lift from my brow. With a blessing of comfort from my three-year-old, I was restored. As we grow in the ways of the world, we seem to forget the knowledge with which children arrive. Setting a goal of cultivation of spirit allows us to welcome back to our conscious memory the comfort of knowing that we are not alone but rather a thread in a fabric of beauty from the divine. Terry Cole-Whittaker, in her book, *What You Think of me is None of My Business*, wrote that we should set goals that are seemingly unattainable to the logical mind: "Realistic goals keep us playing small, safe, and unchallenged …When we set goals beyond our reach, we must depend on God to attain it." As the saying goes, extraordinary people are just ordinary souls doing extraordinary things. Setting a daily goal, looking to the stars, allows us the insight to sit in the stillness with the present and find joy in "the Now."

Meditation today should begin with the phrase "spiritual goals." What is your heart's desire? As you become in tune with the beating of your heart, contemplate your purpose.

Write down what spiritual goals did you discover in your meditation?

Leaders do two things extremely well: They are aware of their gifts, and they use their personal power and vision to share those unique gifts with the world. They cause their gifts to become a force for good.

Donna Zajonc

In her book, *The Politics of Hope: Reviving the Dream of Democracy*, Donna Zajonc calls for a more interdependent and collaborative approach to politics. In the field of peacemaking and conflict engagement, these are terms that are standard in our language of practice. Zajonc believes that the field of politics is the last frontier in a growing global movement to uncover a better way to exist on this planet. She imagines a world in which its governance is influenced not by political parties' interests, rhetoric, or fund-raising requirements but by a political conversation that focuses on honor, integrity, and the search for the common good. John Lennon, in his poetry of lyric in the song "Imagine," envisioned "that the world could live as one." Imagine. John Paul Lederach, in his book *The Moral Imagination: The Art and Soul of Building Peace*, writes to four stories of individuals making a difference in different parts of the world engaged in conflict. Speaking at a local retreat, he called on the attending practitioners to become aware of their personal power, the ability to be a force for good, and to be a part of changing the course of human interaction one case at a time. True political leadership is so rare in the grand scheme of things, but every now and then, a Mandela, Giuliani, Sadat, Gandhi, Meir, King, Aurelius, or Plato walks onto the global stage and uses power, vision, and position to lead us to greatness. In our work, one day at a time, we can be great leaders, holding a torch on the dark path out of the forest of indecision and into the light of agreement. Do not take your role lightly. Know you who are, become aware of your gifts, and use your personal power and unique gifts with those who enter your circle of influence.

Meditation today should begin with the word "leadership." As you sit with the your thoughts this morning, let your mind become still and free of the noise pollution of the surroundings. Let your thoughts on leadership be revealed to you.

What thoughts images came to you in your meditation? Give form to those thoughts, in words or sketched images.

Being a monk in the world requires embracing a spirituality of engagement and not withdrawal, not a spirituality where you are off in a cave somewhere praying.
Brother Wayne Teasdale, *The Mystic Heart*

I have often wondered, what are the prayers of monks, yogis, or people of constant prayer? Prayer was introduced to me as a 5-year-old in the South as something you had to do to beg for forgiveness or to request a pardon. "Penance" was the word that was used. I thought that meant I was bad, but I was not exactly sure why. Not the most hallowed ground from which to grow a personal relationship with my higher power! Thankfully I discovered my way back by the path of my choosing and not by the road that was suggested to me in my youth. Brother Teasdale, a Benedictine monk explains the process of prayer in a way that makes sense to me. "Engagement" is such a beautiful word, so much better than "penance." Spiritual engagement every day is as necessary as brushing your teeth. I have come to understand that inaction does not mean withdrawal, but perhaps a date with the divine. Inaction is necessary sometimes to operate at our highest level. Perhaps inaction is as great a teacher as action. Generally, a high degree of intelligence dictates a busy mind. Choosing a period of inaction allows that force within us all to become powerful again by replenishing the energy that we expend in the living of our lives. It allows the mind to quiet for clarity. I have come to relish inaction as a gift I am finally willing to give myself.

Meditation today on the word "inaction." Settle into the bones of your being, and feel your breath rise in harmony with the divine force of higher power. Sit in inaction, into nothingness, and receive.

Write in your journal about ways in which you can engage through inaction.

Letting Go

There is no birth of consciousness without pain.

Carl Jung

It seems that I have been letting bridges to the past fall away this year. There is fear in letting go of the familiar. There is guilt in letting go. The bottom of the canyon cannot be seen when we drop the rope bridge and watch it descend into darkness. How we all wrap ourselves in the comfort zone of the sure thing. Is transformation possible if we hang on to static comfort? Can we ever morph into the butterfly if we cling to the cocoon? As Jung suggested, birth of consciousness cannot take place without it. In order to calm my chaos, I addictively controlled the borders to my world. I began my recovery from that debilitating behavior in the mid-1980s. The last frontier in the journey toward successful recovery was the "letting go." Letting go, of course, means letting God. Now, to a control freak, "letting God" is pretty difficult. I have learned that I must awake each day with that mantra. While I am not sure that I will ever be over it, I can look over my shoulder as the bridges fall away and see that I have allowed a transformation.

Meditation today should begin with the phrase "let go." Let go of the stiffness in your lungs this morning. Let go of the need to know. Let go of the racing mind. Let God begin his conversation.

Write a few lines in your journal about the process of letting go in your life. Is there something that you need to let go of today?

We were brought up in a tradition that has now become impossible,
for we have extended our circle throughout space and time.

Anne Morrow Lindbergh, *Gift from the Sea*

As a daughter of the South, I recognize that it is steeped in tradition, such as knowing your pedigree. In my home state, traditions such as Mardi Gras, Jazz Fest, and Shrimp Festivals are wonderful reminders of the unique culture of Louisiana. A rich French heritage still thrives within the borders of Louisiana, so devastated recently by Hurricane Katrina. On my last visit, I saw a sign in someone's front yard that said, "Chirac, take us back, we've been cut loose by America!" Tradition is in evidence in the wonderful humor that permeates the Cajun spirit. They have a saying: "Laissez Bon Temps Roulez!" meaning, "Let the good times roll!"— and without a doubt, the good times will roll again in French Louisiana. Traditions, that are not native to anywhere else in the United States, create an active bond between history and today.

Traditions are present in every culture in our nation. They tie us to values, and remind us of rites of passage that move us from one phase of life to another. Marking the holidays with grace, recalling our higher power at celebrations, showing gratitude to our veterans, and celebrating a life well lived as it makes its transitions are all examples of tradition. Our margins of tradition have expanded to the degree that we must redefine the cultural boundaries. Or are there boundaries? As we are now just beginning to understand energy, the sciences, the brain, the intersection of art and spirit, creativity and thought, is it possible that we must redefine our global home?

......

Mediation today should begin with the word "tradition." Float gently into nothingness through the door of tradition. What do you see as you pass into comfort?

Write down the traditions you love. What new traditions have you created as the world has changed with you?

May today there be peace within. May you trust God that you are exactly where you are meant to be. May you not forget the infinite possibilities that are born of faith. May you use those gifts that you have received. May you pass on the love that has been given to you. May you be content knowing you are a child of God. Let this presence settle into your bones. Allow your soul the freedom to sing, dance, praise and love. It is there for each and every one of us.

A Gift from the Internet

Signposts are reminders on the journey; reminders that we are spiritual beings in the midst of a human experience. This signpost was forwarded to me on a particularly difficult day by a dear friend. St. Theresa's Prayer is such a beautiful prayer. It speaks to the necessary qualities for personal happiness. It is a signpost that reminds me to trust that I am exactly where I should be in my development and growth; allows me to let go of the disappointments in my life; brings a contentedness in knowing that I am valued and loved by the Divine; and references the infinite possibilities that existence has to offer. It is a signpost that is evidence of my personal power. In short, I am reminded of who I am. I decided on that difficult day to print it on a small card and carry it in my folio at work. It reminds me not only of who I am, but also who I am dealing with when peacemaking becomes the task of the day. As each day unfolds and the hubbub of industry calls us to a very different reality, it is easy to forget our true nature. Those who sit before us in discord have forgotten for a moment who they are. The peacemaker is there to remind them and show them the trail out of darkness. I have found that I need to have certain small rituals that bring me back to center during the course of the day. The gift of St. Theresa's prayer is one of those rituals. What signposts have you made rituals in your life?

Meditation today should begin with the word "signpost." As you go deep within the recesses of your mind look for images that remind you of your true nature...just be silent in observation...

Record what came to you in your meditation this morning. List personal signposts that you can place along your path to remind you why are here and who you are.

It is often asserted that discussion is only possible between people who have a common language and accept common basic assumptions. I think that this is a mistake. All that is needed is a readiness to learn from one's partner in the discussion, which includes a genuine wish to understand what he intends to say. If this readiness is there, the discussion will be the more fruitful the more the partner's backgrounds differ.

Sir Karl Raimund Popper

Assertiveness is a great quality, but it also has a bad rap. I think we would have a generally healthier society if we could assert our desires in a way that invited communication. Saying with kindness and respect, "I would love to do that for you, but it won't work for me this week," is asserting a boundary that still allows communication and is respectful of the relationship. Assertiveness is also about permission. Think about a time when someone used competition to get what they wanted. Were they rewarded for their manipulative behavior? How did those affected by the competitive communication react to the reward? Using assertive communication on that same situation, how could you reframe the dialogue to more effectively reach resolution?

Meditation today should begin with the word "assertiveness." Give yourself permission in breathe in an assertive breath...and exhale the fearful breath...sit with certainty in your purpose and personal mission...where does your mind take you?

Look at your communication style this week. How could you more positively assert your boundaries instead?

Risk and Creativity

39

*Every second we live is a new and unique moment of the universe,
a moment that never was before and will never be again.*

Pablo Casals, cellist

Thomas Moore wrote of creativity and soul in his book *Care of the Soul*. He maintained that one cannot truly be creative to the fullest of one's abilities unless they welcome the messages from the darker region of the psyche. When trying to access creativity through darkness, he suggested listening to emotionally dark music, drawing the dark images, writing about the depressive state, viewing dark images of others who have created before you, and entering into a conversation about it. To be able to go to that place which you resist, that is very powerful! To seek the edge of shame and despair in the quest for creativity implies great risk. It also implics risk in creativity. Van Gogh comes to mind when thinking about darkness and creativity. It seems that Vincent could only access his creative gifts in sorrow and solitude, drowning the pain in absinthe. To one who seeks control of emotion, going to the edge for the birth of imagination and creativity does not appeal at all. My first thought as I wrote this entry was, "Imagine what it must feel like to be surrounded by the dark night, to risk fully without the surety of knowing whether the creative act you are giving birth to will be well received." Then it hit me: that is exactly where I am! I am already there, already willing, and I was unable to see that until that very moment. How we have clarity for others so much more readily than we have clarity for ourselves! I am in my dark night; I don't know when the end of the journey will arrive, but I have an idea that if I were not in the throes of a dark-night transition, I would not be writing this down. My friend and colleague, Dana Miller, led the art exercises for our last retreat. The point of the exercises was fun and the release of creativity. The emotions that surfaced were risk and imagination. Could the participants let themselves just move their emotion to the paper creation of a personal mandala? As I watched them engaged in deep creation, I felt my own inertia and mental block against the artistic act. Because I could not risk, I created a mandala that looked like a pizza! If I had been able to realize in that moment that every second is a unique moment that never repeats, perhaps I would have embraced that idea and risked failure and creativity. How easy is it for you to access your imagination?

Meditation today should begin with creativity and the soul. Sit with your soul. Imagine.

Write a few lines in your journal about what came to you in your stillness this morning.

Nan Waller Burnett

Peace, and be at peace with your thoughts and visions.
These things had to come to you and you to accept them.
This is your share of the eternal burden,
The perpetual glory. This is one moment,
But know that another
Shall pierce you with a sudden painful joy
When the figure of God's purpose is made complete.

T.S. Eliot, *Murder in the Cathedral*

Finding purpose in one's life is the personal quest for the holy grail. Viktor Frankl, author of *Man's Search for Meaning*, psychologist, and Holocaust survivor, coined the term "logo therapy" for the mind process that served as his life preserver while surviving the concentration camps in World War II. This ring of sanity was the realization that he could focus on the purpose of his life, find meaning in the thoughts he chose to allow into his mind. During the course of his life, he went on to help others find meaning and purpose in their lives. Rick Warren, author of *The Purpose-Driven Life*, a book that has sold millions of copies across the globe, ties purpose and meaning to a relationship with God. The ancient Oriental and Western philosophers have written volumes on finding purpose in one's life. It does not matter how we arrived at this juncture in our development, or when; it only matters that we explore our purpose and adopt it as a choice born of our own fulfillment, sharing our richness and bettering the planet. Finding the purpose of our existence on the planet gives meaning to the unique qualities we bring into the circle of life. Marianne Williamson's notable quotation declares that we have no business playing small when our gifts and essence are "powerful beyond measure." Money, power, adoration, or zeal for a cause is not the route to purpose. What is your purpose?

Meditate today on the word "purpose." Breathe in the silence of soul, and breathe out the chattering mind. Breathe in the clarity of purpose, and breathe out the confusion of the cause.

In your journal, identify the reasons you chose your work. Is your work tied to your purpose? If you do not have clarity on your purpose, brainstorm all your activities and distinguish how each one brings meaning to your life. See if those meanings help clarify your purpose.

Thou shalt be like a watered garden, and like a spring of water, whose waters fail not.

Isaiah 58:11

Renewal is a necessary part of living. The evidence of renewal in nature is abundant in every spring day. We can choose self-renewal this season. A good self-renewal ritual is daily affirmation, whereby the mind focuses every morning upon attracting the positive. Daily affirmation enhances the heart work of the day. The heart is the symbol for love, and whatever you think you are, you create. Be love. Another self-renewal strategy and a requisite for a well-lived life is to create a healthy body. Our bodies are miraculous and regenerate tissue around the clock. It is always possible to turn around the effects of poor nourishment or inactivity. Today, choose to renew your body by going to the "spring of water" and consume whatever makes you feel healthy. Are you willing to let go of old thinking about the care of the soul and the renewal of the body?

A change in the weather is enough to renew the world and ourselves.

Marcel Proust

Meditate today on the word "renewal." Breathe in the air in the "watered garden"; breathe out the tightness of inactivity. Breathe in the affirmations of the heart, and breathe out the negative judgments of the mind.

In your journal, list several ways by which you can renew yourself. Write one positive affirmation that you can carry in your mind throughout the day.

Compared to what we ought to be, we are only half awake. We are making use of only a small part of our physical and mental resources. Stating the thing broadly, the human individual thus lives far within his limits. He possesses power of various sorts which he habitually fails to use.

William James

William James was a nineteenth-century psychologist who taught at Harvard for many years. He was also a prolific writer. It is amazing to me how, today, science is proving him right. Consciousness can now be mapped in the laboratory through brain science. We are only beginning to understand how consciousness serves as an integral part of the whole person. Medicine is opening the door to proactive health care—fostering the holistic health of the person as opposed to treating the diseased patient. The field of conflict resolution is also moving toward this awakening. We have not been using the entire range of our faculties. Kenneth Cloke and Daniel Bowling have both written about working within the system of conflict, empowerment through attentive, empathic listening, mindfulness meditation, and the willingness to engage in the conflict dangerously. I welcome a new dialogue—a shift from "do it this way" to "be reflective in your thinking," "tap into their energy," "listen with intention," and "bring your own qualities to the table." The agreement by the practitioner to bring consciousness to the dispute is a powerful tool in peacemaking on the planet, one dispute at a time. Tapping into thinking, based in the central core of the brain, allows the generation of information not originating in the pre-frontal lobe of the brain. Bringing your consciousness to the table allows you to "know without knowing."

Meditate today on pure consciousness. Breathe in the energy of inquiry, and breathe out the thinking brain impulses. Breathe in the fluidity of new resources, and breathe out the need to know.

Write a few lines in your journal about your own consciousness. How can you tap into more than what you know right now?

Give me a light that I may tread softly into the unknown? Go out into the darkness and put your hand into the hand of God. That you shall be better than light and safer than a known way.

Read by King George VI of England, Christmas Broadcast, 1939
From a story by Minnie Lee Hoskins

Josh Groban recorded a song from Cirque du Soleil entitled "Let Me Fall." The words powerfully speak to trust and the agreement to let go, to trust that which cannot be seen. My late colleague, Alan, performed an empowering guided meditation coupled with Groban's song to bring closure to retreats for airline professionals after 9/11. The fear that many crew members encountered was paralyzing. Some were reliving the images of crashing airplanes, and the powerlessness they felt was palpable. Alan lovingly led them through the darkness with his words, and ended the meditation with a guided visualization of an angel appearing out of the darkness to envelop them in love and safety. As he painted the image of the angel swaddling them in the fold of his or her wings, the song began. The change in their faces as they ended the meditation was remarkable. Many left with the courage they needed to return to flying, and others left with the courage they needed to retire. Ultimately, we have no choice but to put our "hand into the hand of God." We resist that comfort when we rely solely on our own judgment. It is not all up to us. At certain times, there is no torch to light the way, and each day, we could find ourselves lost in the darkness. To tread into the unknown can be frightening, but as King George counseled his people as English soldiers marched to war, to do so "shall be better than light and safer than the known way."

Meditation today should begin with the phrase "willingness to fall." Slowly take in a cleansing breath, and be willing to surrender to your higher power for the journey into the unknown. Find peace in the stillness.

Record in your journal the experience of your meditation today. Write down one thing you are in fear of today. What can you do to embrace the unknown?

Most of us spend the first six days of each week sowing wild oats;
then we go to church on Sunday and pray for a crop failure.

Fred Allen

I love this quote. It reminds me to not be so serious and to have a sense of humor in everything I do. The quote also speaks to hypocrisy. Today, it seems that piety and hypocrisy reign in religious dialogue. It does not matter what continent you are on — someone proclaims to have the answers for us all. Some assert that they are the only ones who shall be admitted to heaven; and others, that their place in heaven will be premium, and the rest of us will be in the cheap seats. Some promise us that, unless we follow certain rules, we shall surely burn in torment. Even as a young child, I did not think that God excluded anyone. To me, the idea that one could treat others poorly or be greedy, then beg forgiveness on Sunday, and then somehow be healed, suggests a higher power that sits in judgment, sounding more like the magistrate of hell. I chose again. I view my higher power to be loving, always available, assisting me in living to my fullest potential in order to share my gifts along the way. My higher power embraces my humanness, allows me to feel human when I am less than perfect. There is no need to beg to "get in." We're in! Heaven's open, an equal-opportunity housing authority for the next chapter. When we notice that we have acted against our values or have chosen in error, we can simply choose again. But "judgment" is the myth here. The feeling that we will be judged by others causes us to act in ways that do not represent who we really are: pious and righteous is the game face; self-judgment is the end result. Hypocrisy is an inside job. Hypocrites espouse beliefs that they do not hold. Hypocrisy is dishonest but human. We are all here searching for answers, and sometimes that searching is misguided. Excavate your authentic inside face, and bring it forth to shine. Choose not to be offended by those who think they have answers for you—and soften your judgment of those people who you think are in the dark!

Meditate today on the word "hypocrisy." In what areas of your life does your walk not align with your talk? Breathe deeply into your soul and choose internal honesty.

Record in your journal one quality or value that needs to be excavated today from your soul so that you can live with more integrity.

Everything flows and nothing abides; everything gives way and nothing stays fixed.

Heraclitus

To become willing to accept the flow of life is among the greatest of human traits. It can also be the key to inner peace. Meditation is a tool that enhances our ability to be open to the present and go with the flow of life. Meditation as a daily ritual trains our frantic mind to center into stillness so that we can listen from the center of our soul. Because change is ever-present in each breath, chaos or observation is the choice of each moment. "Wu wei" is defined in the *Tao Te Ching* as the accomplishment of things by not trying to accomplish them. The intended outcome will arrive when least expected, or in our choosing not to paddle against the river of life. In our attachment to things and their meaning, we set up inevitable inner strife; thus, surrender to the moment cannot occur. Surrendering to life brings joy; fighting your reality brings loss and disappointment. I am a red-headed action figure. Proactive in most areas of my life, I often realize too late that I have been the fish swimming against the current. Frustration and being overwhelmed are common emotions that I wrestle with daily. I will have to set inner peace as a momentary goal for the rest of my time here. What has made that task easier are those few minutes early in the day that are mine alone and not shared. I am learning to forgive myself for the times when I act unconsciously.

Meditate today on the phrase "going with the flow." Breathe in the gentle current of breath, and breathe out the residual tension of resistance.

Write down one thing that you can do today to stop resisting and let your life flow.

We are wide-eyed in contemplating the possibility that life may exist elsewhere in the universe, but we wear blinders when contemplating the possibilities of life on earth.

Norman Cousins

As the baby of the family, I had a particular vantage point of observation. In review of my life, I think that preparation for my future began when I was very young. The nature of observation leads one to the act of contemplation. I remember observing the actions of three older brothers and learning a pressing need for me to know how to duck-and-run. I also had many hours of solitude, perhaps because I had no sister and recall long days when I was responsible for my own entertainment. I remember lying on the grass in the back yard and watching how quickly the clouds moved over me; how comforting the umbrella of the stars made me feel; and I also became familiar with a kind of bottomless questioning I had about the universe. The universe seemed so vast that I could not comprehend it. I quickly dismissed it as one of those things that only God knew; I would have to wait to find out. I suppose that is the moment when I placed the blinders over my peripheral vision, no longer open to the vastness of possibility. However, I did not stop being an observer of life or the people that came into my circle of concern. Eventually I had the distinct impression that change was necessary; it was time to contemplate the possibilities of life on earth. My skills of observation led me into the work of conflict resolution, partly due to my willingness to say yes to the next door opening, but partly due to the decision to live my life with purpose. Look at your powers of observation. What possibilities do you contemplate for yourself?

Meditation today should begin with the word "observation." Observe the stillness; observe the air going through your nostrils into your lungs...observe the empty container...observe the warmth of peace flow into the sacred soul...

List in your journal the images that you observed in your mediation. Can you see a pattern? Can you identify one thing that needs the review of your powers of observation?

How many a dispute could have been deflated into a single
paragraph if the disputants had dared to define their terms.

Aristotle

Our clients come to our table to resolve what they feel is unresolvable. The definition of each client's terms is essential to the process of elucidation, the understanding between souls. If we have the chance to lead the parties out of despair and into the light of awareness, clarification is of the utmost importance. As perception can only be understood in the view of the other's truth, laying the validity of diverse perceptions as a cornerstone of resolution is paramount. Aristotle thought with amazing clarity about the classification of things, ethics, values, education, and honor. Part of his life's work was finding the common denominator of classifications, ordering knowledge, and the process of logical thought. As peacemakers and maestros of conflict engagement, success is likely if we can dig beneath the rhetoric to illuminate the driver of the dispute. Dispute resolution is not a concrete world. Rather, the engagement of conflict is a fluid, volatile, chaotic process, which cannot be harnessed by exerting force. Our management of disputes is possible only through even-handed control. Resolution never occurs permanently when we try to control the outcome. With the simple tool of defining the terms, perception can be shifted toward true understanding, and deflation of the dispute is assured.

Meditate today on the word "resolution." Breathe in a settling breathe of comfort. Take in the meaning of the word "resolution"; think of the word as "re-soul."

Write a few lines in your journal about today's meditation experience. What terms need redefinition in your life? How can you re-soul your perceptions?

*Men occasionally stumble over the truth, but most of them pick
themselves up and hurry off as if nothing had happened.*

Winston Churchill

Denial is a strong attitude to overcome. Denial ensures that you cannot see what is being denied. When we "occasionally stumble over [our] truth" and deny it, our truth tends to follow us like a shadow. Recent research suggests that most of us lie frequently. Some are "little white lies," the ones whereby we convey our regrets to Mom, feigning illness when we really don't want to go to Aunt Sophie's 75th-birthday soiree. But it's the lies we use to convince ourselves that really haunt us. Every soul has truths that reveal themselves in their own timing. Perhaps we are simply not ready to explore a particular pain just yet. At some point, however, we stumble smack into our truth, and we need to stay facedown in it and process the denial into understanding and personal forgiveness. We all have moments of denial; it is part of being human. But, as Mark Twain notes below, it is easier on the memory if we don't lie, especially to ourselves. Life is easier to live.

If you tell the truth, you don't have to remember anything.

Mark Twain

Meditate today on the phrase "truth or dare." Dare to look deeply into your soul for that which you have denied.

Write down one thing you can do today to bring yourself out of denial and into owning a truth denied.

Observe the wonders as they occur
around you. Don't claim them.
Feel the artistry moving through,
and be silent.

Rumi, *The Essential Rumi*

At a retreat for peacemakers, one of the exercises accessed mental artistry through art, through music, and through thoughts. To be an effective agent for change, it is essential to use the whole brain. Staying in logic and rational thought will not get the practitioner to the juncture of understanding between parties. Unfortunately, we train conflict resolution professionals from only one center of the brain - the pre-frontal cortex. When chaos forces the dispute to the edge, the linear practitioner will not find a way out of the chaos. We are all artistic in some fashion. Many have not had the opportunity to push that creativity through the eye of the needle and onto the page. At the retreat, one of the tasks was to create a personal mandala, an image upon which to mediate. Although this excercise intially evoked fear in many, it turned out to be fun and enlightening for all. Listening to your own artistry through creative self-expression allows you to see wonders around you that went unnoticed before. As Rumi suggests, "Feel the artistry in silence." No one can see your unique vision and, if you refuse to sing, no one will ever hear your voice. In the words of Wayne Dyer: "Don't die with your music still in you." Explore and cultivate your artistry; your vision will pass with you if you do not share the wonders of you.

Every time an artist dies, part of the vision of mankind passes with him.

Franklin Delano Roosevelt

Meditation today should begin with the agreement to excavate your artistry. Envelop your soul with a silence of thought, look to the stillness for avenues of artistry.

Write down at least one thing that you can do today to facilitate the cultivation of your creative brain.

Just as you have the instinctive natural desire to be happy and overcome suffering,
so do all sentient beings.... So, on what grounds do you discriminate?

His Holiness the Dalai Lama

It seems that, in the last few years, the efforts of social scientists in leading society toward acceptance and tolerance of other cultures and belief systems have been drastically set back. This has been a source of deep frustration for me. I have felt it is necessary to keep sounding the horn on tolerance, not only in my practice but in my personal life. The deep division that is evidenced in different geo-political camps of thought has created a crevasse of the "us vs. them" mentality on the planet. This division is felt right down to the roots of society; within couples, families, businesses, and societies. I have withdrawn from toxic relationships in my own life. I have noticed I am intolerant of the intolerant. Yet, even in these difficult relationships, I think it is necessary to apply the same tonic of acceptance. As we come together to engage in bringing peace to our fellow citizens through dispute resolution, we need to be a model for tolerance. We need to be judgment free in our practices and afford all people the respect for their journey, no matter what we think of it. Be tolerant of pain, no matter how it is presented to you. Allow people a safe place to grow, respect them for what they experience. Each of us has a road we must follow. Respect them, not only in your work but in your own life as well. In this way, the value of tolerance will spread to raise the consciousness of the planet, one dispute at a time.

Meditate today on the word "tolerance." Breathe in the sweetness of acceptance, and breathe out the judgment of the thinking mind. Breathe in the peace of a loving nature; breathe out the lesions on your heart.

Write in your journal about tolerance. When have you made a decision for tolerance in your life? How often are you intolerant of others? Make a commitment to yourself to express tolerance today. Be tolerant of your process; you are a work of art in creation.

> *It has become painfully clear that a remote sense of spirituality has little or no effect on the way we live as a society. People go to religious services and yet pollute, take excessive profits, encourage wars, oppress, foment political division, maintain racial injustice, and promote their own moralistic agendas at the expense of a deeply moral responsiveness to a world in trouble. It's time to bring spirituality home, close to the heart and connected to an ordinary life.*
>
> Frederick and Mary Ann Brussat, *Spiritual Literacy: Reading the Sacred in Everyday Life*

Our apathy as a nation has a huge price. Choosing the comfort of a static response to the world is no longer acceptable. After centuries of violence and disputes, it is time to seek a better path out of the conflicts scattered across the planet. We have moved so decidedly in the direction of independence and individualism that we risk disconnection from other souls. As peacemakers, our duty is to engage in conflict for the purpose of resolution, one disagreement at a time. The only way to actually be present for conflicts is to be connected with ourselves and the world spiritually. I think the Brussats' statement about the remote condition of personal involvement in our world is true. There is a collective dissonance; a discord between what we show outwardly and who we are on the inside. We have become too distant in our relationship with a higher power. Perhaps we need to consider the opportunity to make an impact in our world. We attempt to teach our children the correct principles but fail to model them. We coach people in resolution and yet do not consistently practice peace in our own lives. We need to move from complacency to commitment, from inaction to proaction. I think that the only way to effectively cross the bridge to human connection is to become connected with our spirit.

Meditation today should begin with the word "impact." What images does the word "impact" evoke in your mind? Sit silently as your mind empties and asks the collective source to fill it with possibilities.

Write down one thing you can do today to impact the planet, one act at a time.

Tapestry

*You see, when weaving a blanket, an Indian woman leaves a
flaw in the weaving of that blanket to let the soul out.*

Martha Graham

I love the metaphor of a tapestry to illustrate the journey of life. I have an affinity for tapestries, and when I see them hanging in museums as works of art, or in fabric shops and other stores, I am drawn to them and want to touch them in awe of the age-old art of weaving. Expressions of creativity have a soul to them. They uniquely tell stories of joy and pain. Martha Graham was an accomplished choreographer, weaving tapestries of dance and movement together for her audience to invest their emotions in and for her dancers to joyfully perform. As the observers became part of the dance, the connection was electric—and that recognition of shared humanity created the opening that let out the soul of the dance. Dolly Parton sings about the "Coat of Many Colors" that she wore to school, despite being ridiculed by other kids, and how that coat, pieced and stitched together with her momma's love, embodied the soul and story of her mother. Today, caress all the fabrics and threads of your tapestry, and all its flaws that have allowed you to see your soul.

Meditate today on the word "tapestry." Sink into your mind and let your unique tapestry of fabrics and threads unfold before you. What do you see? What does your tapestry say about you?

Write down the images that came to you in your meditation. What flaws in your tapestry, that is, what perceived imperfections or mistakes in your journey, became opportunities for letting your soul out?

Creative minds have been known to survive any sort of bad training.
Anna Freud, *The Ego and the Mechanisms of Defense*

Competence seems to be a subject of great concern in our field. How often have we sat in a robotic training session and not been connected to the purpose behind our choice to practice conflict resolution? A truly creative mind can see beyond any set of procedures and regulations and produce something more relevant and inspired than the routine outcome of a standards-driven strategy. Train we must, but in this ever-evolving field of peace and reconciliation, the training is lagging a little behind. An answer to that call is the myriad of graduate and certificate programs being made available to seekers of higher truths in peacebuilding. Students can now delve into dialogue rather than just learn the steps of the process. Competence is essential to the building of a successful practice and requires something more of the practitioner. A certain creative zeal and personal commitment must be present in that soul—hardly the qualities of the compliant practitioner who merely fills out forms and checks boxes, and focuses on billable hours. This is not an occupation for the faint of heart, the casual or apathetic participant, or the ungrounded visionary. Competency is peacemaking, and conflict engagement requires something more of the practitioner. Reach into your soul and find the creative practitioner in you. Unearth and cultivate the rich qualities that you have been unaware you possess. You are already competent. Find your unique voice.

Meditation today should begin with the word "competence." As you agree to silence this morning, search for the competencies you know are yours; feel their value in your bones. Respect your nature, and welcome change.

Write in your journal how you will hone your competencies this year.

I learned about the strength you can get from a close family life. I learned to keep going, even in bad times. I learned not to despair, even when my world was falling apart. I learned that there are no free lunches. And I learned the value of hard work.

Lee Iacocca

An inspiring business maverick who revitalized Ford Motors and saved Chrysler from bankruptcy in the 1980s, Lee Iacocca is a corporate icon. His principles include dedication to family, tenacity, a positive attitude, and hard work. People feel strongly about their principles. The violation of those principles, bring clients to our table. Disrespect, boundary violation, betrayal, and loss are grounds to fight for "the principle of the thing," and are the most difficult to work with. All of us have a set of expectations for those who live within our sphere, whether it is family, business, or nation. To be more fully present for our clients, it is essential that we know the breadth and depth of our own principles. I suspect that many of us have not taken a comprehensive inventory of our principles. If you are aware of your principles, inquire more deeply; if you are not aware of them, take this day to uncover them.

Meditate today on the word "principles." Breathe a cleansing breath, and allow your mind to focus on what is important to you, what has meaning for you. Enter the space with a thirst for knowing.

Write in your journal about the messages you received in your meditation. If you are still unclear, list what you believe to be your principles, and later in the day, engage your conscious thoughts about principles in general.

The Soul should always stand ajar.
that if the heaven inquire,
He will not be obliged to wait,...

Emily Dickinson, *Part Four: Time and Eternity*

Remaining open to the day's unfolding experience brings possibility. If you choose to focus in the moment, the potential for joy and happiness increases exponentially. Anticipation of the unfolding day can be an exciting adventure, and it can offer hope. A posture of openness is receptive and conveys to others that you are approachable. My early decades were largely spent in the labor of learning through the school of hard knocks. I really had no mentor during my twenties, and I chose early marriage out of fear. Although my former husband and I are still good friends and value our experience together, we were so different and lacked the maturity we needed to make that commitment so early. I passed through my thirties looking at the ground under my feet, instead of looking at the joy of the world around me. I was not open to life. I had no sense of my potential or talents, only of my lack and loss. I wove a very negative story around those years, and I lived in that story. Every morning now, I reprogram my thoughts to look for the joy, to remain open to possibility. Openness does not just happen for me; I have to intend it. Today, intend openness for yourself; look for what's working instead of what's not. The ecstatic experience may be just around the corner!

Begin meditation today with the word "openness." Breathe a deep cleansing breath of free movement, and open your arms upward to the sky. Breathe deeply again and release any tension in your lower body.

In your journal, write down the situations in your life about which you are resigned, closed to possibility. What is one action you can take today to generate a new possibility or to be more open to life in general?

I do not believe in the collective wisdom of individual ignorance.

Thomas Carlyle

Remaining unaware is often a choice. We have all witnessed the phenomenon of chosen ignorance in closed cultures, such as religious sects and societies stratified by class, race, or socioeconomics. Around the globe, there are rules of engagement that breed conflict, many of which are dictated by cultural and societal mores. To my mind, we choose to stay in the dark about certain realities, particularly atrocities against humans, so that we don't have to take part in their solution or be responsible for their outcome. The choice to not learn another's point of view is a ticket to the uppermost platform of a self-designed hierarchy. There is comfort in believing that we are right and others are wrong. Per a perceived rank in nationality, race, or faith, we might feel we are entitled to deference from others. Racism is still rampant in our nation as well as in our world. Chosen ignorance breeds more of the same, which doesn't bode well for the future because history can always repeat itself. The pendulum swings far to one side and then to the other to correct the egregious acts of yesterday. The same questions should be asked of both parties in a disagreement, so that dialogue encompassing all points of view can begin. Our clients often come to our table in the dark, armed with their chosen ignorance, and like a scared cat clinging to a branch in the hurricane, they volley their state of unawareness all over the room. Our task then becomes "to love," to sit in non-judgment, accept their fear and projection, and turn it into understanding. To bring ignorance out of the shadows and into the light of personal awareness cannot be done alone. The practitioner requires divine help and the willingness to stay connected to it through the storm.

A great deal of intelligence can be invested in ignorance when the need for illusion is deep.

Saul Bellow

Meditate today on the word "ignorance." In the stillness, look for the connection, the avenue of acceptance. You can traverse the darkness of ignorance if you choose. Envision building a bridge over the gulf of ignorance; ask for guidance.

Journaling about ignorance, what insights come to your mind? In what situations have you chosen ignorance to play small and abdicate responsibility?

*I am willing to expand beyond the limits I have placed on myself
and those I have allowed others to place upon me.*

Iyanla Vanzant

The word "vitality" evokes an image of health and activity. To live a vital life is surely a choice. Energy and excitement are high in vital souls. When I set forth the intention of vitality, I stretch, meditate, take vitamins, eat well, exercise, and try to give something back each day. When I do these things, I get excited; I have more energy and feel more involved in life. My adopted mother of choice, Ilene, has been a wonderful role model for me. She taught me that "if you don't use it, you lose it!" In her eighties, she still walks every day; her mind is sharp; she still drives and is the picture of vitality. Ilene, a breast cancer survivor since the 1960s, never let cancer nor the fact that she had one kidney nor a bad leg get in her way of living every moment fully. Born in Nebraska in the 1920s, she had many tales of survival to tell my children. They adored her "down on the farm" stories. The salt of the earth, Ilene would lecture to my children, "You've got to make your own happiness, kids." I am so fortunate to have had her bless our lives. Today, honor your vital qualities that bless others' lives.

Meditate today on the word "vitality." Breathe in a vigorous breath; feel energy flow through your veins as you begin this day.

In your journal, record your qualities that vitalize you and others, as well as those qualities that devitalize you and others, perhaps by imposing limits. Similarly, record the situations in your life that give you energy and deplete your energy, respectively. What can you do for yourself today that will vitalize you in each de-energizing situations?

But this is human life: the war, the deeds,
The disappointment, the anxiety,
Imagination's struggles, far and nigh,
All human; bearing in themselves this good,
That they are still the air, the subtle food,
To make us feel existence...

John Keats, *Endymion,* Book II

While we try to hold a perpetual vision of hope and opportunity, somehow reality seeps through the cracks in the armor of our perception. In our daily work of peacemaking and building bridges for the weary, the client's pain is the reality, the "what is" we are entrusted with to face and help heal. Sweeping the tears or rage under the carpet of process and making nice does not end the conflict. Certainly, optimism and opportunity is the goal of resolution, but dismissing the reality of the conflict only ensures its return. When we shortcut the rage or sorrow, the reality of pain will resurface to haunt the conflicted soul. In my practice, my intention is to get a healthy dose of every client's reality. I never care about the settlement of items on an agenda. I know that close by, flying under the radar, is the true driver of the dispute. My questions laser in on their truth, their reality, and the discomfort in the room is palpable. All humans bear good qualities in their hearts; I need only to summon that goodness and the attendant ears of each client to hear the pain of the other party. Only then can the conflict truly be expunged.

Meditate today on the word "reality." Breathe in clarity and see with new eyes in search of your reality. Breathe in the clarity of perception.

Write down what came to you in your meditation. What seemingly negative aspects of your reality can you be grateful for because they have taught you to better appreciate the positive?

*[I]f I've failed, others must succeed, because those who do not have power over the story
that dominates their lives, the power to retell it, rethink it, deconstruct it, joke about it, and
change it as times change, truly are powerless, because they cannot think new thoughts.*

Salman Rushdie, "One Thousand Days in a Balloon"

Most of us think we have failed at something during the course of our lives. For me, the
most enlightening awareness I have experienced is that I have the power to change my mind.
Until my late forties, failing to do just that caused me much pain. I lived in a story of my own
design, and the people in my circle of concern dwelled inside that constructed house of misery.
When I finally changed my mind; my life changed before me. I changed my mind about my
practice; my practice changed before my eyes. Every case that comes before me allows me the
opportunity to model for others the choice to change one's mind. It is one of the most powerful
tools I can use in mediation, and it is the one that continues to provide benefit in the lives of
those I teach. Consider your own reality. What choices can you make that lead to change? How
can you change your mind so that your story has a different ending.

Meditate today on the word "failure." Fully experience your reaction to that powerful
word and then transform it into something positive.

In your journal, record your perceived failures and reframe them as successes.

*With a mission statement, we can flow with changes. We don't need prejudgments
or prejudices. We don't need to figure out everything else in life, to stereotype
and categorize everything and everybody in order to accommodate reality.*

Stephen R. Covey, *The 7 Habits of Highly Effective People*

Have you ever felt as though you were on a mission? As though you could not stop until the task was complete? Stephen Covey believes we should all have a mission statement. We should all set forth a plan for life, a guideline for the attainment of goals and the completion of obligations. Developing that statement is not as easy as it sounds. In his landmark book *The 7 Habits of Highly Effective People*, Covey sets forth steps to design the mission for launch. Start with your circle of influence, your vision, your values, your qualities, your gifts, your hopes, your dreams, the things you know you excel in, and the things you would like to improve. Taking this sort of inventory allows you, the author of your life, to be intentional, to set forth your ultimate goal and then allow the day to flow and be lived to the fullest without regard for the end result, because you started with the end in mind. Covey asserts that security, wisdom, guidance, and power are the four life factors that result in success. I think that, every year, we should review our personal mission statement to see if we have followed the trail. Are we living our mission? Are we following our ethics, our dreams, and our hopes? Starting with a mission is a natural precursor to living a purpose-driven life. Many of the clients who come before us are wandering in the wilderness, searching for answers. If we begin with the end in mind, it takes a lot of the guesswork out of life. Conflict is a natural result of mindless wandering. If we are mindful about our work, we can impart mindfulness to those around us.

Begin meditation today with the word "mission." Breathe in the inquiry, and breathe out the uncertainty. Breathe deeply for clarity of intention; breathe out the fogginess of mind.

In your journal, draft a mission statement for the rest of your life. Work on this mission statement for a few minutes each day this week.

The seat and home of the soul is in the heart, the center of the person; it is the heart that nourishes the spirits which know of good and evil. It dwells within the person in the place where life is, against which death fights.

Paracelsus

Becoming centered is the doorway to mindfulness. Focusing on a word, a phrase, the breath, the beating heart, provides a target on which the mind can settle its endless ranting. The Dalai Lama notes that when the mind can be trained to not listen to chatter and to not "fall into the abyss of emptiness," one finds a deep peace, an observant floating awareness, a knowing, that is the mind's natural state. To center the spirit protects the heart, relaxes the constricted bands around its chambers, and allows a peaceful flowing outward through the body. Much research has been done in mind-body connection, and a predominant commonality among many diseases is a lack of oxygenated blood. Breathing often and deeply to clear a foggy mind is a centering skill that brings renewed energy throughout the day. As Paracelsus invites us to the "seat and home of the soul," agree to go to that place where peace may be found today.

Meditate today on the word "centering." Breathe in the willingness to go to the center; breathe out the mind's chatter that fragments and displaces you.

Write down the images that came up in your meditation. Pay attention to your breathing today, and record the times when you notice your breathing is infrequent or shallow.

Opportunity

What is it you plan to do
with your one wild and precious life?

Mary Oliver, "The Summer Day"

"Opportunity" is such a hopeful word. In her oft-quoted line, Mary Oliver asks the reader about an outcome that presumes a successful journey in a positive way. It conveys that we have power, we can make plans, and we can be wild with our precious life. This line of poetry brings to my mind empowerment. The authority to act in one's life is always coupled with responsibility. Do we not have a responsibility to *have* a "wild and precious life"? Should we not endeavor to live each moment to its grandest possibility? I have expressed to my children that they should embrace their lives with purpose. My eldest son was born with many gifts. He is quite a handsome man, with a natural athletic ability in every sport he undertakes. Many of his qualities were part of his character when he arrived. He is a loving, caring, sensitive person—all powerful gifts for life. Not to encourage these gifts would have been poor parenting on my part. His level of energy was not the highest; he easily assumed a posture of laziness. As a teen, he reminded me of myself in my youth, a ship without a sail, unsure of leaving the harbor. Yet he agreed to take two years of his life to live in South America and help those in need. He obeyed his calling, an action that many others choose not to take, and now he has lessons to carry with him. He viewed the opportunity with possibility, and through a tough, two-month immersion program, he gained the gift of learning another language, the social ability to converse easily with strangers, and the realization of how blessed he has been and how privileged he is. He expressed compassion, administered to those in need with a grateful heart, and displayed an innate kindness, which he embodies in his own particular way. He is beginning to see that he has powers buried deep beneath the surface, and it is with great joy that I observe his awareness of those excavated gifts. I know he will be an amazing father. He is beginning to ask the question "What will I do with my life?" We can all begin anew each day and ask the same question. How does your wild and precious life look to you?

Meditation today should begin with the word "opportunity." Breathe deeply into possibility for this day. Cleanse your body of the night's long rest, and contemplate the moments of joyful presence you might encounter today.

In your journal, write down the opportunities you see for joyful presence in your wild, precious day.

Blame

We are aware that blaming and arguing never help us and only create a wider gap between us that only understanding, trust, and love can help us change and grow. This is the fifth of the five awarenesses. Do you make a vow to receive, study, and practice it?

Thich Nhat Hanh, *Teachings on Love*

The blame game is the sport of choice running rampant on the playing field of our mediation practice. Blame is always followed by shame, and shame is the spinning wheel of argument and conflict. When our clients are locked in that scrimmage of conflict, the continuous pounding escalates exponentially. This is where the practitioner of awareness enters the game but not as the referee. As Gandhi noted, "You must be the change you want to see." Trusting the process and understanding pain replaces the whistle and the penalty flag. It is incumbent upon the practitioner to learn the lesson of the fifth awareness before creating the table of peace.

Meditate today on the thought of understanding blame. Breathe in the comfort of safety, and breathe out the adrenaline of the rush. Settle into the breath of trusting the process, and breathe out the internal argument. Be present for yourself as well for as your clients.

Record one way you can intervene in the blame game of your life today. Release the shame you fell from the blame.

*Few things help an individual more than to place responsibility
upon him, and to let him know that you trust him.*

Booker T. Washington

Responsibility is a quality that I recently discovered has been part of my makeup for many years. (It's funny how we can be blind to qualities in ourselves that the world so readily sees.) I have a clear sense of responsibility for many things: the word "duty" comes to mind. I had a definite sense of the job of parenting. Blessed with three children, each bearing a unique set of equipment for the journey through life, I knew that my job was to help them discover their particular talents and learn how to utilize that knowledge while they were gathering their experiences in life. I had a keen sense of responsibility about providing an education for them. I felt a duty to share the knowledge that I had received, both formally and informally, in my youth and adulthood. Having taught at a Jesuit university for many years, I enjoy the welcoming dialogue and community service so present in that educational system, as established by Ignatius Loyola centuries ago.

I have taken many precepts of that religion and left just as many, and all those choices are sanctioned within its walls of learning. But the values of the Jesuit education match my values, a responsibility to share what you know and leave your community improved. As I watched mid-life approaching I decided that I had a responsibility to make a difference, to leave in my wake work that could be a part of the solution and not the problem. I wanted to participate in a forward movement characterized by committed action, to dare to think outside the box, to throw caution to the wind and practice on the edge. Conducting a safe practice never did appeal to me. As I witness the rapidly changing world, time is of the essence. Responsibility calls me to hurry before a collective apathy devastates this planet.

*To let oneself be bound by a duty from the moment you see it approaching
is part of the integrity that alone justifies responsibility.*

Dag Hammarskjöld

Meditate today on the word "responsibility." Ponder the ways in which your responsible nature presents itself to you.

Write down the areas of your life in which you have a clear sense of responsibility. How do you use your life to perform responsibly?

I add my breath to your breath
That our days may be long on the earth,
That the days of our people may be long,
That we shall be as one person,
That we may finish our road together.

Laguna Pueblo prayer

A speaker at a memorial service I attended defined a friend as one who remembers the words to your song and can sing them back to you when you forget the words. Friends are very important to me; my friends are my family. In the inventory of my life, I have noticed that once friends come into my life, they become an enduring part of my circle of concern. I do not have many friendships, but the ones I have are long and deep. When you don't want to stand at the edge of the cliff alone, you have the opportunity to value your friends. When you fear the unknown, you can search behind yourself for the hand of a friend. When you're treading water in the well of depression, your friends reach down into their soul for the strength to lift you out of the darkness. When I can be present for friends, and they for me, our souls bond in a way that confirms a pact made in heaven though forgotten at birth. My "Aunt Fair," my mother's dearest childhood and lifelong friend, has always been there for me, as she had been for my mother. When my mother was eloping, Aunt Fair helped her sneak away by stuffing a wedding dress in a golf bag. Aunt Fair was at my mother's side the day I was born—my middle name is Fair. One of the most remarkable events in my life is when my mother and my Aunt Hilda, who lived thousands of miles apart, died within 20 minutes of each other. When I telephoned Aunt Fair to tell her they had both passed, she said tearfully, "Oh, Nan, your mother and I always said we'd catch hands and go together, but Hilda did it for me." My mother's friendship with Aunt Fair instilled in me a deeply meaningful value. Having no sister of my own, I created one in "Aunt Judy," who has been more an aunt to my children than blood could provide. She is always there for them, and always there for me. On this day, I pay tribute to her, that we may finish our road together.

Meditate today on the word "friend." As you begin your inner journey this day, feel the embrace of the friend who waits in the wings ready to catch you when you are weary. Pay tribute to that friend today.

Write in your journal about your circle of concern. Who needs an ear today? Who needs for you to sing the words of their song back to them?

Nan Waller Burnett

Tact

Tact is the ability to describe others as they see themselves.

Abraham Lincoln

I have no tact. When God was passing out that attribute, I was not present in the room. Diplomacy is a subtlety that was not part of my operating equipment, either. How does someone with no skills of diplomacy be an effective mediator? Practice in an area where tactlessness works in your favor! Working with high-conflict couples in mediation is a place of comfort for me, because I have no fear of offending them. Now, *that's* looking for the silver lining! I do, however, have great respect for those consummate professionals who possess that gift of the verbal soft shoe. I suspect it is a choice. Robert Smith, an attorney mediator in Colorado, is an amazing gentleman, one of those rare ambassadors of authenticity. Truly genuine in his diplomatic style, the remarkable thing about Bob is not that he is a master diplomat but that he never says anything contrived. He always speaks from a place of higher vision; he speaks to the God in people, as if they are the rightful recipients of human grace, whether or not they actually deserve it. I cannot think of a mediation skill more valuable than the quality of acceptance without judgment. It is through acceptance that the transformation of conflict is possible. Granted, I am not tactful, but after I smack the chaotic parties with the two-by-four and show them the mirror, their attention creates the opening for my acceptance without judgment.

Meditate today on the word "tactful." Settle into a path of gentle authenticity, the higher road. Breathe deeply into the safety of the moment.

In your journal, list two situations in which you exercise diplomacy. List two situations in which you repeatedly fall short in the tact department. Identify one place in each of the latter situations where you can accept without judgment.

I never give 'em hell. I just tell the truth and they think it's hell.

Harry S. Truman

Often, the souls who come to my table experience hell right before my eyes. Usually, they have begun the descent before they get to my office, so they arrive with their ironclad story and an arsenal of ammunition. When I reach over the table with my pin to pop their balloon of illusion, their trip to hell is complete. How does the practitioner assist in the client's ascension back up the ladder to a truth-based reality? The answer is simple: no judgment, no disgust, only acceptance of the humanness of emotion. Each soul exhibits the torments of their hell differently. Some clients trigger the other party; some trigger us. The key to truth is in the eyes of the opposition. To make their way out, each must know that they possess the key to the other's ascension from hell: a shift in perception that compels them to disassemble their story and climb up to see the new horizon illuminated by the other party's perspective. Much easier said than done! Success ultimately depends on the mediator's helping each client see that they have choices, and those choices produce different probable outcomes. The mediator presents a reality check: "What will happen if you don't?" "What will happen if you do?" I believe success also depends on the presence of the mediator: the finesse to precipitate the client's descent into hell, the calm to stand face-to-face with the truth as hell, and the discernment to guide them toward clarity and understanding. Just think: if we could accomplish this, one conflict at a time, we could change the planet.

But then it came to me as an insight that I should teach this truth, for it is also happiness. There are people whose sight is only a little clouded, and they are suffering through not hearing the reality. They would become the knowers of the truth. It was in this way I went forth to teach.

Majjhima Nikaya, *The Pocket Buddha Reader*

Meditation today should begin with the word "truth." Discover what your truth is today. Breathe into the comfort of clarity.

Write in your journal what you discovered about your truth in your meditation. In what areas of your life are you living your truth? In what areas of your life are you not?

*The spiritual journey is one of continually falling on your face, getting up,
brushing yourself off, looking sheepishly at God, and taking another step.*

Sri Aurobindo

We come to this earth as a student, innocent and joyous, openly loving, and inevitably become saddled with the human condition as we grow into adulthood. I recently heard the Dalai Lama speak about the choice for happiness. He spoke of the seekers who endeavor to find their inner peace and happiness in another person or in a thing. He concluded that happiness is only found in *this* moment and that we must hold the intention to see it. He believes that daily devotion to prayer and meditation is essential to settle the racing mind, clear the noise of life, and draw strength from the peaceful mind. The key to the door of our inner spirit is stillness. It is with this commitment that we can rediscover the joy and innocence of our youth. If you have ever had the opportunity to witness the Dalai Lama, you know that he exudes joy and openness. Perhaps this state of being is a choice and should be for all of us? But as Sri Aurobindo, India's greatest modern philosopher-sage, wrote, the spiritual quest is not pain-free. We don't always get the answers, or at least not the ones we want. I know firsthand that this journey is laborious and dark at times, while at other times, it is light-filled and clear. There is no destination. Just when I think I might actually become peaceful, I fall into doubt and darkness. In the falling, however, I notice that the trips get shorter, and I am learning to be grateful for the days when I am off-center, knowing that they, too, are part of my spiritual journey. In my ongoing commitment to myself, I now find the fortitude to press forward. Think about your own journey. Do you see that you have been traveling a path you were not previously aware you were on? Today, make or renew that commitment to yourself to still your mind, rediscover your childlike wonder, and courageously walk your spiritual path.

Meditate today on the word "commitment." In the quiet, misty morning of your psyche, can you see the strength of endurance? Breathe into the deep ocean of commitment; let your racing mind settle into the willingness to hear.

In your journal, list the commitments you have and the ones you need to make. What actions do you take, and need to take, to honor those commitments?

We cannot live only for ourselves. A thousand fibers connect us with our fellow men.

Herman Melville

In his book, *The Hidden Connections,* Fritjof Capra, a molecular biologist, built a beautiful bridge between biology and consciousness. He posited the phenomena of life must be understood as part of a larger system. Furthermore, he noted that each cell has a genetic blueprint with emergent properties of the entire genetic system. Complex structures are nonlinear and dynamic, always changing in a waltz of morphology. The energy present in all biological processes is conserved. The mind is not a thing, but rather a process, resulting from an organ; the brain, the structure in which it operates. Consciousness emerges when the mind, in the process of thinking, reaches a certain level of complexity, producing an ever changing stream of thought. Medical science now has the capability to trace this process of cognition by mapping the complex neural firing of synapses on a magnetic resonance image (MRI). Capra noted that consciousness has two processes. The first process of consciousness is a primary function of perception, sensory, and emotional experience. The second process is a higher order that involves self-awareness and reflective thinking based on values, beliefs, goals, and strategies to produce different states of consciousness.

Capra and many others have hypothesized that spirituality is the element of consciousness that cannot be explained according to neural mechanics and emerges from a different center of the brain. I believe the thousand connecting fibers of humanity can be accessed through that emergent field of spirituality. I have felt that connection while meditating and during mediating. Standing in the center with the belief that we are all connected and with a willingness to meld with their heartache and pain, I move toward the center of collective awareness. In that center of collective awareness, solutions are found. This is an area of evolution of the brain that we are only now beginning to understand. Through presence, techniques of meta-communication, and an understanding of chaos and control, practitioners can move into the conflict and lead the parties out of the problem story. If peacemakers can be aware of this power of the mind and hone their intuitive skills, their effectiveness in the ring of conflict is taken to a new level. Have you ever felt the interconnection with others as well as the connection to Source in your work?

Meditation today should begin with the word "interconnections." Feel connected to your body as you follow your breath in and out of your lungs...feel connected to your mind as the thoughts dance across your field of awareness and feel your inter-connectedness with others.

Think of one person with which you feel especially connected. Do you notice times when you feel as though you could read their thoughts or understand them without asking questions? Write about this in your journal.

Unconditional Acceptance

Everything in life that we really accept undergoes a change.

Katherine Mansfield

The quote above embodies the reality of life. Change is the only thing that doesn't change! For one to accept the inevitable is to embrace the fullness of life. *The Work* of Bryon Katie is a form of Socratic dialogue, a process of self-inquiry that leads the questioner toward acceptance of the reality of "what is." After acceptance of "what is," happiness and contentment can be restored as the process of change begins. This acceptance leads to the exercising of choice: "Do I like 'what is' or do I need to make a change in my life?" The shift of one's course is empowering. I am not suggesting that this process diverts us from experiencing conflict. Conflict is a natural form of interrelatedness, a positive state that brings forth dialogue and deeper connection. But how we participate in conflict is what determines whether we live a life of joy and peace or one of lack and limitation. The state of conflict on this planet stems from a general disability of perception: expectations and entitlements in a rights- and rules-based world, and perceived violations or disrespect that lead us to brood in isolation or, on a larger scale, go to war. The crack in our lens of perception keeps us from seeing that we have already been empowered with choice: the choice to accept "what is" or to make a change. In fact, accepting "what is" is the first step in empowering oneself to make a change. "What you resist persists," or as Katie says, "You lose when you argue with your reality, but only every time." Our mind has a way of locking us into reactive causality if we deny reality. Unconditional acceptance—embracing "what is"—releases us from that cycle and allows us to choose again, with love. What aspects of your life, or life in general, do you need to accept unconditionally?

Meditate today on the term "unconditional acceptance." As the silence calms the racing mind, fall into the embrace of the unknown. Breathe deeply as the agreement is made to accept reality and move forward.

Write about one area of your life that seems repetitive. What can you embrace that will allow you to make a different choice and stop the cycle?

To see a World in a grain of sand,
And a Heaven in a wild flower,
Hold Infinity in the palm of your hand,
And Eternity in an hour.

William Blake, "Auguries of Innocence"

Perhaps William Blake discovered in his lifetime that to ponder upon nature is a connection to God. In that vertical moment, it is possible to find joy. In my busy life, pondering nature has often proved to be the rare opportunity I have for connection, to retrieve the sacred from my world. When I surrender to the moment and let my mind wander about the white, sugary sand at the water's edge or through a magnificent field of luxurious Columbine flowers, I notice that time stands still for me. It only takes a moment to honor the thunderous storm bringing sustenance to the plains. The sweet smell of its power fills my nose with peace and hope for the next moment.

Begin today's meditation with thoughts of your universe. Breathe in the fresh breeze of the day; breathe out the tension of night's shallow breath. Breathe in the clean fragrance of morning dew, and ponder the serenity of peace.

When have you found eternity standing still? List a treasure hunt of heavenly views that your eyes can behold today. Be sure to look for them as the day unfolds before you.

Place yourself in the full centre of that flood, then you are without
effort impelled to truth, to right and a perfect contentment.

Ralph Waldo Emerson, "Spiritual Laws"

Chaos is a standard backdrop held against the process of constant change. Change is the standard of life, all things morphing into another form with each breath. Chaos is also the standard in the engagement of conflict. People locked in dispute are enacting a scene from *Postcards from the Edge*, and "the edge" is where the solutions will be found. Successful practitioners feel at home working in chaos, recognizing that the potential for movement immediately follows the breakthrough. In our own life, chaos might resemble a spiked iron ball slamming through our serenity. Perceiving chaos to be a gift of enlightenment rather than a hazard to be avoided increases the potential for remaining calm during the storm. Today, observe those moments of chaos as they enter your life. Find comfort in the promise of chaos.

What a gift of grace to be able to take the chaos from within
and from it create some semblance of order.

Katherine Patterson

Begin meditation today with the thought of "chaos." Breathe in the excitement of promise, and breathe out the adrenaline coursing through your body. Breathe in the information dancing through the "postcards" of chaos; breathe out the fear that repels your desire to stay focused.

Where do you see the chaos in your life today? List the ways you can refocus your energy on "what is."

All things are too small to hold me, I am so vast. In the infinite I reach for
the Uncreated. I have touched it, it undoes me wider than wide. Everything
else is too narrow. You know this well, you who are also there.

Hadewijch, 13th-century mystic poet

The realization that we are somehow all connected can impel us to seek that place of one-ness, whether you attribute our oneness to a culturally specific omnipotent higher power or not. When that communion is experienced, Nirvana, Shangri-la, "at-one-ment" is attained. I have experienced that vacuum of infinite calm when truly connected to another soul. These times of connection do not have to be spectacular occurrences; often, they are ordinary joinings of purpose that can be quite brief. On a recent trip to Boston, a bright-eyed college student from China, only hours in the country for the first time, waited beside me on the subway platform for the "T" to collect us from the airport terminal. In our first glance, the connection was made. I was met by her wide smile and inquiring openness as she asked me for directions to Harvard. Proud of her hard-learned English, she desired to meet her first American, and I was graced to be the one. She said excitedly, "I am traveling to Harvard to meet with other students from all over the world to study Public Health in a one-week intensive course. I have not yet met my first friend, but perhaps it will be you?" The melody of her voice sang to my heart. I adored her and her quest for connection. I thought of my own child in Argentina for the first time and how open-armed Argentineans must have made him feel at home. As I answered her, I felt that tingle of spirit, as though the angel's wings had brushed my arms, leaving the holy moment. "Well, of course you have!" I exclaimed, and we quickly studied the subway map together. I, too, was traveling to Harvard for a weeklong intensive insight course at the Law School. We sat engrossed in conversation for the twenty minutes it took to get to my stop. I bid her farewell and good luck, and told her she was about to meet many new friends. As I stood to collect my bags, she hugged me and thanked me for the help. I smiled all the way to the hotel. I had agreed to "reach for the uncreated" and found a kindred there. When have you experienced that vacuum of infinite possibility in relationship to another?

Begin meditation today with the word "vacuum." In the tranquility of the moment, breathe deeply and reach for the infinite vacuum. Who else do you see in that space?

In your journal, recall some of your first-time encounters that felt like a holy connection. How were you "being" before and during those moments? Be open to entering the vacuum sometime during the day, and pay attention to your way of being as well as that of the other person.

Try to be reasonable in the way you grow, and don't ever think it is too late. It is never too late. Even if you are going to die tomorrow, keep yourself straight and clear and be a happy human being today. If you keep your situation happy day by day, you will eventually reach the greatest happiness of enlightenment.

Lama Thubten Yeshe, *The Bliss of Inner Fire*

To me, enlightenment means freedom from individual suffering. I live my life each day with as much joy as possible and choose to redirect my thoughts whenever I feel a downturn in my level of happiness. I don't wish to attain any specific level of awareness or pass a certain bar of enlightenment for many reasons: I have learned that being good to myself involves accepting that I am a human, and humans have frailties. I cannot embrace my humanity if I spend my time in pursuit of perfection. I have also learned that there is room for all philosophies on this planet. We are different, with diverse cultures, races, genders, ages, and appearances, and that is a beautiful thing. We have as many ways of expressing our unique collections of qualities as we have individuals. I have adopted the notion that we are creations of a higher power; I trust that my higher power has the wisdom to know and love the differences, so I can love myself, too. This has been my journey. Although religion is a wonderful way to collectively share values and beliefs, in my view, it has inadvertently separated us from God. I have given myself permission to find me in God, rather than "God in me." Because perfection—godhood, enlightenment—cannot be attained in this existence, I have learned to be my own sage. I stay in the present moment and enjoy all of life's mystery. I have learned to not judge poor behavior, control, or manipulation in my work, but rather to see that people are simply treading the waters of pain and fear and predictably lack the skills to deal with their emotional triggers. By staying in the present moment, I can always begin again. Each sunrise allows new tolerance for my own humanity, which, in turn, allows me to perceive others with compassion. In his book *Beyond Neutrality: Confronting the Crisis in Conflict Resolution*, Bernie Mayer challenges us to look for a broader application of our talents and skills. I have chosen to share my path with others, not because I am trying to convince others to travel my path, but because I want others to find their own. We all have the ability to become our own sage. We already have all our own answers, and with each new day, our inner peace will bring peace to the planet. The earth is depending on us, the peacemakers, to do just that. "Blessed are the peacemakers for they shall be called children of God." This quotation from Matthew 5:9 says to me, that if we do the bidding of our higher power by having a personal relationship with it, there will still be a planet for the children to inherit. Take good care of yourself and our planet: become your own sage.

Meditation today should begin with the phrase "become your own sage." Relax in the arms of the angels to listen. Communicate to your heart the contented nature of a soul at home. You are a perfect expression of that which you are intended to be.

In your journal, honor yourself for the willingness, the integrity, and the endurance to commit to your daily practice for one whole year. Read the first week's and the last week's journal entries, and reflect on your journey. Embrace exactly where you are as perfect. Thank yourself for the valuable work you do for those in pain.

I keep [my ideals], because in spite of everything, I still believe that people are really good at heart. I simply can't build up my hopes on a foundation consisting of confusion, misery, and death. I see the world gradually being turned into a wilderness, I hear the ever-approaching thunder, which will destroy us, too, I can feel the suffering of millions, and yet, if I look up into the heavens, I think that it will all come right, that this cruelty will end, and that peace and tranquility will return again. In the meantime, I must uphold my ideals, for perhaps the time will come when I shall be able to carry them out.

Anne Frank, *Anne Frank: The Diary of a Young Girl*

A basic belief in humanity underlay Anne Frank's hopes and dreams as she endured the Holocaust in Germany. It was so hard for me, growing up in the 1950s, to imagine her experience as I studied that horrible time in history. America had been fortunate to have the boundaries of ocean to protect it from those who would harm its citizens—until September 11, 2001. That morning, I watched in horror with the rest of the world as the images played in macabre repetition. I grieved the end of our age of innocence, numb from the knowledge that some have such hatred for America and the policies of our government that they would target ordinary souls, like you and me, simply going to work. Anne Frank, and those in similar circumstances, must have faced the same choice between fear and the hope in a basic belief in humanity. Our principles guide us; our standards rule; our morals and ethics must lead us to search out this humanness in each other. Whether we follow the teachings of Mohammed, Jesus, or Buddha, people love their children, care for their parents, and want a life well lived. We are so much more alike than we are different, and if we want peace and tranquility to rule the earth, we must hold fast to our ideals and await the time when we can realize that dream. What do you dream for today? Where can you find the humanity in humankind?

Meditate today on the word "ideals." Breathe a cleansing breath and search your heart for what matters to you.

In your journal, record the ideals that came up during your meditation. How does your life demonstrate your ideals?

*I shall ask into my shell only those friends with whom I can be completely honest. I
find I am shedding hypocrisy in human relationships. What a rest that will be! The most
exhausting thing in life, I have discovered, is being insincere. That is why so much of
social life is exhausting; one is wearing a mask. I [choose] to shed my mask.*

Anne Morrow Lindbergh, *Gift from the Sea*

When I hit fifty, my tolerance for insincerity vanished. In my work, my intuition sounds
the warning bell when requests are made of me that imply a compromise of my impartiality. I
realize quickly that I am being played, and I call it what it is. I have learned to do this with non-
judgment and turn a deaf ear toward the manipulator—and more recently, I have been able to
replace the deaf ear with an open heart. I send love toward the one who attempts manipulation
and an understanding of the emotion that caused their action. I fare poorly, however, when
faced with hypocrisy in my personal relationships. I have been known to toss aside tact and
decorum and doggedly pursue with blunt exclamation, bludgeoning the other person and the
relationship and burning the bridge as I retreat. I am not saying that anyone should tolerate
insincerity and the disingenuous actions of hypocrites, but a more constructive choice is to
speak my truth matter-of-factly and then retreat to my shell of soulful friends whom I respect
and who genuinely care about me. Although I gave up people-pleasing on my fiftieth birthday
and exchanged it for authenticity, I still want to be responsible for how my communications and
actions land for the other person. My work this year has been to contain my red-headed wild-
ness, deliver my communications with the right intention, and retreat with an open heart, not
with fists clenched defensively when I sense a boundary breach. I prefer an emptiness of social
circle over a circle filled with platitudes and banal conversation. My shell is rich with lustrous
pearls of friends who are genuine. Explore your shell today. If you find a hypocrite, usher them
out the door with love. Release them to their path, and wish them all the best as their backside
clears the threshold.

Meditate today on the word "emptiness." Breathe into the floor and feel your body
examine the edges of your physical structure. Release warmth and love for other souls on
their path.

Write down the images that you examined in your meditation. What does your shell look
like? Whom do you need to usher out, who can stay, and whom might you invite in?

The artful denial of a problem will not produce conviction; on the contrary, a wider and higher consciousness is required to give us the certainty and clarity we need.

Carl Jung, "Stages of Life," *The Portable Jung*

Denial is a state of mind. It seems to be the first choice for many, a comfortable room of avoidance, a bypass of the heart. As Kenneth Cloke suggests in his new book, *The Crossroads of Conflict: A Journey into the Heart of Conflict,* all conflict has, at its base level, a deep caring. There wouldn't be conflict if we were indifferent. To desensitize ourselves to the pain of conflict, we deny our feelings of caring. Our "truth" becomes a lie. I learned this acronym in a workshop: denial is Don't Even Know I Am Lying. Of course, we are lying to ourselves—and then, in turn, to others. It is easier, easier than caring deeply for our "deeper truth," our soul. As Freud noted, denial defends our ego from our public face; it's a defense mechanism, a protection of identity. No one escapes the process of denying pain again and again. But if we do not actively seek conviction about our true nature or clarity of purpose, denial becomes the quilt of lies we bed down with every night. One cannot rise above the "cover-up" without the painful process of peeling the onion. The tears of release sting our eyes as the layers of self-deception fall away, and the print of the soul is revealed. The mask of denial can be hung on the wall to remind us that we chose our true purpose over our ego. As Anne Morrow Lindbergh says, "I choose to shed my mask." Seek clarity and certainty of your higher consciousness today.

Meditate today on the word "denial." What do you see along the edges of your mind that needs to come forward to look into the light of your soul, rather than hide in the darkness of ego protection?

Journal about the areas of your life that you need to examine and become clear about. Excavate them; pick through the issues you hold behind the mask of denial. List one thing you can be honest with yourself about today.

We have the power to make this the best generation of mankind
in the history of the world—or to make it the last.

John F. Kennedy

We have been hearing the call to action for decades. The pendulum swings with a regular beat; the metronome of time ticks off the seconds that remain. What shall we do? While we are immersed in the pursuit of happiness, in chasing the elusive butterfly of individual gain, what is happening to our world? The state of conflict and unrest is increasingly palpable. We have compromised our environment. Those who have reached the golden years are fearful that they have not amassed enough to make our life count. But when King Midas in his castle counts up his money, what rings up isn't true richness but a valueless bag of gold. In his golden years, Warren Buffet has decided to give his fortune away; $40 billion can affect a lot of change. Donating most of his fortune to the Gates Foundation to increase a global trust for good, he wanted to leave the legacy of his hard-earned life for the general improvement of the planet. Certainly, Tom Brokaw would qualify him as a member of "the greatest generation." As practitioners on the front lines of conflict, armed with the skills and an understanding of peaceful engagement, we stand ready to answer the call to action. What shall we each do? By simply putting one foot in front of the other, we can enter that ring of life with a quiver full of arrows ready to pierce the hard of heart and bring them, one by one, into a deeper understanding of peace. As John Paul Lederach writes in *The Moral Imagination*, it only takes one person deeply connected in a village to affect the safety and well-being of an entire region, one village at a time.

Begin meditation today with the phrase "the best generation." Settle into your body and find comfort and balance. Breathe deeply into the fold of humanity and join the ranks of the leaders of peace.

In your journal, write one thing you can do this week to make a difference in your village.

The universe is but one vast symbol of God.

Albert Einstein

My belief in a higher power originated with my contemplation of order in the universe. How could there be such perfect order in everything—the inter-connectedness of human bodily processes, the combinations of energy we discover in physics and chemistry, the processes of plants, the orbits of the heavenly bodies—if not for divine creative forces? My brother Michael emailed me a photograph taken from the Hubble Space Telescope of the Helix Nebula, and the subject heading was "The Eye of God." I felt a warmth come over me, a sense of truth, a feeling of being connected, the realization that we are not alone. Abandonment is a false state of mind created by the ego, that causes many of us to slip into depression. The order of the universe is a comforting truth that gives a sense of being "at one with," even when it's too immense to perceive through our senses. We can distinguish the webs of connection present everywhere—a circulation system of the beating heart of awareness. Choose awareness today.

Meditation today should begin with the phrase "order is a symbol of God." Choose stillness of the mind; float on the deep breaths of thought; feel the connection ever-present in your heart.

Write down the web of thoughts that connected through an order that arose in your meditation.

Out beyond ideas of wrongdoing and rightdoing,
there is a field. I'll meet you there.

When the soul lies down in that grass,
the world is too full to talk about.

Rumi

I returned from a seminar filled with peace, clarity, and delicious ideas, deeply inspired by the extraordinary presence of the group. Excellence in practice is what the participants were in search of: mastery for mediators. We all left that week with renewed passion, possibility, and opportunity, "too full to talk about" it, but post-seminar emails flew around the group. Armed with innovative collaborative knowledge and the permission to combine energy in alchemy with those drawn to our table of transformation, we were eager to rise above the "ideas of wrongdoing and rightdoing," and ascend to the field of our inter-connectivity. I am thrilled to join my colleagues in the shifting of the paradigm in peacemaking and conflict resolution. Take a moment this morning to review the nature of your work. Are you prepared to take the next step in building a rich practice? That step begins with the care of your soul. As you search for excellence, go where the river of innovation cuts deep into the soil to produce a lush field of sweet meadow grass. Go where "the world is too full to talk about": the field of peace.

Meditation should begin today with the word "excellence." Slip into the common field of light and energy warming your veins. Sit with the word and become peaceful.

Write down the images that came to you in your meditation. In what areas of your life do you demonstrate excellence?

*It's a funny thing about life; if you refuse to accept
anything but the best, you very often get it.*

Somerset Maugham

Perfection and perception of experience intersect in a strange and wonderful way. Human beings are rarely "being"; a truer phrase would be "human doing" or "human having." Doing has created a "perfection syndrome" of emulating those around us for the clues on how to perfect our process of living, which sets in motion a perpetual state of striving that leaves us empty and feeling that we are not good enough. As Eckhart Tolle states, in *The Power of Now,* "We never quite get there, always rushing toward perfection wherever we go." The striving prohibits thriving. Similarly, having created a culture preoccupied with the accumulation of goods, property, and treasures; materialism has become the state of our being. In the above quotation, I think Somerset Maugham implies a nuanced way of existence. Accepting nothing but the best is not about the striving, the doing, or the having; rather, if you embrace "what is"—what currently is "being" in your life—the funny thing about life is that your acceptance of "what is" creates the openings to attract and receive what you want. Accepting your current state of being, moment to moment, clears the path to the things you want to do and have. As Wayne Dyer says, "Just be." You are perfect in your current experience, and your current experience is perfection.

Meditate today on the word "perfection." Ponder this word of striving and attainment. Breathe deeply into your soul, and embrace "what is."

List the areas of your life in which you seek perfection. How can you change your perception of your current experience?

The great gift of human beings is that we have the power of empathy.

Meryl Streep

Daniel Bowling held a teleconference for the members of the Spirituality section of the ACR in the summer of 2006, in which he suggested the listener embody peace for the clients. "We can't expect to bring peace without being the peace." I felt a surge of negative contradiction come forth. My initial thought was, "Well, that is easy for him to say!" To me, Daniel appears close to perfect. His persona is always peaceful, carefully measured, and still and his thoughts are well-reasoned. "But what about the rest of us wrestling in the trenches with the judgments of our human thought processes. The rest of us can't be that perfect!"

Thankfully, more rational thought followed my exclamations, "Daniel is further on his path that you are, Nan. It is no big deal. You can be human, judge, and choose again." I'm still at the place in life where I need a back door to escape my critical mind! I do think it is important to have empathy for ourselves in the humanness of our judging mind. I do not think one can sit at the table with conflicted clients who are laden with triggers, acting out their dance of pain without judging them. Minds judge. Let it go and choose again. With this line of reasoning, I can let myself off the hook of seeking perfection and arrive at the same intersection as Daniel does in his peaceful way. Through choosing again, I can get to that place of empathy for the tortured soul that sits before me. Even as I choose not to judge them, I understand it is impossible to not stand in the emotion that conflict triggers. You cannot be in conflict without being in pain. When my initial judgment passes, then I can embrace their humanness by embracing my own. After all, Webster defines empathy as "the imaginative projection of one's own consciousness into another being." We cannot arrive at the place of empathy without dancing our own waltz first.

Meditation today should begin with the word "empathy." Go to the stillness and embrace it. Allow your soul to bubble forth from the collective connective energy. Through the acceptance of your own soul, feel the connection with those who appear before you. Think about your process of empathy today. How do you arrive at acceptance of the client where there are?

What is one thing that you can do to enhance your performance at work today? Identify one thing you can focus on to gain more empathy for your own process.

Discovery

If we were to discover a complete theory of cosmology,
we might come to know the mind of God.

Stephen Hawking

Discovery is such an exciting occurrence in the mystery of life. The act of personally uncovering brand new knowledge must be such a delicious feeling. The intersection of science and spirit, of energy and essence provide a plethora of discoveries for those on the spiritual journey. Stephen Hawking's positive statement about cosmology invites the reader to search: for more information; for more wisdom; for more clarity about our particular responsibility; to discover our purpose in the grander scheme of things. It prompts one to ask, "Can we truly know? Will the mysteries of life be revealed through science, through spirit, through energy?" The mind of God melding with the mind of man elicits a vision of mysterious alchemy. To truly welcome discovery, you must embrace mystery. My path of inquiry leads me to accept mystery and open to new discoveries by simply being present and releasing any expectation that I should have the answers.

Meditation today should begin with your current mystery. Take smooth calming breaths and allow yourself to drop into knowing...what do you seek? What can you see? What do you discover?

Write down the recent discoveries about your personal path that you were able to see in your meditation.

Ethical man — a Christian holding four aces.

Mark Twain

In writings from Plato to Twain, one sees that ethics has been a topic of interest and discussion through the millennia. What is it about human nature that would cause one not to be ethical? I think most would agree that moral values and principles are talked about frequently, yet evidence of that moral code seems in rare supply.

Take a closer look at how you handle ethics in your decisions with your fellow humans. Honor those ethical decisions that you have chosen to become a part of your character. Be introspective about the ways you can become more ethical. What about in our own field? At the table of resolution, part of our job is to move parties through the process of ethical decision-making. How often do you get the feeling that, in their need to protect their interests, they would lie in a heartbeat? How do you coach parties in ethical behavior and ethical decision making in the field of peacemaking and conflict engagement?

....

Meditation today should focus on the word "ethics." Agree to fall into stillness this morning and honor your ethical character.

Write in your journal one way that you can improve your ethics today.

> *I do my best to transform rage into creative expression and effective work.*
> *But it would take more than a lifetime to finish this bit of alchemy in*
> *which I mix my genuine innocence with my undeniable darkness.*
>
> Thomas Moore, *Dark Nights of the Soul*

Jung wrote volumes on the "shadow self," the reverse side of the public self. In society, we are raised with the values of kindness, caring what others think of us, and doing for the less fortunate in a selfless way. What about our negative thoughts? Byron Katie says that we internalize them, mistakenly assigning them "to who we are." We are not our thoughts, but denying that we have those thoughts leads to insanity, neuroses, and depression. Thomas Moore notes in the above quote that we need to embrace our darker side, our true emotions of rage, discontent, and anger. He theorizes that the planet is violent because we develop only the bright side of our personality and avoid the dark side. The violence is the acting out of rage on the planet. He believes that not embracing and exploring our darker humanness causes addictions, emptiness of soul that leads to depression. Often our rage is transferred to the relationships we engage in and is actually projected onto others to avoid owning the rage. When we try to contain rage in the resolution of conflict, whatever the context of the relationship, we collude with societal norms in continuing rage on the planet. Although we think we are powerless in the area of peace on the planet, we are powerful beyond evaluation. Whatever we do to effectively deal with rage, validation of the soul is immediately achieved, and the world is changed one conflict at a time. How do you deal with internal rage: do you avoid or validate your own soul?

Meditate today on the word "rage." Breathe in the permission to be human; breathe out the rage in your heart. Breathe in the humanness of your being; breathe out the denial of anger. Sit with the validation of who you really are: a human expression of soul, not perfect but real.

Write a few lines in your journal about rage. Can you work with rage at work, or do you move for containment? How can you honor the emotion of rage in every area of your life?

> *Consciously, deliberately, then, I abandoned my academic career. For I felt that*
> *something great was happening to me and I put my trust in the thing which I*
> *felt to be more important,* sub specie aeternitatis. *I knew that it would fill my*
> *life, and for the sake of that goal I was ready to take any kind of risk.*
>
> Carl Jung, *Memories, Dreams, Reflections*

Frances Moore Lappé and Jeffrey Perkins, in their book, *You Have the Power: Choosing Courage in a Culture of Fear,* wrote about how fear drives this country. Advertising executives cultivate it, politicians control voters through it, news media instills it and preys on fear for ratings, and parents use it to protect us when we are developing and often in unhealthy ways. Fear causes us to stay in dead-end jobs, to stay in dead relationships, and to make daily decisions for "what is safe" in response to fear. It takes real courage to move outside of the fear and be willing to think outside the box. Lappé and Perkins suggested that we use the vast energy we generate for fear to move forward and transform negativity into positivity. Carl Jung reached a point in his successful career where he dared to place advancement ahead of fear of what his academic community might think of him and to risk his reputation and move into controversial philosophies. When doing spiritual workshops, often my co-facilitator and I would have participants do a fear exercise that underscored that the major choice in response to fear was either "Forget Everything And Run" or "False Evidence Appearing Real." The collective discovery was that we would rather put on our track shoes than face down the fear. Lappé and Perkins believe we need a societal dialogue about fear. I agree: bringing sensitive or buried topics to the surface shines a light on fearful thoughts and vaporizes them. We have no need to be a minimalist society, with only so much of the pie to divide. We need the courage to generate abundance. Our culture has not provided us with optimistic perceptions about abundance. America is very much like a huge dysfunctional family, a culture ensnared, in an escalating spiral of dependency on fear, causing us to dive into addiction (e.g., work, food, substances, religion, or relationships), and act out our denial, which in turn launches us into shame, then guilt, then isolation, all due to what? What do we fear? The impetus for writing their book came after Lappé and Perkins asked a new immigrant what he thought of America. They were astounded to hear, "You Americans are all afraid of each other." Courage is necessary for all areas of life. It takes courage to be a parent, to be a leader, to be a maverick, to trust a power greater than you. Where can you find courage?

Meditate today beginning with the word "courage." Become willing to surrender to your inner voice for risk. Breathe in the limitless energy you know you possess; breathe out the fear of the mysterious unfamiliar.

List your courageous acts this year. Become familiar with the courage you already have. How can you act on your courage today?

A word fitly spoken is like apples of gold in a setting of silver.

Proverbs 25:11

A wisely chosen word, at the precise moment of opportunity, is the premium artistry of a conflict practitioner. Clarity is the gift the practitioner can bring to the circle of conflict. Lucidity, the goal in conflicted communication, is to articulate in eloquent terms the root cause of discomfort in a way that brings forth the solutions. Understanding the intention of an opponent often reveals a road out of the forest of fear. In my practice with high conflict clients, I am always searching for the treasure trove of reality hidden under the surface dialogue. A question I frequently ask is, "What is under the fear? ...the anger? ... the rage? ... the disconnection? Asking the client to be very concrete with the other is a powerful way to bring clarity to a conflict. "What is she doing when she is trying to control you?" or "What does he look like to you when he is a jerk?" As the light returns to the eyes of the client, and the awareness of clarity rises, the lines of pain in a tortured face smooth with understanding. Those are the moments when you know the word fitly spoken has graced the table of resolution like a setting of silver.

Meditation today should begin with the word "clarity." Agree to dwell in the stillness with silent speculation and welcome the personal clarity that you need to be effective in your day.

Write down the images that came to you in your meditation. What do you need to become clear about your life, your work, your purpose?

Be generous in prosperity, and thankful in adversity. Be fair in thy judgment, and guarded in thy speech. Be a lamp unto those who walk in darkness and a home to the stranger. Be eyes to the blind, and a guiding light unto the feet of the erring. Be a breath of life to the body of humankind, a dew to the soil of the human heart, and a fruit upon the tree of humility.

Bahá'u'lláh, The Bahai' Faith

Those drawn to the engagement of conflict are innately vessels of kindness. As a "breath of life to the body of humankind," practitioners stand with the awareness that one can be safely lead from a conclave of conflict to the soul of solutions. With a passion for the work, kindness takes the form of coaching; teaching from experience and moving people forward to embrace a future of hope. Kindness does not necessarily mean that a person is meek or passive. Kindness does not have to mean that one only says the correct thing, has the perfect response, or is always polite in request. Sometimes kindness means that you stand with the other in opposition and agree to embrace obvious differences occurring in human interaction.

What kindness does mean is that you perform without judgment. Kindness means you agree to bring light into a darkened room filled with negative emotion. I suspect I had the idea that striving for perfect behavior was desirable due to my upbringing in the South; manners were very important. Saying something that might hurt someone's feeling was strictly taboo. The problem is I was always striving; it was never possible for me to quite get there. I suppose the problem I had with saying the perfect thing at the perfect time was that it seemed disingenuous to me. Trusting the kindness of others was a problem for me, the ones who were flawless in their behavior; are they too kind? Those around me appeared to me to be in "la-la land," sailing down the river of denial, safe from challenging the current reality of life. For this reason, it is difficult for me to accept praise or compliments without logically running them through my linear mind or intuitive impulses. I am noticing that when I recognize kindred spirits, I trust them immediately. It has to do with my perception of their kindness. I also recognize that there are many people who do genuinely love first and ask questions later. Think of the acts of kindness that you have extended to others, just because they cross your path.

Meditation should begin today with the word "kindness." Be a "breath of life to the body of humankind, a dew to the soil of the human heart, and a fruit upon the tree of humility." How does that feel to you?

Write in your journal today your thoughts about kindness, both personal and professional.

Growth

Relationships are the Holy Spirit's laboratories in which He brings together people who have the maximal opportunity for mutual growth.

Marianne Williamson

Accepting my adversaries as angels of information who help me to discern my truth and purpose is a difficult concept for me to consider. But, what if it is true? How do I accept the person who thwarts my efforts is bringing some nugget of clarity to my path? Or, the one that frustrates me the most is my greatest teacher? How much effort goes into the struggle of who was right and who was wrong? We feed the fire of the victimhood through the labor of self-defense. But where is the growth occurring when we are in denial? Taking the position that maximum opportunity can be realized through mutuality, or simply asking the question, "what is the lesson I need to learn here?", can transform an adversarial situation to one of possibilities.

Meditation today should begin with the word "growth." Sit with the thoughts of constraint for a moment and then let that hardness drain into the well of acceptance. Allow the intention of growth to run over the borders of your mind, to be open and accepting.

Decide to open up today. Write a list of angels of adversity in your life and think about the gifts they may have brought you today.

If you yourself are at peace, then there is at least some peace in the world.

Thomas Merton

Have you ever been in a room where an open, genuinely loving soul changed the energy? Before he retired as a partner at our firm, we had the pleasure of that experience every time Charlie Turnbo walked into the office. He has a welcoming air about him; he never judges anyone. He has the gift of conversation that makes you wonder if he shouldn't be running for office. He surely would have stumped the panel on *What's My Line* as the most unlikely person to have worked for much of his life as a warden in the federal prison system.

We began a training program at our firm for uncoupling parents, to teach them more effective conflict engagement. One of the lessons of acceptance he taught, with great compassion, was that all parents have the right to be in the lives of their children- even mothers serving prison time for crimes. "We only have one mother and we need to be able to love her, no matter what the circumstances." I can just see Charlie on visiting day, greeting all these precious children with love and sunshine as they walked through the doors of the prison. He was at peace, and on that day, he brought peace to broken families by radiating his love and acceptance to everyone who was near him. We only have power over our moments, one at a time. Through these moments when we are at peace, we can bring peace to the world.

Meditation today should begin with the word "peace." This morning, let peace drift across your mind and feel the calmness inside. Touch the warmth of peace with your breath…float into the reservoir of inner peace.

Write down one way that you can choose peace today. How can you affect the energy in one encounter today? How can you embrace the humanity in all souls?

*Treat the Earth well: It was not given to you by your
parents; it was loaned to you by your children.*

Kenyan proverb

Each one of us has only a few decades on this earth. If we consider posterity and ponder for a moment the world our great-grandchildren will have, the loan may seem more valuable. There are so many beautiful reserves, parks, and forests that we can enjoy, where we can find peace and tranquility. Lately, taking care of Earth has been reduced to a debate over whether we are actually ruining our world with pollution. This argument confuses the issue. If you build a home and never paint it, or clean it, or perform regular maintenance on the structure, how will it look in 30 years? Look around you this day and take in the beauty of this earth. Consider the loan.

Meditation today should begin with the word "earth." What does that word represent for you? Sit silently for a few moments and give your thoughts a place to be home.

Write down one thing that you can do today to conserve the beauty of the earth and repay the loan of tomorrow's children.

*I remind myself every morning: Nothing I say this day will teach me
anything. So, if I'm going to learn, I must do it by listening.*

Larry King

Being the eternal student is an enormously rewarding experience. One is never bored. There is always new information emerging. Larry King has made a career out of 'listening to learn' by asking the right question, at the right time, to extract the right information to satisfy his inquiring mind. Mining the client's stories for information is part of the set of skills of every practitioner; some are more proficient than others are. To approach inquiry with the intent to learn brings an authenticity to questions that illicit trust. To be truly interested in a story that you have heard a thousand times can be effectively accomplished only if you embrace the client with the intent to understand. We are the vessels of hope for our clients. To listen to their story as though it is the first time you have ever heard it, is to embrace the storyteller with unconditional acceptance. I think the only way we can be present in those situations is to purposely empty our minds of the background noise and intend to listen, intend to learn. It is in the intention that connection is made.

Meditation today should begin with the phrase "listen to learn." As you sit quietly, empty your mind of the morning tape playing in your head- let go of the list of 'to-do'. Find that space which allows you to listen with unconditional acceptance.

Write down one thing that you can do today to be more connected to one that is significant to you. What can you learn through listening?

Here's a task: Be the bearer of only good news today. In living out this task, note whether you find it difficult to maintain. And if so, discover why within yourself.

Caroline Myss and Peter Occhiogrosso

In daily conversation, we often do not realize how negative our speech becomes. Caroline Myss is an extraordinary individual - a medical intuitive who works with individuals in pain - and with hospitals on cases that are hard to diagnose. I love her assignment in the above quote. We like to think we are generally positive in our approach to life. But to inventory, for just one day, the dialogue we speak can be quite revealing. In brief therapy, the practitioner tries to get the client to do just one thing that is different for two months. The paradigm shifts through behavior! Try the experiment today: take note of any internal or conversational dialogue of a negative nature and transform it. Is it possible to bring only good news to the world for just one day? At the end of the day, review your experience. Was it is easy to recognize negative dialogue? Could you catch yourself slipping into negative, even if it was only in agreement with another who is negative?

Begin meditation today with the word "positive." Melt into the morning with a release of negative thoughts and external dialogue. In the distance, see the rising light of a new paradigm of thought.

Write down the impressions from meditation this morning. At the end of the day, return to your journal and write down your success. If you could not turn the negative to a positive each time, write down your thoughts about why.

*Meditate; engage in daily prayers, read uplifting books, commune with
Mother Nature—in some way try to remove yourself from the discord
of the everyday world that invades your sense of inner peace.*

Stephen R. Covey

Although Stephen Covey did not introduce any new concepts in self-improvement, he was a master of the way he ordered and taught those concepts. In *The 7 Habits of Highly Effective People*, his writing was immediately applicable to all readers, from children to seniors. He shifted the paradigm of how people looked at personal productivity and time management. He gave us tools for keeping on track in a fast-paced world. The above quote tells of a different kind of time management. He advises the readers to set spiritual time aside to feed our hungry hearts with sustenance each day. He speaks of replenishment- to drink from the well of inner peace each day and to create a free zone of sanctity for the soul. Today, consider the fundamentals of living a full life. What can you do today that will improve your mental and spiritual existence?

Meditate today with the word "fundamentals." Review the fundamentals of your daily routine as you slip into the reservoir of peace. Let the morning become a sanctuary of stillness. Enter the zone of tranquility. Regenerate your day.

Make a list of ways that you can improve your day. Review your current daily routine and take note of anything that is not working for you.

Sometimes our light goes out but is blown into flame by another human being.
Each of us owes deepest thanks to those who have rekindled this light.

Albert Schweitzer

Communication between true friends is clear, non-judgmental, and accepting. A friend is one to whom you could say, "I didn't mean to kill her...but it just happened." A true friend would say, "Now what do we need to do for you, so you can process this fully and do the right thing?" Although this is a ridiculous example, it embodies the rare quality of kindred friendship. I have friends who would absolutely stand by me as they walked me into prison if I egregiously violated the law; expressing sorrow for my choice as they delivered me for my penance. Having such a friend makes one feel rich and empowered. A true friend will say, "are you sure you want to handle this situation like that, or do you need to make a different choice?" The bargain struck when lifelong friendships begin is often intuitive and unspoken. Although some deep connections are made through common experience, other kindred souls come into our life just deeply *knowing* who we are. I like to think that a kindred friend represents an agreement made before life began, to honor and travel a path together.

It is when you give of yourself that you truly give...
Through the hands of such as these God speaks,
And from behind their eyes, God smiles upon the earth.

Kahlil Gibran, *The Prophet*

Meditation today should begin with the words "kindred friend." Whom do you need to honor today: someone from a decade long past or someone you just met; someone who is always present for you? Meld into presence with the spirit of that kindred soul and breathe deeply into your lungs in search of the soul connection.

Journal about how can you honor your kindred friendships today.

*Laughter gives us distance. It allows us to step back from
an event, deal with it, and then move on.*

Bob Newhart

Current research tells us that our longevity depends, in part, on the ability to be happy and find joy in life. Laughter and humor sometimes provide clarity and perspective as well. It is essential one's life not be taken too seriously. I have a circle of supportive friends in which we bandy around the phrase "Get over yourself; life is here to enjoy!" Humor can be the time-out from a life too heartbreaking to process. I remember in the year following 9/11, I hungered for a Chris Rock or Robin Williams comedy special. My sadness was so deep that I actively sought escape. In search of a respite from reality, I chose humorous cinema. As with anything, it can go too far. Some people use humor to avoid unpleasant feelings. At some point, we also need let go and embrace the sadness of a situation. Today, think about laughter. What role does laughter play in your life?

Meditation today begins with the word "laughter." Smile your way into stillness this morning. How does joy feel to the muscles in your face? Where is the joy into your soul?

Write down the images and feelings that came to you in your meditation. Today, take note of how laughter feels in your body.

*If you can learn a simple trick, you'll get along a lot better with all kinds of
folks. You never really understand a person until you consider things from
his point of view...until you climb into his skin and walk around in it.*

Harper Lee, *To Kill A Mockingbird*

One quality of a successful peacemaker is to be able to slip on the shoes of both the powerful and the underpowered, and then hike around for a while. Understanding the perception of another soul allows one to help redirect a narrative. Re-scripting the stories of communities, parents, partnerships, patients, tribes, or employees activates a personal line of inquiry that leads *the lost* back to *the found*, whatever the venue. Tunnel vision is a common state when people are in opposition to one another. The expressway out of darkness is illuminated by intentional acts of compassionate insight.

Meditation today should begin with the word "insight." Sit in silence with the word and identify what it represents to you. Rejoice in what was lost is now found.

Write down the insights you had in your meditation. How can you gain insight into another's pain? Is there a misunderstanding in your life that could benefit from compassionate insight?

> *...I would like to beg you dear Sir, as well as I can, to have patience with everything unresolved in your heart and to try to love the questions themselves as if they were locked rooms or books written in a very foreign language. Don't search for the answers, which could not be given to you now, because you would not be able to live them. And the point is to live everything. Live the questions now. Perhaps then, someday far in the future, you will gradually, without even noticing it, live your way into the answer.*
>
> Rainer Maria Rilke, *Letters to Young Poet*

Reflection is such a passive word. Action is much more like home to me. Actually, reaction would be closer to the truth, frantically trying to understand, to control, to attain or to reach the next plateau. These are all reactions to the lack of trust in a higher power and connection with myself. Since we began formal education, we have been taught to constantly improve our *self,* and therefore to identify with our ego. Reflection can be scary, like letting go of the wheel while driving 80 miles an hour. As we careen down the expressway of living, we miss the love waiting just beyond the shoulder, in the clearing of the forest, in the reflection on the lake, in the still of the distant mountains. To observe in stillness can feel uncomfortable and risky. What will happen if we choose to "live the questions," observe our thoughts, and let identification with our ego slither away? Just be and "live your way into the answer."

Meditation today should begin with the word "reflection." Observe your breath, let it settle deeply into your lungs, and do not seek anything. Allow yourself to float into profound awareness and be open to reflection.

In your journaling today, reflect on what is "unresolved in your heart." How do you "live your questions"?

Integrity

Human fallibility being what it is, victory and truth do not always go together.
Therefore, if you have to always win, you can't always be true.

Rabbi Rebbe Nachman

Human imperfections prevent us from truly being present for each other. We are all students, evolving or not. I think we are socialized to be fighters at heart. As Americans, we have built our nation on military superiority. Today, the planet is in disarray. Power dynamics are in flux. When one has all the power, is it necessary to pre-emptively wield that dominance? Our integrity as a nation is at stake. Our individualism is coveted more than our community is. We set boundaries that lead us to the incorrect notion that *to win* establishes us as the *top gun*, and to seek another's truth is rejected categorically as weakness or passivity. To have victory at the expense of others, are we not compromising truth?

To maintain personal integrity and the integrity representative of our nation, we must risk *setting truth first* instead of winning at any price. This not for ourselves but for the greater good. Our integrity and personal presence then can shine through. We are free to choose, to be powerful, and to be empowered. If we inventory our integrity and improve it, we will improve our planet.

Meditation today should begin with the word "integrity." Breathe honor and honesty into your body and sink into the comfort of your own presence.

In your journaling, contemplate the Rabbi's statement, "if you have to always win, you can't always be true." Consider your own life. How can you embody personal integrity in your life today?

All religions must be tolerated…for…every man must get to heaven his own way.

Frederick the Great

Religions are collective organizations of worship and community. Coming together to find communion with a higher power is a beautiful and wondrous feeling. I, however, rejected religion at the age of six. Unfortunately, in my ignorance, I also rejected God with it. As I look back, I remember the instant when I made the decision. It was All Saints Day and my catechism class was outside the nave of the church, lined up like little dominoes. While waiting for Sister Philomena to signal our walk of worship, I studied a framed poster on the wall just above the holy water urn. A loving Jesus was smiling at four little children whom he held in a wide embrace. Little birds hovering above them were witness to the love. One was a little red haired boy, another a little African girl, then an Indian boy, and finally an Asian girl. I smiled back. Jesus did love us all. The frankincense filled my nose as we began our procession and the long walk toward the altar. Looking around in excitement, I noticed the last four rows. I saw only black people. After I passed these rows, a few empty ones were evident. Only white people filled the rest of the rows. I didn't know the word hypocrisy at six, but something similar rang in my head. That day I rejected religion for being hypocritical.

After a few decades, I acknowledged that God was close to me and I could no longer ignore Him. I began to search for communion. I recognized that although Catholicism was doing the best it could, it did not resonate for me. My next choice also turned out to be another dogmatic religion of exclusivity. Again, I left, yearning for balance and tolerance in life but not finding it in those faiths. I was 35 before I came to terms with what Frederick the Great noted in the 18th century, everyone "must get to heaven his own way." Today, I have found communion with souls who share my beliefs and values. I have learned that although all religions are beautiful not one has cornered the market on God. Tolerance and acceptance are my religion of choice; I have made peace with my religion of birth and found I what I needed inside me.

Meditation today should begin with the word "religion." Embrace the peace of communion and breathe empowering breaths of acceptance of all souls who are in search of their Source.

Write down in your journal what the word religion means to you. Write down what spirituality means to you. Make a list of ways that you can honor and embrace those who walk a different path to God.

*This is the true joy in life, the being used for a purpose recognized by yourself as a mighty one; the being a force of nature instead of a feverish, selfish little clod of ailments and grievances complaining that the world will not devote itself to making you happy.
I am of the opinion that my life belongs to the whole community, and as long as I live it is my privilege to do for it whatever I can. I want to be thoroughly used up when I die, for the harder I work the more I live. I rejoice in life for its own sake. Life is no "brief candle" for me. It is a sort of splendid torch which I have got hold of for the moment, and I want to make it burn as brightly as possible before handing it on to future generations.*

George Bernard Shaw

To a man whose life's work was a joy, contribution was his most important legacy. George Bernard Shaw's work was his passion, his way of being involved in the pulse of the earth. He viewed his contribution as that of a presence on the hill, holding a torch for others, for them to reach their own pinnacle of personal contribution. I think peacemakers and conflict professionals are quite like Shaw in their passion for their work; ours is a legacy of making a difference, one day at a time, one dispute at a time. In order to contribute in the field, I think one must look for the thread of hope, hold in the imagination that peace is possible, and stand on the edge of reason. The extraordinary individual who is willing to make the contribution that changes a community, a country, a region, could be you. Take note of the daily contributions of your work. Give thanks for the willingness to stand on the edge and participate fully.

Meditation today should begin with the word "contribution." Settle into your breath; sense the cadence of the air bringing life giving contribution to your body, your heart, and your soul. Know your life to be a "splendid torch...[and] make it burn as brightly as possible."

In your writing, explore what came to you in mediation. What have your contributions been? What do you want your contributions to be? How will you make your life a "splendid torch?"

The Sibyl with raving mouth utters solemn, unadorned, unlovely words, but she
reaches out over a thousand years with her voice because of the God in her.

Heraclitus

When agreement is made to welcome those in pain to your table, you "court the dangerous."
One never knows when the "raving mouth" will sling toxic sludge toward the intended target.
Dealing with that rage day in and day out, laden with triggers of sorrow and defensiveness for
our own psyche, can create dissociation from our own heart and soul, at work and in our own
life. We can become so numb, so non-reactive, that we run the risk of dehumanizing our fellow
human or becoming inhuman and robotic ourselves. Also, courting the dangerous can cause the
reverse. Unaware of the psychic negative energy we have absorbed, we may rave at our loved ones
or others, drown our pain in alcohol or other addictions, or forget who we are. When I witness
the "raving mouth" at work, when the ire triggers my own, I have learned to keep my eye on the
God in them. To realize their pain, the loss, the free-falling flight from fright, allows compassion
to come forth and embrace their sorrow, contain the fear, name it, work with it, and help them to
release the voice of the God in them. Are you willing to court the dangerous? Can you stand firmly
in your place at the table and know that the voice will be heard if you are willing to provide the
sacred space and safety required to bring it forth?

Meditate today on the word "danger." Breathe in a cleansing breath of air; breathe out the
fear of the unknown step. Breathe in the willingness to stand in the face of danger and the
comfort in knowing you are not alone.

Write one thing that you can do today to enhance your willingness to court the dangerous.
What might be stopping you? What is helping you to get to that place?

If one advances confidently in the direction of his dreams, and endeavors to live the life which he has imagined, he will meet with a success unexpected in common hours.

Henry David Thoreau

Success is the journey, not the destination. To "advance confidently" is the piece that I found most difficult. I was so busy *doing* in the early part of my life, I never realized that I could dream. To "advance confidently" was only possible for me if I faked it. When I look back, I am so glad I was willing to fake it. I simply agreed to place one foot in front of the other and be led on a path. In retrospect, I see that there were angels along my road from whom I received strength for the next segment of the race. Pretty soon, the terrain looked different to me. I was seeing a landscape that I could have never imagined and the ride was rich and meaningful. I was granting myself permission I didn't know I had. I just said *yes*. My point of view altered, my lens of perception cleared to envision new things. I think it was the willingness to see abundance, to be successful; it called to me from somewhere on the fringes of my memory. For a moment, consider your own path. What success lies on the shoulder of your road that you need to be willing to see?

Meditation today should begin with the word "success." Visualize your successful self as you begin your renewal this morning. Breathe with a sure cadence. Become quiet and receive.

Write down your successes. What is a goal you have set that you have not attained? What is one thing that you can do today to be successful?

Learn the craft of knowing how to open your heart and turn
on your creativity. There is a light inside of you.

Judith Jamison

Often, our habits are ones of protection, which, by their nature are guarded and restrictive. Habits can be broken and new ones can replace them. We have so many that reinforce our negative ways of thinking. Choosing to cultivate positive-heart-habits is easier than one might expect. The spirit rises to new heights of awareness when the chains of the bad habits are removed. Kahlil Gibran wrote, "When you are sorrowful look again in your heart, and you shall see that in truth you are weeping for that which has been your delight." We want to hold onto and repeat the joys in life, but all things are impermanent. Instead of choosing to embody love, we protect our heart against the pain we experienced when that particular joy of the heart ended. When we restrict our hearts, we sentence ourselves to a deadening of emotion and decrease the possibility that we will experience love again. Could it be that we fear that which we desire? The only thing required for a change to positive-heart-habits is a willingness to acknowledge that which we fear and dispel it with our light inside which shines so brightly.

"To love for the sake of being loved is human; but to love for the sake of loving is Angelic."

Alphonse de Lamartine

Meditation today should begin with the phrase "habits of the heart." Breathe with intention of discovery...fill both chambers of your lungs with the air of willingness and let your fear subside...

Inventory your habits of relationship. List times in your recent past when you have chosen to restrict your heart and withhold love. What is one thing that you can do today to create a new habit of the heart? How can you risk? How can you be angelic?

*To be vital, awake, aware, in all areas of our lives, is the task
that is never accomplished, but it remains the goal.*

Brother David Steindl-Rast

Webster defines essence as "ultimate or intrinsic nature; prime character; that in being which underlies all outward manifestations." My friend, Melinda, has coined her own word, "energessence," which she defines as the essence of energy that is within each of us. I interpret one's essence to mean one's spirit, one's source. Our essence often resides underneath our defense mechanisms. Our task is to reconnect with that essence. Essence is a part of the word essential, which means ideally perfect, complete, or important in the highest degree. As Brother David Steindl-Rast noted, the task of reconnection may never be accomplished but remains the goal. Our purpose is to connect with that essence and through it manifest abundance in our lives. The act of seeking out our vitality of essence remains the impetus for meditation and self-discovery. Without connection to our essence, we are not able to uncover the unique gifts we have to offer. As a mother, when I look at the essence of who my children are, I have a vantage point of wisdom they do not have. I see my eldest child as having the essence of spiritual and artistic expression as part of the fabric of her soul. I see my second child as having the essence of heart in application to all people at the core of his being. I see my third child as having the essence of endurance and fortitude, and the stamina of spirit to be a lifelong seeker. I am sure that my children do not have the perception I have in my unique role as their mother. My belief is that God has a similar vantage point about us as spiritual manifestations. I think God has information for us that helps to make our purpose clear. It can be found through searching for insight into our essence. How can you act today to discover your essence? In what areas are you already awake, aware, and vital? Where is your "energessence"?

....

Meditation today should begin with the word "essence." Silently go within with your song of sacred searching. Sit and listen for the still voice of your essence.

Write down all the qualities that you readily recognize as the essence of your being. Tonight when you return to your solitude, write down the news ones that you unearthed today.

God has no hands or feet or voice except ours and through these He works.

Teresa of Avila

The job of the peacemaker is to uncover that voice of caring. Eliciting concrete information is the key to illuminating the source of caring that is at the base of every story. Through clarification, we enlighten the other's listening ears, providing an opportunity for intentions to be declared. I don't think that people who come to this work do so without having compassion as a quality. In realizing what *we* care deeply about, we bring the power of understanding with us to the table. Knowing the first step is to delve into the reason for the caring as well as the details driving the issue, allows a practitioner to build a bridge over the river of conflict. We are truly doing the work with spirit. When we convene a sacred space, the souls of the conflicted arrive for transformational healing. We are only the vessel, the medium through which love of God passes through to arrange the engagement of solutions. As Mother Teresa said, "through these He works."

Meditation today should begin with the phrase "angels of caring." Wrap your lungs around the morning air as you settle into your soul work and feel the beating heart of angels of caring for your soul and for your soul path mates. Care for those who are desperately in need of peace.

How can you embody the care of the angels in caring for yourself? What does it feel like to take care of your *self* first? What is one thing that you can today to care for your soul?

If you wish to know the divine, feel the wind on your face and the warm sun on your hand.

Buddha

Once we embrace stillness and enter into mindful thinking, each day brings new awareness of everyday grace in the simplicity of life. One of the first awakenings occurred when I pulled into my office parking spot and spotted a robin curiously observing me. I was struck by how inquisitive and alert robins are. In my mindlessness, I would have never had the time nor desire to sit for a moment and commune with the mother robin out foraging for her babies. I said aloud, "Well, she and I have a lot in common. Foraging for my children still is not completed and they are all in their 20s now!" She stared at me with peace, unafraid as I stepped from my car. She stood firm on the median, cocking her head to the left and right, and I could swear she was smiling (if birds can do such a thing). A steady joy rolled across my heart and, in that moment, I felt the peace of God. Since that time, I look for those moments. I am amazed how many moments there are, and how many I have missed looking down, in a hurry, living my frenetic mindless life. How is mindfulness changing you? Are you finding the Divine in ordinary things?

Meditation today should begin with the phrase "divinely ordinary." Embrace the sacred time of stillness and agree to see the edges of your mind. Breathe into the fog and search for divinity.

Write down the images you saw in your mind's eye. List the opportunities that you have this day for mindfulness and finding the divine in the ordinary.

The greatest discovery of my generation is that human beings
can alter their lives by altering their attitudes of mind.

William James

Attitude is everything. It has almost become a cliché. When teaching conflict theory, one of the overhead slides I use is "4 Ways to Handle Conflict." When I get to number three, "Change Your Mind About the Conflict," I spend a great deal of time explaining perception and attitude. I am always amazed that 90% of the class still operates under the notion that things are black and white, "Of course others should see things their way." I suppose it is human nature. But the act of changing your mind is astoundingly easy once a resolute choice is made to do so, and attitude changes along with it. Miracles occur often when successfully transforming your attitude; attitude is everything. How empowering is the notion that we can change our lives by changing our mind? If practitioners of peace can change their mind, then we can coach others through that process. What do you need to change your mind about today?

Meditation today should begin with the word "attitude." Change any negative attitude you have about meditation today. Give meditation a new name, like 'floating', and envision meditation as something else. Breathe with inquiry and take a new journey.

Write down the images you saw on your journey. What is one attitude that you can alter today?

*If we fill our lives with people simply to keep from being alone,
we've assembled not a circle of friends but a cast of extras.*

Jesse Jennings

I think the magic carpet ride of the computer has moved us to outer space and not to *The Alhambra*. It is hard to feel energy through email. It seems that we are bombarded with information of an impersonal nature. It can make for a very lonely existence. In search of human companionship, we aim for the comfort of friends but often end up with a cast of characters who give the boozers at the *Star Wars* bar a run for their money. In amazement, we hear ourselves asks, "How did we get here?" We are shocked back into reality and retreat to the valley of loneliness. So, what is the answer to loneliness? I think the answer is to love your alone time. Turn solitude into inner peace. When we run from *what is,* we are running from a powerful opportunity to learn from living. To embrace that time of inner peace is to accept our spirit. When we melt our fear of being alone with the warm love of energy, we find in the quiet soul that we are never alone. When we pop our head out into the world, we fill with peace and inner beauty and find a field rich with others who are just like us. Synergy is created with the melding of light filled souls. You will attract others on the same path and never find yourself in the *Star Wars* bar again.

Meditation should begin with the word "loneliness." Softly walk in solitude toward your alone time with renewed focus; welcome each breath as you ascend the stairway to heaven. Angels who travel with you are waiting to enlighten you and in your solitude, you agree to surrender.

In free association, write down all the feelings behind the word lonely. Reframe one feeling of loneliness present in your life right now. What is one thing that you can do today to not feel lonely?

Expect the unexpected or you won't find it.

Heraclitus

The clarity of thought that Heraclitus shared in the sixth century BC is amazingly applicable in today's world. His inspiring words always provide a fresh perspective whenever I read them. Considered one of the pre-Socratics, he may have been the first philosopher to suggest that opportunity and possibility lay firmly in the camp of creativity. Heraclitus believed that the cosmos was dynamic, flowing, and ever-changing—and that he was a part of that energy: "Everything flows." His brilliant use of metaphor and paradox riddles our imagination with excitement. He walked the streets of the once-Greek city Ephesus, one of the best preserved sites of ancient ruins that still stand today, on the western coast of Turkey. An Ephesian of royal descent, Heraclitus was an introspective intellectual. Through his writings, he instructs us to wake up and discover what is happening around and through us. An ancient guru of self-awareness, he counsels us "to search unto your self." His words cause one to reflect and drop expectations of how things should look or be. His epigrams have been studied for over two millennia as an exercise in creative thinking, often to provide different pearls of wisdom for each soul who reads them. When pondering your life, what expectations do you have of your world? Are they getting in your way of experiencing that world fully?

A wonderful harmony is created when we join together the seemingly unconnected.

Heraclitus

Meditate today on the word "expectation." Observe your breath flow in and out of your lungs. Drop your expectation of this meditation. Be in your body and notice your breath, your thoughts, and your breath again.

Write down one expectation you have about your life that you can chose to drop today. Is there an expectation that you can adopt?

You are what exists before all stories. You are what remains when the story is understood.

Byron Katie

The tales we weave are quite often woven to deceive. But, who are we deceiving? I love the story of the Venetians during the Renaissance. The Masquerade was a Venetian custom of throwing the last hurrah, a celebration before the season of Lent. Although in many cases, through the ages, it became more an exercise of debauchery than clean fun, the idea was to enjoy the last party of the season without anyone knowing who you were. Elaborate masks were created out of paper maché and were ornate works of art, chosen to represent the alter ego, the "Mini Me." Unfortunately many of us cast a "Mini Me" in the starring role of our script. "Mini Me" runs rampant in our lives, masking who we really are, wrecking relationships, and turning love away at every opportunity.

Somewhere along the line, we began thinking that we think we really are our "Mini Me." We attend the celebration of life in our finery but are wallflowers reticent to show our dance card. We are waiting for the right moment to begin truly living; the right look, the right person to show up to relieve us from the hell of loneliness. That moment is now. There is only one moment, this moment. Everything else is a script. Are you waiting in the wings with your script in hand and your mask of finery firmly in place? Has your "Mini Me" rehearsed the carefully written lines for a flawless but disingenuous performance? Or are you ready to drop the mask and start living another story; the one of empowerment, of personal awareness, contemplation, and transformation. The moment is now. As Katie said, "You are what remains when the story is [finally] understood." You do not need a "Mini Me" adorned by an ornate mask. You are beauty and presence personified.

Meditation should begin with the word "script." Erase the lines on the page and agree to become whole. Breathe deeply and intensely, and cleanse the memory of the "Mini Me". Breathe in a vision of beauty and be the presence of your true essence.

Write down the images that came to you. Can you lay down your script and live in this moment?

All things are not only in a constant state of change, but they
are the cause of constant change in other things.

Marcus Aurelius, 1 A.D.

As we wade into the swirling energy of emotion at the table of resolution, the power of our presence injects a different energy into the space. A single question, hanging in the air above the conflict, can float down and dissipate the tension as if by magic. I happen to think the divine works through peacemakers all the time. We are willing. We are passionate. We bring hope and possibilities to those in need. We are agents of change.

Meditation today should begin with the words "agent of change." As you settle into our morning ritual of peace, feel the power of that phrase and welcome it. Breathe deeply, open to awareness and possibility.

Write down an instance of your success as an agent of change. Explore what it means to you to be an agent of change.

Symbols

*Each symbol is articulated, vivified, or deadened, by the image that
represents it. A symbol cannot appear at all unless in an image…Symbols
become images when they are particularized by a specific context,
mood, and scene, that is, when they are precisely qualified.*

James Hillman

Every image has a construct of meaning to us. These constructs bring differences in images
to each personal canvas. Certain symbols and images appeal to me. The symbol of the fleur-de-
lys is all over my house. I am drawn to that symbol in a mysterious way. I think, for one thing,
it represents my home state Louisiana. To me, the lily flower represents accord, an offering of
peace. I am also moved by other symbols, such as when I see our nation's flag or hear "America
the Beautiful." I am drawn to the Chinese symbols for mindfulness, chaos, listening, and peace;
so lovely to me in their brevity of appearance and depth of meaning. I am heartened when I
see mountain wildflowers; they remind me of abundance. I am comforted by flowing water as
a symbol for tranquility. I am exhilarated when I hear Mozart's *Requiem;* it reminds me of God
and of power. Think about the symbols and images that come to you. Notice how different they
might be from others you know. As peacemakers, our responsibility is to help draw portraits of
experience from one party to the next. How is this done? It is done through the art of metaphor.
In your work ask questions of meaning.

Meditation today should begin with the word "symbol." Sit in silence and allow symbols
to rise to your awareness. Gather a garden of deep purple violets into your mind and feel
the lushness of spirit that accompanies your thoughts.

What symbols did you see? What do they mean to you? Write them down in your
journal.

There are only four questions of value in life, Don Octavio: What is sacred?
Of what is the spirit made? What is worth Living for?...and, What is
worth Dying for? The answer to each is the same: only Love!

Don Juan De Marco to Don Octavio, *Don Juan DeMarco*

Only four questions of value in life? Could it be that all of our machinations to explain this world can be simplified to these four questions? But somehow, they ring true upon hearing them.

Is it possible that we only need to love? Not in the romantic sort of way, our culture defines as the bandage for depression and misery, but the kind of love of which the great spiritual teachers spoke. Is the sanctity of "love one another" so holy that it gives meaning to every life? Four questions of value to each human soul. Four questions to ponder. Today, consider these questions and search for your own meaning.

Meditation today should begin with the words "the sacred." Sit with the sacred and breathe in the slow cadence of peace. Share the sacred images of the mind with the sacred breaths of life.

Write down the answers to these four questions for your life. What is of value to you? Can you find love as the source of all that is valued?

The wise man does not speak in the presence of one who is greater than
he in wisdom; he does not interrupt the speech of his companion; he is not
hasty to answer; he questions and answers properly, to the point; he speaks
on the first point first, and the last point last; regarding that which he has
not learnt he says: "I have not learnt; and he acknowledges the truth."
Philip Birnbaum, *Daily Prayer Book: Ha-Siddur Ha-Shalem*

John Paul Lederach, the great peace builder, wrote in his book, *The Moral Imagination,* of four stories in different areas of the world in which the decision was made to end violence by one person. Their act of respect affected great change in the community. These four stories have at their core respect – respect for human life, respect for the elders, respect for power, and respect for community. As written in the Jewish prayer book, acknowledgment of truth and deference for those who have attained greater wisdom is the very definition of respect. Lederach's thesis question in his book was "How does constructive social change happen?" He believes that there is a critical moment, a turning point when opportunity produces a window for union. His hypothesis is that each instance has an opportune moment of creation, of collusion, a conspiracy of love, if you will, to draw the line in the sand at the edge of tomorrow. To say, "Because I respect life, no more violence." He speaks to a resolve to dissolve the hatred, to throw the differences into the shadows and to bring forth light to the similarities. To say, "I respect you," speaks of an agreement from one soul to another. I think it is possible, one soul to another, to change the world. It is time to restore respect in the world and within each of our relationships.

Meditation today should begin with the word "respect." Revel in the reverence of your soul and be contemplative this day, breathe in respect for your path.

Write down the images that came to you in meditation. Find one thing that you can respect about a person whom you do not think you respect. What is one way that you can teach respect today?

If you want to know the past, to know what has caused you, look at yourself
in the present, for that is the past's effect. If you want to know your future,
then look at yourself in the present, for that is the cause of the future.

Majjhima Nikaya

Eckhart Tolle in his book, *The Power of Now,* notes that we are always frantically rushing from one thing to another, one place to another, one person to another. In that race, we miss our lives. We miss the present moment. We walk around with a metaphorical scroll. As we consider every decision, our logical mind rolls out the scroll of our history to see how to protect ourselves; to be safe from choosing the wrong thing, being in the wrong place, or avoiding what has hurt us in the past. In the next millisecond, we roll out the scroll of our future to see where we are headed. What goals must we complete? What thing do we need to obtain?

History no longer exists. The future is not yet here. If we live in the past and spend all our time planning for tomorrow, we miss the experience of the present. I often ask clients, what will happen to you if you stop right now, in this moment, and take account of the wonder of it all? Each day lived in the present moment is the laboratory for peace, the chance for love, and the moment of happiness. To understand that to, "look at your self in the present, for it is the cause of the future," is the key to inner peace and the only chance we have for true happiness.

Let there be nothing behind you; leave the future to one side. Do not clutch at
what is left in the middle; then you will become a wanderer and calm.

Sutta Nipata

Meditation today should begin with the words "living in the now." In this moment, breathe deeply into the present moment and find gratitude for a beating heart, a passion for work, a love of your presence...

Write down the things that you can do to find gratitude in the present moment. Record the instances of grace and inner peace that you noticed during the day.

Peace, the other name for home.

Kathleen Norris

I have spent this year creating an altar of peace for my soul. After a difficult decade of conflict engagement, I knew I needed it. My home office has become my sanctuary. It is a warm, book filled space with a sturdy oak altar upon which to create the words in my soul. I welcome conducting client phone calls for lengthy intake sessions, so we can enlighten our connection before it begins in person. I correspond from my home office, draft documents, meditate, pray, read, and relax. I only go into my formal offices for mediations, meetings, and to teach. Then, I again retreat to my peaceful sanctuary. The other name for it: home. I begin each morning in the same ritual way. The consistency comforts me and brings me strength for whatever the day presents. As I descend from my home altar, I give thanks for the peace that awaits there for me when I return. Keeping a simple sanctuary has become renewing for me. Is there a place in your home that you can carve out from the edge of a busy corner; a delicious room that can be fashioned into a womb of warmth for your soul? Look around today and construct a sanctuary of simplicity from your home.

Meditation today should begin with the word "simplicity." Keeping simple depth in your breath, breathe from your belly and seek the simple solutions to your life. Go to that place of stillness and be the peace you seek.

Write down the elements of a sanctuary of simplicity. What is one thing that you can do today to create simplicity in your life?

Things do change. The only question is that since things are deteriorating
so quickly, will society and man's habits change quickly enough?

Isaac Asimov

When I consider the state of affairs in the world and how quickly they are deteriorating, I understand why our field has recently stepped forward. Bernie Mayer in his book, *Beyond Neutrality: Confronting the Crisis in Conflict Resolution*, calls for conflict professionals to step up to a higher order of work. Mayer argues for a change in terms from conflict management to conflict engagement. In his appeal to the field, he issued a challenge: we must become a force in changing the planet. I agree. We no longer have the luxury of arguing about method or approaches to practice. We must heal the rifts in disciplines and styles of practice to reach for deeper wisdom, wider inquiry, and the courage to go to the edge with clients. I feel it is necessary to speed up our development as a field and be ready to undertake the next major crisis. As Asimov asked, "will...man's habits change quickly enough?" We must be ready, willing, and comfortable in the role of going to the edge to find creative solutions. And, above all, we must be tolerant and welcome our differences.

Mediation today should begin with the words "urgency and willingness." Breathe in the sustenance that you will need to travel the road of engagement and breathe out the reticence to risk. Breathe in the desire for involvement. Feel the urgency to become a part of the solution.

Write down one thing that you can do today to engage conflict more effectively. Is there a way to for you to become involved in creating a more peaceful community?

You are a primary existence. You are a distinct portion of the essence of God, and contain a certain part of Him in yourself. Why then are you ignorant of your noble birth? You carry a God about within you, poor wretch, and know nothing of it.

Epictetus

Margaret Wheatley, author of *Finding Our Way: Leadership for an Uncertain Time,* wrote that nothing in the universe exists as an isolated entity. Indeed, everything exists in the context of relationship of inter-connectedness. Bruce Lipton in his book, *The Biology of Belief,* studied the biological webs of life and made the same comparison to human behavior. Planck, Einstein, Wilber, and many others have written that, through quantum mechanics, we now know that all energy is conserved in the universe, everything can be broken down into holons, the smallest of particles, and nothing is ever lost. It is through these interdisciplinary theories that we understand how we, as humans, can collapse the barriers of separateness and move toward each other as valiant warriors waging peace against the narrow view that we are separate from each other, separate from God, separate from the planet which we inhabit. What do you need to do to realize that you are powerful beyond appraisal?

Meditation today should begin with the word "inter-connectedness." Breathe in the blessings of common union and breathe out the feeling that you are solitary, alone in the world.

Write down the images that came to you in this meditation. How can you feel more connected today? What is one thing that you can do to move into wholeness and a holistic practice?

To be credible we must be truthful.

Edward R. Murrow

Truthiness—that which one holds to be true regardless of what is supported by fact.

Stephen Colbert, *The Colbert Report*

Our perception is our truth. To be credible in our profession requires that we bring our truth to our performance at work. Think about how persuasion and truth in our culture impact your life. What can you do to feel more connected to your own opinions and not be dependent on being part of the herd? Are you involved in group think, or do you reason new theories and ideas out on your own? How much *truthiness* do you buy at face value without researching? How does your process of critical thinking affect the values and ethics with which you live your life? If you were more present to your reactions to outside persuasive opinion, how would that affect the way you practice?

Meditate today beginning with the word "persuasion." Open your airwaves to accept the air into the corners of your body. Coax the energy from within to rise into consciousness and settle your mind around persuading yourself to just be.

Examine ways in which your culture has persuaded you to take certain positions. List one thing that you can do differently today to persuade yourself to become less reactive and more proactive.

Maybe we should remember that God dwells within us, even when
we are in the basement, not just on the mountaintop.

Margaret Stortz

I believe even as the depths of depression visit us on the path of life, as surely all of us have experienced, we are never truly left in isolation. Waves of misery pour over our ailing heart, bringing the memory of familiar pain. That is the perfect time to remember we share a deep spiritual connection with a higher power. A more hopeful message is that we can choose to grab the hand of our higher power and, together, sift through the heartbreak. Should we desire an alternate reality, it is ours for the asking. One of my meditations is, "Please let me understand the trigger and learn the lesson quickly. Please help me correct my thinking so the pain will dissipate." I believe that God has made me that promise; I only need to remember it. I don't think I will ever be free from the fall of my spirit, but the trip gets shorter every time. I have confidence in that promise, and I know the sun will rise tomorrow. I can choose again. What does your relationship to your higher power look like to you? Do you need to explore that relationship? Do you need to let the stillness this morning define the safety net for you? When you descend, how do you correct your thoughts?

Meditation today should begin with the words "you are never alone." Go the place of peace and stillness. Breathe in the deep comfort of surety and breathe out the dark inner thoughts. Uncover the treasure of promise. Do you feel the promise of higher power?

What do you need to ponder today to discover the depths of your being? What are your limits? How do you correct the depression and come out of the darkness? Can you feel comfort in knowing you are never alone?

*Purposeful giving is not apt to deplete one's resources; it belongs to that
natural order of giving that seems to renew itself even in the act of depletion.
The more one gives, the more one has to give – like milk in the breast.*

Anne Morrow Lindbergh, *Gift from the Sea*

Anne Morrow Lindbergh viewed giving to others as a natural state of renewal. I whole-heartedly agree. Abundance is not a tally of personal wealth or resources; it is a state of mind. Abundance is a perception of a spiritual nature. A common philosophy is that more you share, the more you have. When we approach life with a question of increase, are we bargaining with the distributive model? I think it is quite possible that when we practice from a place of minimalism, we live a minimal life and have minimal work. When we think, "What is in this for me," we draw exploitive people into our lives who take advantage of us. Wouldn't it make more sense to approach life with gratitude as a general state of mind? We should not be calculating our possessions but instead the many blessings we already have, observing how we are being cared for, and noticing how people show up to assist us in our journey. Giving freely is an act of love. We renew and replenish our world by loving. Give someone a boost, and you will be lifted. Help someone who may be sad and you will feel joy. Giving freely is a form of abundance. It is a natural order of giving. The return is immeasurable and your life will look different to you.

Meditation today should begin with the words "give freely." Give yourself permission to breathe freely and deeply…allow yourself to notice the abundance that you have…time will stand still…you will be renewed…give freely to your soul, the inner peace which you deserve.

Write down the messages that came to you in meditation. Identify one opportunity for you to renew your abundant life by giving freely today.

People are constantly trying to use you to help them create
the particular illusions by which they live.

Thomas Merton, *Conjectures of a Guilty Bystander*

Often, we live in illusions that appear real and cause us to be fearful. Fear is justified only to the extent we fail to recognize the illusions, for they are true only when we want them to be true. As a broker of conflict engagement, I am presented with the veil of illusion every day. When fear is high, trust is low. The environment is ripe for illusions to rise from the living laboratory of the story-bound dispute. Illusions are investments deposited by the clients into the story of the pain caused by another. The only way to dispel the considerable investment made by parties is to help them withdraw all future deposits of fear. When attack is the first move, retaliation is the second. Illusions do not bring peace.

When you interact with another, an illusion is part of this dynamic. This illusion
allows each soul to perceive what it needs to understand in order to heal.

Gary Zukav, *Seat of the Soul*

Meditate today on the word "illusion." Breathe in the clean air of clarity, and breathe out the invested illusion of yesterday. Breathe in the desire to uncover illusion; breathe out the freedom from the fear.

List the illusions you may be holding in your life. Write a line or two about the ways by which you can begin to see clearly and to let go of the pain.

We are stardust, we are golden, we are half a million strong,
and we've got to get ourselves back to the garden.

Crosby, Stills, Nash and Young

What if the physicists are right? We are stardust. What if the vibrational theorists are right and we resonate and communicate on levels that cannot be seen? What if it's possible to have the walls collapse between us? What if we tap into an unexplained energy? What if we are not human beings having spiritual experiences but rather spiritual beings having a human experience? We *are* stardust, we are golden, and "we've got to get ourselves back to the garden." What if our free agency caused us to leave the garden and live in this dream, which can sometimes be a nightmare, of living on earth? Somehow that makes more sense. The famine, diseases, and wars are not allowed or brought by a higher power to be feared but are the product of one who is not yet awake to the realities of who we are. I like that story better. Stardust sounds a lot more fun to me than flesh and bone and then you die and its over.

Over the five decades of my life I have thought a lot about God, trying to reconcile my relationship to Source while rejecting most of the religious interpretations I've heard. In critical thought, I used my analytical mind trying to make sense of things of a spiritual nature, but never my heart. In the last few years, my journey has changed. It has become clear to me the dream we are living is not a nightmare, but can be joyful, peaceful, and quite powerful. In the tumultuous cacophony of life, it is sometimes necessary to shut out the noise and embrace the wonder of each moment. I have discovered that I only have one chance for happiness and that is in this moment. "The garden" is, for me, that state of awareness I find in the early hours of the day—the time I set aside each day to take care of my soul, renew my sense of purpose and passion, and make preparations for work. Think about your own journey. Do you need to get back to the garden?

Meditation today should begin with the word "stardust." Can you embrace your part of our universe? Breathe deeply and feel the power of that breath as you go back to your garden for a few minutes...

Record the images from your garden. What is one thing that you can do today to realize your state of golden, of stardust, and find your garden in the moment?

Man's judgments of value follow directly his wishes for happiness—
they are an attempt to support his illusions with arguments.

Sigmund Freud

Attribution theory forms the basis for assigning meaning to life. We categorize events and thoughts by the value that we place on them. In *Blink,* Malcolm Gladwell wrote about *thin slicing,* the nanosecond of judgment our mind slaps across all incoming information to evaluate first impressions of people and events. We form judgments to support the argument that justifies our illusions of meaning. When clients sit before us, their reactions are often quite apparent- a glance, a tightening of the lips, a furrow of the brow. But to what are they reacting? Sometimes people take the trip into orbit alone, they've assigned a faulty reason to a perception of the other's behavior. As a conflict professional, our task is to uncover the *wishes for happiness* the argument represents. What is the expectation that was not met? How do they perceive the other person is preventing them from attaining happiness? What about in your own life? What do you attribute to the behaviors of those in your inner circle? When are you offended? A clear inventory of our personal path, leads to a clearer understanding of those whom we assist in their wishes for happiness.

Meditation today should begin with concentration on the words "wishes for happiness." Silently ponder those wishes that repeat in your narrative. Can you envision a negative judgment transforming your wish into happiness?

List the images that came to you. Write the meaning you attributed to those images. Can you recognize your wishes for happiness?

Is it possible to appreciate yourself, including your imperfections, just as you are?
Alice Walker

The age-old process of self-acceptance is one that most of us never quite complete. I think that accepting yourself is important to inner peace and happiness. Is it possible to truly accept yourself if you cannot embrace the imperfections and recognize the humanity in your personal characteristics? While growing up, I never felt particularly powerful, but I had these sheers fits of power leap forth from my persona apparently from nowhere, or so I thought. I blamed myself for not knowing my place and for not fitting in, while admonishing myself thinking, "Who do you think you are?" I was in my 30s before I acknowledged my power as a great quality, not the shadow role to which I was playing. I learned to use my power in positive ways, for the betterment of myself and for the good of others: *Power with Ethics*, one of the great courses in life.

When I brought my daughter into the world, I recognized that she too was very powerful. As she anxiously anticipated the ending of the dryer cycle, dreams of victories in far off lands danced across her mind. I remember one day at the tender age of three she looked at me and said, "Mom, do you ever take pictures with your mind?" Deep introspection had begun at a very early age. Noticing my imperfections as a parent, she would bring me back to earth with her precocious observations by saying "You're not the mother of Jesus you know!" Realizing my own power was in denial, I vowed to change that process of generational dysfunction by teaching her. She *was* powerful and that power was a good thing. I taught her not to deny it. I taught her that she should use her power wisely, never harm anyone with it, or hurt them by overpowering. She practiced often on her sweet brother, failing miserably most of the time, but loving him deeply through her abuse, making decisions for him, telling him to jump when ordered. Looking back, she made him feel secure and, perhaps, insecure all at the same time. Honing her powerful skills as she grew into a beautiful young lady, she learned to have deep respect for him, for his innate ability to love first and ask questions later, to be gentle and kind with those who need it, and to have a calm and peaceful center, while she wrestled with her dragons, taming the dragon to a docile benevolent soul. She is now using her power for good. She is beautiful, inside and out. She has stepped into the light and is learning to ignore her interior scrutiny of imperfections. What about appreciation of your power? How do you own your power? Can you choose to embrace it?

....

Meditation today should begin with the words "appreciation for power." Breathe deeply into the rigid pockets of your lungs and feel the power of your humanity...rest with the beauty of all of those lessons.

Write an attribute list, positive attributes first. Then make sure you list all the qualities that you think are denied. Choose one that you can embrace today.

Nothing in life is to be feared. It is only to be understood.

Marie Curie

How much of life is spent in misunderstanding? How much of life could be welcomed if we chose not to fear the unknown but to understand? The major role of a peacemaker is to help those in communication and perception breakdown get more information. More information reveals intent, and intent brings understanding. Understanding reduces fear and increases trust in the other. A solid understanding of someone or of a situation sounds like such an easy thing, but in reality it can be quite difficult. Think of things in your life that are hard for you to understand. For me, it is how people can stand only in their truth and ignore another's perception. I have disdain for narrowness, fear, and minimalist doctrine espoused in the name of fairness. But in truth, it just brings up for me my intolerance of the intolerant. How different am I? Through not understanding others, I get in touch with my intellectual snobbery. In truth, I am intolerant of stupidity. I am intolerant of those who do not think for themselves, but follow as sheep through the valley on their way to slaughter. It is easy for me to not seek to understand them. Perhaps instead of fearing the opinions of those who are different, I should understand myself better?

Meditation today should begin with the word "understanding." Settle into your chair with a clear intent on understanding...images will come to you as you breathe peacefully...seeking...

Write down the understandings that came to you in meditation. Are they understandings about yourself, or those with whom you are in relation?

I am extraordinarily patient, provided I get my own way in the end.
Margaret Thatcher

In the hurried rush of life, it is easy to become impatient. Patience has been my lifelong struggle. When it was being issued I must not have been in the room, and I am honestly quite certain that I will never master it. I am in the process of learning that meditation and connection with myself are two things that, historically, were missing from my toolbox and contributed to my struggle with patience. A permanent intention of mine is to, at minimum once a day, connect to my inner source and remind myself to be patient.

Meditate today on the word "patience." As your active mind approaches your breath, allow it to rein in your racing thoughts and sit in patience, watching your mind slow in the stillness.

Journal about three areas of impatience you notice in your personality. Focus on ways that you can work toward patience in those areas.

We receive three educations, one from our parents, one from our schoolmasters,
and one from the world. The third contradicts all that the first two teach us.

Charles Baron de Montesquieu

Daniel Bowling writes about the three phases of professional development for a practitioner. The first is *doing*: practicing our skill set until we achieve proficiency. The second is *knowing*: we expand what we know and become a more advanced practitioner by applying theory and using our knowledge in a reflective way. The third phase is *being*. Bowling notes that, when we are comfortable with the knowledge of our field, we can hone our personal qualities to meld with knowledge in our practice: do we have the qualities of acceptance? are we passionate? do we have patience? are we creative? can we easily adapt? do we have a general optimism about the inevitability of change? The questions we ask about our state of being comes from a different base of knowledge. Bowling posits that, unless we develop these qualities in our practice, we cannot be truly successful in the practice of making peace and conflict engagement. As Baron De Montesquieu noted, the third education that we receive from living in the world contradicts the first two. If we choose introspection, by living in the world we discover who we are. We grow out of the mapping of our parents, the drilling of the schoolmaster, and become reflective in the world. Bowling noted that unless we develop the third process of reflection, our presence never develops past the first two processes of education. How does your practice reflect your qualities?

Meditation today should begin with the words "doing, knowing, and being." Just agree to sit and be...feel what your existence is...breathe quietly and completely into your body and feel the edges of your energy...

Write down the images just being brought to you. Where are you in the evolution of your practice? What can you do today to enhance the qualities you have and move toward a reflective presence?

Follow Your Bliss

Follow your bliss and don't be afraid, and doors will open
where you didn't know they were going to be.

Joseph Campbell

The Power of Myth was a documentary made by Bill Moyers for PBS in the 1990s; a series of interviews with the great anthropologist and educator, Joseph Campbell. Campbell made amazing journeys throughout the world studying over 400 tribes and indigenous peoples, searching for the commonalities in their beliefs and mythology. He discovered the similarities were striking. Tribal cultures in completely different parts of the globe, with no pattern of migratory uniformity had threads of parallel beliefs and comparisons too alike to dispel as coincidence. He wrote of these discoveries in the book *The Hero with a Thousand Faces* in 1940. At the end of the series, Moyers asked Campbell for one piece of advice he would give to those who are looking for meaning in their life, and his wonderful thoughts about *following your bliss* resulted. He was speaking about the choice to remain open, to be content to sit in the moment and wait for the door to open. He discovered this philosophy not only in the living of his life, and to a large extent gave credit to his work. In the pursuit of our human connections, the discovery of similarity in our tapestries of beliefs was proof to him that we are so much more alike than we are different. The simplicity of *follow your bliss* is inviting. Can you wait for the next door to open? It will not be in the place you expect it.

Meditation today should begin with the word "bliss." What are you doing when you feel blissful? Imagine that bliss for a moment, allow your mind to feel blissful, and permit your face to feel the smile that naturally occurs when you follow your bliss.

Write down all the things you feel when you *follow your bliss*. What is one thing that you can do today to follow that joy?

I feel that merely to meditate on compassion is to take the passive option. Our meditation should form the basis for action, for seizing the opportunity to do something.

His Holiness the Dalai Lama

Being proactive is the natural compliment to mediation, as The Dalai Lama so poignantly observes. The world is in need of active peacemakers and conflict practitioners. Precise images and clarity of thought comes to us in meditation. The road becomes clear. If we do not wish to leave the state of happiness and comfort caused by the inner peace of a meditative life, then we cannot use the gifts that we have been given to make the world a better place. Our circle of influence is wider than we sometimes think it is. Wayne Dyer noted in his series for PBS, *Inspiration,* to be in the room with one who exudes love and acceptance is joyful and uplifting to the spirit. Resonance is improved in that circle of influence. To be in the room with those who bring low energy with them, makes one want to run. Have you ever been with someone who totally drained you? It can often make one want to flee. But to run from those souls does nothing to raise the consciousness of the planet, does nothing to improve our ability to see another's point of view, does nothing to influence peace. It is important to note that letting others drain you is a choice, easily missed, but a choice none the less. Those souls are the ones which we should bring up with us, the ones we must force ourselves to stand with in the room. To be able to raise their vibrational energy is a matter of protecting your own, while letting the force of your essence shine brightly in the face of darkness. They are lost. Use your influence on the path, circle back and give them the choice to see a different reality. Then be willing to go forth without them. A higher power will handle the rest.

Meditation today should begin with the word "influence." In stillness, just be…accept your calling to be proactive when you are complete…

Write down three ways that you can influence your path today.

*The ordinary acts we practice every day at home are of more
importance to the soul than their simplicity might suggest.*

Thomas Moore

Staying close to home can be a very spiritual experience. In the simplicity of performing the everyday tasks of living, we nurture ourselves and kindle the fire of a warm hearth. Making a pot of tea, working in the garden, reading in a favorite corner, or putting photos of the children in albums are all accomplishments "du jour." I find that when I have ventured forth in the world of frenetic activity. I must come back to home plate and touch base. I am soothed by classical music, spiritual music, soft jazz, and opera. I love to gaze toward the western horizon in the late evening and see the sun settle behind the mountains. I also need internal time to be alone and take inventory of my musings throughout the day. It seems the older I get, the more downtime I need. Maybe the adrenalin chip in my computer is getting weary. Puttering around the house makes me feel grounded. The simplicity of grabbing the dogs and taking an afternoon hike is so replenishing to my spirit that it immediately restores me. What are the simple things that soothe your soul? What can you do in simplicity for your spirit?

Meditation today is the first act of "simplicity." Agree to sit in stillness and float into nowhere.

Write down in your journal one simple date that you can keep with yourself this week. Will you go to the nursery, hike, sit in the library, attend a concert?

We are the music makers,
And we are the dreamers of dreams…
Yet we are the movers and shakers
Of the world forever it seems.
We, in the ages lying,
In the buried past of the earth,
Built Nineveh with our signing,
And Babel itself with our mirth;
And o'erthrew them with prophesying
To the old of the new world's worth;
For each age is a dream that is dying or one that is coming to birth.

Arthur William Edgar O'Shaugnessy, *Ode*

O'Shaugnessy wrote this poem in the 19th century. I chose this quotation especially for this topic because it represents to me many theories of science. Not only does the poem embody the theories of creativity, complexity, and chaos, it also addresses systemic and quantum theories. A circular process draws connections to the images that I see in my mind's eye when I hear this poem. I think "For each age is a dream that is dying or one that is coming to birth" is our true reality. Quantum theory tells us that all energy in the universe is conserved. Quantum physics tell us that all matter can be broken down at its smallest level into holons (Wilber) and that energy moves in a wavelike fashion, a sea of chaotic movement. We are part of that energy. As interventionists, we can tap into the common energy of uncertainty and through creative movement toward the center of a conflict, work with the complexities present and the chaos of the system to bring the parties into a transforming resolution. We are the rank and file, the army of *movers and shakers* of this planet, the *music makers* of the new song for the dance. We are part of the solution, of the quantum reality, and believe that as boundaries collapse, a new age comes to birth.

Human beings, vegetables, or cosmic dust, we all dance to a mysterious
tune, intoned by the distance by an invisible player.

Albert Einstein

Meditation today should begin with the phrase "quantum thought." Feel the energy course through every cell of your body, feel the resistance of your body in your effort to be still…float in the cosmic energy of the waves of the sea of change…

As your brain draws connections toward the center of your conscious mind, write down how you see yourself as a part of the system of energy in which you live and work.

Rune of St. Patrick

At Tara today in this fateful hour,
I place all Heaven with its power,
And in the Sun with its brightness, and in the snow with its whiteness,
And fire with all the strength it hath, and lightening with its rapid wrath,
And the winds with their swiftness along the path, and the sea with its deepness,
And the rocks with their steepness, and the earth with its starkness:
All these I place by God's almighty help and grace,
Between myself and the powers of the darkness.

Ancient Celtic Prayer

The Rune of St. Patrick was written in the 5th Century. The ancient mystics had an extraordinary view of the world in which they lived. The ancient mystics drew often upon nature and its power when embracing the fullness of their existence. I think the mighty power of darkness has perhaps been harmfully embellished over the ages. Over time, the metaphor of a devil, or fallen angel as mythological, has become a literal interpretation for many. I feel that this literalism has served to move us farther apart from a relationship to a higher power, as it implies we helplessly lay in the shadow between the power struggle of an omnipotent God and Satan. This is not a choice that leaves me with a warm feeling. In this prayer, St. Patrick summoned his strength and aligned himself with the power of nature but against what fateful hour? I think the *fateful hour* is the hour of choice. The power of choosing is a moment-by-moment occurrence. My beliefs are that I enjoy free agency. God has endowed every human with free agency, the power to choose. The power of darkness symbolizes to me the choice of alignment with the ego not the choice of love and sharing that heaven signifies. When faced with the choices of your reality, what powers do you summon to provide sustenance for the journey between the ego and the love?

Meditation today should begin with the words "higher power." What meaning to you assign to those words?

Write down the feelings that come up when you contemplate a relationship with a higher power. If you choose to deepen that relationship, what can you do today to that end?

To aspire and attain to this you must recognize that you have, by nature, the requisite ability within and then cultivate those qualities which will let it develop.

Ernest Holmes

Self-worth is an easy concept to understand, but is it far more difficult to actualize than most are willing to admit. All of us have areas in which we are confident of our abilities and other areas in which we are blinded to our true worth. I think that few attain true comfort with worthiness. Perhaps it is our culture or our internal tape of negativity that scrolls continuously through our minds. Sarah Ban Breathnach in *Simple Abundance,* recommended to the reader that a daily record of gratitude is necessary for one to truly access self-worth. When we look for and recognize our gratitude for the worth of events, things, or people, we can more readily see worth in our own journey. Ernest Holmes, author of *Science of Mind* reminded us to realize that worthiness is part of our natural set of abilities and that focus on the cultivation of those qualities results in esteem of the self. He noted that one need only remember that fact for the process to unfold. What parts of your personality do you not value? In what areas do you lack a feeling of worthiness? Goethe suggested that a necessary quality for achievement is to hold yourself in higher esteem that you currently envision. To positively envision a high level of worth causes it to become reality.

For a man to achieve all that is demanded of him he must regard himself as greater than he is.

Johann Wolfgang von Goethe

Meditation today should begin with the word "self-worth." As you agree to become still this morning embrace all the qualities of your being...realize that your journey has brought you to the perfect place for discovery...

Make a list of the areas of worth that you recognize about yourself today. Make it a long one.

Hear me four quarters of the world – a relative I am!
Give me the strength to walk the soft earth,
A relative to all that is!
Give me the eyes to see and the strength to understand
That I may be like you…
Great Spirit, Great Spirit, my Grandfather,
All over the earth the faces of living things are all alike.
With tenderness have these come up out of the ground.
Look upon these faces of children without number
And with children in their arms
That they may face the winds and walk the good road
To the day of quiet.

Black Elk, Medicine Man, Ogallala Sioux Nation

Native American traditions have embedded in their memory a natural congruence with the earth and the elements. For centuries, they were taught by their elders to understand a connection with all things, to embrace their spiritual path, to value their children. In Western cultures, there seems to be such a separation from the planet. We appear to be much more involved in acquiring than conservation. It also appears to me there is a pervasive emptiness in the hearts of our people, running frantically in search for the unknown. In comparison, members of native cultures more readily accept their place in relation to the earth, feel more at home in nature, and gather sustenance from oneness with the land. In his prayer, the great leader, Black Elk sought strength to stay connected to all that was dear to him. I think this is evidence that staying connected is hard work for all people, regardless of their enculturation, and connection must be cultivated in daily life. In this way, native cultures are much like Buddhist and other Oriental cultures, who understand the necessity for strength in the journey. To "walk the good road to the day of quiet" speaks to me of the quest for peace, to *walk the good road to peace.* Are you connected to something? Do you feel congruent with your world?

Mediation today should begin with the word "congruence." Breathe deeply in the tranquil air of morning…do feel that your spirit is melding with our environment? Feel connected to your body, connected to your breathing…connected to your soul…

Make a record of the images in your meditations. Identify one thing that you can do today to feel more congruence with your world.

For my thoughts are not your thoughts, neither are your ways my ways.

Isaiah 55:8

Leonardo da Vinci wrote that all knowledge has its origin in our perception; all of the knowledge, in perception? Now that is a powerful statement. It says that all knowledge is subjective, open to interpretation. If there is one thing I teach clients every session, it is to imagine for a moment that there is no *truth*, no black and white. There are only shades of gray and differences in perception, divergences in their current reality, and that they are locked in conflict. This awareness, that all knowledge is subject to interpretation, is the doorway to understanding. The key to success in intractable conflict is to coach people to be able to agree on that, if just for a moment. Now this is easier to do when reshaping another's reality, but when faced with choices of interpretation in our own lives, it gets a little more difficult. Our lens of perception is locked in the same room with attribution and meaning. As we assign value to incoming data we are subjectively interpreting that data. Our analytical mind is a judging machine, and we lace the interpretation with triggers of fear and early historical experience. Consider for a moment how difficult it is for us to successfully view a situation with a different perspective; this allows us to have empathy for the triggers and perceptions of our clients. Toward that end, review your perception about a significant relationship; it may be at work, a familial relationship, or a love interest. Think about how you could view that person differently. What would it take?

Meditation today should begin with the words "subjective interpretation." What does your mind's eye see as you go within this morning? Cleanse your lens of awareness with each breath and with intention see a different view.

Write down in your journal one area of your life that you can interpret in a different way. Can you change the way you view one thing today? Don't worry about whether it makes sense to you, just do it. See how it feels to imagine one person in a different light. Example: "I wish would be more loving." Change the perception... "_is more loving, I just can't see it yet." Now ask, "What would it take for me to actually hold this perception? How would that person look to me if I could see them as more loving? What would they be doing? What would I be doing?" Write down your answers.

Nan Waller Burnett

True genius resides in the capacity for evaluation of uncertain,
hazardous, and conflicting information.

Winston Churchill

This quotation makes me think of the task set before a skilled mediator. A mediator must create a space through which the creative act can emerge and solutions can find their way to fruition. In my view, field independence is another requirement for genius in the practice of a mastermind. A requirement for the mastermind in peacemaking and one that is risky is the ability to stand with the strength of self while evaluating uncertainty in intractable conflict. Those who are unwilling to risk cannot let the ideas flow from the unknown source of genius. The mastermind gives birth to ideas every time a selection of question is made. Transforming conflict professionals are of this same stock; the stock of genius, of willingness, of possibility, and of imagination, the mind of a master of the trade. They are the artists of opportunity.

Meditation today should begin with the words "the mastermind." Breathe in the exciting air of your personal genius...agree to let the risk of this moment fill your mind with creation; the creation of opportunity and the development of your mastermind.

Write down one way that you can bring your skills and artistry forth today. How can you create through imagination, a possibility for development of the mastermind that did not exist yesterday?

A visionary is one who can find his way by moonlight, and
see the dawn before the rest of the world.

Oscar Wilde

To hold a vision of something not-yet-realized is a gift. Visionaries begin with the end in mind. They hold the possibility of solutions, which the conflicted cannot envision. A visionary is one who knows of the rising sun, when the clients can only see darkness.

Ken Wilber is one visionary of our time. His writings about classification, psychology, spirit, and philosophy are extraordinary. Reading Ken Wilber's works is a journey through an astonishing reality. His is an exceptional mind, and he presents ideas with remarkable vision and clarity. His extraordinary writing began in his early 20s, exhibiting an unusual ability to extrapolate information others have not mastered after decades of living. By 40, he had published multiple volumes of brilliant work. I think there are many ordinary people who have visionary talents, perhaps not as stark as Wilber's but the ability to display and hold a vision for others so that solutions can more readily be seen. Beginning with the end in mind, they hold the possibility for solutions which envision collaboration that the conflicted cannot see. One who holds the vision of the rising sun, when the clients can only see darkness.

Meditation today should begin with the word "vision." Pay attention to the visions that arise in the breathing of the morning...let your mind see the possibilities, the opportunities in the early morning...

What visions came to you in meditation? Write down the vision of the day. Check your writings from the morning this evening for accuracy. Write another sentence or two about the day.

United your resolve, united your hearts,
May your spirits be at one,
That you may long dwell
in unity and concord.

Rig Veda

I love this quotation. This Hindu prayer is so simple in its application, so succinct in words, it sounds like music to my ears when I repeat it. I usually say a prayer of cleansing before I meet with clients. The prayer asks my higher power to allow me to clear my mind of the noise and chatter of my own reality, so that I can be present for those whom I assist. "That you may long dwell in unity and concord" is such a beautiful request for the future of a relationship, business or personal. The antonym is disarray, the condition in which people in conflict find themselves when they arrive at our offices. What about the unity in your own life? If you are peaceful in your life, why do you think that is so? If you are in disarray, what needs to be returned to your heart? What do you need to return to inner peace? What choices can you make that allow your spirit to be as one?

Meditation today should begin with the word "unity." Draw the unison of breath into both lungs...breathe deeply into your soul and feel complete...agree to float with the word unity this morning...

Write down in your journal a few lines about unity and what the word means to you. Are you in disarray or concordance? Where is the unity in your life?

A diamond must be cut before its light can shine out.

Harzart Khan

Challenges lie in front of us with every breath. As we arrive in this existence, we are the beauty of the rough-cut diamond: pure in content, a veil of mystery upon our crown. As we develop, the world we know often further clouds our brilliance instead of enhancing it. We are taught fear to protect us. We are taught to struggle for everything. We are taught to protect our interests, our hearts, and our creations. We are taught the rules and regulations for living, and to color within the lines. Religious education is often laden with guilt-ridden messages intended to control behavior. All this mapping and programming causes many of us never learn who we really are. Many of us never develop our creative intelligence, our spirit, or our ability to love for the sake of loving. When we choose to embrace the challenges of each day, we surrender to a higher creative source. To surrender allows the softness of the jeweler's cloth to buff out the rough edges and bring forth our brilliance. We discover we are meant for love, for greatness, and to improve the condition of our lives, our home, and our world.

Meditation today should begin with the word "challenge." Surrender this day to brilliant and beautiful essence of who you are. Become willing to move toward each breath of resistance and surrender to the deep folds of your body.

Write down the challenges that you see in front of you today. How do you surrender to your innate beauty and brilliance?

If you wish to make an apple pie from scratch, you must first create the universe.

Carl Sagan

Although it is difficult to face a mountain-sized problem, determination can bring creative solutions to fruition. To be resolute in staying 'in the moment' is the kind of determination necessary to create the universe. When we choose to see how abundant life is, resources are created. When we choose to love and move into each other, rather than withhold in fear and recoil, we draw love into our universe. It takes a great deal of determination to climb that mountain, but in reality after the first decision and take the first step, the rest simply becomes part of the apple pie.

I was once working with a colleague who I sensed was wired with a minefield of carefully buried triggers. My intuitive reaction was harsh; to withdraw and protect myself from the explosion. In that moment, I made a decision to move forward in the *sizing up* dance that seemed to be in play instead. Miraculous energy surrounded the situation and after trust was installed as a foundation of our work, we moved forward together with creative collaboration. We're creating apple pies from scratch!

Meditation today should begin with the word "determination." Have determination to stay connected to your breath and to your body this morning. Be resolute in your effort to float among the lilies of the field.

Write in your journal of one instance where you can remember the choice to move forward instead of recoil. What area of your life is in need of determination today?

To practice properly the Art of Peace, you must: Calm the spirit and
return to the source, cleanse the body and spirit by removing all malice,
selfishness and desire. Be ever grateful for the gifts received from the
Universe, your family, Mother Nature, and your fellow human beings.

Morihei Ueshiba, founder of Aikido

Tom Crum wrote *"The Magic of Conflict"* in the 1990s. He described the art of Aikido, one of the martial arts, as a dance of conflict, but with a very different outcome. He outlined the process of training the mind and body together to perceive conflict in a new light. Energy rearrangement is also part of that art; alignment of positive energy to reflect back negative energy, used to transform the pair of dualists. This is a powerful concept: ground the energy to the earth to cleanse the soul and transform.

An injury to my neck in the early 1990s caused a sad retreat from my very active body. I had to learn to respect the limitations of my injury, yet vowed not to have the injury own me. This was a delicate balance of care of pain vs. ignoring the pain. I was angry for many years about my otherwise healthy body being permanently altered. I chose to cleanse my anger by making peace with the injury and instead considered the ensuing experience as a gift and a blessing. The neurosurgeon's treatment plan did not appeal to me in the least and would have left a significant scar. My choice proved to be a positive one; now, 14 years later, I have a manageable injury that lets me know when I've not relaxed my body enough. I refuse live in the consciousness of the impaired. Instead, it's rather like living in the South with mosquitoes- a permanent fixture in the landscape, you just accept them, shoo them away, and get on with your life.

Meditation today should begin with a deep breath of cleansing peace. Focus on the words "engaging anger." Exhale the tension of anger held in the memory of your body...choose anger as a friend of information and the opportunity to choose again.

Write down your thoughts in free form about anger. How do you use anger? What is one thing that you can do differently today to release anger from your body?

The coming of the Messiah does not depend upon anything supernatural;
rather it depends upon human growth and transformation when people
realize that the Messiah is not someone other than themselves.

The Baal Shem Tov

We are our own savior. How profound! The above quote from the Jewish scriptures teaches the reader that one must grow and be transformative in their approach to life. *We* must be our savior in this world. We must be proactive and not passive in the nature of our work and of our life. I chose the above quote because it reminds me of a joke I once heard from my dear Jewish friend, Milton. Abie went to Synagogue every Saturday without fail. When he would pray in earnest, the request went something like this, "Lord, it is Abie, your faithful servant. I have been to your house every Saturday and I keep the commandments, please Lord, help me win the lottery." Nothing. No response. Undeterred, Abie would return to the Synagogue every Saturday and repeat the prayer. Nothing. No response. Many fruitless Saturdays later, he bowed his head in deep prayer and implored the Lord to help him win the lottery. Dejected, Abie arose, the last one in the Synagogue and as he began to leave, the Lord spoke to him. "Abie... help me out, buy a ticket." I love this story. Although wonderfully humorous, it reminds us that it is imperative we do our part. We must prepare the way for our success, our spirituality, our life through love and action. As we accept this calling, we are transformed. When we agree to grow, we do become our own messiah, our own savior.

Meditation today should begin with the word "profound." Thoughtfully breathe through the outer reaches of you body and search for the wisdom today that you need to meditate with...

In your journal today write one thing that you can do today to be proactive in your life. How can you be your own savior?

Whatever we are waiting for...peace of mind, contentment, grace,
the inner awareness of simple abundance—it will surely come to us,
but only when we are ready to receive it with an open heart.

Sarah Ban Breathnach, *Simple Abundance*

The first step in building a holistic practice is putting yourself first. When we don our own oxygen mask first, before rushing into the conflict with oxygen for others, we ensure that we will be present for all of life. When we are whole, we have the gifts of attention, clarity, love, respect, and inquiry for ourselves as well as for others. The willingness to receive abundance, grace, contentment, and inner peace allows us to reveal to others that potential in them, the opportunities that may be present in their portfolio of possibility. To shift others from problem focus to solution focus and to hold that sacred space open for engagement in a respectful and honoring manner, is a gift of immeasurable worth to those entrenched in the pain of dispute. If we have been drawn to this work, we must make the choice for holistic practice or we cannot survive long enough to be successful in our endeavor. We need to be willing to learn to trust our instincts, to establish a strong bubble, a boundary of protection, to care for ourselves before we help others, to develop our intuition, and to learn how to be compassionate with ourselves. These tasks are only possible if we make time for them every single day. What can you do today to commit to yourself?

Meditation today should begin with the word "care." Go into your heart this morning with the arms of forgiveness and the agreement to provide the sustenance you need for your journey.

Write one thing in your journal that you can do today to develop a holistic practice.

*Therefore you must always keep in mind that a path is only a path; if you feel
you should not follow it, you must not stay with it under any conditions...
Does this path have a heart? If it does, the path is good; if it doesn't, it is of no
use. Both paths lead nowhere; but one has a heart, the other doesn't. One makes
for a joyful journey; as long as you follow it, you are one with it. The other will
make you curse your life. One makes you strong; the other weakens you.*

Carlos Casteneda

When I approached my 40s, I began to look to the meaning of my life. My professional career was not one that made the best use of the gifts that God gave to me. My children would soon be ready for their own flight. What did I see as meaningful beyond that of raising extraordinary children? What would be left as a record of my life? What work would be a labor of passion? I wanted to leave the planet a better place than I had found it. A student of history, I believed my history professor when he said that empires rarely survive 200 years. Realizing that America had passed the benchmark, I was drawn to the engagement of conflict. Our diverse planet has many more similarities than differences, but conflict seemed prevalent. I thought, "there has to be a better way to co-exist, to live without fear, to embrace the joy." I began to move forward without a clear plan. But a path appeared, one that resonated in my heart and soul. I had missed so much of my life looking down at the road in fear of falling. I wanted to see the view. Choice appears in the distance as we approach every decision. I have learned to welcome the fork in the path without fear. I look for clues in the periphery. What door has opened? What window is shut? Who has walked into my life recently? Why are they here? What lesson is this bringing me? Does this feel right? Does this path have a heart? Will it make me strong?

Meditation today should begin with a vision of divergence on your path. Take in the beauty of the landscape. Feel the sound of your heart calling to you, quietly rumbling in your soul. In your stillness, do not be afraid to see what is newly planted and find the path that calls to your heart.

Write down the images that came to you in meditation. What is presenting itself to you this day? Who has entered your life? What is one thing that you can do today to be clear about the path with a heart?

Let the honor of the student be as dear to you as your own, and the honor of your colleague be like the reverence due to your teacher, and the reverence for your teacher be like the reverence for Heaven.

Philip Birnbaum, *Daily Prayer Book: Ha-Siddur Ha-Shalem*

If we treat others with respect, even if our critical mind does not think that they deserve it, how would our daily experience of others be changed? The quote above is the golden rule repackaged. To treat others with respect, then respect will be returned to us in immeasurable honor. I once taught a workshop where I was accosted verbally about a point of view by one of the men in the group. I was taken by surprise but explained what I meant, dismissed it, and then went on with my training. In the next few minutes it happened again. I sensed that he clearly had an issue with the training, either in the way I was presenting it, or with me. I had to make a decision, as I was feeling my walls of protection activating; my force fields went up. Again, I sidestepped the disruption and waited for the right moment to be proactive. Finally, it was time for a break. He remained in his seat as the room cleared. I went over to him and with great respect and a little humor, I asked him if I reminded him of his ex-wife. He got the inference and immediately moved to dispel any appearance of malice. I apologized to him for unintentionally offending him in someway and he also apologized to me for having taken such a strong position of the topic, stating that he had forgotten *he was not in charge of the workshop.* Our respectful conversation allowed him up to make the self-observation that perhaps he thinks he should be in charge all the time. We traded understandings and mutual respect. In that moment, he transformed and offered me great respect the rest of the day. How can you use the Jewish tradition of "honoring the student" in your personal relationships?

Meditation today should begin with the word "honor." As you become silent and feel the morning air pass through you, notice how your lungs honor your body. Honor your humanness...respect your soul and your innate goodness...

Write in your journal about honoring yourself. What are some ways that you can feel that self-respect? How can you honor another today?

Who are the learned? They who practice what they know.

The Prophet Mohammed

The Koran details the life of Mohammed. I think in addition to the ethic of practicing what we preach, this passage also speaks to the ability to influence those around us. By practicing what we know, we exert a great deal of influence on our environment. Daniel Bowling, in his article "Bringing Peace into The Room," noted that in order to truly be effective in our role as conflict interventionists, we must cultivate the quality of presence. Through presence, we are able to work in the sacred space of conflict to more effectively assist the parties in solutions. It means we can increase our ability to influence the situation. Daniel Bowling asserted that if we are learned in our profession, we "must embody that quality of presence and bring all of our personal qualities to the table." We must practice what we know. As The Dalai Lama noted, "Without inner peace, it is impossible to have world peace." Without presence it is not possible to influence the world around us. Think about how you influence the world around you today.

Meditation should begin with the words, "practice what you know." Quietly go to the place in your mind where true meditation can occur...how does thought influence your behavior?

What areas of influence did you recognize in your meditation. How can you use your knowledge today and practice what you know?

It is your work in life that is the ultimate seduction.

Pablo Picasso

Working is my escape from life. I live in my head most of the time, and in this season of my life, relating to others has taken a backseat to creations of the mind. I suspect that I am in a transition, perhaps a dark night of the soul, but I do not naturally search for social interaction. I really miss being social. The femme fatale, a major archetype of mine, played front and center during most of my youth. But I find myself caught between the craving to share fun and the worry that I will be bored to death. In the struggle of choosing one over the other, I miss the present moment. Meditation, for me, has become a metaphor for acceptance, the willingness to welcome whatever shows up before me, no plan, the abandonment of an agenda, and a daily reminder to connect with the real me and not my brain. I also recognize that meditation is permission. In embracing myself, I can embrace other souls with genuine love for them in the moment. In my work, I search for the purpose of my life. Work can be quite seductive. I am so interested in what I am doing, that those in my inner circle who are not in the field don't know where I have escaped to. Review your work habits. Are you overworking?

Meditate today on the word "work." What images come to you? Are you frantic? Let it spiral downward. Are you engaged? Be fluid in your movement toward the center. Are you peaceful? Float in the inner comfort.

Write down or draw the images that came to you in your meditation. Do you see a way out of frantic overwork into a more balanced work life?

Happiness is when what you think, what you say, and what you do are in harmony.

Mahatma Gandhi

As Gandhi noted, personal harmony is complete integration of the mind, body, and soul. When peace is the standard, harmony is easy to maintain. Many times I have craved that feeling of harmony and could not get to the inner peace I so desired. In retrospect, I see that, for the most part, walking the talk is a requirement for true happiness. I once saw a Discovery Channel special about the recent brain research done on Buddhist monks practicing mindfulness meditation. A prevailing happiness and joy on their faces almost made me think they were taking drugs. Once I started to meditate, I began to see why they were happy. I will never have the discipline of a monk and the hours to meditate, but the 15 minutes a day I have to practice has made a tremendous difference in my life and my work. Noise inside the head is common for all of us, but I usually have a choir with no one singing the same tune. Meditation helps me tremendously. I can more easily reflect on that noisy choir and insist all my voices use the same sheet music. I don't really have to work too hard in meditation to achieve this; the agreement to be still naturally results in a sweeter resonance in my head. Meditation allows me to choose harmony easily. Happiness is more a part of my natural behavior now that I work for full integration of my thoughts and my voice. I am walking the talk. Are there areas of your life in which you desire more harmony?

Meditation today should begin with the word "harmony." As you sink into your meditative pose, feel the comfort of your energy in harmony with your thoughts... breathe deeply into the morning with the thought of happiness...

Write in your journal about the feelings that you experienced in the meditation. Were they balanced? List the feelings that arose and think of one thing that you can do differently today to create more harmony and inner peace in your world.

What is a weed ? A plant whose virtues have not yet been discovered.

Ralph Waldo Emerson, *The Fortune of the Republic*

Emerson's words talk about how all elements of creation have positive attributes in the precious ecological balance. But when I read this quote, it reminds me of the most important skill that an intervener can employ: the skill of reframing. Reframing is nothing short of artistry. To be able to paint the dandelion as an exotic wildflower has the potential of changing the entire dynamic in the circle of conflict. One of the most effective qualities of a peacemaker is the skill of posing the right question at the right time. Practice makes perfect in our business, and experience increases our creativity. However, I think it is also acceptable to risk saying the wrong thing in reframing. One concrete metaphor may resonate with one party and not with the other. We can keep trying until something does resonate. When faced with looking at the weeds in our own garden, our vision is more skewed. Discernment is difficult, but to try to see for a moment the point of view God had when creating the weed; it might be okay just not to know.

Meditation today should begin with the word "reframe." What painting in your mind's eye needs a different frame? Breathe in the willingness to venture forth with new perspective...

Write down what areas of your life in need of reframing. List those areas of pain and try today to do one thing that might make the reframing more successful.

Nan Waller Burnett

Every man's work, whether it be literature or music or pictures or anything else, is always a portrait of himself, and the more he tries to conceal himself, the more clearly will his character appear in spite of him.

Samuel Butler

I review my life and think it a pity that I spent so many years of it trying to look good to others. In group therapy in my 30s the therapist said, "You know, you are a Steel Magnolia. The Southern beauty encased in a layer of steel to protect yourself. Why don't you just let it go, until your makeup runs down your face, and risk looking bad for one minute." You guessed it- I was pissed. I never even went to the mailbox without my makeup; I was certainly *not* going to blubber in front of strangers. I masked my emotion and mustered some flip comment back to her in an effort to maintain my composure. But she was persistent and not afraid to risk with me. "You make me sick," she finally retorted. I lost it. I let my tears flow and makeup run until the snot ran down my face. In that moment, I began my journey toward authenticity and learned that I had been an actor in own life up until that moment. She became my mentor and her voice served as my choir until I could finally hear my own. I remember that day as my wake up call to life; the day I stopped trying to conceal my humanness. My portrait was repainted and it took two women. One risking to be the angel to a soul crying for rebirth, the other, risking a masked reputation to answer the call.

Meditation today should begin with the word "reputation." Go deeply inside and be willing to risk removing that beautiful mask that it took so long to create...breathe the cleansing air of support in your lungs; nourish your skin with the flush of forgiveness...

Write today in your journal about how concerned are you with your reputation. How concerned do you need to be? What is the worst thing that would happen to you if you dropped your mask of image and quit making reputation your standard?

The self is the sum of the different roles the person plays.

William James

Identity is not a static property of personality. Reinvention of the self occurs throughout the life span. A loving parent, the ever present friend, a strict disciplinarian, a diligent worker, a grateful child, a creative volunteer, the helpful neighbor, closer of the deal, the maker of dreams, or the self-pitying one who isolates—all are examples of roles and hats we wear at different times in our life. Identity is an ever-changing transformation in the microcosm of personal growth, and occurs every day.

I have always taken issue with the desire of psychology to use the medical model to classify every behavior. It seems self-serving to me. Why do we do this? Only one thing is accomplished; individuals are pigeon-holed into behavior seen as unchanging. In my role as an intervener in conflicted relationships, I can never take the position that a client is in a certain classification of behavior: "Well, they are traumatized." or "He is narcissistic." or "She is a borderline." They all lead to a single assumption: "They will never change." Instead, I stand in the possibility that identity is only a clue to solutions. People can and do have the ability to change. Without that reality, there is no room for transformation. As William James noted, "the self is the sum of the different roles;" a unique creation of energy, matter, and spirit; in short, individuality. Can you embrace your identity as a precious gem of creative conglomerate? If you can, you will have success in the true resolution of conflict.

Mediation today should begin with the word "identity." Clear the air of personal doubt...embrace the unique expression of energy that you are...gather the hats of your life...place each upon your head and encircle the spirit with the tapestry of experience you uniquely embody.

Write down the visions of different hats that came to you in your meditation. Identify how many roles comprise the uniqueness of you. What is one thing that you can do today to give form to those hats, to understand them, and to embrace them?

The first key to wisdom is constant and frequent questioning, for by doubting
we are led to question and by questioning we arrive at the truth.

Peter Abelard

Peter Abelard was a monk in France during the 12th century. He was part of the movement perceived as a great threat to the Catholic Church. A learned man, he saw the key to being wise was in never ceasing to question. It ended up costing him his life. Through his refusal to stop speaking about intellectual freedoms, he became a symbol of the times. The power of his writing is such that it is still widely read today, more than 800 years later. Our personal truth can only be understood through critical thinking and "constant and frequent questioning." Introspection about one's own life brings a clarity that is not present unless we question ourselves relentlessly. It helps us discover the errors of the past that we do not wish to repeat, and to be able to forgive our actions or the actions of others. To question relentlessly leads us to transformation of the self.

Meditation today should begin with the words "question relentlessly." This morning look to the stillness...breathe deeply into the questions...what needs to be realized...what needs to be owned...what needs to be forgiven...

Write down the list of questions that came to you in meditation. Choose one area of your life that you would to review to receive more clarity about this day.

Problems are only opportunities in work clothes.

Henry J. Kaiser

Clients come before us with problem-saturated stories. In the murky waters of discord, they cannot see the clearness of the water. It is necessary to search for clues contained within the client's narrative of the story. We must start the dialogue to address the problem with solution-focused language. Providing a mirror that reflects the possibility of a better future allows the client to feel more hopeful. One day as I prepared for mediation, a woman entered my office heavy with palpable fear. She was 45 minutes early and moved through the door, the heaviness of the dispute evident in her drooping shoulders. Wearing the burdensome coat of a victim, she explained that no one understood her— they all believed her husband. She feared he would get parenting time with their child. He was, after all, manipulative and cunning in his persuasion of the judge, the advocate, and the lawyers, especially hers. Her only hope was that she get to my office first and make me understand the gravity of the situation. She implored that he should not be allowed near her son. Further, she said, "He has chosen to leave me and no one wants to make him pay!"

After explaining to her the nature of my role, I gathered my wits about me. Although tempted to slip her into the category of 'client from hell,' I made a different choice. I took a risk, and with empathy I moved toward her. I softly asked, "Tell me what happened to you, sweetheart?" She momentarily hesitated; unsure of what to say next. "Well I just did!" she replied, and started to recant how all of her life others had tried to overpower her. I stopped her in mid sentence and said, "No, that is not what I meant. I meant what happened to you when you were young that would cause you to want to keep a child from his father?" The floodgates opened. Forty minutes of grief and sadness poured from her abandoned heart. The release of hysterical divorce trauma deflated her rage and allowed her clarity to come forth. No one had ever called her on her tirades; they all had tried to contain it, not really listening to the cries from within. The professionals at that table saw a very different person that day. She was willing to drop the drama and love her child enough to let a part of him go. In that release, she loved herself, maybe for the first time.

Problem saturated stories can be converted into opportunities but it takes hard work and a great deal of risk. When your own life is in review, can you see past the murky waters of problems to the clear water? How do you help your clients see problems as "opportunities in work clothes?"

....

In meditation today, transform the weight of "problem" into the lightness of "opportunity." In each breath release the problem …with each breath, inhale the clarity of the waters of opportunity…

Make a list of your problems from yesterday's memory. Shred them. Make a new list of opportunities you have for today. Make at least one of them a reality.

Nan Waller Burnett

If you practice an art, be proud of it and make it proud of you. It may break your heart,
but it will fill your heart before it breaks it; it will make you a person in your own right.

Maxwell Anderson

Ken Cloke's article, "Why Every Conflict Breaks Your Heart," has a powerful proposal to the conflict practitioner. He notes in the ACResolutions Magazine, Fall 2005, that every dispute is a spiritual crisis at the source. He wrote to the deeper part of the practitioner's being: to understand conflict as a calling; to handle conflict from a more mysterious, intense level of compassion; and, to build accord from a higher place. He presents the role of peacemaker and conflict practitioner as a sacred role of creative intervention. He proposes one only need to be willing to perceive conflict from a different perspective and work with compassionate attention. As Maxwell Anderson says above, your artistry "may break your heart, but it will fill your heart before it breaks it…[and then] make you a person in your own right."

Through the selection of questions that empower, to the intuitive sacredness of each reframe, the genius of communication shines through in every soul who agrees to sit with presence with other souls who are rapt with pain and drowning in fear. If you are willing to go to their hell with them in every instance, you will be the artist who leads them from the self-imposed prison of skewed perception to the clarity of understanding. In that act of willingness, you will be made a stronger person in your own right.

Meditation today should begin with the phrase "artist of caring." Today in the stillness of the morning, agree to search for the artist that you already are, the creativity of you. With each breath push away the haze of doubt and accept the creative energy waiting for your purpose.

In your journal, write down the evidence of artistry that has already made you who you are. If a conflict has broken your heart write about it.

The curious paradox is that when I accept myself just as I am, then I can change.

Carl Rogers

Carl Rogers was the father of humanism in the field of psychology. He changed the way that practitioners perceived their patients and the normal transitions of life. Patients became clients. The entire field of mental health morphed into a new system— a holistic view of the human-being, not the medical model from the Freudian era. Rogers' main thesis is open embrace and complete acceptance of the clients, in a positive affirmation of humanness, allows change to unfold naturally. Just thinking about how I used to run my life always looking for more information, a better way to do things, more efficient ways of ticking off the list of life, in order to become improved... it wears me out. The paradox is that acceptance must come first before change. I'm not suggesting that improvement is a negative quality, but perhaps the agreement to just be and to accept the what is of life, brings illumination and transformation before any act of improvement can kick in. Do nothing and change will follow: a paradoxical hypothesis for certain!

Meditation today should begin with the word "paradox." Breathe into the confusion... breathe out the misinformation in the midst of clear thought...embrace the paradox of life...accept yourself first...change will follow.

Write in your journal today of the paradoxical issues in your life. Can you choose one paradox to embrace today?

The world has achieved brilliance without conscience. Ours
is a world of nuclear giants and ethical infants.

General Omar Nelson Bradley, 1893-1981

The accuracy of this statement by World War II army hero, General Omar Nelson Bradley, is striking. A technology as frightening as anyone could have ever imagined torched an entire region of Japan, maiming and imprinting a nation for generations. Worry for the future of the planet came to him in that moment. Gen. Bradley's words speak to an urgency to gather our ethical considerations and review them in earnest before proceeding. Are we still ethical infants? The unfortunate state of world affairs would certainly suggest that. We, as peacemakers, must put ourselves in a position to affect change on a world stage. I suggest that we have a higher calling to fulfill and a sacred energy is moving through those who answer the call. Our brilliance is recalling its conscience. Every time that we reach an accord for those in pain, we contribute to the collective consciousness of positive energy and make a real difference to change the "ethical infancy" status of the world.

Meditation today should begin with the word "ethics." Sit with the thought of ethics, not in the pejorative way, but in an inquiring manner...breathe in the brilliance of the morning and combine the two in unison and purpose...

How can you improve your personal and professional ethics today? How can you undertake your practice with the intent of raising the ethical bar on a case by case basis?

Life can only be understood backwards, but it must be lived forwards.

Søren Kierkegaard

Wouldn't it be wonderful if we could live backwards? Well, maybe not. However, it would take the guess work out of it! Life feels scary when trust is the missing element of living life in the forward mode. If we could only trust that perfect events will unfold exactly as they should, then understanding would be in place from the beginning. Envision knowing that you are performing exactly as you should be for the lessons that need to come to you today; knowing that as you look in the rear view mirror, you had executed actions that were flawless for the situation. These would bring you peace, would they not? You are exactly where you need to be. Welcome the comfort that comes from living in this very moment. Your life is perfect, your actions are correct, you are living in the moment of now— the only moment there is.

Meditation today should begin with the words, "looking in the rear view mirror"...in your mind's eye, encircle the now of this day with new awareness. Breathe deeply through your body and into the floor...feel the air fill your lungs with perfection...you cannot do anything wrong today...

Write in your journal the thoughts that came to you while you were in meditation...if you feel error this day, know that it is perfect...where is the lesson? Feel gratitude for the perfect lesson.

When you close your doors, and make darkness within, remember never to say that you are alone, for you are not alone; nay, God is within, and your genius is within.

Epictetus

I think it is wise to "close your doors" often and spend time with spirit. But, sometimes we shut our doors in shame or isolate ourselves to avoid letting others know we are in a dark place of depression. In those times, to know we are never truly alone is a comforting thought. Genius, for me, was the decision to embrace life; to have wisdom of the heart. When I look back, I now realize that most of my genius was called forth in times of darkness and despair. In the early years post-divorce, each day felt like, in some way, my children were compromised. It was a hellish experience. Above all else, I have a maternal nature. Nothing is more important to me than the health and well-being of my children. I sought solace in counseling. My therapist said to me, "Stand tall Nan and know that you are their mother. Love them and do not be afraid to show them who you really are. They will love you for your courage." It took over 10 years for me to know that she was right. During that time, I had no choice but to trust that certainly I was not alone. Had it not been for that experience, I would not have the deep faith that I have now. Their father has changed over the years too. I now realize that his behavior during that time was based in his fear of losing them.

My work is a passion of the heart, but has become my wisdom of the heart. I intimately know the fear, anger and doubt my clients are living with. I can stand beside them, without flinching, because I too know the walls in that room. My wisdom of the heart was brought out past the depths of pain. Is there a painful room where you go? If you look closely you will see that your spirit is melding with your higher power and as Epictetus wrote in the 1st Century you will find your 'genius within'. Find the wisdom in your heart. Wisdom of the heart provides an opportunity to call the genius forward but may be lost if we remain in the consciousness of darkness as dreadful.

Meditation today should begin with the word "genius." Breathe a cleansing breath and agree to sink down into the depths of the darkness to discover your spirit...

Write in your journal the images that came to you when you were in deep thoughtful meditation. Do you have peace? Can you go to the darkness and know that you are never alone?

A good relationship has a pattern like a dance and is built on some of the same rules. The partners do not need to hold on tightly, because they move confidently in the same pattern, intricate but gay and swift and free, like a country dance of Mozart's. To touch heavily would be to arrest the pattern and freeze the movement, to check the endlessly changing beauty of its unfolding. There is no place here for the possessive clutch, the clinging arm, the heavy hand; only the barest touch in passing. Now arm in arm, now face to face, now back to back — it does not matter which. Because they know they are partners moving to the same rhythm, creating a pattern together, and being invisibly nourished by it.

Anne Morrow Lindbergh, *Gift from the Sea*

What a beautiful image of the dance of life! Anne Lindbergh wrote with great clarity on the realities of dancing within the vortex of human energy. Often, in relationship, we cling too tightly and arrest the pattern, constraining the creativity, altering the beauty of any moment. As we get older, the comfort of sharing life with that partner allows more fluidity, more individualism, and more creation. Perhaps the fear of the unknown is lessened. Possibly, as it matures, the ego becomes less greedy. The invisible nourishment of the soul increases as the dance occurs, an embodiment of sacred creation, so rare and yet limitless allowing the true nature of a person to unfold. To hold onto too tight to the euphoria of physical love results in forgetting the spirit of the person contained within the physical body. Can you envision the dance of the relationship as a rhythm of two lives unfolding?

Meditation today should begin with the words "rhythm of dance." Feel the cadence of your breath rhythmically moving in and out of your lungs...feel the constant beat of your heart providing a percussion of symphonic harmony...allow your breath to flow in your mind...

Take an inventory of relationships that are on your journey at this moment. Which dances are fluid and free? Which are difficult and mechanical? What is one thing that you can do today to embrace more fluidity in that difficult relationship?

The more compassionate you are, the more generous you can be. The more
generous you are, the more loving-friendliness you cultivate to help the world.

Thich Nhat Hanh

Generosity is not merely a conscious choice; it is a natural behavior of the heart. To be generous speaks to abundance. Sharing things close to your heart, such as books, food, or a peaceful place is one of the great joys of an abundant life and practice. If you choose work because of the monetary nature of things, you will live only in the consciousness of attainment. We spread what we share with others: if we spread love, we receive it; if we spread compassion, we receive it; if we spread our gifts with generosity, we receive generously; we receive what we are willing to give. Abundance is a natural by-product of generosity. Abundance is a natural cause-and-effect of love, compassion, and generosity.

Compassionate generosity is a direct result of heart-work. Heart-work is a decision to exercise a moment-by-moment choice to see the world in a different light. In heart-work, the more you practice with generosity, the more work you create, the more abundance you feel, the more joy to enjoy. Look to this day with generosity.

Meditation today should begin with the word "generosity." Fill your lungs with the air of cleansing love and open your heart to the work of the soul. Ask for energy to separate from the ego mind and join with the spirit...breathe deeply and be generous with yourself...feel your worthiness deeply in your soul.

Write in your journal all the ways that you were generous with others last week. List all the acts of kindness, compassion, generosity. How can you be more generous with yourself today?

The greater the danger for most of us lies not in setting our aim too high and
falling short; but in setting our aim too low, and achieving our mark.

Michelangelo Buonarroti

Michelangelo spent years on rough scaffolding in the rotunda of the Sistine Chapel, shaking against the forces of gravity to hold his arms up to pour his genius onto it's ceiling, to coax the visions of a heavenly existence out of his brilliant mind. He remarked that he did not sculpt the David out of the marble; rather, the David was always there, entombed in a sarcophagus of Carrera marble, waiting to be freed. It has been said that artists achieve greatness through the medium of pain. The Renaissance was a period of great freedom and great pain for the masters. It is hard to imagine, when studying the brilliance of his artistic mind, that Michelangelo ever doubted himself or his work. He was, in fact, quite tormented with achieving his mark. Never fully satisfied with the results of his work, he fought depression and perfection his entire life. When we set our aim too low and we hit the target, complacency can set in and cause us to languish unproductively. Most of my early years were spent aiming too low. I did not agree to a journey of transformation because it sounded fun. I began the journey born of great pain, fear, and depression. Since I have agreed to say yes to the results of my choices, I stand amazed at the breadth of the target. What about achievement in your life? Are you enjoying the results you desire?

Meditation today should begin with the word "results." Go deeply into breath with the search for discovery in your life...breathe out the cloudy uncertainty...breathe in the clarity of purpose you desire...

What would you like to do next? What results are you looking for? Journal about the results you desire today.

A relationship of trust is shaped in the primal ambivalence of love and hate.

Sam Keen

When working in the area of interpersonal conflicts or business conflicts often we encounter the poison of the heart. Relationship poison is the alchemy of love and hate acted out in a negatively intimate dance of anger and pain. Many couples come to us in deep intra-psychic pain, which taints every relationship of which they are a part. They mirror a hatred for themselves and project misdirected poison onto the other. How is it possible to go from poison to trust? Humans are reaction machines and rarely understand when they are locked in such a predictable and repetitive system. Understanding human dynamics is important if you hope for transformation of the conflict. I go a little further. I want transformation of the relationship. I would have to achieve transformation if I have the goal of trust.

The antithesis of trust is fear. Fear must come down if trust is to rise. Fear can only be handled through inspection and dissection of the emotions and triggers which cause fear. A skilled artist of conflict engagement accomplishes this task through questioning, digging deep within the triggers to the heart of the pain, to make concrete for the other the clear intention and not the reaction. In Wayne Dyer's book, *The Power of Intention*, he wrote about taking offense. To be willing to understand, to be willing to transform, the parties must "stop being offended." This involves the safe, sacred circle of engagement, the empathy of an angel of mercy sent to the heart of the conflict to drain the poison of reaction from the conflict and replace the poison with a deeper understanding of intention, and hopefully trust. Do you have relationships of a poisonous nature? Do you have people in your life that trigger you? Clean house in your own life; and you will know the way to assist others in cleansing the poison from their life.

Meditation today should begin with the word "poison." Trust your lungs today that they will breathe the sustenance of air and energy through your body...trust that you can see a different reality in the context of the relationships of which you are a part...sit with the mantra of trust...trust that you will see the way to clarity...trust that you will remove the poison from your mind.

Write in your journal the images that came to your meditation. Do you see poison in your relationships? Can you see one way to correct that poison today?

One day when I was feeling like a motherless child, which I was, it
came to me: that feeling of being a part of everything, not separate
at all…I knew that if I cut a tree, my arm would bleed.

Alice Walker, *The Color Purple*

When the walls of our imagined reality collapse, sometimes we can see another reality, one that exists in the background. Celie, the long-suffering heroine in *The Color Purple*, lived during a time when fairness to blacks, and women in particular, was not part of the landscape. Looking at the quality of her life, Celie had no choice but to allow those walls to collapse and reveal an advanced reality. In that moment, she was part of the tree, part of the oneness of life, part of the collective energy of spirituality; it was something greater than her flesh and bones, more than her thoughts could ever imagine. At times when we feel motherless, an opportunity presents itself. Go forward into possibility. Physical existence is a strain for the spirit. We are spirit first. Flesh and bone is, after all, only temporary. What is the glue of life that holds your reality together? Are you an empty vessel with no connection to anything? Or are you like Celie, part of a parallel existence that connects with the oneness of all. The glue that holds our construction paper reality in place merely needs of the freedom of thought to allow parallel realities to be seen.

Meditation today should begin with the words "the glue of life"…as you inhale this morning let the walls of separation collapse and meld with the core of your essence… choose another reality and breathe deeply in oneness and renewal…

Write in your journal about the feeling of separation you have. Now write of one instance that you can think of where you became part of the whole, as the tree.

*Whenever you see darkness, there is extraordinary
opportunity for the light to burn brighter.*

Bono

The musician from Ireland, Bono, has never been content to sit on stacks of money and not respond to the deep problems on the planet such as poverty and the rights of children. He chooses to use the blessings of resources he has amassed in the recording industry to allow his light to shine brightly in the world. He widened his circle of influence to include the oppressed and hungry. He works tirelessly to shine his light into areas of the world that are easily forgotten, such as Darfur. Each one of us has an avenue of light to share within our communities. I don't know anyone in this field who does not share their talents and time doing pro bono work for the less fortunate. As a field of peacemakers and engagers of conflict, we have widened our circle of influence through our work. The opportunity for influence is presented daily. Put the peacemaker in a room and the opportunity is already there.

I love the experience that comes with the blessing of teaching. Anyone who teaches knows there is no money in doing it. When I go into that classroom, I am confident the reason I am there with those particular students is to use the opportunity for transformation. After 7 years, I know it works. Regularly, I hear from former students that something they learned in my classes changed their relationships, changed their view of conflict, or that they have used the principles they learned to become a force for good in their circle of influence. At the end of a training at Harvard, Ken Cloke gave an inspirational closing in which he admonished the participants to "go forth and change the world. The world is counting on us to do it. We have the knowledge and the skills to effect change in every arena." Widen your circle of influence today. Shine your light on one who needs you today.

Meditation today should begin with the word "influence"...bring peace to your body this morning by silently gathering renewed energy to the cells...let the cells influence your consciousness...let your consciousness have influence on your circle of love...

Write down the images that came to you in meditation today. List all the ways that you can have influence in your world this morning.

Boundaries

When we truly care for ourselves, it becomes possible to care far more
profoundly about other people. The more alert and sensitive we are to our
own needs, the more loving and generous we can be toward others.

Eda LeShan

In my experience, it seems the major reason for conflict in a close relationship is boundary violation. Conversation increases the awareness of potential violations, leads to preventive measures, and delineates boundaries; it is about letting others know where we start, and they should stop. Personal boundaries are hard to define, especially in close relationships. If we do not know where we begin and another ends, we trample boundaries unknowingly. Rigid boundaries prevent people from having a voice, keeping true dialogue at bay and adding to the development of avoidance loops. Loose boundaries cause us to speak for others, make decisions we have no business making, let others direct our lives, and enhance the victim archetype in relationships. The first act in relationship must be to care for our own soul. Be generous with yourself today. Discover the boundaries of your energy, the essence of you.

Meditation today should begin with the word "boundary." Fill the boundaries of your lungs with soft full breath. Where are you in the field of energy? Take care of your soul in this meditation...feel it...

Write down the ways you establish and maintain your personal boundaries. What is working well? What areas need more attention? How do your personal experiences help you at the table of resolution?

Value your power of judgment…and this power promises freedom from self-deception, friendliness with others, and harmony with the will of heaven.

Marcus Aurelius

I have extraordinary clarity when it comes to the issues of others. In my conversations with clients, I frequently tell them, "You already have all of your answers, but I might just ask you the right question that would unlock that answer." However, when it comes to discernment in my own life, it seems that things are often in the shadows. I suppose it all comes down to trust. Do I trust myself? Meditation is beginning to help my foggy mind open to clarity and find "harmony with the will of heaven." Just as I tell my clients they already have the answers, each day I work to remember that same advice is true for me too.

Meditation should begin today with the word "discernment." As you breathe softly and fully, what do you need the answers to? Think about discernment in your life. Sit with the thoughts that float over your consciousness this morning…

List the areas of fogginess in your personal life right now. Where do you need clarity? Take an inventory of your ability to know your own truth.

The most beautiful experience we can have is the mysterious. It is the
fundamental emotion which stands at the cradle of true art and true science.
He to whom this emotion is a stranger, who can no longer pause to wonder
and stand rapt in awe, is as good as dead: his eyes are closed.

Albert Einstein

Einstein was able to embrace the mystery of life, to sit in amazement and stand rapt in awe. The creation of his genius could come forth when contemplating the wonder. There is so much to learn in this age of information, so much to dream about, so much to become emotional about, so much to consider miraculous. Einstein noted that, if we do not have full access to our emotion, we are as good as dead. When I first began my therapy practice, I worked for a police psychologist, John Nicoletti, treating officers and their families in family counseling. I remember counseling a couple who were having trouble finding time together in the business of raising their family. The wife was desirous of more fun in their marriage, and he could not comply. She internalized this as evidence that he did not love her. I remember asking him "What sounds like fun to you?" He went home and thought about it. When he came back the next week, he said it was an extraordinarily difficult question to answer and that he had to look through magazines for ideas. This darling man was so separated from his emotional center, due to the horrors he witnessed doing his job, that he could no longer experience joy or fun. I often use humor in counseling, and while he thought I was funny, it looked painful for him to smile or laugh. Most of the time he looked like a dead man walking.

Post-traumatic stress has a huge affect on those who live through trauma, especially police officers, doctors, firemen, and military personnel. Often the pain is too great, and repressed feelings actually begin to destroy the neural connections in the amygdala of the brain; it becomes easier to die a little each day. The ability to pause and wonder about the beauty of life around us becomes difficult. How many of us have the occupational hazard of trauma? Or in our lives underwent trauma at the hands of those who are supposed to love us? I suggest that, as peacemakers and engagers of conflict, we can unwittingly absorb the negative emotion of our clients if we do not protect our soul. Then, we too will become unable to stand rapt with awe, with our eyes as good as dead. Compassion fatigue is the beginning sign. If you recognize the daily damage of this work and don't move to care for yourself, then you could be like the police officer who could no longer smile - as good as dead, your heart closed. Stand in amazement this day at the wonder of the mystery.

Meditation today should begin with the word "amazement." What are you amazed by? Fill your lungs with wonder and look for the mysteries ...feel the peace of the morning... the wonder of the dawning of the new day...

Write down in your journal one thing that you can do today to experience the mystery. What how you will prepare for work today in a way to maintain that sense of wonder?

The good mind chooses what is positive, what is advancing, - embraces the affirmative.

Ralph Waldo Emerson

Mind training involves restructuring the chorus of critical thoughts constantly cascading from a frantic mind. We are programmed early with stale thinking, the don'ts or shouldn'ts of life which keep us in the consciousness of fear and guilt. Emerson suggested that advanced thinking, positive in nature, is a 'should' to be supported. A positive affirmation is a healthy tool because it affords us the opportunity see with new eyes. "I'm open to new ways of thinking" is a positive affirmation. "I perform my duties to the best of my abilities", is an affirmation of performance. "I'm exactly where I should be in life" affirms the journey. As Emerson noted, "the good mind" can choose again and be trained to find value in all actions. I remember a cacophony of disharmonious rhetoric reeling through my mind in my 20s. As I entered my 30s, a calling to maternity softened the noise as I struggled to build self-esteem in my children. I noticed the positive messages were changing me as well and made a real difference in my children. When I was 40, my children were into their teens and became critical of me. The old critical messages began to replay and were reinforced. I launched an active program to try to reverse that old tape. Reprogramming of self-talk must be an intentional act. Restructuring the mind is possible in less than 3 months if the desire is strong. Endurance is the key. A daily ritual of self-care is necessary if the mind is to learn a new way of thinking that does not involve negative fear, guilt, and critical thought. Review the processing of your mind. Do you need to undergo a restructuring? How can you affirm the uniqueness of you?

Meditation today should begin with the word "affirmation." Affirm your body with the sustenance of life...fall into your body with the fullness of breath...sit in silence and affirm the essence of your being.

Write down a negative message that often plays in your mind. Burn or destroy the list. Write down three positive affirmations that you repeat to yourself this day. If you become entrenched in your negative thought, ask a friend. Friends can always see the beauty in you.

Flexibility

Be open, be available, be exposed, be skinless. Skinless? Dance around in your bones.
Wallace Stegner

A bag of bones dancing around the room is a humorous thought. Can you imagine being so loose that you could dance with freedom and allow your spirit to soar? The first two steps to availability are: to be willing and to be open. These release your spirit to be free so that you can fly through the cosmos. Then, with a song in your heart, the dance of life becomes a magic carpet ride and each morning is filled with anticipation. "What will happen today?" becomes the question of wonder for the morning. "Who will show up today? Who will call? Who will show me grace from God? Who will help me heal old wounds? If you want to jump out of the bed in the morning, then be flexible. If you want to find joy in the day's promise, then expose your vulnerabilities. If you want to know there are no limits to love, then be open. If you want to feel your formlessness, then be skinless. Dance around in your bones and feel the day awaiting your soft touch; unwrap the gift of life.

Meditation today should begin with the word "flexibility." Expand your body with the air of the morning…feel the flexibility in your soul and rise in anticipation of the day…

Write in your journal about your flexibility. What does that image bring to your mind? What is one thing that you can do this day to increase your flexibility in your life?

The ultimate value of life depends upon awareness and the power
of contemplation rather than upon mere survival.

Aristotle

Intentional reflection is necessary if one is to become aware and rise above the noise of physical survival. The intention to contemplate one's actions is the first step in discovering the value of life. I suppose my intention was set forth when I was young. Certain patterns of my family of origin were not palatable, and I did not want to repeat them. Much like eddies in a stream, an alcoholic family system get stuck in repetitive behavior. Addictive behavior and denial are the standards of the system. I was determined to outgrow my family system. I set forth that intention as an act of survival. It had mixed results.

In retrospect, I think my household morphed into our own brand of addiction, addiction to rage, addiction to alcohol, addiction to food and nicotine, and my own personal addiction, control. To be in chaos caused me to try to control everything around me in a desperate desire to settle the tension in my body. Did it work? Not only did it not work, it caused me to live in the consciousness of great frustration and pain. I lived in a world of constant tension. I began my recovery from relationship addiction and codependency in my 30s. In one way, I think my control addiction served me well. It compelled me to learn to let go; to trust the process of life; to make spirituality a priority. Now, I see the broad circularity of life and embrace not only my addiction to control, but my family of origin. It was also the key to rising above it; I created a platform of something newer and more effective; a higher path to living. It made me a better mother, a better partner, and a better practitioner. Today, through contemplation, I am able to bless my journey, live in the moment, and fully awake in the anticipation of tomorrow. I have learned to value my journey, all the pain, all the joy, all the beauty of my higher power.

Meditation today should begin with the word "contemplation." Sit in observation of each breath… breathe high into your throat…deeply into the floor…expand your mind from side to side…embrace the entire history of your tenure on earth…

What did you discover as a result of your morning meditation? List all the lessons that your family of origin brought to you. Is there one personal value that you need to contemplate today?

And blame the mote that dims their eye, each little speck and blemish find; To our own stronger errors blind.

Benjamin Franklin

It is easy to see the mistakes of others; we have a particular vantage point of clarity when analyzing behavior on their behalf. It is not as easy to see painful behaviors which arise from our own actions. When events trigger us, we tend to keep the ache and agony in the shadows, where avoidance saves us from the painfulness of review and ownership. Coming out of the darkness into the light is a choice. To live an extraordinary life, it is necessary to come to terms with our qualities which we find hard to acknowledge. The quality of our life is determined by our willingness to be conscious.

I tend to deceive myself about the transitions of life. I don't seem to be willing to let go of any chapter of my life with ease. As relationships change, I have a mote in my eye about abandonment pain. As friends move away, I have buried myself in work or refused to process the pain of missing them by denying the value of that friendship to me. As children grew and left my care, I declined the opportunity to view the transition as a normal part of development and sank into the shallow water of sadness.

A function of maturity is letting go of the notion that once things become a part of your life they are permanent. Nothing is permanent. The very idea of permanency is self-deception. There is freedom in coming to terms with impermanence. To embrace the idea of impermanence causes me to stay safely in the moment. Now, I look at each day and value the friendships I have in this moment. I treasure each stage with the children. I value the history of a relationship that has changed into something which I did not expect. The willingness to embrace all of the mistakes of yesterday, to know that, at the time, they were perfect for my own development, brings me out of the shadows of a forest of self-deception. Are there buried feelings in your life that you need to excavate? Go through that treasure chest, process the reality of those feelings, and remove the mote from your eye.

Meditation today should begin with the word "self-deception." Agree with each deep breath to reveal any pain that needs to be processed...be unafraid...know that you are not alone in your process...float with new awareness this day...

Write down a list of the all of the areas of deception which came to you. Pick one to concentrate on and agree to excavate the relics of that painful memory this week. Embrace the reality that comes with moving from the shadows into the light.

Sharing

My bounty is as boundless as the sea,
My love as deep; the more I give to thee,
The more I have, for both are infinite.

William Shakespeare, Romeo and Juliet

The intention of sharing love usually comes with a right of ownership or an expectation of something in return. When the intention changes and is realized in the form of choice, the nature of the relationship can grow and become a sharing of an inner love that is waiting to get out. The wife of one of my former business partners is always in a deep state of sharing her love, with everyone, all the time. When I first met her I observed her curiously. I thought to myself, "She is either the most insincere person I have ever met or she is the most deeply genuine one." The condition of our inner sanctum is reflected in our ability to outwardly share, and have a deep sense of respect and love for others. Beverly reflects her inner sanctum of love and has a way of making everyone in a room feel the presence of love and acceptance. She embodies "love thy neighbor;" Beverly is the real deal and a joy to be around. Drawing from a reservoir deep with love, she shares her bounty in every contact. I believe that Beverly makes a conscious choice to do this with every person, every day. Like most of us, her life has not been without its grief and sorrow, but the intention to choose to love has enriched her life tremendously. Coming from this place of security, she knows the reservoir will never end.

When in a significant relationship, the risk seems greater. Once the decision is made to open the heart, and we become vulnerable, as the chance for rejection is always present. An intention to choose love and share love must be adopted for the trust to build and the fear to subside. No one can be owned, relationships end, but in love we can move on to something deeper, something boundless. We can stand with a higher power and the significant relationships that are meant for us will appear from the shadows. Think about your significant relationships today. Can you share your reservoir of love, knowing that it will never cease to be abundant?

So my voice becomes a breath and a shout. One prepares the
way; the other surrounds my loneliness with angels.

Rainer Maria Rilke

Meditation today should begin with the word "sharing." In the solitude of the morning breathe deeply into the 'One' center...you are never alone...your untapped reservoir awaits, it only requires your decision to choose to share your love...

What relationship came to you while in your meditation? Write about the relationship and the sharing of love.

Transformation cannot occur without transition. This is a transitional period of liminality when things are barely perceptible – a personal rite of passage, from sleepwalking to awakening. The process is the reality and it cannot be rushed.

Sarah Ban Breathnach

Transformations have been the most difficult periods of my life. I wish I had been taught early to expect transitions. Much like a receiving a gift, unwrapping of the future holds a reward of awakening despite the pain of an evolving soul. But I was not taught to expect transitions. The fear of the unknown paralyzed me most of my life. The "what-if" and the "should-haves" appeared as minefields in the battle of living. I was terrified of one wrong step and that I would pay for the decision for the rest of my life. In a misperception of safety, I remained sheltered from living. In an effort to teach children to be successful, the natural way of the world is left on the sidelines; the game of winning becomes the lesson. What are we trying to win? Is it the lottery, the most profitable practice, the most money, the most successful children, or the biggest house? Life is hard, the mountain will never be fully reached, but when we live in fear of catastrophe, the awakening can never occur. The process of emotions and events is necessary to get through the transition, and the process cannot be navigated swiftly. I have learned to keep paddling my canoe through the rapids of the river.

Ban Breathnach is right: any rite of passage is all about the transitions and holds the formula for awakening. Pushing the pain away from consciousness is the reactive nature of sleepwalking. Helping our children and each other, we should be focused on the transitions, for in the transition the transformation of awakening has the opportunity to unfold. My sleepwalking days are over. I want to be fully awake for the rest of the ride.

Meditation today should begin with the phrase "transition to transformation." With each breath feel the potential of the moment, feel the pauses, feel the pain...breathe out the constriction in your soul...breathe fully forward into the future moment with a new consciousness of awareness...

Write about your most recent transformation. Did you experience a painful transition right before the light shone through?

Nan Waller Burnett

There are two ways of spreading light;
To be the candle or the mirror that reflects it.

Edith Wharton

Leaving a legacy is a blessing to the ones you value. Legacy is more than something of monetary value but rather a record of the richness and depth of one's experience. It is something that people do not think about until they are old, and many times it is too late. One thing that can assist in preserving the legacy as a living document is to have a record of your life. The things that seem important to you in your youth may not look the same when you reach your 40th birthday or your 60th. As a reminder of what was important at that time comes in the form of journaling or taking annuals notes in review. Make it a true record of a life well lived. Record the benchmarks of your life to gauge progress and personal growth. We are the candle. Our journals also let us be a mirror for our loved ones making the path well lit. How will your loved ones remember you? As one who was a seeker of life with all the blessings afforded to you? Did you use your gifts and talents completely to enrich the world? Did you provide an example to your family and live with a zest for life? Our children need to see that we dream; that we search for something better. Spread your light by leaving the path for discovery; a legacy of knowing where you are going and being fully present while you journey through the joys of life. They, in turn, will do the same!

Meditation today should begin with the word "legacy." What is your legacy? As you go to that quiet place of serenity, look at your life and credit yourself with all the wondrous things that you have already done…with each breath know the second by second existence of right now holds the answer…

Make a list in your journal of all the things that you will leave behind you on this earth to those you love. Is there anything that is missing from the list that you would like to accomplish for the legacy ledger? What is one thing that you can do today to make that happen?

Interdependence

Dependent people need others to get what they want. Independent people can get what they want through their own efforts. Interdependent people combine their own efforts with the efforts of others to achieve their greatest success.

Stephen R. Covey, *The 7 Habits of Highly Effective People*

Peacemaking, I think, requires the recognition that the sum of the parts is greater than the whole, and that a larger vision can be realized when individuals operate independently to combine their efforts toward a shared aim. Intercultural communication theory tells us that Eastern society has been regarded as collective and communal, while Western society has traditionally been thought of as highly individualistic. I take a different view: the pioneers and the founders of this nation who crafted our Constitution took great care in helping the masses and creatively including our global neighbor. In the settling of the colonies and the frontier, when neighbors had trouble, folks gathered around to contribute what they could. Our nation's settlers had to be interdependent to survive, and that spirit of interdependence produced a governing document that still guides our nation today. No single soul could have produced that enduring text. In the last century, the American corporate model has been shifting to truly reflect the value of authentic employee involvement and team building. As mediators and peacemakers, we are natural systems workers. We act to illuminate for the opposing parties their mutual dependence to resolve the conflict, and the necessity of interdependence to recreate relationships. In this way, we act interdependently with our clients to seek creative solutions that engender soulful expressions of peace locally and, ultimately, globally. Search your soul today and discover the interdependence that is evident in your world.

Mediation today should begin with the word "interdependence." Breathe a collective breath of all souls, and feel the release from the depths of your lungs.

In your journal, list the situations in your life in which interdependence does or would better support you than independence or dependence. Identify the people in those situations with whom you have or should have an interdependent relationship.

A man to carry on a successful business must have imagination. He must see things as in a vision, a dream of the whole thing.

Charles M Schwab

For the mind to languish in the delicious state of creativity, it has to have permission. The mind must be trained to go to that central place of whole brain thinking that envisions a dream. The permission to create comes from a desire to experience all that life can provide. The intention to cultivate fertile brain soil is enhanced by a daily practice of *going* within. Eckhart Tolle, in his *Gateway to the Now*, wrote of three gateways to deeper consciousness. The first gateway is to be connected to the body. He noted that most people look down and see the body as something they have. The mind is so noisy that our entire focus is on the mind, and it is untrained. Connection to the rest of the body, first in a meditation, allows a focus on the rest of the aliveness and energy that is experienced in the other processes of the body.

The next gateway is the gateway of silence, a willingness to be still long enough to let the structures of the mind collapse, and the agreement to go to the languid pool of energy that resides within you. To open to the essence of higher power that is experienced when the stillness speaks rather than mental noise. Alertness is enhanced in this gateway. Attention to silence is an agreement to shut out the mental noise that holds the mind's attention.

The third gateway is the gateway of acceptance. Access to the creative center of the brain is completed by embracing what is already present in your life. All pain and misery is caused by argument with reality. Suffering is caused by refusal to accept what is occurring right now in your life. To say yes is to fully accept that which is presenting in your life. It also means saying yes to whatever crosses the path. The full acceptance of this moment, the Now, is to surrender to reality. Through surrender and the third gateway of acceptance, inner peace is possible. When these three steps are followed in a daily meditative state, the creative center of the brain is fully opened clarity is possible. Imagination and intuition clasp hands and go forth together to make the dream a reality. Creativity and transformation reside in the same languid pool of energy that is you, your purpose, your willingness, the connection with you and your higher power.

Meditation today should begin with the word "dream." Breathe deeply into your body and feel all the other processes that are occurring...feel the blood coursing through your veins...feel the digestive processes awakening this morning...feel your creative center...go into the silence and accept your vision, your purpose...surrender to the Now and say yes as you agree to sit in stillness...

Did you see clarity of vision and feel a dream of success? What can you accept today that will allow you to embrace your dream?

I have one life and one chance to make it count for something . . . I'm free to choose what that something is, and the something I've chosen is my faith. Now, my faith goes beyond theology and religion and requires considerable work and effort. My faith demands — this is not optional — my faith demands that I do whatever I can, wherever I am, whenever I can, for as long as I can with whatever I have to try to make a difference.

Jimmy Carter

Jimmy Carter has been a proactive force for good in the world since he left the Presidency. The above quote speaks to his conscious choice to pursue humanitarian endeavors. Making an impact in the world is a calling for him, an example of his faith in action. Often, calling and purpose are confused with image. In the professional world, the creation of a practice can result in the pursuit of reputation or an identity aligned more with what we do, rather than who we are. With this false focus on image in the mind it is easy to stay in the consciousness of mental noise, build a statue of ourselves, a persona that does not feel or forgets to experience life. Separation of the professional self from the spiritual self is felt as an isolation of the soul. When we are separate from our essence, we are not whole, not fully integrated, and we cannot be a force for good in the world. We become working zombies in the pursuit of things and image, empty vessels of want, depressed, and not present in life. No one enters their profession without wanting to make an impact. To achieve inner peace, it is necessary to disconnect for a few minutes every day from our achievements or who we project in the professional world. Think about your achievements. If we put as much energy into being available to ourselves as we do into our public image, we would emanate happiness and appreciation not only for ourselves but for those around us.

Meditation should begin today with the word "achievement." With every breath look at your 'being' in review...breathe in awareness and breathe out old ideas about your 'doing'...let the stillness reveal who you really are...

What images of your professional persona came to mind? What images of the being of you came to you in your mind? List them both on separate sides of the paper in your journal.

No voice; but oh!
The silence sank
Like music on my heart.

Samuel Taylor Coleridge

This morning as I watched the sun hit the deep purple mountains, infusing them with the brilliance of western red, I felt joy flush through my veins. Appreciation of the beauty of the wilderness brings me such solace. Nature's holy cathedral is my place of worship this day. The silence envelopes my soul as the gradual illumination of the day fills me with the sacred music of the heart. Where can you go today to feel the comfort required by the soul? Is there a corner of your home that is yours alone? Is there a patch of land in the yard where you can cultivate serenity? Do you drive to the library? Do you walk in the wilderness and sit on a rock to commune with the divine? Does the river run by a carpet of flowers in a park near you? Can you climb to the top of the building to be closer to tranquility? Is there a holy church that welcomes you with the embrace of peace?

Meditation today should begin with the word "solace." Sit and feel your fingers warm with the energy of the soul...agree to become still to discover your source of renewal...

Make a list your places of solace. Make a date with yourself this week, to go to that place alone.

*We are already looking at Spirit, we just don't recognize it. We
have all the necessary cognition, but not the recognition.*

Ken Wilber

Ken Wilber, in *Grace and Grit*, a memoir cowritten with his wife the year she passed away, wrote of the presence of spirit that already resides within each and every one of us. With great compassion and vision, the two lovers recorded this deeply emotional and personal journey. Wilber noted in this book that we only need to realize we are looking at spirit in each and every person. The problem is that we do not choose to recognize what we see. We adopt instead the reflection of the world around us, forgetting we are spirits in human casings. When we are faced with conflict in relationship, it is easy to lose sight of the divinity in all people. It is easier to see flaws and to judge rather than to connect with their spirit. Mindfulness helps us remember that we are all divine representations of spirit. Meditation brings up inner peace, even if it is only for a few moments. I think it is important to remember the goodness that resides within us. When we take care of our soul every morning, we judge less, accept more, and recognize the divinity in all.

Meditation today should begin with the word "recognition." Appreciate the soul within your body...breathe deeply with acceptance of your humanity...comprehend the stillness of your mind...let it float...

What qualities about yourself do you need to recognize today? Give recognition to one in your family with whom you are at odds.

*Serenity is ours when we allow the angels to quiet the turbulent
forces of life and leave our souls in deep peace and stillness.*

Deepak Chopra

The Gyuto Monks of Tibet sing single chords which create a resonance not of this earth. Huston Smith, the theologian, noted on a trip to Northern India to study Tibetan traditions, that when he heard the monks chant, it sounded like spiritual technology meant to match the wavelengths of God. The effect is that of hearing multiple chords, although only one note is sung. As the chords are sung, Smith described it as though the power from heaven is sprinkled onto the individual wavelengths of sound to create the harmonic music of a resonating symphony. The mono-melodic chants deepen the meditation of all who gather to partake in the earthly audience of heavenly sound. Smith noted that when the meditation deepens, the walls between God, the monks, and the sound collapse into one holy chord, and there is no boundary between heaven and earth. I begin each day in the same peaceful way. Prayer and stillness quiet the noisy mind. I listen to spiritual music such as classical, Asian instrumental, and sometimes Gregorian Chants, much like the chords of the Gyuto Monks. I, too, have on occasion experienced the same collapse of boundary between the physical and spiritual world. When that happens, I notice the turbulence of human life ceases, and I am left for a moment in deep inner peace. It makes all the difference in my day, and I am clearer, more loving, and more connected to my soul. Think of the rising light of dawn. How can you embrace serenity more fully?

Meditation today should begin with the word "serenity." Allow your angels to help quiet your frantic mind…listen to the internal bell of resonance ring forth with stillness…go to that holy place of depth…notice your perception of physical boundary…agree to let the walls collapse…

Write in your journal three ways that you can invite serenity each morning. What is one way that you can bring peace to others today?

We cannot cure the world of sorrows, but we can choose to live in joy.

Joseph Campbell

One only needs to switch on the television or open a newspaper to learn of sorrows of the world. It is not possible to cure the strife and sadness reigning on earth. But there are sources of pleasure all around us. Choosing the focus of our attention can be the difference between inner peace or inner strife. Watching the summer sky for evidence of the divine in a meteor shower is a chosen focus. Wayne Dyer noted, "When we change the way we look at things, the things we look at change." Suddenly watching the summer sky at night is eye candy of the heart, to be unwrapped with anticipation through attention and awareness. We focus our minds in a certain way and the intensity of the focus sharpens so we can only see that upon which we focus. In the summer, I have the blessing of a high mountain retreat to enjoy. I have no television, I cannot get a clear radio signal— I have designed serenity. At the end of the summer, I find the lack of information of current events has not caused me to miss much of anything. Although I feel deeply sorrowful for those who must live within the structure of war and misery, I do not have to dwell in their sorrow. For that time, I choose joy. I take every opportunity when presented to help those who cannot help themselves, and I relish the moment when the eye candy appears at the edge of the forest, a delicate fawn grazes contentedly next to her mother, and all the sorrow of the world is lost to me. As I choose inner peace, I trust that my energy is working toward a world where we no longer struggle to survive. Can you find a moment to let go the misery of the world and choose joy?

Meditation today should begin with the word "joy." Feel the smile rising up out of your throat...breathe into the smiling folds of your face...know that you have you focused on your soul...deep energy within the heart of joy for your moment in the now...

Make a decision that today you will choose joy when confronted with misery. Tonight write about that instance of focused joy.

*Who could be set free while he imprisons anyone? A jailer is not free, for he is
bound together with his prisoner. He must be sure that he does not escape, and
so he spends his time in keeping watch on him. The bars which limit him become
the world in which the jailer lives, along with him. And it is on his freedom that
the way to liberty depends for both of them. Therefore hold no-one prisoner.
Release instead of bind, for thus are you made free. The way is simple.*

A Course in Miracles, W, Lesson192

We have been mislead by the lyrics of love ballads, by romance mythology, by constrictions imposed on us through social mapping, that we are owned by another person when we fall in love. In the first years of passion, discovery of common interests and the experience of being a couple, we bathe in the delight of a perceived oneness. As familiarity settles in the relationship, the passion subsides and the commitment begins. Coupleships are not free from misery. Problems with relationship show up in the form of expectation, neediness, and ownership. When expectations are not met, neediness may be magnified and cause conflict to arise. As a divorce mediator, I see much sadness and sorrow in the uncoupling of families and unmet expectations seem to be the root of the sorrow. Often the unspoken feeling is, "You were never there for me." Many times the heartache is caused by deeper need than sharing of love; it is about a person who has been abandoned through the action, or non-action, of another.

Successful partnership starts with each person being complete and having a deep relationship with their source. Then each can accept a partner exactly as is, traverse the rocky hill of adult development and growth and allow elasticity within the walls of the commitment. Generally, unconditional love is thought of as something we express only for our children or animals. A deep compassion is required if we are to provide unconditional love of our mate. This does not mean that every partner we choose is perfect for the entire earthly experience. Some matches are not based on common values nor do they bring peace. The requisite value of any relationship should be honesty. When you are romancing a stone and it does not work, uncoupling can be the only choice. True release from the pain of uncoupling comes with unconditional love for the soul of the other and genuinely honoring their divergent path. Review your relationships. Are you honoring the relationship by maintaining your connection to your source? In what ways are you holding deep compassion for them? Are you allowing elasticity? What are you not saying? Are you romancing the stone, do you need freedom?

Meditation today should begin with the word "romancing the stone." Feel free to breathe deeply into your lungs and release the bands around your heart...sit in silence and provide the solace your soul requires...you are the one who builds the bridge to your own completion...

What images came to you in the meditation? Do you see an open space? Or do you see a stone wall? Are you creating one? How can you build the bridge to your own completion? How different would your relationship look if you could do that?

While you are proclaiming peace with your lips, be careful
to have it even more fully in your heart.

Saint Francis of Assisi

Saint Francis was considered an odd bird growing up in Assisi, a small hill town in Umbria, Italy in the late 12th Century. He marched to the beat of his own drum. Very different from the noble family of his birth, he heard a calling from another place not of this world. He was a compassionate man and felt the pain of those less fortunate. He was highly in tune with nature and animals. One legend about St. Francis is that he tamed a vicious wolf outside a monastery. In 1205, he was 20 years old and fighting to defend Assisi from the nearby Perugians, when he felt deeply that peace should reign on earth. The war affected him so much that he chose to answer the call to live a different life. He divested himself of all possessions and took vows of chastity, poverty, and obedience. He lived a life that was the embodiment of those choices and had many followers. He died at the age of 44. The Prayer of St. Francis is used widely today as the prayer for peace and improvement of the planet. Gandhi's "you must be the change you wish to see", is a paraphrase of St. Francis's doctrine. Today, he is revered and recognized as the founder of the Franciscan order of Monks, the Patron Saint of Animals, and the Saint of Acceptance and Great Compassion. For practitioners in the areas of peacebuilding and conflict engagement, the writings of St. Francis remind us not to judge and to live the life we espouse. When considering your life's purpose, what do you need to experience more fully in your heart before you can be more effective in your work?

Meditation today should begin with the phrase "be the change." Recognize your role as an agent of change and breathe in the fresh ideas of the morning. Breathe out the rules and analysis, and then breathe in the willingness to be open. Breathe out the constrictions of identification of the ego.

Write down in your journal what you see as your role in your work on this planet. Does it match your purpose? What do you need to do today to become more aware of your role in conflict engagement?

Expression

[Expression] is the alchemy of language, the transformation of life into
simple art, the sublimation of experience into thought. If you don't write,
then paint or sing, or at least talk frankly and openly to your friends.

Thomas Moore, Care of the Soul

We all have unique talents and diverse avenues of self-expression. Often those gifts lie deep, treasures on an ocean floor, waiting to be hoisted to the light. If you don't perceive yourself as artistic, you may not have taken inventory of your exceptional gifts to share with others. Some share their wisdom through poetry; some through visual art; some through written opinion or oration and debate. When teaching adults in professional studies, I anxiously await the gifts that my students bring to me. There is always a rare nugget of value I find in each one as they share their experiences in class. What distinctive gift do you have that you can shine your light upon?

Meditation today should begin with the word "expression." Breathe in the promise of a new day, and sit with the irreplaceable gifts you already possess.

In your journal, list the gifts you can honor within yourself.

Separation from God is like a well; Remembrance of God is the rope.

Rumi

The great teachers of the spirit traditions have always taught one lesson in common; that our misery comes from the feeling that we are separate from our higher power. When we pass through the veil of birth, we forget. As we enter the physical form of our body, the reality of our being before we arrived begins to fade from memory. Jesus, Mohammed, Buddha, Zoroaster, and others taught that our pain is relinquished when we remember who we are. I love the quote from the Jesuit, Pierre Teilhard de Chardin, we are "spiritual beings trying to be human." I felt pure truth when I read that for the first time. In some ways I think it is easier to be human than to remember that we are spiritual. I think of those souls whom we assist in conflict and I sense a deep well of misery; people struggling to feel loved, to feel worthy and to feel peaceful. It seems to be in the struggling that we feel the emptiness, the trying to get there, as Eckhart Tolle noted. Where are we going? Why are we struggling? Are we such empty vessels that we cannot ever feel that what is, is enough? Mindfulness in daily life helps in the trying to remember. The agreement to feel at one with a higher power, to embrace the mystery of life will lead us out of the deep well by taking the hand of God. As you look at your morning, of what struggle are you now aware? Do you feel alone, separate from the whole? What do you need to do for yourself today to remind you that you no longer need to struggle?

Meditation today should begin with the word "struggle." Release the tension in your arms as you breathe deeply...give up the trying to and just be present...just feel the warmth of your beating heart...there is no need to struggle against any force...just be.

What you have been struggling with lately? What have you noticed in your world that seems heavy, tiresome, in need of cleansing?

I come from the East, most of you [here] are Westerners. If I look at you superficially, we are different, and if I put my emphasis on that level, we grow more distant. If I look on you as my own kind, as human beings like myself, with one nose, two eyes, and so forth, then automatically that distance is gone. We are the same human flesh. I want happiness; you also want happiness. From that mutual recognition, we can build respect and real trust of each other. From that can come cooperation and harmony.

His Holiness the Dalai Lama

One of the elements in analysis of conflict is recognition of mutual interdependence. Where do the interests of the parties intersect? In his speech, The Dalai Lama addressed areas of commonality, the space where human diversity meets human similarity. Perception is everything; as Leonardo da Vinci noted in the 15th century, "All of our knowledge has its origins in our own perceptions." From the area of mutuality, we can "build respect and real trust" and narrow of the channel of fear in which we, as humans, seem immersed. To shorten distance between commonality and diversity is a key element of resolution. The entryway to trust lies opposite the door to fear. Open and honest sharing of information is the only way to successfully change perception and to shorten the distance. Moreover, respectful communication and permission to be heard can only be extended by choice. We know this is the last thing that people in conflict want to do. Our role in peace building and the engagement of conflict is to bridge that gap, to insure the perceptions are understood and the speech is decelerated to allow understanding. Helping others is about our ability to illuminate the path. In your own life, where do you need to shorten the distance to understanding? Is it in your family? In your friendships? In your loving relationships?

Meditation today should begin with the phrase "shorten the distance." Agreement to be still is an agreement to commune with the divine within you...breathe the spirit into the center of your being. Who resides there with you as you shorten the distance?

Write down the images that came to you in your meditation. Where can you shorten the distance today?

*There is a fountain of youth; it is your mind, your talents, the creativity
you bring to your life and the lives of the people you love. When you
will learn to tap this source, you will have truly defeated age.*

Sophia Loren

Sophia Loren, at age 71, is still considered the one of the most beautiful women in the world. As she noted above, she believes beauty comes from the inside out. I remember hearing that when I was a young teen. I also remember thinking it was crap. At that age we are so concerned with fitting in and looking our best all the time; actions worshiping the "God" of appearance, not inner beauty. In the quest for flawlessness, we allow the magazine photographs to decide our beauty and worth. Men have been caught up in the image game as well. Often the more disciplined gender, they race, lift, and pedal their way to eternal health, sculpting their sinewy muscles to new levels of definition each week. It makes you wonder whether it is health or vanity they seek.

Men and women who realize that ageless beauty is an inside job, take a more holistic approach. It is not that they don't exercise and eat well but, as Sophia said they also pay attention to emotional and spiritual health. Inner beauty grows from within, glowing with a radiance that cannot be attained from a bottle or the right number of repetitions on a machine. Emanating from a place of self-acceptance and a heart filled with love and respect for all, both men and women remain ageless beauties regardless of the changes over time. Tapping into the source of inner love and beauty is the true path to agelessness. What do you need to concentrate on this week? As you view the silhouette in the mirror, is it more repetitions, a more expensive face cream, or is it care of the soul on which you need to work? As you accept the inner beauty of your soul, you will view radiance in the mirror that you could not see before.

Meditation today should begin with the words "ageless beauty." Breathe deeply the life giving oxygen that keeps your tissue radiant...breathe out the old negative self talk that leaves your skin sallow and turned downward with tired age...accept the illumination of the soul as your new face, not a mask of cover but a glowing eminence of your heart.

Make a list of all the things about your appearance that you dislike. Burn or destroy it. Now make a list of all the luminous qualities of your heart and soul.

Nan Waller Burnett

Life is a spell so exquisite that everything conspires to break it.

Emily Dickinson

Emily Dickinson saw beauty all around in 19th century America. In her brilliantly written prose, she embraced the simplicity in the gifts of life. When reading her words it is easy to see myself melting into a light that surrounds and permeates my physical boundaries reaching for a deeper glowing boundary within. As I gaze out of the window on my high perch in the Rockies, I notice the gentle hills so lush and green protecting the majesty of the purple peaks behind them. I notice black and ginger colored butterflies, and periwinkle blue dragonflies skimming across the gently rippling lake in front of the hills. I hear red-throated hummingbirds buzzing around in the feeder and see magnificent stellar jays soaring on their decorated graph-like wings from tree to tree. On my morning meditation walk, I noticed there were buttercups of a deep radiant mango color and ruby Indian paintbrush wildflowers on the edge of the outcropping above me. The air was so sweet and so filled with life! As in Dickinson's images of the pastoral splendor of the landscape, I feel the depth of my beating heart and the connectedness of my earthly soul with heaven when I view the panorama around me. I feel just as she felt; life is so exquisite. I know the summer is drawing to a close; the first shimmering aspens are beginning to turn bright yellow. The morning air has a crispness of aroma from the lodge pole pines that stand sentry to my Shangri-La. I know that very soon autumn will conspire to break the exquisiteness of my summer high in the mountains. I release my hold on that vision of peace and welcome a new spell, one of falling into the autumn with a part of the exquisite memory with me.

Meditation today should begin with the word "exquisite." Welcome your awakened perception, and completely relax. Know that your experience is rare and unique. Breathe deeply and notice your breath disappears in peace and stillness...enjoy the exquisite experience of the morning...

Make a list of the things that are the most beautiful to your senses. Notice them when you see them during this day.

In the long run, we shape our lives, and we shape ourselves. The process never ends until we die. And the choices we make are ultimately our own responsibility.

Eleanor Roosevelt

The years that First Lady Eleanor Roosevelt spent in the White House were less than ideal. Much trial and tribulation, not only in her marriage, but in the country and the world weighed heavily upon her. The choices she made were evidence that she refused to give up, even as outside influences threatened her purpose. Also, she noted the process of development and improvement never ceases. This hopeful statement reveals a belief in opportunity and possibility. The blackness and whiteness of life simply does not exist. A million shades of gray are evident in the tapestry of experience. We are shaped by our choices and the beauty of choosing is that you can choose again. Truly accepting the idea of "choose-again" is freedom from the prison of a self-imposed perfection. Mistakes are human; we are human and we make mistakes. One only need to awake with the dawn of the next morning and to grant the permission that is necessary to choose again. Most of the pain and misery we feel in relationships is felt through an imaginary dance. We are taking our turn on the floor alone and projecting pain and misery onto those who stand close enough to us to mirror it back to us. How can the shape of one's life be improved by the decision to choose again? What choices do you need to make today to give yourself permission to choose again? What choices do you need to point out to your clients as they arrive steeped in the misery of the cold prison walls?

Meditation today should begin with the word "choices." Breathe in freedom of choice...breathe out the constriction of self-judgment, breathe in the possibility of a new perception...breathe out the sadness contained in a finite world...

Write in your journal the images that came to you in meditation. What choices do you need to make today to live a more hopeful, jubilant life?

Since we cannot change reality, let us change the eyes which see reality.

Nikos Kazantzakis

Change is a constant. Why are we taught that we live in a finite world with rights and wrongs, reduced to black and white? Why are we taught to buck change and seek sameness? The comfort zone of uniformity in experience causes us to languish in stagnation. The universe demands a kind of morphology in energy, as sustenance for eternity of the life cycle. We are compelled to follow a trajectory of orbit that we cannot control. This does not however, keep us from trying to control it. As the youngest child in an alcoholic family, I adapted to life through the addiction of control. I controlled the environment around me to feel safe. My other siblings chose three separate addictions. In my self-constructed prison of control, I effectively shut out living. The only goal I had every day was to calm my guts from churning; and any change threatened my tummy. I was 35 before I awoke. The light began to glimmer on the horizon, and I learned the painful truth of addiction from the cradle. A hard lesson to learn is that you have to spend the rest of your life committed to not acting out the addiction. Each morning I perform a ritual devotion of releasing that which I cannot control…which is everything. Training my frenetic mind can only be mastered through surrender. When I hit my 50s, I began to surrender to the ritual of prayer and meditation. I welcome the day with the prayer of serenity, express my willingness to live differently, and meditate for clarity and peace. As a result of this daily practice, my life has changed, but not without the burning pain of a few dark nights of initiation. These were passages of which I am now grateful and review earnestly for wisdom, but at the time loathed beyond measure. Passages through dark tunnels are frightening and force you to surrender to God. Now, for a control freak this is not a painless journey! There is a line in the workbook of The Course in Miracles that says "Where would you have me go today, what would you have me say and to whom?" I look to the day for the wondrous changes that will occur. What is your destiny? What changes do you need to welcome to realize your joy, to welcome grace, to feel the closeness of God? Open your heart to change and achieve your destiny.

Meditation today should begin with the word "change." Breathe in the wind of change and breathe out the fear of surrender…breathe in the willingness to be vulnerable… allow your breath to blow open the gates of control to embrace the change that awaits you…

Write in your journal about the feelings you have for change in your life; just the feelings. I feel about change. Choose one of those feelings and think of one way that you can be open to change about that feeling today.

We are not human beings trying to be spiritual.
We are spiritual beings trying to be human.

Pierre Tielhard de Chardin

My early view of the human experience: a journey of trial and tribulations, misery and pain, dotted with moments of joy and peace. I have now begun to feel that de Chardin was right but my road to this understanding was not an easy one. My spiritual journey was not chosen by me; rather, I felt thrust onto the path, kicking and screaming for release. I now ride in the back seat of the bicycle, the tandem bike; the one where I am never alone but feel safe with God. My definition for spirituality is the individual experience with my higher power or source. Webster defines spirit as "the breath of life, conceived as a kind of vapor animating the body, or, in man, mediating between body and soul." To be spiritual, as defined by Webster is "of the soul or its affections as influenced by divine Spirit." For me, to be spiritual is to find connection to peace beyond thought and the chattering noise of my mind. I find connection grounds me throughout the day, instead letting my inner voice rant and rave for control of the world. Moving into spirituality means a type of concentrated solitude and deliberate moment-by-moment release. I no longer argue with my reality, for very long anyway. When I think of my spiritual journey as it relates to my practice, I see visible evidence of mediating between body and soul. When I take those first minutes of the day to remember who I really am, what I really am doing here, I also notice the connection I have with the people who are placed along my path. I share and they share with me and together somehow we meet in our bigger, mutual existence, the one of spirit.

Meditation today should begin with the word "spirituality." Invite your spirit, your inner core, with each breath to speak to you...go to that place where your humanness vaporizes and you become the spirit that you are...

In your journal today, write down the clearest path to spirituality that you can envision. Take one step on that path to spirituality today.

Replenishment

I will tell you what I learned myself. For me a long,
five or six mile walk helps. And one must go alone and often.

Brenda Ueland

In the morning after I meditate, write and prepare for the day, I must leave my desk and commune with nature for 30 minutes. It may be blustery or gorgeous, but I must go. My peace depends on it. I do not have the luxury of the 5 or 6 mile walk as in the quotation of Ms. Ueland above, but I grant myself the time I have to proceed with my work, and my work includes the 30 minute walk. When in the middle of two intense sessions with clients, I need to leave the office and walk, no matter the conditions, no matter the time. I find that I cannot continue with the tasks of the day if I do not grant myself the freedom and peace of movement. Replenish the body, the mind, the heart, the spirit, and you will return to the table with the attentiveness and effectiveness required for the kind of work we do. I do my deepest walking meditation with my animals. For the puppies, it is a grounding event; getting ready to go, I only need grab the leash, and they respond with glee and excitement. I know dogs can smile. I see that broad smile as they return to their internal Artemis, huntresses of the forest. My little spiritual friends have a way of pointing out the beauty of God's mysteries. We hike through wildflowers and rocks layered with the colors of power: deep purple, sage green, iridescent charcoal, and terra cotta pink. We notice a giant boulder with the most delicate edelweiss sprouting from a tiny fissure at the top. We stop and smell plants and observe flying creatures of both the avian and insect variety. As for me, my stiff and tired body is in need of re-patterning; my weary eyes desire the magnificence of the lush green meadow, the deep azure lake and the mountains glowing with the radiance of the sun. Can you find the time to replenish your soul this day?

Meditation today should begin with the word "replenish." Breathe in new life to your sleepy lungs...breathe out the stiff, stale air of the night...breathe in renewal and peaceful energy...go to the stillness of your mind and quiet the thoughts of the last moment...

Write down three ways that you can replenish your soul each day. Make them a commitment to yourself this week.

If you separate anything from the connection and continuity of either the parts or the causes, you disturb the whole. And when you are dissatisfied with life, you disconnect yourself, and this causes, as far as it is your power, breakage, and disruption.

Marcus Aurelius

Daily events of living consume us. When things are painful to review in our lives, often we bury ourselves. We go through the motions, filling every moment with things to do in order to dull the senses. In addition to control, I have recently discovered another addiction, workaholism. I realize that Marcus Aurelius' ancient counsel still applies to living today: perhaps we need to separate from that which is causing dissatisfaction. I can excuse my workaholism by attributing it to the kind of work I do, as a small business owner, mediator, educator, writer, mother, mentor, and friend, but that would be a lie. Until a few years ago, I never took time for me in the mornings; rarely spent time convening with the divine, seldom sat with my spirit to just be. In search of something missing, I just decided to be busy, all the time. In the act of busyness, I depleted my reserves in body, mind, and spirit. Busyness is the act of avoidance. Perhaps I was not taking an inventory of how my life was already abundant; or, maybe I wanted outside forces to be the cause of my busyness and then I could be a victim of the busyness. But in the act of a full out marathon, I was not removing the obstacles in order to be open to the flow of creation and soul. I could not find my peace within. To say, "Yes" to peace and stop the crazy incessant movement is the anecdote to the busyness. If we do not choose to balance our energy, we cannot be the peace we wish to bring to those in conflict. We move into the addiction of running from the divine and into the arms of misery and emptiness. We miss the special moments of life: the butterfly chasing the puppy; the singing of a grandchild out in the garden; the clouds reflecting smoky waves of peace over nightfall; or the love from a friend waiting to receive us. What are you missing in the act of busyness? Do you need to dismantle the parts of the busy wheel and instead ride the magic carpet?

Meditation today should begin with the word "busyness." Disengage from 'the list' as you go within this morning to float along a more peaceful plane. With each breath take the time for you and heal from the frantic pace of yesterday, the push to pull. Go within and be busy-less.

Write down the list of the 'to do's' that came to you in mediation. Set them aside. Now write down a list of things that you can do for your peace. Choose one from the second list for every 4 hours of your waking day and make sure it happens. Finish your 'to do's' when you feel like it.

Nan Waller Burnett

*So we see that one of the keys to the game of living is to become aware of the ways
in which we are demanding that people be different from the way they are.*

Ken Keyes

Marital therapists will tell you that one of the major causes of marital discord is unmet expectations. Amazingly, we do not talk about what our expectations are before we commit to another. Commitment is miraculously supposed to give us the powers of mind reading. Unfortunately, our minds do not work that way, especially when we are in the wonders of a new of relationship. We feel understood by that person, or at least their attention and behavior would make us feel understood, and connected in passion or oneness of purpose. Likewise, expectations are not spoken of in other close relationships. Our business partners should also be able to read our minds. Most relationship energy is wasted trying to mold, fit, cram, or stuff a partner into our idea of what we expect in that picture frame of a perfect relationship, or business partner, in-law, or neighbor. In reality, we cannot demand that people become anything other than they are. To change another in the course of relationship never works and we spend a great deal of time in the annoying act of unsuccessful restructuring. Acceptance is a better use of energy.

In helping clients resolve differences in close personal relationships, peacemakers and conflict practitioners need to begin with inquiry of expectation. Having clients draw a concrete diagram of what the expectations are, bring clarity to any dispute. No demands are what acceptance looks like. This does not mean that one needs to accept and live with behavior that does not bring peace and joy. It means the expectations we have of ourselves need to rise. Asking for what we need in a relationship is the opposite of avoidance. Every person approaches conflict with a certain degree of avoidance; our clients desire peace but do not have the skills to get there. The skilled facilitator of conflict engagement is the master of understanding. We need to recognize and release our own personal desires and expectations to settle the case in mediation, knowing they are often unrealistic expectations. We provide the questions, they provide the answers. Think about the expectations that you have for your role in personal relationships and also in the resolution of relationship strife.

Meditation today should begin with the words "unmet expectations." Go to the quiet reservoir of mind and look within. Have your unmet expectations been reviewed? Breathe in the inquiry you need today to bring clarity to your own relationships and breathe out unrealistic expectation.

Write down all the expectations that you have in significant relationships. My partner should . After you write down all the shoulds, write down the answers to this question: I should . Come back to the list at the end of the next week and see if you were successful in looking at relationships in a different way.

Allowing for improvement, while not existing in perfection, I am a work in progress.

Julia Cameron

Julia Cameron wrote of her singular journey in *The Artist's Way.* Cameron's "work in progress" metaphor can also be applied to relationships. Empowerment is having the freedom, the authority, and the responsibility to act in your own life. We have a skewed sense of relationship in our culture. We think that, somehow, when we choose a mate for life, we should be joined at the hip; however, except in rare cases of a perfect affinity for exactly the same interests, most couples follow different paths at different times. Unrealistic expectations and boundary violations are the main reasons for emotion to bubble up in relationships. A general lack of communication skills adds insult to the injury. Often, we find ourselves fighting over the wheel of the one car. If we were trained to be on the same highway but in different cars, we would be more empowered in our relationships. When clients come to us with the victim story, one of the most effective tools to use is to illuminate the path to empowerment. Embedded within a perception of powerlessness, clients lack the skills to resolve their issue or are too emotional to be rational.

The dance of power is an element of conflict that can be subtle and misunderstood. Every move made within the negotiation communications of conflict, whether tactical or reactive, applies pressure to a system. Every move a neutral makes can change the trajectory of the system. The system is always in flux. Parties who are not present can also influence the system. Low power tactics are used by avoiders, and high power tactics are used by competitors. Avoiders and low power tacticians are under the mistaken impression they are powerless against the forces of the higher power tactician and need empowerment. Think about your ability to be empowered in your own life: when do you use low power tactics and when do you use high power tactics in relationships? Can you set boundaries? Becoming empowered is a process of choosing again. Reintroducing yourself to choice and spiritual freedom is the way to a joyful mind and a happy nature. Reacquainting ourselves with the spiritual path holds the key to self-empowerment.

Meditation today should begin with the words "empowerment in relationships." Go to the place of stillness and peace. Imagine your relationships having the quality of peaceful coexistence. Breathe a soft pillow of comfort around your view of your close relationship. Imagine all is well, all the time.

Write down the areas in your life where you feel you are empowered in your relationships. Now write down the areas where you feel powerless. What do you need to ask for? Do you need to set a boundary in a loving and gentle way?

The answers are questions in disguise, every new answer giving rise to new questions.
Abraham Joshua Herschel

The context of a message is the pathway to insight. Context holds the pearl of one's truth—it explains the pain experienced from one heart to another. Context is the part of dialogue which gives meaning to the words. As the quotation illustrates, all the questions we ask in search of solutions bring forth answers which point to new questions. Context paints the picture and makes the intent concrete. As we string these pearls of perception together, disputants can rise from ignorance of meaning to indulge the other person with awareness of their intentions. The artful posing of the question takes focus, experience, and wisdom on the part of the inquirer. Hopefully, the result is to find peace amid the wreckage of previous misunderstandings. Conflict explains the pain, context explains the meaning, one with the power to explain away the other. The art of reframing the toxic language of the speaker in pain is to provide safe passage of the harmful words through questions posed by the practitioner. Each chosen word is weighty in possibility. Each inquiry has illuminating power. Consider the context of the questions you pose today. There is power in those choices. Possibility dwells within the choices. Consider the context of the questions that you ask yourself today. What question, self imposed, holds the key to understanding and the release of personal pain?

Meditation today should begin with the word "context." Feel the air of the morning enter your body. Breathe in with inquiry and breathe out with confidence. Give yourself permission to go within and ask the right questions, for you and your clients. What question do you need an answer to today?

Write down a question that came to you in your meditation. What can you do today to bring light to the pain that came with the question?

Transcending violence is forged by the capacity to generate,
mobilize, and build the moral imagination.

John Paul Lederach

John Paul Lederach, in his book *The Moral Imagination*, wrote beautifully of transcendence. He posited that in order to transcend cycles of violence we must be willing to explore different principles. We must understand the landscape of our situation. Be willing to explore the creative process—to "venture into the uncharted territory" of discovery and imagination, and to embrace mystery. We must be willing to harness the genius of the creative spirit, and to welcome the paradox of living side by side with inherent differences. In order to transcend anything, we need to be willing to stand deeply in the mud of the problem and be willing to drag it to the edge. The edge for me is a synonym for creativity. This is where chaos undergoes metamorphosis. Lederach noted that many of the great scientific discoveries were made creatively through "serendipitous insight." When in the process of mediation allow serendipitous insight to flow.

Mediation today should begin with the word "transcendence." Breathe deeply forcing your lungs to upward heights and feel the resonance of the word transcendence in your body as you say it with intention.

Write down what the word transcendence means to you. How does the word manifest in your practice? What does it mean in your personal life?

> *How wonderful it is that nobody need wait a single*
> *moment before starting to improve the world.*
>
> Anne Frank, *Anne Frank: The Diary of a Young Girl*

I sat amazed when I read this hopeful thought, filled with promise from a 14-year-old child, who we know had her life taken from her. As she wrote from her prison of temporary safety in Amsterdam, she could see the inter-connectedness in life. Her extraordinary words still ring out to generations of the future; it is heart-stirring optimism from a child of God who was executed because was considered sub-human by the nature of her religion. A gentle, sanguine approach to the world, hopeful in her desire for improvement, kept her solitude peaceful. When I think of her words, I think it remiss of me not to immediately spring to my feet and try to effect change today. As I write, "Somewhere Over the Rainbow" through the angelic voices of IL Divo ring out from a CD on my computer, and I see her sweet face in the midst of my thoughts; I know she is at peace. I envision her sitting over the rainbow and smiling. She improved the world during her short reign on earth. She didn't wait for a single moment. How about you?

Meditation should begin with the word "involvement." Breathe deeply and meet your breath with purpose. Envision your breath gently mixing with hers this day and take from the collective energy, of which she is a part, sustenance of the life energy to improve your world.

Write down the images and the thoughts you experienced in meditation. How can you be involved and improve the world today?

There is perhaps no phenomenon which contains so much destructive feeling as moral indignation, which permits envy or hate to be acted out under the guise of virtue.

Erich Fromm

Webster defines virtue as "moral excellence." The first definition found in the dictionary is, "One of the order of angels." Plato named the cardinal virtues as fortitude, prudence, temperance, and justice. To examine these four virtues provides insight into our standards of practice within our field, as well as in the conduct of our lives as ethical souls. Courage, strength of mind in meeting adversity, and endurance to the end, the elements of fortitude, are evident in our job description. The ability to conduct oneself reasonably and with skill is the virtue of prudence. Moderation in all things is the virtue of temperance, the act of restraint in behavior. Conforming to the truth of things is justice. A balanced fairness is what we seek as the change agents of disputes. A virtuous person is one who accepts another without judgment. Fromm spoke to the hypocrisy of one who judges in the name of virtue.

In the world of academia, so closely aligned with ego, there is a great deal of judgment. Our own field is suffering greatly under the weighty burden of moral indignation about the "right" way to practice. I call for each of us to identify and release the ego from our work. The practice of peacemaking and the engagement of conflict is an inside job on the part of the practitioner. It is an art: creativity mixed with experience. Everyone's canvas will look a little different, but that is what makes the world beautiful. Moral indignation within our field is counterproductive in our endeavor to bring solutions of peace to the planet. All spokes on a wheel lead to the hub. Acceptance of every spoke is necessary to put emphasis where it is needed—moving the field forward.

Meditation today should begin with the word "virtue." Breathe in the courage to see deeply into your soul and breathe out negative thoughts. Breathe in acceptance and breathe out righteousness.

What are there avenues open to you to flourish in the cardinal virtues? How can you be more courageous today?...more accepting, enduring, and fair?

Nan Waller Burnett

Hide not your talents, for us they were made. What's a sundial in the shade?
Benjamin Franklin

A well-known television commercial reminds us that a mind is a terrible thing to waste. The musing of the mind is so creative when given fertile ground to sprout wings of innovation and discovery. Benjamin Franklin and other great thinkers from the past, Einstein, Leonardo de Vinci, Plato, Aristotle, Ptolemy, Galileo, and Mozart, all had one thing in common— a general curiosity. They lived in the consciousness of wonder. It seems that in these times we live, time for discovery is sorely lacking; life is lived in the fast lane. A sense of wonder and creativity is found in the stillness that comes with every morning's practice of going within. Taking the time to quiet the mind and construct new avenues of patterned thinking allows a thirst for invention to arise in the dry mouth of monotony. Each and every one of us has unique talents that remain a hidden treasure if we do not take time to discover them. If the sundial is in the shade, it does not accurately reveal the time. The gem of a perfect idea, an act of caring, a creative way of problem solving, a wrenching portrayal of the human condition in drama, artwork from the divine, or arms to hold the weary will not come forth if we hide our talents. We spend so much of our developing years comparing ourselves to others that often we never walk across the bridge to self-acceptance. Our talents were made for sharing, to improve the world in which we live. If we never draw our light to the surface, it will never be shared. Move your sundial into the light today.

Meditate today with the word "talents." Go to that place of creation and rest, deeply into your thoughts and breathe in the collective discovery of an endless energy. Breathe out the fear and drink from the well of possibility. Come out of the shadows and create.

Review the images that you saw in your mind's eye...quickly write them down. What can you do today to begin to share your talents?

When you become the master of your thinking, you become the master of your life.
Ernest Holmes

Deepak Chopra, MD explains in his book *Quantum Healing* that because your body is a field of intelligent energy, you have the power to influence your physical health. He believes that through focus on the positive generation of thought on the cells, we can keep ill health in check and bring increased vitality of life. It seems that some of us live in a state of eternal ill health, while others live vibrant healthy lives. Mind, body, and spirit research has shown that our bodies are more responsive when treated with a holistic approach. Howard Gardner in his work in multiple intelligences noted that we have up to seven different processes of intelligence. Daniel Goleman brought the knowledge of emotional intelligence to us. Ken Wilber, Danah Zohar, and others have brought us the notion that we have spiritual intelligence. Chopra believes that we can have medical intelligence through a multi-phased approach to health. Now, through the technology of brain scans and MRI, we can map the electrical processes of the brain in many different process of thinking. We have concrete evidence that different parts of the brain respond to positive, healthy thoughts, meditation, prayer, and optimism. We have conclusive evidence that treating cancer patients with a holistic course of treatment produces positive results. It all boils down to one thing. To be the master of your thinking is to create a more positive experience during your time on earth. Joy is welcomed. Exercise your intelligence, be the master of your thoughts.

Meditation today should begin with the word "intelligence." Embrace the entire field of your intelligences this morning. Welcome the logical mind as it allows you to traverse the earthly experience; now, breathe out the logic. Breathe in the emotional intelligence and give thanks for the wave of emotions that keeps us in touch with humanity. Breathe in your spiritual intelligence and connect with the collective creative energy you need to keep your body a temple for your soul.

Write down the thoughts that arose in your meditation. Did you find negative thoughts? Write them down. Did you find positive thoughts? Write them down. Give thanks for all the intelligences that you have to make your life a whole one.

Believe nothing just because a so-called wise man said it. Believe nothing just because a belief is generally held. Believe only what you yourself test and judge to be true.

Buddha

Meditation grants the award of knowingness. In the stillness, we can extract the wheat from the chaff. Critical thinking only does not do it for us any longer. Problem solving and decision-making are too linear to provide us with the breadth of information we need to discern our truth from the truth of others. As the Buddha noted, you must be able to believe in your own powers of discrimination, to distinguish between common beliefs of a culture and personal beliefs. Validity requires an asking of the soul. The *ring of truth* must confirm our intuitive processes as well as our logical thought. For this reason, it is imperative that we hone our individual powers of prayer, so that we do not swallow the truths of another as our own. Meditation can be the vehicle we use for that journey. We can always agree to worship in community, but we must have a special individual relationship with our Source to understand what our purpose on earth. To be valid in our reactions to life, we must live in the consciousness of awareness and we find that validity through meditation.

Meditation today should begin with the word "valid." Breathe in clearness of thought and breathe out with force to cleanse the lungs. Breathe in a sense of wonder and breathe out stiffness in the body.

Journal today about what seems valid to you. When you hear the ring of truth how do you recognize it? How do you discern the correct choices in your life?

*I gain strength, courage and confidence by every experience in which
I must stop and look fear in the face... I say to myself, I've lived
through this and can take the next thing that comes along.*

Eleanor Roosevelt

Generally, dispute resolution has been a field of denial of emotion and fear, with a focus on containment and settlement. We maximize the gain, we minimize the loss. This is hard to do if you are focusing on emotion and fear in particular. Clients arrive at our table filled with fear. They are afraid of the unknown, of losing whatever the dispute is about, and of facing the opponent. If we fear anything, it is time for inquiry. Allow inquiry to reach through to the depths of fear and dispel it. Having the courage to face that which makes us afraid is a very freeing experience. When you face it with inquiry, the feeling arises, is explored, diffused, and finally goes by the wayside. That line of inquiry should look something like, "Why, what, how, and when am I afraid?" On a deeper level ask, "What is the first step out of that feeling?" As Eleanor Roosevelt noted once you've "lived through this [you] can take the next thing that comes along." What runs you? What stops you? What frees you?

Meditation today should begin with the phrase "facing fear." Sit in stillness and count your deep breaths as you contemplate that which makes you feel despair.

Think about the things of which you are afraid. What runs you? What stops you? What frees you? How can you use inquiry to dispel fear and face it? List the things in your life right now that are discouraging to you. How have you been discouraged in the past? How can you use inquiry to dispel the feeling?

Peacemakers

Let the peacemakers arise in the four corners of the earth and practice their trade.

Frederic and Mary Ann Brussat

There is a rising up occurring in our field of conflict resolution. I feel a certain energy pulsing through the dialogue and a power of practice that has not had been there before. I sense a coming together, a movement toward the center from many spokes. Collaborative lawyers are moving the field, mediators changing the field, educators are affecting the field, and the judiciary is stirring the field. An interdisciplinary inter-connectedness is pouring in from the dialogues in the great academic universities. Cultural anthropologists are finding a meeting of the mind with jurists and legal scholars. The language of the psychotherapist is in tandem with that of inspired attorneys. Communications specialists are training educators; philosophers are moving to match politicians. From "the four corners of the earth", the peacemakers are rising up to "practice their trade." As Rumi notes, "we will meet each other in the field and our souls lie down in that grass together." Are you ready to join those moving toward the center of the field?

Your meditation today should begin with the words "maker of peace." As you consider the peace of the morning air coursing through your lungs, wrap your breath around your blessings and express gratitude for this moment of your life...the moment you rise up and make peace for the planet.

Write down the efforts you make in peacebuilding. What is one way that you can make peace with yourself today? What is one way you can further peace in your community today? How can you be a channel for peace in your own relationships?

*All the evidence available in the biological sciences supports the core
proposition that the cosmos is a specifically designed whole, with
life and mankind as its fundamental goal and purpose.*

Michael Denton, PhD.

Disorganization of the universe is a great source of wonder and excitement. Is it possible that we realize it is not disorganization or chaos at all, instead it makes perfect sense? We will discover in this lifetime, that science and spirit meet in the circle of knowledge to dismiss the age of reason forever. For all of our efforts at measurement, quantifying the unknown, developing hypotheses, categorizing, and qualifying humans scientifically, is it possible there is a question that science and reason cannot and could never answer. Will we finally see a benevolent higher power standing at the end of the rainbow of rationale awaiting our return to source? Wayne Dyer notes in his book *Spirituality*, we are all part of the same life force. He wrote the emptiness that many feel is because we do not feel any connection to that source. As we gaze up to the universe in wonder and excitement, a feeling of significance or smallness can permeate the questioning mind. But in search of cosmic comparison, the molecular scientist, the neuroscientists, the physicists, the holistic healers, and theologians are coming toward the center of understanding. The current theory is that we are part of a purposely designed whole; we are comprised of ever-changing energy, a collective consciousness. We have purpose after all. In review of your wondering about the cosmos, enter your meditation today with a sense of excitement…agree to become open to new revelations about the fabric of life.

Meditation today should begin with the word "cosmos." As you go toward the stillness of the morning and breathe deeply the nectar of energy that is abundant in life force, source. Breathe out any feeling of smallness and breathe in connection and acceptance.

Write in your journal today about your relationship to the heavens, the higher power, to yourself. What is one thing that you can do today to make that connection felt within your heart?

It seems rather incongruous that in a society of super-sophisticated communicators, we often suffer from a shortage of listeners.

Erma Bombeck

A major reason for the failure to understand is that our minds are constantly focused on our preparation of the next response. We are locked in a perpetual state of responding because we cannot quiet our racing thoughts. We do not stop to focus on the message. When clients come before us in conflict, the quiver of arrows lies beside them at the table, ready to shoot down any potential accusation lobbed their way. I once had an injured Dad before me, his mouth on ripple-salvo, blasting every request the Mother made with lightening speed. He was well versed in his story of self-righteous blame. I could not slow his volleys. I sometimes keep the power point fired up, on reserve and ready to break craziness at the table. I took a deep breath, asked silently for guidance, trusted my gut, and flashed up on the screen, the Chinese symbol for listening. The symbol for listening is comprised of the symbols for ears, heart and eyes; a beautiful character of art in white on a peaceful background of blue shown down radiantly on this seething man. I said, "Read the words to me." "Why?" he replied. "Because I want you to," I retorted with authority. He complied. I then asked him if he was listening to her at all. He responded that she didn't "deserve to be listened to because she is a liar." Further, he noted that his entire life with her had been a lie because she had never loved him, she just used him. The opportunity for true healing awaited me like a gift, wrapped in golden paper. "Tell her how you felt when she left." Without the strength to lift another arrow from his quiver, he broke down with grief and sadness, filling the room with the grace of a reality finally spoken. He poured his heart onto the table. I asked her to respond to his deep rejection, and she responded with great compassion, "I never intended to hurt you. I did not know how to ask for what I wanted. I felt that I could not be heard. I have great respect for you as the father you are to the children." That litany of reality stopped him cold. As he listened deeply to her, he realized that she was also sad. In his perpetual monologue, he discovered that he had been taking the trip to hell by himself; he chose again in that moment. In review of your significant relationships, do you need to recommit to deeply listening?

Meditation today should begin with the words "perpetual monologue." Breathe in the desire to listen deeply and breathe out the racing monologue of mind and feel the peace, breathe in stillness.

What is one thing that you can do today to become a better listener?

What is life? It is the flash of a firefly in the night. It is the breath of a buffalo in the wintertime. It is the little shadow which runs across the grass and loses itself in the sunset.

Chief Blackfoot

When I read the above quotation by Blackfoot, it reminds me to notice every second of each day with new eyes. As I sit perched in my mountain office in the high country of Colorado, the expanse of the Continental Divide before me, I watch the azure sky responding to the setting of the sun. It transforms the sky from radiant magenta and blushed pink to violet, purple and blue-gray, and I flashed back to the sky of my youth. In the Deep South, the air is heavy and sweet with the smell of honeysuckle and fresh grass. The sky suspends weighty clouds of whipped cream as they lumber across the firmament. I remember lying in the yard, somewhere in the back of my mind was the urge to get up, afraid to have the chiggers bite me, but unable to move as I watched the slow dance of the earth; amazed that it was actually moving. What a journey I have had! I have also seen many valleys since that time. The difference is that I have come to be comfortable while in a crevasse wrought with information, in a way that I could never have imagined. In the earlier years, fear always drove me. I spent years in the '*yikes*' mode; afraid of the bottom, expending much energy in avoidance. Now, when I see the shadow approaching, I know the peaks and valleys of life are a part of every journey, every experience. I have felt my sense of wonder return. I await the surprise. Who will be sent my way? What re-connections, what new connection? What lessons do they hold for me and I for them? As I sit and watch the sky before me, I embrace the mystery.

Meditation today should begin with the words "peaks and valleys." As you take in the fresh morning air and your lungs rise to fulfillment, notice the peaks and dream of the high points, the day you graduated, the day your children were born, the day you bought your first house...and as you exhale the peaks, embrace the emptiness of your lungs as they rest in the valley with anticipation of the next peak.

Make a list of as many of your peaks as you can recall in rapid succession. On the opposite side of the paper, make a list of the as many valleys as you can. Ponder the list today. What is one thing that you can do to prepare you for the next valley?

Optimism

Let your hook always be cast. In the pool where you least expect it, will be a fish.

Ovid

It seems the world is comprised of pessimists and optimists. Cheerfulness is a character trait and yet it can be cultivated and nurtured as a choice of the soul. Optimists have a certain confidence about them, a brightness of personality that draws others towards them. Given the task of assessing whether the glass is almost full or almost empty, they will always choose the perceptive fullness of any point of view. Webster defined optimism as, "The doctrine the world is the best possible world, that reality is essentially good, the good of life basically overbalances the pain of it." As Ovid wrote in the 1st Century B.C., one should always remain open to possibility; just around the corner the prize awaits. An optimistic outlook on life greatly improves the experience of it. Optimism is proven to be a quality of those who can beat life-threatening illness, enjoy success in business and raise healthy children. Remain hopeful that solutions are possible, and you will be effective in your job. Hold the view that all outcomes are within reach, and you will be able to assist the parties in finding the light of day in resolution. Optimism does not support a finite world of black and white. Rather, optimism supports the view of infinity. If one expends energy looking for why something will not work, reality will be an unsolvable problem. But if one remains hopeful, the creative juices of possibility pour into the mind and transformations can occur in any application to life. What about your personal life? Are you an optimist or a pessimist? Take an inventory of your relationships. Uncover the optimism today.

Meditation today should begin with the word "optimism." As you go that place of peace, let the open mind search for the brightness with confidence and breathe the light air of optimism into your lungs and breathe out the stale air of doubt and pessimism.

Write down in your journal all the things that you can think of about which you have doubts. Now write down all the things that look hopeful to you. Search for a new area of hope and optimism today.

Sorrow

The deeper that sorrow carves into your being, the more joy you can contain.

Kahlil Gibran

The reservoir of emotion that one holds deepens over time. Engraving a story of loss upon the heart, sorrow fills the soul with regret and misery. But as the emotion pours into a river of pain, a release of sadness and sorrow can bring the joy of tomorrow. The heart is elastic in its ability to hold a multitude of feelings. As Gibran notes, the elasticity creates more room for joy to return. I am reminded of Garth Brooks' song, "The Dance." Those who sit in sorrow miss the chance to dance in their life. I had my heart broken when I was in my early 20s. It carved a pattern of protection into my heart for years. I lived through a painful divorce where my character and spirituality were maligned. I had to wait 14 years to find out that my children knew who I really was and recognized my values and virtue. Memory of pain can cause a heart to reflexively respond with protection if one does not deliberately set out a course of correction. Sorrow is the mournful cry; the tears of the heart. We can set forth a pattern as though sorrow is the normal state of emotion. Depression is the abnormality. Joy is the first order of the heart. One has to set forth the intention to fill the deep engraving of grief with the blissful, beguiling enchantment of the soul. One needs to invite the magic of jubilance, coax the magnetism of charisma to charm the soul, and create a new pattern of delight in the heart. There is an abundance of room for the myriad of emotion to pass through the folds of a vibrant heart. What corrections of thought do you need to make today? What intentions need to be set forth?

Meditation today should begin with the word "sorrow." Have the courage to breathe deep joy into your lungs by choice and breathe out the restrictions of yesterday. Fall into the embrace of an angel as you deposit your sorrow within the folds of the wings of mercy. Choose joy this day and know the heart is elastic with expandability.

Write in your journal all the ways that you have chosen sorrow in the last week. Write down the times when you have experienced joy. How could you have chosen joy on the sorrowful days?

In every generation, we thank thee and recount thy praise – for our lives
which are in thy charge, for our souls which are in thy care, for thy miracles
which are daily with us, and for thy continual wonders and favors.

Philip Birnbaum, *Daily Prayer Book: Ha-Siddur Ha-Shalem*

Gratitude stands at the gate of appreciation. Gratitude brings the awareness an ordinary day holds evidence of the blessings received. I remember my mother saying, "You should always count your blessings, things can always be worse than they are." At the time, it seemed a trivial thing to say, without meaning to a young person with no first hand experience that life can be difficult. As I began to keep a gratitude journal, I noticed my attention became focused on the positive things in my life. Relationships I had once considered trials had a new meaning for me. I was able to embrace fully the daily reality of my life when I counted blessings in my satchel. My focus centered on the beauty of my world, my divinity, and the positive blessings already present in my life, rather than the wave of misery formerly at the core of my concentration. I love this beautiful Jewish Prayer. It is expansive in its focus to the wonders of living and addresses all the possible matters for which we can be thankful. Also, it acknowledges prior generations, a stalwart tradition in the Jewish faith; reminding present generations to instruct their children in the traditions of the fathers. Prayer in any religion is a beautiful ritual. Requesting an audience with the divine, a connection, an owning of internal equality brings each inquirer peace in the moment. Imagine of your day unfolding in way that illuminates the gifts and blessings for which you can give thanks.

Meditation today should begin with the word "thankfulness." Today I allow my consciousness to concentrate on honoring the lives of others. I breathe into my body the grace of knowing all that I should be thankful for and this intention will set my course for the day with peace and I am willing to be thankful.

Quickly list a column of gratitude. Look again. What is missing from your list? Stop three times today and give thanks for what is in front of you in that moment.

*People are usually more convinced by reasons they discovered
themselves than by those found by others.*

Blaise Pascal

Often, we cannot see the reality of a situation because we are blinded by desire. We may desire to be right, be invested in a particular outcome and/or resource, or perhaps just to win over another. Pushing our point across the table at our adversary only brings resistance to the engagement. A couple I recently worked with were divided about their two children, both lobbying for what they envisioned as the desires of each child, unable to see their own pain and triggers were escalating the conflict higher up the ladder of animosity. They had married young, and he was her self-appointed protector, shielding her from the dog-eat-dog world of business and responsibility. He was an administrator, the educated breadwinner, providing nicely for his family and controlling every move they made. In his perception, he had served well: after all she was uneducated, unskilled in the ways of the world. He had set her up nicely in a beautiful mountain house, and she drove beautiful cars. An authority figure with tunnel vision, he saw her as a ninny, unable to do life without him, shallow, and histrionic; a teenager really. He soon met a trophy of a woman in his working life. She was beautiful, owned her own company, had efficiently raised two children who were both in college on full scholarships, and was always seeking self-improvement. He was head over heels in lust with her. He began to plan an exit strategy. Much the same way as he had controlled their marriage, he began to control the exit; telling her to get a job, get an education, get off your _____; "Be a role model for your children for God's sake!" Safely ensconced in his tunnel, he built a case for disengagement. Even after the divorce, he tried to tell her how to do her life. Her view of her life was very different. Through the years, she felt that she had been so controlled she could not grocery shop without his consent. She felt smothered and constrained, and she feared his ability to win every argument. She never trusted him. Now, in divorce, they were armed with efficient attorneys; he, of course not taking the advice of his and she, of course, standing firmly behind her new protector; neither listening to my reasoning or admonishments to refocus on their children. Tunneling vision, they failed to hear the warnings of others. In the end, they destroyed both of their children, one seeking distance by refusing to speak to either, and the other vacillating between parenting the mother and thoughts of suicide. Such is the work before us in the engagement of conflict in families. What about your own world? Are you in a relationship with a tunneler? Are you tunneling your vision in some way?

Meditation today should begin with the words "tunnel vision." Agree with each breath to look again at your relationships...go on a voyage of discovery this morning. What can you see?

Write down in your journal any adjustments you need to make in your perceptions about your relationships.

Your soul suffers if you live your life superficially.

Albert Schweitzer

When we feel really despondent over events in our life, the natural tendency is to try to escape the hurt. There are many ways that we can evacuate our heart. At the root of all pain is the feeling that we are not good enough, or that we will be or have been judged and found deficient. One way to escape those feelings is to live life on the surface. Albert Schweitzer notes that simply living in "the doing" of things provides a superficial existence which lacks the depth necessary for real growth or happiness. Skimming the surface of life and failing to ride the wave, both of peaks and valleys, manifests a walking death while the body is still alive. A dissonance of emotion occurs, restricting the flow of electrical energy to the amygdala, the brain's emotional processor. As the separation of the self is reinforced through continued separation from higher power, we become humans doing, not human beings; mere robots in life. Another way of escape is to dive into what I call "othering." "Othering" expresses itself in parasitic relationships. As Rumi says, "You are the source of your milk. Don't milk others! There is a milk fountain inside of you. Don't walk around with an empty bucket."

Know in your heart that you are the source of your own milk, your fountain is awaiting your command; it will tap a creative source of soul that will never be depleted. Living is not for the faint of heart! To not live the life you were given is a tragedy. Don't stay on the surface where it is safe and even. Dive deeply into the essence of you and know that you are light filled energy. You draw into your heart those who will enhance your journey and make the experience rich and full.

Mediation today should begin with the word "escape." Sit in the quiet corners of your heart this morning and escape the fear of a superficial life. Dive into your lungs with each breathe and embrace the adventure of the unknown.

Write in your journal today five ways that you can dive into life rather than escape today. What is one thing that is stopping you?

He who has a 'why' to live for can bear almost any 'how.'

Freidrich Nietzsche

Expectations, desires, dreams, and wishes are all intricately tied to hope. Hope is also a breath away from trust. The word implies an optimistic view of the future while trust is reserved for the outcome. Hope has a futuristic element to it. To hope for something means that, perhaps it doesn't already exist. "I hope the weather is good today. I hope things settle down in the Middle East. I hope I don't end up alone." These are all wishes for the future. Also, hope has a connotation of happiness and fulfillment. My daughter was three when we prepared for to trip to grandma's house. We boarded a bus for the terminal at the airport and a pilot in uniform followed us onto the platform. She took a long look at him and said, "I hope he knows how to get to Salt Lake City!" We begin to hope early in life. Hope is not necessary if focus can be placed in the moment. That which is already occurring in life is perfect, there is no need to wish or hope for it not to be happening, it is just what is. As Nietzsche noted if one is familiar with purpose one can embrace any "how" that is already here. What things do you hope for? What current moments do you need to recognize, as the hopes of yesterday?

Meditation today should begin with the word "hope." Sit with the word quietly and contemplate the hope in your heart. Breathe form into the hopes. Breathe out any attachment to the outcome and go to the place of knowing that is peaceful and safe.

Release your hopes on the wings of the dove. As they fly away from you know that they will manifest in the moment of the now. Write in your journal the images that you saw in your mind's eye in your meditation.

Nan Waller Burnett

*Happiness is spiritual, born of Truth and Love. It is unselfish; therefore
it cannot exist alone, but requires all mankind to share it.*

Mary Baker Eddy

We are so invested in the thoughts of the mind we often do not realize that our soul knows a deeper truth. Inspiration comes from deep within our soul. To become inspired is to bring forth happiness. If I affirm in my soul that I am worthy of inspiration, I will become inspired. For me inspiration comes through choosing again. Happiness is one emotion that is felt through the conscious intention of choice. Webster defines inspiration as to "take in air, to breathe." To focus on the literal meaning of the word for a moment, imagine that inspiration is followed by the words, "choose again." Inspire yourself with a long breathe and say "I will choose again." For me, this is a very empowering practice. The inspiration comes into my mind now without prompting, especially when I feel anger arise: "choose again." This practice proves to me that whatever condition I may be experiencing at the time is not permanent and through my exercise of choice, I can become inspired to be happy. Mary Baker Eddy was the founder of the Christian Science Church. She notes in her writings that happiness is of the spirit and a result of love. One is drawn to share it with others. My dear friend, Carol, who I have counted on frequently for inspiration, was recently visiting me in the mountains. We were talking about our collective journey through the transitions of life and when we reflected on why we were, perhaps, more content than some of our cohorts. She said, "on a deep level the soul always knows, and I think we have made choices for happiness when we had to. We have allowed our soul to do its thing." Those words had a ring of truth for me on that memorable evening. As I gazed out onto the meadow, the sun sank slowly behind the peaks, and I reflected on the circle of life, realizing that as "souls doing their things," Carol and I had traveled that path together. We have shared tribulations but, more importantly, we have shared a thirst for knowledge. We chose the road to joy and inner peace, and as Robert Frost says so well, "that has made all the difference."

The soul is never...not doing what it needs to do.

Carol McFadden

Meditation today should begin with the word "inspiration." Infuse your lungs with the sweet sustenance of happy thoughts. Stimulate your brain to flow with thoughts of joy and radiant the light of those thoughts throughout your body: breath, inspiration, breath...Awaken, breathe and stimulate your mind to choose the road of peace and find those who travel the road with you.

Write down in your journal any instances of inspiration you have noticed recently. Were there any faces that you envisioned in your meditation? Do you know them? Then write down any other feelings that arose during the meditation. Look for the evidence that you have can choose inspiration at any time.

*It is good that the philosopher should remind himself, now and
then, that he is a particle pontificating on infinity.*

Will and Ariel Durant

I am consumed with Ken Wilber. Without question, he is the modern philosopher of our time. A remarkable mind in search of answers of the grandest nature, he never stops processing the wonder, the mystery. I sit amazed as I read his words; one can almost feel the firing of synapses. The first book of his I read was *A Brief History of Everything*. Now, really, who would attempt such a project? Dumbfounded as I turned the pages, his very linear mind had communicated to my very circular patterns of thinking. Doubtless he already knows that he is a particle pontificating on infinity. For according to quantum mechanics, that is exactly what he is. I am now a true *Wilberian*! He could care less about the established view of scientific approaches to reasoning. . Like the Mozart of philosophy and psychology, he is willing to simply stand in his light and speak out with unabashed confidence. Not one to leave a stone unturned, he has performed research of such depth to back his reasoning, and one is hard pressed to disagree with him.

In *Integral Psychology*, he related one story of his thirst for knowledge. He recants a story from early in his career. He was in an antique bookstore and discovered a copy of Gustav Fechner's work, *Life after Death*, 1835. He was astonished to read in this early work that Fechner, who had always been credited with making psychology a true science by developing a method for scientific quantitative measurement of the mind, wrote of deep consciousness and three phases of life. Fechner posited that man lives three times, first in birth, second in dying, and third in universal spirit. Wilber was flabbergasted to find that Fechner's true philosophy of life was mind, soul, and consciousness. Fechner is recognized for his contributions but only about scientific measurement. Wilber asked "Why had no one told the story of Fechner's true thoughts on consciousness and the mind?" Wilber made it his mission to enlighten the world about Gustav Fechner. If you are not familiar with Ken Wilber, I invite you to become a *Wilberian* today. He is a model for expansion of the mind and for being a particle of infinity with divinity.

Meditation today should begin with the word "philosophy." Go to the place of wonder and breathe deeply into your consciousness. Bring life force to your creative mind. Determine what you believe to be true. Do you need to question what is considered to be normal in your field? Do you need to uncover a deeper truth within yourself?

Write in your journal today about your sense of mystery and wonder. Examine your personal philosophy. Discover what is really important in your life.

The privilege of a lifetime is to be yourself.

Joseph Campbell

Shame drives so much of the human experience. Shame is the one of the quadrants in the formula for interpersonal conflict; what I call *the box of conflict*. When one perceives shame or blame, one always responds with defense and protection. We tend to bury the memories that trigger shame in us. They surface when someone in our circle of concern, often an innocent bystander, shatters our self-protective glass with a comment or an action. While leading women's empowerment groups, I worked each week with the self-loathing that shame brings. One gray autumn day, a successful, pretty woman of 35 finally decided at the end of the sixth session to share for the first time. She recounted the torment of her soul. She had lived in deep shame over an abortion that she had when she was 20. It was her first year in college, filled with promise and preparing for a career in medicine, she lost her virginity to a young classmate, also 20. On her first sexual experience, she had become pregnant. Filled with shame, she had never told another human being after she had left the clinic. She never even told the boy. She checked herself into a motel north of the college town and sobbed for 2 days. After naming her unborn child and begging God to forgive her, she buried the pain, sealing it for years as a festering shame. She revealed her truth in group that day, shaking with grief and self-hatred within the safety of bonded sisters. Not one flutter of sound could be heard in the sacred circle. I motioned for the group to act upon their empathy, and we all moved without words to the center of the circle, placing warm hands of love and understanding on her rigid body. After several minutes, the flood of pain was released from her heart. Then, the tears of two group members began to flow. They related, one after the other, their own stories of shame and self-hatred, and released the floodgates of the hellish water of shame. In the sharing of shame, other members also found forgiveness for their own perceived transgressions. As Joseph Campbell noted, we are privileged to be ourselves. Why then, is it incumbent on us to harbor the deep secrets of shame for a lifetime without embracing our humanness? Honor your path today. Know that your life experience is holy. Treat yourself today as one who is deserving of self-love, not the shame of self-hatred.

Meditation today should begin with the word "shame." Breathe out release from the dark molding hatred and breathe in the divinity that dwells within your core. You have nothing be ashamed of and know that as humans we are doing the best we can at the time with the knowledge we have at the time. Breathe in the embrace of acceptance.

Write in your journal all the things that you have been ashamed of in the past. Burn or destroy the list. Write down all the things that you honor about yourself. Flag this page and review the list everyday for 30 days.

Internal peace is an essential first step to achieving peace in the world. How do you cultivate it? It's very simple. In the first place, by realizing clearly that all mankind is one, that human beings in every country are members of one and the same family.

His Holiness the Dalai Lama

Accordance is the act of bringing agreement or an act of harmony. As the Dalai Lama noted, we must be peaceful ourselves to bring peace to others. Another other criterion for success in building peace is to understand the inter-connectedness of all creatures in spiritual energy. On one occasion, a father came in several minutes before the mother and wanted to prime me for the session by telling me how manipulative she really was. Early arrival with that intention is not uncommon. On that particular day, I had spent 20 minutes reading a spiritual path book and meditating. In the past, I might have ushered him into the waiting room, instructing him to be mindful of the fact that I was a neutral and should not speak to him before the other parent arrived. But on that special day, I was serene, open, and showed interest in what he had to say. I listened in peace, asked him questions about the nature of his fear, and with peaceful energy, I brought him to higher reasoning about the necessity for children to have the experience of their mother no matter what he thought of her. In his heart, he knew this to be true and by the time the mother arrived, we were spiritually prepared to begin to resolve their problems in accordance with what was in the best interest of the children. With my questions I was able to draw a metaphorical picture of inter-connectedness for him and in a miraculous way, without knowing, I knew exactly how to do it. These are the gifts which a willingness to be peaceful brings to the circle of conflict. Think about accordance in your life and in your practice.

Meditation today should begin with the word "accord." Breathe harmony into your lungs this quiet morning and breathe out the unsure breaths. Breathe in the silken peace of prayer.

Write down in your journal one way that you can be more peaceful today. How can you bring accord to those in painful conflict? How can bring peace to your soul?

Grace strikes us when we are in great pain and restlessness....
Sometimes at that moment a wave of light breaks into our darkness,
and it is as though a voice were saying: "You are accepted."

Paul Tillich, *The Shaking of the Foundations*

Grace is given for the asking. We can summon grace through stillness and listening with an open heart. Grace can become a quality—it has become so in many holy people—but if you are painfully trying to morph into another kind of butterfly, as I am, you will not likely attain a constant state of grace. I can only hope for periods of grace, moments when I am granted that inner acceptance. I can then extend grace to others, the glowing feeling of which I can only describe as true love of self. I am sure we have all felt that feeling at some point along our journey. If we can remember the exact details of the loving act of kindness that precipitated our feeling of grace, perhaps we can register it in our reflexive psyche. Moments of deep sadness, moments when we helped one in need or reversed a negative situation, point toward where this ever-present feeling of grace is stored. Look deeply into your soul and locate your reserves of grace. As Tillich states, where is "that moment a wave of light breaks into [your] darkness"?

By grace I mean inner harmony, essentially spiritual, which
can be translated into outward harmony.

Anne Morrow Lindbergh, *Gift from the Sea*

Meditate today on the word "grace." Breathe softly into your soul this morning, and give yourself permission to feel the comforting arms of grace.

In your journal, record the times you felt and extended grace. Replay those memories throughout the day and extend your feeling of grace to others.

For the sense of being which in calm hours rise, we know not how, in the soul, is not diverse from things, from space, from light, from time, from man, but one with them and proceedeth obviously from the same source whence their life and being also proceedeth."

Ralph Waldo Emerson, "Self-Reliance"

Waking up to life can be as though we are experiencing the planet for the first time. Some of us find awareness in noticing for the first time the luscious fragrance of a peony, the smell of a newborn baby, the power of a thunderstorm, the crisp air and anticipation of an autumn morning's rush hour, the awe of a spring sunrise. Stop and allow those experiences to come to the forefront of your mind each hour of this day. Feel the energy of being alive in the moment.

Meditate today on the word "awareness." Breathe slowly and fully, becoming still, and feel your breath in your body.

Write in your journal about awareness. What did it feel like to tune in to your awareness of each moment, of the "Now." What sensations did you feel when meditating this morning?

I want first of all to be at peace with myself. I want a singleness of eye, a purity of intention, a central core to my life that will enable me to carry out these obligations and activities as well as I can. I want, in fact to live in grace as much of the time as possible.
Anne Morrow Lindbergh, *Gift from the Sea*

When I read this quote of Anne Lindbergh's, the first thing that came to mind was what a beautiful mission statement she had developed! Wouldn't it be an extraordinary goal to set as the work of the soul each and every day? I think that, perhaps, she also speaks to a larger issue than just her personal fulfillment; rather a deeper personal ethic and doctrine of living that brings fullness to the experience of life. The goal is not to acquire, nor to collect, nor to receive the adoration of your peers but to, in retrospect, be able to see that you lived in grace as often as you possibly could. To *"live in grace"* is the outcome of inner peace. A *"purity of intention"* is the outcome of choice. To have a *"singleness of eye"* is the outcome of concentration. A *"central core"* is the acknowledgement of a soul grounded daily in the connection to a higher power. These are the principles of fulfillment that she chose to serve as her mission. What about your mission? Do you have a statement that sets forth your principles of life? Would it bring clarity to your purpose?

Meditation today begins with the word "principles." Listen to the chords of music coming from your breath...center on the harmony of your beating heart...go within and discover your personal code of living...

Write down the list of your principles that you set forth as your blueprint for life. Is there one principle that you can work on today that will make your day sing with jubilance?

Behavioral psychology is the science of pulling habits out of rats.
Douglas Busch, PhD

Often within the doctrine of our field, one has the sense that somehow how our work can be measured and taught in a finite way. "Yes, of course, you are doing this correctly." or " No, you should never have asked that question." I have always felt that conflict practitioners should be trained in introspection and conflict theory as well as their own personal conflict styles before any concrete application of process should be taught. Mindfulness, meditation, and personal awareness are all components of introspection. Practitioners should be aware of their own response to conflict before attempting to apply someone else's model of resolution. If we want to create a different type of interaction on this planet, then we have to drop the scientific behaviorism. While it may be true that one only needs to hold the space open and sacred for a resolution to occur, this would imply a couple of disputants that are primed and ready to settle given the right conditional surroundings. I don't agree. If we are not mindful of our process, we will determine the fate of the outcome of the disputes by the very nature of our questions, unconsciously eliciting the desired response in our *trained rat* minds. Daniel Bowling encourages us to bring presence to our work with conflicted souls at the table. If we are not present at the table, can we truly be present to the parties? Think about your training today? Were you trained in the skills of presence and mindfulness? Can you make that choice for today?

Meditation today should begin with the word "presence." What behavior is required of you to be present in your work? What behavior is required of you right now as you agree to become open and aware? Go to that place of inner peace. Breathe deeply and just be.

Write down the ways that you already perform your job with behavioral awareness. How often are you truly present in your work? Commit to being more open and present in your work today.

Just trust yourself and, then you will know how to live.

Goethe

It sounds straightforward: trust your work, trust your skills, trust your abilities. But to truly embrace that inner soul, and fully accept what we find inside is much, much harder to do. To seek that place of self-trust is essential if we are to connect with our source of energy. In my youth, I trained my mind to discount my inner voice and the urges of intuition I regularly felt. One year I took on an intern, a bright, quick-minded practitioner with natural skills and an extraordinary ability to question effectively. We always met before the mediation began and went over the intake from the case. After mediation sessions, we would spend 20 or 30 minutes debriefing. He would frequently ask me two questions. "Where were you coming from when you asked that question?" it was as if you were a laser beam coming from nowhere. I was not in the same place that you were. I want to understand how you got there." I could not answer him. The other question was, "With all the risks that you take, how can you trust yourself so confidently that you are on the right track? What if you are wrong?" Again, I could not answer him.

From these questions I became aware how my spiritual path had transformed not only the way I practiced, but also my level of self-trust and confidence. I discovered that my daily path of morning ritual introspection and meditation had allowed me to access a core energy that renewed me, and it cleared the way for information that I had no way of knowing. I frequently had words pass through my lips that had not crossed my line of conscious thought. I remember thinking to myself, "Where did that come from!?" I believe there is a collective energy that we as practitioners can tap, if we are attentive to the knowledge that comes from that process. If we are open, we find solutions that we could not normally access. I believe it is a form of spiritual intelligence, one that can be cultivated through daily ritual practice. My self-trust, the ability to trust intuitive hits from others, has grown exponentially. As a result of my introspection, I have reconnected with trust of the self and trust of the soul, and as in Goethe's words above, it has caused me to trust myself. I have rediscovered how to live in the process. Think about your level of self-trust today. Review your thoughts about trusting the inner voice.

Meditation today should begin with the word "self-trust." As you take the soft, pillowy air into your lungs this morning, let your mind rest on thoughts of inner trust. Feel the trust of your intuition, and of your ability to reason from the heart.

Write down in your journal that ways that you already trust your process. Now write down the ways that you can improve your level of self-trust. What is one area of self-doubt that needs brought to the light?

Unusual travel suggestions are dancing lessons from God.

Kurt Vonnegut

Have you ever just wanted to go to the airport, not knowing where you might end up? Too scary? Most airline families have experienced these unusual travel suggestions from the Universe while being bumped off one flight after another. My family and I had some of the most exciting times when soaring off to a city we had not intended to visit. It is in these serendipitous moments that life unfolds and brings opportunities of unplanned joy. One evening at Charles de Gaulle airport, after a 747 was canceled, and it was clear that if we were to ever see the USA again we would have to get to another city to depart, we made the decision to leave Paris by any means available. We were not alone, there were several other airline families in the same dilemma. We made pacts to travel together and my husband, ever the Captain on and off the job, took control of reprogramming our departure from France. We descended into the bowels of the airport to the train depot, bought tickets on the Eurostar and within 30 minutes were racing toward London with lightening speed. As we enjoyed cocktail hour aboard the bullet train, we celebrated our fraternity in the United family, bonded, and knew each other's stories before we reached a drizzly, cold London a few hours later. Still in the lead, Captain Bob led us onto the tube to our stop at the hotel. He talked the night manager into letting aircrew and ground crew alike check into dry, empty, quarters for the evening. We all met again a few moments later and enjoyed a meal together at midnight with our newly made friends. One thing you learn when you are an airline family is to roll with the punches. Many years later when the events of 9/11 changed the industry forever, that reality was brought home again. Stripped of their pensions after decades of flying, many airline industry employees had to learn to trust the travel plans of God in a more direct way. Trust in a higher power has been an essential component of finding peace in a terrifying world. Can you roll with your punches? When God presents you with new travel plans are you ready to roll?

Meditation today should begin with the word, "flying." Using flying as a metaphor for life, breathe into the stillness and let your spirit soar to new heights. Become quiet as your mind empties of fear, and you embrace what life unfolding has to offer you.

Write down the times in your life, when you recognized the need for a new direction. What do you need to do today to prepare yourself for the next unexpected turn of events? How can you remain aloft in the turbulent times of your life?

Though you have broken your vow a thousand times, come, come again.

Rumi

Rumi reminds us of a promise made before time began, that we are always welcomed back home in spirit. The promise of a higher power welcomes us back with all of our human frailties, again and again, regardless of stumbles and mistakes in the journey. It is a comforting thought. I think that perhaps the most difficult part for me is self-forgiveness. To release a deeply rooted self-hatred is only possible through knowing that we are accepted. Even though we are human and, therefore, break our vows time and time again, God will always welcome us back. When I am able to get underneath all the internal criticism, I find the root of the hatred is my incessant review of every error I have made. I am much harder on myself than my higher power would ever be. I know that no matter what my children do, I always love them. I am able to forgive them their developing nightmares that cross the boundaries of my pain and grief in releasing them to their God. I am, after all, only their earthly parent and in the spiritual sense, they are my brothers and sisters. "Come, come again" is an invitation of love to be extended, no matter what the past circumstances, no matter the current time. Rumi reminds me the promise of life is all about love. When I awake, I know I must reprogram my critical mind to love myself first, so that I can love others. I must make that promise first to myself.

Meditation today should begin with the word "promise." As you breathe in the promise of the day, remind your soul that you can stumble, make an error, and choose again. Breathe out the hesitation of the heart and extend yourself this day.

Write in your journal the promises that you can make to yourself today. Deliver on one of those promises before noon.

The Bible refers to God's Spirit as the 'ruah', the divine wind, or breath,
hovering over the primordial waters of chaos. [Genesis 1:2]

Brother Wayne Teasdale

Wayne Teasdale is a mystic, a lay monk, who lived his life within the cacophony of our bustling civilization, while seeking inner peace and communion with the divine. In his book, *A Monk in the World*, he wrote of his search for the divine within, while carrying on a very human life. In the second chapter of his book, "Intimacy with the Divine," he explains his journey. Although I was not introduced to his work until I read about him through the work of Wayne Dyer, I discovered that it was also my journey. Teasdale outlines, with great clarity, the necessary steps in the creation of a daily practice. The contemplative soul awakens to consciousness with daily spiritual practice and must pursue, with intention, a state of receptivity that can only be cultivated with consistent action. Teasdale's personal ritual of contemplative practice has many elements: "Contemplative meditation, which includes walking meditation, sky meditation, and prayer; 'lectio divina', or spiritual readings; contemplative reflection; and allowing for daily periods of stillness, silence, and solitude." Teasdale referred to the centering prayer, developed by his mentor, Father Thomas Keating, and noted that it always lead him to a profound form of mystical insight. I agreed to follow this path. The miracles that I have seen, and have been part of, continue to amaze me.

In the act of writing this book, quotations have been sent to me at the perfect time, books have been recommended to me by others, and prayer and the reading of other books have provided instant verification to me that I am a vessel for something greater than I. I bear witness that many others are traveling with me, some I do not know yet, but I awake in the morning excited with anticipation knowing that I will know them soon. I have been the vessel continually for the embodiment of spirit at the table of conflict, and I know it. For this reason, I am intensely passionate about the necessity of spiritual practice for peacemakers and the conflict practitioner. Your life will change as a result of this work; it is your choice as to whether you allow it to exhaust you or renew you as you bring peace to the planet, one case at a time.

I constantly have intuitive insights into the hearts of people, what they are going
through, and what they need. I seem to know these things without effort. I take
no credit for this...Contemplation opens the door much wider and gives me a
different way to look at the gifts of wisdom. It helps me experience this illumination
and realize it as a process of holistic perception that results from grace.

Brother Wayne Teasdale

Meditation should welcome a richer exploration of your soul. Delve deep into your dreams of peace. Embrace intimacy with the divine.

Write down all the ways that you have learned to become intimate within this year.

What plays mischief with the truth is that men will insist upon the
universal application of a temporary feeling or opinion.

Herman Melville

Cynics abound in our world of rational analysis. However, cynicism has its attributes and is a good quality for many occupations. We rely on cynics to be skeptical, to have basic distrust for that which appears on the surface, and to probe the facts and doubt the results. Without them, our world would not run as efficiently. Without the cynics, we would not be able to hurl men toward the heavens in spacecraft designed by the cynics and the skeptics. While the visionaries may have dared to go, the cynics brought the project to fruition. The danger in the universal application of one truth to another context is that we may miss the obvious in the development of the hypothesis. The universal application of principles, regardless of the discipline, causes us to be prone to tunnel vision. To draw conclusions from a situation in one context and then apply those in another can be a slippery slope of logic. While intuitive hits are dismissed as not originating from rational thought, they originate from an area of the brain that develops from creative process, rather than data based analysis. In the field of peacemaking and conflict engagement, we need whole brain thinkers. We need those who doubt the obvious and those who dare to go forth combining spiritual truth with formal practices. I believe that one way to have extra reserves of *knowingness* is to be open in every moment of encounter with the senses. We can accomplish that by building an introspective practice. As Aristotle taught his disciples 2,450 years ago, "Know thyself." The holistic practitioner can discern with all areas of the brain by developing a deep spiritual intelligence. Cynics are known for crossing the *T*'s and dotting the *I*'s; holistic practitioners add the "*I*" to mediation and stand in the "*I*". Think about your truths.

Meditation today should begin with the word "cynic." Explore the word this morning in your deep awareness. Does your negative chattering mind play mischief with your truth? Deeply breathe the cleansing air of the morning as you quest for process of your truth. As you empty your mind, find the peace that resides within.

Make a list of cynical or doubting qualities that you have. Make another list of intuitive qualities that are part of your personality. Identify one area of your life that you can apply more holistic processes of thought.

*All you need is deep within you waiting for you to unfold and reveal itself. All you have
to do is be still and take time to seek for what is within, and you will surely find it.*

Eileen Caddy

Eckhart Tolle, in his audio programs and books, paints a vivid picture of the frantic human 'doing'. "I saw all these people rushing from the subway through the streets trying to *get there*", he noted as he recalled his first time in New York. "Where are they all going so quickly, what is the rush?" I know what he means. I also know I am that person of which he speaks. We have been bombarded with so many choices that we cannot possibly slow down and enjoy the ones that are before us. People I know have expressed that same feeling of exhaustion as I have felt. In my haste to take all of life in, not missing one event, one chance for career development, I end my day flattened. I still strive to prepare that Betty Crocker meal that my mother slowly and lovingly prepared from her '*kitchen world*' of the 1960s and 1970s. We end up spent, empty and left with a feeling of want, of what we cannot be sure. Eckhart's work was the major part of my spiritual path in 2003. I listened to the CD's *Stillness Speaks* and *The Power of Now*, for an entire year during my walking meditations. This practice served to rearrange the negative thinking of my patterned mind. I never got tired of hearing his calm words speak to me walking through the falling leaves, the sparkling snow, the blooms of early spring or the warmth of the Colorado summer days of that year. The first 2 years of my journey were difficult. I found myself not wanting to continue and forcing myself each morning to practice the ritual; through sheer determination and the fact that once I say I'm going to do something, by God, I'm going to do it (one thankful quality of healthy ego.) I am so glad that my shadow self showed herself that year. In the stillness, I found a deeper life. Open to the stillness I found forgiveness. From the stillness I found my practice soaring. In the stillness, I found God.

Say the word "stillness" today as your mantra. Sit in folded peace on your pedestal of promise and repeat the word over and over, stillness...stillness...stillness. Connect with your inner joy, in stillness.

Write down three ways that you can be peaceful through stillness today, regardless of what is on your calendar.

Nan Waller Burnett

Conscience

Give me the liberty to know, to utter, and to argue freely
according to conscience, above all liberties.

John Milton

Conscience is the inner thinker. It also embodies the intention to be morally correct and have responsibility for one's own thoughts. Webster noted that conscience implies a feeling of obligation and a quality of character of right action. Our conscience is the voice that speaks in the stillness during the mental firing of rational thought. We vote our conscience in elections; we listen to our conscience every day.

In 2001, I was vacationing on the Danube River when the one-hundred-year flood occurred. The cruise director was from Hungary, not part of the same company that operated the river cruise, definitely not a graduate of conflict charm school, and no doubt had her hands full trying to handle 100 whining Americans. After a couple of days of being stranded in Regensburg, Germany, she was in over her head, and just shut down mentally and emotionally. One elderly lady, a diabetic from Florida, was in a melt down and kept asking to go home. The cruise director kept ignoring her, lumped her into the 'whining American' category, and paid no attention to her real medical needs. In military fashion, she retorted, "No, it is not possible for you to leave the ship. You will get nothing refunded." I could that see the elderly lady, her frail body crippled with her sincere fright, was going to go over the edge. I listened to my conscience telling me to disembark, call the American company who organized the trip and lobby for relief for this lady. At first I got the packaged response. Undaunted, I asked to speak to higher authorities and, eventually, they agreed to arrange for her to be transported to the airport for a return to the United States with a full refund. Sometimes we just need to listen to that voice of conscience ringing in our heads, and bust a few boundaries to do what we feel is right in a bad situation. Conscience is the voice of the rational mind, but it represents a deeper voice calling to us from a hearty soul. Uncovering wisdom from your spirit is the next level. How does your conscience direct your actions? Can you dig under the rational thought and hear another voice quietly speaking to you?

Meditation today should begin with the word "conscience." Awareness is bringing consciousness to each moment. See the safety of trusting the process of life. As you contemplate a deeper level of awareness ask, "Is there something deep inside of me that I am unwilling to see?" Today, bring awareness to deep conscience.

In your journal, explore the ways you can bring awareness from your spirit to your conscience of rational thought.

Something inside us can transform suffering into wisdom.

Rachel Naomi Remen

Suffering is prevalent in every human experience. As Scott Peck noted in the opening line of *The Road Less Traveled*, "Life is hard." Theologians of many faiths believe that through the instances of suffering we are presented with, are the lessons we need to explore and the endurance we need to find the answers. From these hard choices, we learn to traverse the raging waters of adversity and forge to the other side of inner peace. One of my mentors once told me when I presented a particular problem, "Ah, a great opportunity! What is the lesson for you in this?" Feeling my pain was being trivialized, I stood aghast at his insensitivity! Of course, in the end he was right; always in retrospect do we see the wisdom. The eternity of youth never allows us to see how quickly the life experience passes, opportunities for growth slipping between our fingers.

Suffering is never pleasant for anyone. If we are successful in reframing a problem into something of opportunity and potential growth, then time we spend under its burden is shortened and return to inner peace is then possible. A lesson from the daily practice of the Course of Miracles is, "Let me recognize that my problems have been solved." The lesson teaches there is only one problem, separation from higher power, and that problem has already been solved through grace. We only need to remind ourselves of this. One explanation that made sense to me when I heard it was, we only need to realize who we are and we feel the peace of God. As Remen noted, "Something inside of us brings forth the wisdom to transform us in that 'holy instant' of realization." When I remind myself of this, this trip to hell gets shorter, my peace returns quickly, and I can quiet my frantic mind.

Be ye transformed by renewing your mind.

Romans 12:2

Meditation today should begin with the word "suffering." Breathe a deep cleansing breath and know the worst thing that can happen has already happened. You only need to choose to rise above the present adversity and know that you have the ability to transform in this moment right now. Breathe in the new choice you have just made and feel peace.

Write down three steps to peace for anything that causes you pain today.

Service is a part of the rent we pay for the privilege of living on this earth. It is the very purpose of life, and not something you do in your spare time.

Shirley Chisholm

To be of service to others is part of every spiritual creed. We do not exist in this field of energy alone, and we must be available to use our gifts, talents, and skills for the common good. Being in service to others is about giving. We give because we can, because it is needed.

I listened to a radio broadcast on National Public Radio one day; it was a short documentary made by a college student from New Orleans who interviewed survivors from Hurricane Katrina. Rather than focusing on the devastating losses, she focused on the blessings. The student detailed instances of strangers who crossed boundaries to help others, many separated from their family members. She interviewed a lady who had 11 people in her van, five were total strangers whom she discovered trying to cross a partially submerged bridge on the outskirts of New Orleans. Enveloped in the arms of benevolent strangers, they found love extended to them, friendship, and a dry place to rest on the long journey to Houston. The lady pulled into the gas station just on the other side of Lake Charles, LA. A man at the next pump rushed over to her, asked about the escape from the city, and said, "You sit there. This tank of gas is on me." They traveled on to Texas and stopped at a Denny's. As the haggard 11 slowly moved their exhausted bones through the door, a retired man and his wife got up and told them all to order whatever they wanted to eat and something for the road; he would "be honored if they would allow him to pay for their food." The radio show continued on with story after story of strangers coming from the edge, wings folded under their earthly clothes to be angels of mercy to those who they did not know and would probably never see again. I felt deep emotion as I listened to these accounts of one's humanity to others. "Service to others is the rent we pay for the privilege of living." What a wonderful blessing of being human.

....

Meditation today should begin with the word "service." As you go to the stillness this morning, feel the energy that is coursing through your body, breathe into the mercy that you feel for others...breathe out the isolation of the heart...go to that place of unconditional love...

In your journal, reflect on ways you are in service to others. Today as you watch the hours unfold, look for an opportunity to serve others in need. Write the events of the day in your journal tonight.

A new scientific truth does not triumph by convincing its opponents, but rather because its opponents die, and a new generation grows up that is familiar with it.

Max Planck

It seems to me there is a basic dissonance between that which we are taught in our youth and the discoveries that are made during our lifetime. I see this reticence to embrace the unbelievable as resistance to change. Max Planck, a brilliant scientist of quantum mechanics, must have felt extreme frustration as he tried to impart his new theories to the old school of Newtonian physicists. Each field of learning has the same sort of dissonance running through the literature, regardless of the subject. Molecular biologist, Fritjof Capra built a bridge between biology and human systems in his book, *The Hidden Connection*, introducing webs of growth. It explores a hypothesis that all molecules are emergent properties of a system and that life has evolved from an unbroken continuation of an entire autopoietic network. All cells are dynamic with the ability to evolve in a catalytic reaction. He suggests this growth, this creativity of the cell, is a key property of all living systems. Incorporating complexity theory in biology, he posits that there is inherent creativity and the possibility for morphological change in all cells. Translation: we all have the ability to transform at any moment given the right conditions. Within the confines of relationship, our behavior is dependent on the internal and external forces of autopoietic dynamics. Possibility is another word for this phenomenon in our personal development. One movement on the part of one member of the system can change and transform the rest of the system. Do we have to wait for another generation to begin exploring and using this newly uncovered basic truth of human interaction?

Meditation today should begin with the word "science." As you sit in silence this morning, breathe deeply into the unknown and embrace the discoveries of your consciousness. Float in the stillness and be peaceful with your mind. Know that you have the desire to learn new knowledge and the ability to apply it.

How has your knowledge of scientific truth had an impact on your practice? What do you need to do to alter the process of your practice today?

To hold, you must first open your hand. Let go.

Lao Tzu, *Tao Te Ching*

Conflict arises because of an attempt to control. Every conflicted interaction, every communication is a subset of the intent to control and an exercise of power in the moment. The exchange of differences moves us to disagree, to vie for control of the argument, the outcome, or the person. In my experience, we control to make ourselves feel safe. When we are in control, we gauge the unknown to be manageable. When we win, we present evidence to ourselves that our point of view or reasoning is sound; a whisper of "I'm worthy. My mind is more rational," is reflected back to us in the victory. But in the quest for control, we trample boundaries, seek validation for correct thinking, and rob another of their point of view. Responses to this push and pull dynamic cause the other to withdraw, give in, give up, or fight. It is no wonder that an intricate dance of enmeshment arises from the interaction. With pained and bruised feet from this terrible dance, our clients come to us for help. As in the wisdom of the Tao, we must first release. Whether that relationship is in business, family, with a former love, an aging parent, or a neighbor, we invite our clients to disengage so we can escort them back into solutions they desire. When in the interactive dance with others, how do you perceive your steps to the dance? Become familiar with the way you control or respond to control in your personal relationships and then you will be able to recognize the dance in others.

Meditation today should begin with the word "control." Take in a cleansing breath and release the control of your lungs to expand to new depths. Open your mind and breathe in fluid thought. Breathe past the controls of your logic and settle into the stillness of inner peace.

Write about control in your life. How do you control others? How do they control you?

As long as you believe what you're doing is meaningful, you can
cut through fear and exhaustion and take the next step.

Arlene Blum

To risk is to take a chance of loss. Arlene Blum is a mountaineer who climbed Mt. Everest. For her risk was everything. She proved to herself that she had endurance. She pushed herself to the edge, risked loss, and triumphed over her body. Often, perilous journeys through conflict take us to the edge. This is true in our practice and for our own lives as well. I cannot possibly work with souls in conflict without assessing the minefield, or in this case, the *mind field*. I must empty my mind of my own agenda, invite the help of my higher power, and dive into the abyss of identification with the ego to explore my way out. I then have the courage to risk and to take a step into the d(anger). I have permission to move with confidence certain that, if I reach a wall, I can readjust and approach with a different frame of wisdom.

I once had a couple in front of me locked in an avoidance loop and going nowhere. She had taken over 10 years to gather the courage to move out of the relationship, which for her was empty. A series of illnesses, real and imagined, had tethered her to him as his lifeline and perpetuated their stagnant relationship. She was drowning. She vacillated between short periods of permission and long periods of pity. Unaware of the story of sadness in which he lived, he was confused. He continued his denial and his dance of illness, knowing on some hidden level that if he stopped, she would leave. Unable to move past the debilitating guilt, I decided to risk his mask of ego and urge her to move toward revealing her truth. I invited her to take him by the hand, sit knee-to-knee, and look deeply into his eyes. I asked questions which led her to praise him for his parenting of their girls, to thank him for 17 years of marriage, and to inform him of her deep sadness about his illness and tragic events of his life. The tears began to flow before any further words could be uttered from her trembling mouth. He, too, allowed tears to drain his broken heart; he knew what she was going to say. He listened in sadness as she continued in a prayer of her heart, and then simply said, "I know." His denial had been pierced in a way that he could no longer avoid. He released her, and they held each other in an embrace of deep appreciation. The ritual of dissolution was complete. The risk bore the fruit of resolution. As Arlene Blum noted in the quotation above, find a way, not only in your practice but also in your own relationships to cut through the fear and exhaustion, and risk taking the next step. Your life will have new meaning.

Meditation today should begin with the word "risk." Breathe full courageous breaths of fresh strength. Breathe out the stale air of the "safe" path to resolution. Breathe in the marvels of risk and know that rich possibilities await you with the release of ego.

Write of risks that you have already taken in your work. What risks do you need to take in your life? Write down your perceptions and opinions of risk. What is one thing that you can do today to risk your heart?

> *If you see in any given situation only what everybody else can see, you can be said to be so much a representative of your culture that you are a victim of it.*
>
> SI Hayakawa

Victims of 'group think' abound on the planet. In our youth, we are acculturated into the views of our parents and community through a normal developmental process. We then move toward adopting our own views and to being the masters of our own thoughts, or maybe not. I have been a member of a couple of groups that have altered my opinions on issues earlier in my life. Independent thinkers process issues with a more critical eye. The great political divide in this country has resulted from two distinct camps of group thinkers, who, spewing forth rhetoric heard over the airwaves or on cable news shows, often adopt whatever they are told to believe without critical thought. A requisite quality of a peace and conflict practitioner is to think outside the box of norms. Clients arrive in thought disarray, unable to find their way through their emotionally charged firing of synapses without guidance. A thoughtful line of questioning can produce a line of answers that are more carefully considered. We must also critically think our way through the literature in our own field. A multi-disciplinary field produces practitioners of an eclectic sort who addresses conflict engagement in many different ways. Which way is right for you? Careful consideration and introspection can assist in determining which approach to take. What about your own life? It is extremely important for practitioners to know who they are as humans before choosing another's approach to the practice of this field. Are you a critical thinker? Make sure you are not a victim of your group. Know that you are unique and worthy. Your practice will reflect a tolerant approach to all thoughts.

Meditation today should begin with the words "critical thinker." As awareness brings consciousness to each breath I take, I review my life. As I breathe out the unsure or cloudy thoughts in my mind, I welcome the fresh air of inquiry. With increased awareness, I see that it is safe to trust my process of thought.

As you contemplate your level of awareness, ask yourself: "Is there something deep inside of me that I am unwilling to see? Am I thinking through the logic with my own unique process?" Today, bring awareness to your thinking and process.

Let's put the 'fun' back in dysfunctional!

Merry Englebreit

Humor is a wonderful tool in the engagement of conflict. With a little finesse and alert social antenna, we can turn a conflict around with humor alone. It is a little harder to have perspective about our own stuff, when we are alone and mired in the muck of a down day. I have found that if you can sit down and find a reason to laugh when you would rather cry, the absurdity of the negative energy soaring into emotion can boomerang positive energy back to your heart.

After an unusually emotionally charged couple left my office one day, I sat sadly focused on my shoes in the chair, unable to move. My energy drained, I sat for a few minutes pondering what exactly had triggered my sadness. Was it their misery or mine? Suddenly, I thought of a time when I was in a therapy group around the mid-80s. The therapist had confronted me about my perfect makeup and persona and said, "You are like a Steel Magnolia. You're terrified of not looking good!" Speechless, I felt the blood flush through my cheeks and wanted to crawl under the carpet. In that moment, my mind tracing the root of the trigger, I burst out laughing at myself. Here I was twenty years later sitting with the 'shit fairy' as though it was yesterday! Not much has changed but the motive. Now I can let their sad energy separate from mine and choose fun instead. I still like to look good, only now I do it for me and not for others; huge difference! What about your life? How can you put the present fun first, and not the memory of your dysfunctional past? In review of the journey, it is good for the soul to honor and know that we traveled the path in a way that was perfect for our growth.

Meditation today should begin with the word "fun." Feel the corners of your mouth smile as you go to that place of memory. Breathe in honor for the journey past. Breathe out worry about the future path. Rest in the fun of the moment, just with your connection to the divine.

Write down all the fun things that you can do this week, to remind yourself not to take the journey too seriously.

Breathe. Let go. And remind yourself that this very moment
is the only one you know you have for sure.

Oprah Winfrey

Surrendering to the reality of 'this moment' is what meditation is all about. Meditation is the emptying of the chatter of the mind. In the connection to the peace that resides within the stillness, surrender comes more easily. With the practice of surrender comes acceptance of that which we cannot change.

Meditation was very difficult to make part of my daily ritual. As a control freak of over 40 years, I have mastered 'take charge' and multi-task down to a fine science. Surrender is not my reflexive move. Fight or flight is much closer to the first response for me. Through discipline of mind and daily attention to self-care, I have seen my life change dramatically over the last 6 years. As each day unfolds, I take note of the slight but forward moving change through journaling. My frantic life is not any less frantic but I can more easily direct the craziness and choose again. Letting go has become my mantra. Acceptance follows in tandem fashion. I see clients fighting reality everyday, as if a salmon swimming up stream- breathless, they fight against the current, flailing and twisting with no success. One cannot be an instrument of peace without first-hand knowledge of the process of surrendering. As they drag their weary bodies through the door of my office I must be the embodiment of surrender to be effective in bringing them out of conflict and into peace. While surrendering is less painful than fighting the current, to let go is very scary to a control freak. With my relationship to higher power being the focal point of my path, I have learned to trust that I am never alone. Before I could release my death-grip on control, I had to know there was a power greater than I. In that knowingness dwells deep joy. We are never alone. As Oprah noted above, "this moment is the only one we have for sure," but it is also brings immense comfort. Surrender to your practice, surrender to soul, your source exists in the reservoir of energy that awaits you.

Meditation today should begin with the word "surrender." Let the tension in your muscles release and settle next to your warm bones. Breathe deeply, release your tight chest, and accept the sustenance of the oxygen. Feel the floor beneath you as you welcome the magic carpet ride of surrender to new heights of awareness.

In your journal, write down five ways that you can surrender to your higher power today. Make one area of surrender your focus for this morning.

Freedom is what you do with what's been done to you.

Jean-Paul Sartre

Live long and prosper. The Vulcan blessing by Mr. Spock embodies the meaning of the word thrive. Webster defines thrive as "to prosper by any means, to grow vigorously." When I think of the word thrive, I think of one who operates on many levels, fires on all cylinders, one who is able to reach the apex of Maslow's mountain of self-actualization. To thrive is to overcome the hurdles of life as they appear. *What's been done to you*, no longer constrains the freedom of your soul; rather you rise above the circumstances of misfortune and own the freedom of release from events not of your choosing.

My youngest son is one who has chosen to thrive rather than be a victim of his circumstance. A premature baby, a result of an emergency birth, he was born navy blue and fighting for his tiny lungs to stay inflated, his very first battle with the *'done to you'* of life. He was late walking and talking, stuttered and needed speech therapy, needed help learning to read, had no social antenna for the playground at Montessori, and yet was in possession of a very high IQ. He was the very young victim of divorced parents at a mere 22 months old, had developmental lags, ADHD, could read faster upside down and backward, was known for low academic output, but a very keen sense of humor and a quick mind. When I looked at the mountains this child faced, I also saw that he was tough and resilient. At a very young age, I saw in him the guts to climb and never stop. I chose not to accept mediocrity from him. While on the surface, it seemed cruel, even to me, I knew from somewhere deep in my soul that this kid could thrive and could actualize in a way that would have Maslow rising from the next world to applaud his determination. I pushed him to excel, pointed out to him his quick mind, and underscored *his story* of overcoming adversity and trials. He left my house at 18 for college, but not before having a stroke. It seems that as an infant, in a compromised body struggling to recover from a difficult entry into this world, a tiny hole in his heart never had the chance to close. A blood clot was hurled from his heart to both hemispheres of his brain. Angels of mercy must have been standing over Taylor. He dodged two potential bullets of damage and recovered from the stroke unscathed. With only two stitches needed in his leg vein, the doctor repaired his heart, and he set off for college. He will now enjoy the success he was destined to achieve. Thrive Taylor! Live long and prosper.

Meditation today should begin with the word "thrive." Breathe deeply as you choose to change your focus and deploy the life raft of practice to change your state of consciousness. Breathe out the old stories and usher in the new ones, empower your soul to thrive.

Write down in your journal a list of all the times that you can remember that you have been able to thrive in the face of adversity. Think of a decision that you can make today to have freedom from what's been done to you.

Nan Waller Burnett

The journey of spiritual growth requires courage, initiative,
and independence of thought and action.

M. Scott Peck

We must always be in the pursuit of peace and in the dawn of each day reprogram our endlessly thinking mind. Initiative is necessary for pursuing any path of spiritual development. Christian contemplatives, such as Father Thomas Keating, view the journey to higher power as not a dual, but rather a singular consciousness with God. Fr. Keating believes that we are not separate or external to God; instead, we have an internal connection to God. He further notes that spirituality is a process of trust in God, and when we take the initiative to surrender to trust, we undergo a "refashioning of our being, a transformation of our pain and woundedness." This commitment to oneself and to the journey takes determination and the initiative of the heart. Another element of the path is humility. Humility is an element of introspective insight. Humility defends us from falling into the ego or self-deception. Daily cultivation of contemplation protects us from falling from the safety net of self-care. Taking the initiative to meditate and pray according to your comfort, your way, your time, your unique expression of higher power provides solace to the soul. Former Judge Leland Anderson once facilitated a session at the Rocky Mountain Retreat about the mythical path and finding yourself in the law. He also noted that the path is one of compassionate action and if we are not careful, the cumulative sadness of the work can slow down the road to joy; we must take the initiative to continue to grow through pain. Access your initiative, courage, and independence, and press forward with diligence in the care of the soul.

Meditation today should begin with the word "initiative." Settle into your skin with the initiative to reach down into your soul and unite with the divine...feel your resistance to release the control of the stream of consciousness racing through your mind...trust the path.

Write in your journal what the steps to your personal path were before this year. Now list the steps to your personal path today. Is there anything that you need to initiate into your daily ritual to make the journey richer?

Diversity is the perfection of the universe.

Saint Thomas Aquinas

Harville Hendrix notes in his book *Getting the Love You Want* that we seek out the person who helps us finish our issues with our parents. Opposites do attract and it seems that when these folks get to our table they have perfected the dance of dysfunction to new levels. But, perhaps Saint Thomas Aquinas is right, in our diversity we are the 'perfection of the universe.' Is it possible that we meet beyond the veil of remembering to find that perfect person to help us learn the lessons we need to learn? All relationships revolve around power and communication. The party who has the least amount of power tends to be a passive person, fraught with imagined and real atrocities, they avoid any confrontation, and in so doing they create a great deal of unhappiness for themselves. They add fuel to the fire of conflict. Clients avoiding a problem and the people they perceive have caused it, is the nature of much of the conflict we see in our work. Rather than dealing with the issues as they arise, the passive type runs. Passivity plays right into the hand of the aggressor and competitive type personality.

The laws of attraction activate both ways. According to the perceptions of the passive person, boundary violations are the central point of wrongdoing. Aggressors are drawn to passive people. Aggressors may test the limits of situations or others to see if they can bust those boundaries. Often this dance of aggression is unconsciously thrust into relationships due to learned behavioral patterns prior to the relationship. Passive people often fail to set any boundaries at all and may lack the ability to ask for what they want. They would rather let others make the decisions so as not as to assume responsibility if things do not work out. A victim stance in the relationship is often firmly in place.

Passive people can be intimidated by the actions of aggressors in the face of manipulative anger and feel quite guilty when faced with manipulative hurt. Passive conflict can be the most difficult to affect if the connection to inspiration with intention is not in activated. In the perfection of a divinely ordained moment, a line of inspired questions can uncover the true nature of the dance. When couples with diverse characteristics are dancing the conflict cha-cha, go within and smile. Angels are present; they just don't know it!

Meditation today should begin with the words "passive conflict." Go within and ask in what ways do you get involved in the passive conflict dance of love? Be still and know the answer will come to you in the silence. Breathe deeply and cleanse your lungs until the breath takes in a dance of its own.

Make a list of passive behaviors you have displayed in the last week. How can you choose again?

Nan Waller Burnett

Creativity arises out of the tension between spontaneity and limitations,
the latter (like the river banks) forcing the spontaneity into the various
forms which are essential to the work of art or poem.

Rollo May

Creativity is the soul's music, coaxing a melody from the mind; a choral performance of the unique human qualities bellows forth from deep within. Because the human mind loves to categorize and label types of thought, a natural process results, one that is linear and finite. When we insist on the black and white thinking of the rational mind as our only measure of data, we become the *Johnny One-Notes* of thought. We confine ourselves to one way of living, one way of being, one way of knowing. Whole brain thinkers bring forth a symphony of experience; an evocative creativity that seduces the mind to dance with the soul.

Rollo May was an experiential therapist. He was a master in the wizardry of psychodrama, integration of the voices within and other forms of cathartic release of human emotion. Psychodrama is spontaneous connection with the inner stream of consciousness, giving wings to deep emotion, opening the box confining the soul, and allowing flight to spring forth from the creative center of the self. With the release of emotion, the bonds of limitation are broken, and the music of the soul sings out through all thinking levels of the person, thus allowing integration to occur.

Webster defines spontaneity as "proceeding from a native internal tendency without constraint." The experiential therapist has no agenda, no plan, and no singular approach to unlock the satchel of sorrow that each soul carries. Instead, the therapist waits for inspiration, for an impulse, for the hair on the back of the neck to stand erect, and moves with lightening quickness to meet the emotional clue as it presents itself. Reaching down into the gullet of grief, the experiential therapist grabs the pain and turns the guts of the client inside out while holding them in a reverent embrace of safety. After the buried treasure is unearthed, the client can claim the denied grief and choose to strum the instrument of joy rather than hear dissonant chords of grief. Spontaneity is required of the practitioner and of the client. Together they sing the songs of the soul as they resonate from the depths of despair. Can you be spontaneous? Can you sing the songs of your soul in your life? Can you reconcile your limitations and act with spontaneous creativity to bring forth your art of the soul?

Meditation today should begin with the word "spontaneity." Silently sit in solitude. Breathe slowly and bring forth the music of your mind via the soul.

Write down any spontaneous acts of creativity that you have noticed in your personal life in the last week. List them on one side of the page. On the other side of the page, write down any spontaneous acts that you have created in your work.

*Those who do not know how to weep with their whole
heart don't know how to laugh either.*

Golda Meir

Grief can be a paralyzing emotion. The grip of anguish swallows the soul in a way which is often hard to transcend. In Golda Meir's words, one can find the promise of leading a life with the full range of emotion. She notes that living with the whole heart is a necessity. If one cannot cry, one cannot laugh. No tears, no joy. Most of us spend our energy trying not to feel pain. But when one recognizes deep grief, it is much more productive to allow the river of tears to flow than to squelch a howling heart. We process the emotion deeply and then it is released allowing us to feel the circularity of life. Jubilance rises from the sorrow to replace a grief stricken day with a joyful one. There is a line in Macbeth which tells us to express the grief in words— do not deny the grief, rather the flight of emotion is possible only on the wings of the words. Making grief concrete lays bricks of the road upon which to travel from misery to joy. The process is important. Denial of grief ensures the road will be long and hard. Grief rules the heart and cuts deep into the tissues of memory, eventually even manifesting itself in the body. Denial causes stagnation, the grief grows, and the possibility of depression leaves an imprint in the cells. Give yourself permission to cry loudly when the wave of grief attempts to drown you in misery. Give yourself permission to laugh heartily when the jubilance overcomes you in delight. Feel every emotion as it rises in your breath. Grief will no longer lead you into depression. As John Bradshaw noted in the 1980s, "The worst thing that can happen to you has already happened."

*Give sorrow words; the grief that does not speak whispers
the o'er-fraught heart and bids it break.*

Shakespeare's Macbeth

Meditation today should begin with the word "grief." Notice the memory of your heart as you think of grievances in your life. Feel the tingle of tears burst to the surface of your nerves and allow the tears to flow if you feel them. Let the sorrow escape from the memory of your mind and breathe a cleansing breathe to clear our remnants of grief.

Write down all the reasons you have to be joyful on one side of the paper. Now write down all the reasons you have to feel grief and sorrow. Compare the list. Pick one sorrow and choose again, make the sorrow felt and then know joy.

He who is able to love himself is able to love others also; he who has learned to overcome self-contempt has overcome his contempt for others. But the depth of our separation lies in just the fact that we are not capable of a great and merciful divine love towards ourselves.

Paul Tillich, *The Shaking of the Foundations*

Many people exist within a constant cycle of fear of performance, fear of criticism, fear of acceptance, or a myriad of other worries. The first step in disabling this destructive cycle is to afford ourselves the olive branch of inner peace and love of self. Why is this so difficult? I think even the most confident among us experience periods of self-loathing. This routine is a continual play of recorded tape, the recounting of disappointments or embarrassment in our personal history. When we play this internal tape over and over, we sabotage the chance to experience real love in this life. Real love begins with self-love. Unless we love who we are, we commit ourselves to a cycle of using relationships to mirror disappointment and shame. History is over. The prior moment does not exist anywhere in the present. The present moment is the only opportunity for self-love. Begin to build the bridge that seals the separation of the heart. Love yourself. One of my mentors in group therapy, Verna Salmon, uses in her work the phrase "Fake it 'til you make it!" You will see immediate results.

Meditate today with the thought of love for yourself. Breathe in affirmations of love; breathe out the loathing of a lonely heart. Breathe in the warmth of self-acceptance, and breathe out the feeling of separation. Give yourself permission to change your perception of who you are.

Write about the areas of life that you have not been able to embrace with love. In what ways can you honor yourself today? Make a commitment to find ways to embrace those unloved parts of you today.

Intuition is a spiritual faculty, and does not explain, but simply points the way.
Florence Scovel Shinn, *The Game of Life and How to Play It*

The great sages encourage us to develop intuition. While many of us are naturally intuitive, most of us are so conditioned to use reason and logic to evaluate incoming information that we have closed the door on intuitive messages. In order to cultivate intuition, it is necessary to make a personal agreement to succumb to silence, to be still, to meditate for clarity. Intuition happens as a result of connecting with a collective energy found at the core of our being. In the past, I have been able to "know without knowing." This knowingness is much easier for me to access when I am working, seeking solutions for others, than when I seek personal answers to the confusion in my own life. I give myself permission "to know" for the greater good of all my clients, but I experience a cloudiness in my thinking about my own life. How about your own journey? Can you receive more clarity today?

Begin meditation with the word "intuition." See where it takes you.

Write down examples of information that you have received through intuition. Observe any intuitive information that you receive this week.

A human being is part of the whole, called by us "universe," limited in time and space. He experiences himself, his thoughts and feelings as something separated from the rest - a kind of optical delusion of his consciousness. This delusion is a prison, restricting us to our personal desires and to affection for a few persons close to us. Our task must be to free ourselves from our prison by widening our circle of compassion to embrace all humanity and the whole of nature in its beauty.

Albert Einstein

Self-made prison cells can be unlocked by their maker. Discerning exactly how to dispel that optical delusion can be hard to do. We are taught that we live in a world of lack and limit. Our biological urge to win the *survival of the fittest* game, leads us to believe that we are in competition with each other. When we view our lives holistically, we seek a larger picture. Choosing abundance over scarcity changes the scenery. Gratitude for the abundance in life forces a different picture within the eye of the mind. The landscape is greener; the mountains, tall against the azure sky are calming; the lapping of the ocean more inviting. Consideration of Einstein's philosophy, that we are part of the whole, widens our view as well as the range of possibilities. His prescription for accepting ourselves as 'one of the whole', is to love openly. To have compassion for those who are not traversing the same terrain is the key to cohabitation on this planet; it leads to the creation of a garden, not the self-made prison that we construct in our minds. There is always beauty to behold. Surrounding us is an endless reservoir of love and energy from the collective of humankind. Your job in life is to extend yourself, expand your mind, and tap the keg of energy awaiting your attention. It has always been there for the asking; the choice is to receive.

Meditation today should begin with the word "holism." Take a whole, deep breath into your lungs, and fill with energy from your source. Expand with life affirming vigor and powerfully slide into your meditation.

What is one way that you can allow yourself to feel the collective energy? Free associate words on the page that come to you. Do you see clues for action today?

Come and rejoice, what was lost is found.

Il Divo

Rejoice is a word that has a spiritual connotation to me. The feeling of joy, the act of rejoicing is such elation, an exalted ride on the wings of an eagle. When my friend, Alan, passed away, I chose a lovely song by Il Divo for the memorial video presentation of his life. He led a life with such clarity, such wisdom, and for me to be present at his passing was a gift. As he took his last breath, a gaggle of geese flew over his home singing in harmony a happiness that was apparent to all. It was as if he were carried to the heavens on the wings of the geese. The experience reminded me of this song. My friend Dana remarked on that luminous day, "It was as if Alan was saying, come on… this is no big deal, I'll go first…no need to fear." The lyrics to the song "Rejoice" still resonate in my head.

"Where did I misplace my faith?
Where did I set it down?
How did I forget what this was about?
So, come and rejoice, come and rejoice.
What was lost is found; you don't even have to make a sound.
What was lost is found."

The lyrics are such a beautiful reassurance that we continue on, God is waiting for us to return. Complete with our diploma of life tucked under our wings, we finally realize the blessings of this life came in the form of the relationships of which we were a part of; the angels sent to travel with us on the journey of earth. Rejoice, what is lost is found. Alan was my angel, and he left many gifts with me before he moved on. He gave me my mantra "choose again." He made me understand that I am not my thoughts, that everything happens in perfect fashion, the people come to me on my path are angels sent to assist in the journey, and that life was meant to be joyful. Rejoice, what is lost is found. Bless you, Alan. You are loved.

Meditation today should begin with the word "rejoice." Give gratitude for the air that you breathe, embrace the breath and realize that you are living a beautiful journey. Sit in peace and feel the joy of the connection deep within.

Make a list of all the reasons that you have to rejoice. Remember these sources of joy all day.

The stream of consciousness resembles a river flowing toward the sea. The surface of the river stands for that level of consciousness that we use to attend to daily life…the river itself stands for the spiritual level of consciousness…we begin to experience the awakening of spiritual attentiveness…the depth of the river stands for the true self and the Divine Presence, the source from which our life emerges at every moment.

Father Thomas Keating

Ken Wilber notes, in his book *Spectrum of Consciousness*, the journey toward awareness is a multi-layered, symbiotic process happening on different planes of awareness concurrently. We expand and deepen ourselves not in a straight line but rather in a repetitive circular fashion. As Father Thomas Keating writes, in his book *Intimacy with God*, deeper streams of consciousness can be cultivated by realizing our true nature— at our core we are part of divinity. But we must first enter the water. The water is metaphorical for the journey. Wayne Dyer suggests that without the intention to self-actualize we often languish and do not complete the mission. Therefore, we must set aside those precious few moments every day to look beyond the surface of the waters of awareness, to become familiar with the ritual of introspection, renew our commitment to seek out our core, who we truly are in spirit, in energy and to intend to seek the depth of personal knowing. The masters above tell us that we are infants in development of the mind. What if we are now in a tangible evolution of the mind, an expansion of the processes of the brain to develop spiritual intelligence? If we are, in the extension of the mind, we extend the abilities of humans to make major transformative shifts in paradigms. Moving toward harmonic streams of consciousness, humans can move mountains, bring peace, and change the way we relate to each other. But, the journey cannot first be taken on a global scale. The journey, in my view, must be scaled internally by developing the spiritual relationship. Think of your streams of consciousness today. Are you floating on the surface of the water, or are you ready to submerge your intentions to the depths of your soul?

Our consciousness is as immense as the heavens above. Our hearts are equally vast in their capacity for love, kindness, compassion, mercy, and sensitivity. Sky meditation uses the image of the heavens, or a natural reality to achieve a spiritual and psychological realization. It is a powerful tool for reawakening.

Brother Wayne Teasdale

Meditation today should begin with the phrase "streams of consciousness." Go the place of stillness and breathe the cleansing air of the mind sweeper. Sweep through the floating thoughts as they journey from the brain and fire along the way. Feel the synapses fire bringing you awareness.

What images and thoughts came to you in meditation today? Write down where you are in your journey, on the surface, in the water, or connecting to your true self? What is one thing that you can do today to make that journey expand?

Shall be a dawn made of all the air I ever breathed.

Saint Geraud

I learned to breathe deeply at 9,000 feet in the mountains high above Denver. My physical therapist told me that I was naturally a shallow breather and I should learn to breathe more deeply to relax the muscles around a neck injury I received in 1994. This was my wake up call. Do you think I listened? Not a chance! It took me 10 years of wrestling with the injury, literally grabbing me by the neck. The injury proved to be one of my greatest teachers. I learned over the years to dance within the confines of the constriction. I now use that lesson to access a deeper consciousness. Conscious breathing heightens attentiveness and deepens relaxation simultaneously. To be wide awake to awareness and completely relaxed at the same time is the goal of the seeker of inner peace. The more you relax, the more you explore the unconscious. To bring alertness and relaxation together, is to be relaxed and conscious at the same time. While relaxing, we can breathe our way to higher states of being; to engage in full, free, powerful breathing and yet remain in a state of total relaxation, this is a fundamental step of breath mastery. The more peace you have, the more power. You will experience a true awakening to life and love, to joy and peace, and to your creative energy. Follow the path the breath takes when it comes into you. Clear the way for the breath so that it meets no resistance. Breathe in a powerful steady rhythm for several minutes. Open, relax and expand your chest. When you open and expand your mind through breathing, it resembles a dance, a flow of energy; the lungs are a partner to the process, instantly responding. This fills the space that you create with spirit. As you create a beautiful dance, open and expand it to the movements of the body and feel the energy coursing through the body... inviting, allowing, receiving, and accepting. When you open and expand your mind, the breath rises and responds to the flow as it soothes, strengthens, and calms your beating heart. I now know the steps to this dance by heart, in my heart. It is the dance of surrender.

Meditation today should begin with the word "breathe." Flow...breathe...dance...be peace. Rid your riddled body of tightness and open it to love and calm acceptance. Surrender to the breath.

Keep a journal of your breathing, just for this week, to become familiar with how and when you breathe deeply.

Nan Waller Burnett

There are three ways of seeing life. In one, people stick fast. In another they go to excess. In the third, they see correctly. In the first way, people take pleasure in all the things of life—in possessions and happenings, in families and continuation. When a teaching is proclaimed that advises non-attachment and going beyond the dictates of the self, their heart does not leap up and they are not drawn to it. In the second way, people are afflicted by hatred of life. Just as attached to life, they nonetheless revile it and make a bad thing of it to excess. In the third way, people see life as it is—forever being and ceasing to be. They accept it willingly but are not attached and do not despair. It is they who begin to know the unconditioned.

Itivuttaka Sutta

The life journey is about integration of all the parts of ourselves; deepened awareness of all levels of consciousness. As the Dalai Lama teaches in his book, *Transformation of the Mind*, deep concentration enhances our ability to control our negative thoughts. The advanced course for living is often brought on the wings of adversity, pain, and suffering. Within the constructs of the rational mind, we try to suppress emotion as an antidote to calm the racing mind. It is, however, the rational mind that needs to be controlled. We need to bring all emotions to the surface, examine them, and understand the reasoning under the emotion. Emotion results from sensations, triggers, and memory. It is in this state that our clients arrive at our door. Conflict embedded in interpersonal relationships, are always a result of an interpersonal trigger. Conflict lies in the perception of violation of some sort. These misperceptions arise from the constructs of the mind. The practice of discipline of thought produces mindfulness. Through mindfulness, we gain power over our mind, understand choice and can exercise control over the thoughts on which we allow our brains to rest. It is necessary for the practitioner of peace and conflict to be the first to take the journey. If the change completes the practitioner, the practitioner can change the field. If the field is changed, the world view is changed, one conflict at a time. I decided that I needed to give myself permission to complete my process by listening to the urging of my inner voice. Earlier that year, I had held the first pilot project, a retreat for practitioners. The words, "Change the practitioner, change the practice" kept running through my mind as I prepared the design format for the retreat. We can only understand how to effect positive change by understanding it first hand, through our own process. What do you need to do this year to become the consummate professional that you aspire to become?

Meditation today should begin with the word "integration." As you begin your morning ritual of cleansing the mind, breathe in awareness of all the parts of you. Gather all streams of thought into the inner sanctum of your holy soul.

Write down the streams of consciousness as they appeared before you. In quick fashion, make a list of words that are important for your journey.

In the midst of winter, I finally found within me an invincible summer.

Albert Camus

In the 1980s I was able to access the vision of my inner child for the first time. This was an especially painful although enlightening event for me. I had a vision of a little auburn haired angel with large brown eyes and deep sadness, too deep for a 5 year old. In that moment, I got in touch with the need to take better care of myself, for in many ways I had missed proper development. I had been going through the motions of life for 30 years and was not actually alive. This precious little girl was frozen in my adult body and fairly often throwing temper tantrums to get out of the prison of the interior. I buried one painful memory after another with a busy life and looking completely outside of myself for any joy and happiness. At the tender age of 35, I was stuck in the death of the winter landscape. My entire life lay before me, already looked over, a dead end road. I didn't realize at the time that I was just beginning. By going within and experientially bringing forth the great tears of the face of the angel, I found the summer, long and invincible; the place where the sun never ceases to shine. Have you looked to see the angel you are? Can you find that child and love your essence wholly? Hold deep reverence for the journey of darkness to the light of summer.

Meditation today should begin with the phrase "inner child." Turn back the pages of memory and envision the precious child you were. Place the honor which is due at the foot of the angel. Embrace the path. The path is perfect. Breathe deeply into your awareness and swaddle the child that is you in your arms.

Write in your journal the memories necessary to complete your tribute to the inner child. What is one thing that you can do today to care for the child within?

Stories are medicine.... They have such power; they do not require that we do, be, act, anything—we need only listen. The remedies or reclamation of any lost psychic drive are contained in stories. Stories engender the excitement, sadness, questions, longings, and understandings that spontaneously bring the archetype...back to the surface. Stories are embedded with instructions which guide us about the complexities of life. Stories enable us to understand the need for and the ways to raise a submerged archetype.

Clarissa Pinkola Estés, PhD, *Women Who Run With the Wolves*

People live in a self-constructed story. Sometimes that story was handed down by the expectations of loving and well-meaning parents, assembled from the ruins of a life they themselves could not, or chose not, to live. Sometimes that story was pieced together as a protective quilt of defense against the unknown. Whatever the assembly derives from, exploring narratives provide practitioners with a wealth of information about the people in front of them. Narrative language, rich with clues about how to support a healthier journey, how clients insulate from pain, or how they live their lives, provides threads that can be woven into a new reality, into a tapestry of a promising tomorrow. We agree to walk in our clients' footsteps when we ask questions that allow images to rise at the table of resolution. To be truly clear and present for our clients, I think it is necessary to uncover our own narratives, to explore the drama playing on the stage of our own lives. To be actively restructuring our own problem-saturated story allows us to move onto the client's stage with empathy and clarity, a partner in the transformation of their story. To truly understand another's pain, is it not necessary to walk the same road? Now as this spiritual path is nearing its end, how successful have you been at creating new narratives in your life? Has this made it easier to understand your client's story?

Meditate today on the phrase "self constructed story." Who is speaking to you? Breathe in clarity and understanding, and breathe out uncertainty and doubt.

Write a few lines in your journal about "your story." When asked "So, what's your story?" What do you say? How do you share your life's path with others? What is one thing you can do today to be clear with yourself about that story? What is one part of your story you wish to rewrite today?

What people get admired and appreciated for in community are their soft skills: their sense of humor and timing, their ability to listen, their courage and honesty, their capacity for empathy.

M. Scott Peck

The above quotation by Scott Peck reminds me of the qualities that David Hoffman and Daniel Bowling outline in their book, *Bringing Peace into the Room*. These qualities are the blessings of the peacemaker. Both of these gentle souls embody these qualities in their every day dealings with people. I think when people are drawn to this field they already have these characteristics in their nature. We often focus our awareness on what we need to do better or what is lacking in our job performance rather than focusing our talents and blessings. But I do not have the same presence that Hoffman and Bowling have. In my intellectual assessment of myself, I know that I have very different qualities; however, I can see with my heart that those qualities are as equally valuable. Humor is something I rely on in every mediation session I hold. Although my approach is not attached to outcome, I am very directive and use confrontation often when trying to affect a negative system. My approach is based on systems and chaos theory; my foundational philosophies tell me to enter the center of the scared circle to keep it flowing. I need humor to make that happen. If my timing is not accurate, humor can have the opposite effect on moving the system forward or giving it a well needed break from the tension. I have the courage and the honesty to be forceful in highly conflicted situations. I have to listen well in the beginning of the information exchange. I must develop empathy and rapport with the couple before the mediation begins. Without trust, they cannot place their faith in the process or in me to impact their system effectively. It has taken me many years to embrace my unique set of qualities and see them as blessings, rather than view them with a critical eye. I suppose that I am in that body of practitioners who are in the process of developing presence; cultivating the serenity I need to dance with other souls with less confrontation and more grace. But I am sure of this; my sessions are perfect for these reasons: I ask for a blessing before the couples arrive, I practice under the mantra of 'do no harm', and I go to the center of the circle with total concentration when the parties are in front of me. I do my best, and I have faith that I am working with people who have been sent to me for a reason. This is my blessing. Will I continue to improve my methods? Yes, I will. How about you? What blessings do you possess? Where are you in the developmental process of character cultivation?

Meditation today should begin with the word "blessings." As you agree to sit in the sacred space of your energy, breathe the cleansing breath of blessed oxygen for your soul. Go to the place of renewal when you can see your efforts as a blessing.

What are your blessings? Write them down in quick fashion. Give gratitude for your characteristics that allow you to be successful in your work and in your life.

The disease of self-hatred is epidemic is our culture...this disease has to be healed in some degree for the spiritual journey to develop because the spiritual journey is the surrender of our selves and of our self-identity. If we don't have a self, we don't know what to give.

Father Thomas Keating

Father Thomas Keating refers to separation from the ego in the above quotation. The ego, the critical mind, speaks with a critical voice; the spirit speaks from the soul. Self-hatred is pervasive in the human condition and blocks the path to spirituality because of the disparaging thoughts about who we are which leaves us feeling unworthy. I agree with his assessment. Within each day, every soul finds a little bit of heaven and a little bit of hell. Some days we are depressed. We are not our depression and to identify with depression creates a deeper state of depression. Depression is a wave, and if we stand firmly planted on the beach, the wave, the depression will not drown us. I always ask clients, "What is under that depression, what drives the feeling of the deep dark place?" Our identity is not what we do. Our sense of self is so wrapped up in performance that we place high demands on our abilities. Only those souls who understand they are made of and embody the essence of a sacred energy can master their minds. They are the ones who can say to the stream of negativity, "take a hike, I *am* worthy." Self-hatred motivates us to set trip wires that protect us from outside criticism, and it is no wonder, we already do a bang up job of criticizing ourselves. Emotional band-aids are carefully placed around the soul of one who thinks the voice to listen to is the critical voice. What percentage of the population has these bouts of self-doubt, and self-hatred intertwined with the psyche from time to time? 100% of us must choose again every day. Even the most balanced individuals, those with a healthy self-image, have moments of doubt and judgment, even embarrassment. We must go within, embrace the spiritual self and give it a break from the brain. Our brain serves us well. We can assimilate information with our thinking organ; we can make flash decisions, evaluate data, and use the creativity of the thinking brain to improve our lives and the lives of others. But we have made a huge error in thought: we think we are not worthy because we believe the thoughts we think. It is the great lie of the ego mind. Think of your sense of self and make another choice.

When you become the master of your thinking, you become the master of your life.

Ernest Holmes

Meditation today should begin with the phrase "self-identity." Mentally embrace your mind with forgiveness and cleanse the cells of your being with a warm breathe of absolution. Go within and remember the body of spirit, not the thinking brain, represents who you really are.

Notice the negative thoughts that came across your mind in the beginning of your meditation. Write them down. What is one thought that you could choose today to redirect your critical mind?

I was an integral part in each experience, but only a part, and the experiences were unspeakably larger than me...every single person and thing fit together like puzzle pieces gliding into place.

Margaret Stortz

Margaret Stortz's words rang true to me when I read them, and also speak to me of the Integral Approach. I find the energy of the whole inside of me during and after entering a deep meditative state. *Integral Approach*, pioneered by Ken Wilber, is based on an inclusive, balanced wholeness in which all parts come together to make a greater holistic experience. I could experience a calmness and peace that lasted for hours, no matter what the nature of the 'incoming' activities in my day. This allowed me to hear and act upon my inner compass. Now, I notice when someone is sent to me with a lesson I need to learn. I become aware of when people are sent to me for assistance. I know I am not clairvoyant. I am simply listening to that inner compass, the one that aims to my true north. I understand that we really do need each other through the journey. I would have never been able to be in touch with my inner compass without the ritual practice of meditation and self care.

Meditation today should begin with the phrase "inner compass." Find the energy riding on each breath and flow with the wave of air that aerodynamically lifts you towards your true north.

Write down in your journal the times that you noticed your inner compass. Watch for information with different awareness arriving this week in the form of the connected energy of all who you meet on your path.

All the troubles of man come from his not knowing how to sit still.

Blaise Pascal

Eckhart Tolle is a master at imparting the wisdom of the living in this moment. By focusing on *this moment*, the racing mind is trained to float and not to flit. By focusing in *this moment*, the stillness the body craves is granted just by the asking. I underwent a 2 month mental reprogramming by listening to Tolle CDs on my autumn walks through a wilderness trail. I noticed that when the 2 months were up, my mind wanted desperately to return to the mental madness preceding the trial rewiring. I devised two methods to refocus. First, I decided not to beat myself up for my brain wanting to return to that which it does best, race. Second, I gave myself permission to be human, to laugh at the simplicity of *"we are not our thoughts,"* as Tolle beautifully explained in *The Power of Now."* In the forgiveness of those acts, my inner critic is silenced. You see, I have this critical person who lives in that racing mind and tries to control my thoughts, many of which are negative. Much like the air traffic controller who speeds through the language of coordinating airspace or an auctioneer on clearing day, my inner critic wants to analyze and point out every imaginable disapproving thought I have and brand me with a scarlet B for bad, as quickly as the thought occurs. I used to live in my mind, unconsciously. Now I observe and do not judge the thoughts. My brain is only firing away as it is supposed to, synapses speaking frantically to each other. I am thankful I have such a quick and racing mind. Thanks to Eckhart and the simplicity of his work, I now have tools for remaining in the *Now.* Awareness is such a liberating experience. Can you stay centered in awareness today and return your thoughts to peace when the brain does its thing?

Meditation today should begin with the word "now." In this moment breathe in the peaceful thought...breathe out the frantic one...observe your mind as it want to write the laundry list for the day...forgive yourself...you are not your brain...you 'now' have power over these thoughts...right 'now'...in the stillness...in the clear permission of each breath...

Write down in your journal the thoughts that wanted to fill your mind when you sat in stillness this morning. What is one way that you can connect with the peaceful mind today?

Really great people always see the best in others; it is the
little man who looks for the worst—and finds it.

Samuel Taylor Coleridge

As a therapist, I always operate in my practice with the mantra, "do no harm." The golden rule of a psychotherapist is to never make a situation worse by your entry into the system. Peacemakers already know that in the work we do, conflict is the standard. We enter the system to provide the impetus for systemic change with the disputed relationship, whether business or interpersonal. I reject in theory the need to classify people. I must always search for solutions and I find that classification gets in the way. If I do not hold this standard, no solution is possible. I can see the best in others while at the table by choosing to see a deeper soul who is perhaps profoundly compromised with no skills to rise above the misery they conspire to create. If I cannot be hopeful, I will do harm to the system. I stood in amazement during one conference when I heard a practitioner give a detailed account of a bloodletting that occurred in mediation. He remarked that he "simply just let it happen" and took a passive back seat with the remark, "Well, it was their dispute and if they want to pay me for a day's work to continue to fight, I'll sit and follow them around the room all day." I think that his approach is harmful to the system and perhaps unethical. It is harmful to the practice. It is harmful to the practitioner. The work of conflict and peace building is more an art of creativity than a step-by-step process. If you look for the worst in people, you will find it. If you hold the belief that people in pain, on some level really want peace and may not know how to stop being abusive, you have a shot at changing the system. And you do no harm. What relationships do you have that need a closer look? Do you passively react in your relationships? Do you harm someone through passivity or judgment? Are you critical of your own soul? The principle of "do no harm" applies to seeing the best in ourselves first, and then we can see the best in others.

Meditation today should begin with the phrase "do no harm." As you go within to the silence this morning, remember not to harm your own soul. Embrace the fullness of your being. Breathe deeply into the collective energy that can renew you.

Write down any changes that you need to make in your approach to your job, your relationships, or your soul.

Nan Waller Burnett

Healing occurs when we begin to hear the dirge we sing and question its validity.

A Course in Miracles

Many shy from the spiritual path because of religious education and the guilt and shame it conditioned us to feel somewhere along our path. For most of us, our exposure to religious education is also where we learned values and morals. I think it is necessary to have a connection to our center, whatever form that takes. I found that I needed to reconnect to the roots of my faith. As we meet clients locked in conflict we undergo our own form of healing. We are triggered by the events and the variables of others' stories as they are recounted at our table. For this reason, it is generally important to heal before you can heal others. Admittedly, many of us may heal with our clients instead. To me, that is not really an obstacle. If I take the view the people before me are destined to be there, boundaries are well delineated between my triggers and theirs, and I can deal with my own stuff later, then I can hold the view that it is not necessary to be perfect before we begin to work miracles in the area of conflict. It is only necessary to be open to introspection and to embrace what is coming up for everyone at the table. When I do my review after the case is closed, I always contemplate the lessons I learned within, assess what I should look for or say or do next time, and then I handle my "stuff." If you find that you have been too busy to listen to the remnants of the dirge singing in the background, it is time to stop and carefully take note of the melody. Is it a broken record? Is it a violin of sorrow? Is it a cello of change? Or do you hear a trumpet of transition? Whatever the melody the orchestra of life is playing for you, see if it still matches your current reality? Life cannot be lived without our hearts being broken a little bit in every relationship. Healing our broken hearts takes time. Healing will bring the inner peace necessary to bring peace to your soul.

Meditation today should begin with the word "healing." Lift your open wounds to the light and feel the healing wind of energy flow through you. Open your mouth and take in as much of the soothing breath as you can deeply into your lungs. Listen quietly for the gentle melody of peace off in the distance.

Write down in your journal the healing that you need to have. List the people you know with whom you need to close the chapter of pain.

What it lies in our power to do, it lies in our power not to do.

Aristotle

The choices we make determine the quality of our experience. We exercise our free will each day. We have the will to choose freely that which makes us strong and healthy or that which is destructive and harmful to us or others. This act of freely choosing is what brings forth the genius, produces the uniqueness of each individual, and creates the soul in all of us. Our free will makes us human. Recognizing free choice is empowering. Often, it is necessary to make the wrong choice to fully understand the lesson. In my early years, I found it very difficult to forgive myself for making the wrong choice; I made a lot of left turns. My defense mechanism for reconciling this dissonance was to adopt the victim role. It was easy for me to feel like a victim. After many years of my self-imposed sentence in the victim's dark forest of pain, I became determined to live differently. I worked to find my way out through choice, roads leading in all directions, and through trial and error, I made my way back into the sunshine. Many people who I met along my journey are still in the forest. My mentors stand in the sunshine and beckon me to join them. As a therapist, it seems to me to be more difficult for my clients; there are so many more choices than we ever had in past ages. The joy of riding the wave of information results in relationships that lack quality because we sit in front of a machine much of the day. Hooking yourself to the computer can result in isolationism, loneliness, a deep emptiness that requires a conscious journey back to humanity. One intervention for exercising free will is the scheduling of fun; making a date with oneself to partake, to enjoy, to experience that which too many choices has robbed us of: human contact. Free will is always available for the exercising. Why do we find it so difficult to realize that powerful act of change is available to us all the time? Aristotle's wisdom of the ages can still be perfectly applied. What obstacle is stopping you from exercising free will in your life? What lies in your power to do, in which you are paralyzed to change?

Meditation today should begin with the phrase "free will." As you go to the place of peace deep inside of you, take a long slow breath of inquiry. Connect with the center of your soul and ask, "What is stopping me?" Breathe out the cloudy unknowingness and breathe in the clarity of knowing: Your free will always resides in your power. You only need activate the choices it will bring to you.

Write in your journal today all the blessings of freedom you have personally activated in your life in the past. In the next paragraph write down all the things that you would choose if no one had any input in your decisions but you. What is one thing that you can do today to keep a barrier from stopping you?

Nan Waller Burnett

There is a destiny that makes us brothers; no man goes his way alone.

Edwin Markham

I have always had a difficult time working in a singular fashion. It is not that I can't work alone; much of my time is spent within the borders of my mind, and I love solitude, but the work is a little harder. My output is so much better when I am working in tandem with others in a synergistic way. Synergy, as Webster defines, is "combined effective action, or yielding to energy without resistance." I love that definition! Yielding to combined energy is a perfect way of working, with no resistance. An agreement to flow with the divine is a wonderful way of thinking about synergy. It reminds me of a streaming dance of fluid motion. I have had the privilege of working with many exemplary individuals. The best of those experiences can be described as the fluidity of the dance. I agreed to co-present at a national conference with my dear friend Michael Aloi. We prepared for our presentation through teleconferences and by sharing our power point presentations back and forth via e-mail. The night before the presentation we met for about 20 minutes to go over the timeline. The next morning my body wanted to remember the jitters, well rehearsed from a lifetime of doubt, but for some reason, I was filled with a calm knowingness the presentation would go well. As we entered the room for the set up, an electric quality of synergy swirled around the two of us, and we performed a graceful dance as though we had been working together for years. I like to think the presence we experienced was because we were on the same path and we recognized that when we began to develop the presentation. I embrace the notion that none of us goes our way alone; a destiny greater than the two of us prevailed. There was a willingness to be present for each other and work together in the dance. Have you experienced a synergistic relationship with others along your path? As Edward Markham wrote of in the words above, is there a destiny that makes you feel like you have found a soul you have traveled with before?

Meditation today should begin with the word "synergy." As you inhale the breath of the morning, feel the synergistic movement of the body in the act of living and go deeply into the soul for inner peace and renewal this morning.

Write down the times that come to your mind when you have experienced a synergy with others on your work teams or in your relationships. What qualities did those relationships bring to your work or your life? What is one thing that you can do today to bring combined energy with no resistance to your work or your relationship?

*We either make ourselves miserable or we make ourselves
strong. The amount of work is the same.*

Carlos Castaneda

People have a myriad of ways of coping with the discouragements of life. Many of these coping mechanisms are harmful to our nature and our soul. There is really only one way to cope with sadness or anxiety about something, and that is to get to the place where you can choose again. Rather than face the fear of the unknown, many cope through the addictive use of substances, such as food, cigarettes, pills, alcohol, or mood enhancers, to dull the pain of life. Shopping, religion, relationships, work, and sports are others ways to cope with adversity. As Carlos Castaneda noted, the amount of work that we put into not feeling our pain is the same amount of work that we endure when we process our pain. There is only one healthy road to cope with pain and that is to work through it, acknowledge it, surrender it to a higher power, and choose again. Coping with life through addiction is manifested when you use something outside of yourself to soothe the pain. The act of self-medication produces an emotional dependency that leads to physical dependency through the release of brain chemicals. Addictive behavior is circular, looping in and out of shame and self-medication in a never ending cycle. It is important to note that daily spiritual ritual can become an addiction as well. I have known people who cope with emotional addictive behaviors by jumping straight to "give it up to God." One of the problems I have with spirituality, as a first course of pain removal without first processing the emotions, is that there is an inherent danger of spiritual bypass. When you jump straight to "give it up to God," you run the risk of short-circuiting your humanity. In a spiritual bypass, the residue of guilt and sin are left as an indelible mark on the psyche. We assume a posture of the sinner; we think we are flawed, and therefore, we lie at the foot of God and give the pain straight to Him. I feel although, in the end, that is exactly where we have to go, we must first recognize our humanity. Life can be painful. We need healthy ways to cope, and the good news is that each time we travel through the pain, the trip through the process gets shorter. As in mediation, the process is very important. Much like in active addiction, denial becomes the standard if we do not go through the process. As Joseph Campbell's noted below, in order to cope with life successfully; you must take the first step.

*I have found that you only have to take one step towards
God, and God will take 10 steps toward you.*

Joseph Campbell

Meditation today should begin with the word "coping." As you sit in peace, clear your mind of the clutter of the morning and look instead deeply inside to the core of your being. How to do you cope with adversity?

Write down all the positive ways that you cope with emotional events in your life. Now write down all the negative coping mechanisms you have in your toolkit of denial.

Start by doing what is necessary...then do what is possible.

St. Francis of Assisi

As the hustle of the holiday season, fades into memory for this year, remember your daily practice and intentionally focus on a new commitment to the path. When the mountain looms large above our horizon, it is easy to become discouraged. At times, it can feel as though there are too many hours in the day, too many reasons not to prioritize, too much work to begin. One effective tool in conflict resolution is fractionation. Try using this tool in your personal life. Find one thing you can do this hour to chip away at the mountain. Break down into pieces things that can be accomplished one at a time. As St. Francis counseled in the 12th century, begin by "doing what is necessary."

In order to scale the mountain, it is necessary to nourish the spirit and make time for contemplation. Open to your sacred place inside as you consider the mountain of work before you. You will restore the mind, the body, and the spirit. Contemplation brings the spiritual practitioner to direct awareness that cannot be attained through cognitive understanding, but rather through grace. Look at what is before you and see possibilities instead of burdens. Reflection, not analyzing thought, and intuitive questioning through the heart makes the path up the mountain visible. Accepting the reality of the tasks at hand brings renewed energy to begin. When we look forward, we break free from restriction into an effective, engaging path of action. Set the intention to begin anew in the coming year with peace and promise.

Meditation today should begin with the phrase "looking forward." Breathe in renewed energy for the journey and breathe out the hopelessness of yesterday's view...settle into the peace of the morning...

Write down in your journal a list of the tasks at hand. What is one way that you can fractionate the tasks today? Prioritize and choose three things that can be accomplished this morning and then review the day again in your journal this evening.

Live out of your imagination, not your history.

Stephen Covey

As professionals, we are in the business of assisting our clients with solutions of peace. The problem for many is they are currently living their history, their story of some source of violation. It is difficult to invite change to any system when the participants are stuck in the dance of repetition without knowing it. The question is: How do peace and conflict professionals intervene and transform people during the course of one or two sessions? The use of solution-focused language in the line of questioning can frequently bring forth answers that escort the client from the room of disaster to the ballroom of imagination. Stephen Covey has wonderful suggestions in his series of the 7 *Habits of Highly Effective People.* One idea to spark the imagination is to focus on a different reality and the reality is born in the action of creation. Imagination does not live in the past; imagination is an act of creation that is always performed in the present. To actively focus on the creation of another reality places the energy in a powerful mode. When the lens of perception is shifted, the focus of the eye sharpens to see a distinct picture of another landscape. Given the variables of each case, how can we know what questions to ask and when do we ask them? Spiritual practice begins with putting the state of your energy first through the act of renewal. Start solution focused practice intervention at home by intervening in your own life. Are you living out of your imagination or your history? How can you change the creation of imagination in your life? Adjust the circularity of the lessons that are presenting in your life by changing the dance step of repetition. If you can perfect reading your own heart, you can read the hearts of others.

Meditation today should begin with the word "solutions." Breathe deeply in search of solutions and seek your soul's code. Breathe in the words of the heart as you read the questions of the soul then imagine a different story.

Write down the solutions that came to you in your meditation. Live one today.

Compassion is keen awareness of the interdependence of all things.

Thomas Merton

The difference between cooperation and competition is motivation. A choice between the two, coupled with the level of avoidance, determines the approach to disputes as well as the outcome. But what conditions cause the constructive or destructive process of conflict resolution? Morton Deutsch, author of *The Resolution of Conflict,* said that all conflict is determined by the way that parties in a conflict are interdependent with each other. The degree of interdependence in a given situation depends on the state of the relationship. If the relationship is positive and mutually interdependent, then cooperation is the dominant approach. If the relationship is negative and mutually interdependent, then competition is the dominant approach. It naturally follows then, that one requirement for cooperative behavior relies in compassion for one's fellow man.

Thomas Merton suggests the awareness of interdependence is compassion. Compassion for the pain and emotions of the other party will determine not only cooperation, but the desire to be collaborative as well. Sympathetic attunement to the distress or misfortune of another is easy to do when one is not involved in the dispute. We are not so zealous about cooperation when we perceive that another is usurping our boundary or wants something that we perceive as valuable and scarce. To instruct parties to take a step away from the emotion and treat the problem as separate from the issue, was the cornerstone of Roger Fisher and William Ury's work in *Getting to Yes.* What about your own interpersonal conflicts? Can you easily step away from the emotion of boundary violation or scarce resource and be cooperative? When we teach those who arrive at our tables for assistance in the resolution of their conflicts, with what we have already learned, a path for resolution becomes clear. We then can become keenly aware of our own interdependence with the other. Think about the current conflicts you have in your life. When can you choose cooperation?

Meditation today should begin with the word "compassion." Go to the stillness of the morning and breathe in compassion for your journey. One who chooses work in conflict and peace building does not travel a level path. Breathe in comfort for your own process in conflict and breathe out the notion of perfection. Allow yourself to be human in all things and travel the path before your clients arrive.

Write down a list of all relationships or areas of conflict in your life this week. On the other side of the paper write down the ways that you can have compassion for yourself in the expression of those emotions. Find a way to recognize your opportunities for cooperation. Spend some time in healing one of those relationships today.

Destination

I always wanted to be somebody, but now I see that I should have been more specific.

Lily Tomlin

When we think that, perhaps, we have missed the mark of our potential, it may cause us to question the where we are now. Life is not a destination but the joy of the journey. I recognized quite early that I had an internal locus of control. Simply, an internal locus of control means that you feel that you have the ability to be proactive in your life: make decisions, shift course, choose again. Standing at the water's edge, one who is proctive can stand in the waves without being pulled down. In contrast, one with an external locus of control feels they are at the mercy of the tide: life does them, they don't do life.

I am consumed with seeking balance, and now think acccpting the gifts of each day is more important than grasping desperately for them. I have the luxury of choosing again, instead of being at the mercy of the tides. I now know and accept that we only need to show up and do our best. We have no control on the outcome of any given experience. The results lie in hands that are greater than ours. I love the above dryly humorous quotation from Lily Tomlin. It is so representative of the human experience. It gives us a glimpse of the divinity of prayer. It also says that we should do our part and ask. Think of your view of self against the world. Is it about the destination? Or is it the journey in which you relish?

Meditation today should begin with the word "destination." Listen to the bell chime... where is your spaceship taking you? Breathe deeply with wonder and anticipation of the journey. Breathe out the air in the deep black bottom of darkness.

Write in your journal today about your sense of self. Give form to the idea of who you think you are.

To your tired eyes I bring a vision of a different world, so new and clean and fresh you will forget the pain and sorrow that you saw before. Yet this is a vision in which you must share with everyone you see, for otherwise you will not behold it.

A Course in Miracles, T, *Chapter 31, v 8*

The end of this journey offers the possibility to review the completed path. This ritual of self-care has afforded the opportunity for introspection, growth, and renewal. At times, the voyage has been painful or a desire to take flight has arisen. The practice of daily attention with intention to your soul has also evoked feelings of joy and inner peace along the way. Devenio restituo pacis is a Latin phrase that means, "to come to restore peace." As the passage of one year gives way to the newness of the next, how will you restore and refresh yourself? How can you come to restore peace to your family, your work, your community, and to all global citizens? We all share this earthly experience where so many are in pain. We are one in purpose. If we are successful in finding the path to peace each day, and choosing again in our own lives, we can impart to others the way of inner peace. As the journey for this year closes and ends where the path began, the circle of all things living brings with it the hopefulness of tomorrow. Make a difference in your life today. Make a difference in the world. You have the skills and the artistry to do so. Share your gifts and come to restore peace.

[your] song will echo through the world with every choice...For we are one in purpose.

A Course in Miracles, T, *Chapter 31, v 10*

Meditation today should begin with the phrase "devenio restituo pacis." Settle into the crisp morning air and feel the anticipation of the New Year. Breathe in the regeneration of the winter's frost and the hopefulness of spring...exhale the cleansing air of sharing your knowledge of inner peace.

Review your journal this day. What will you take with you into the New Year? What will you leave behind? How can you share this path with others who may be pain? In the crusade for making peace in hearts and in the world what can you alone do to further the resolution of conflict?

References & Suggested Readings

A course in miracles (1976). Glen Ellen, CA: Foundation of Inner Peace Press.

Alter, R.M. & Alter, J. (2000). *The transformative power of crisis*. New York: HarperCollins Books.

Angelou, M. (1997). *The heart of a woman*. New York: Bantam Books.

Aurelius, M. (1945). *Meditations*. Walter J. Black (Ed.). Harvard Classics. Cambridge, MA: Harvard University Press.

Aurobindo, S. (2000). *Essays on the Gita*. Pondicherry, India: Sri Aurobindo Ashram Publications.

Ban Breathnach, S. (1995). *Simple Abundance: A daybook of comfort and joy*. New York: The Simple Abundance Press.

Ban Breathnach, S. (2002). *Romancing the ordinary*. New York: The Simple Abundance Press.

Bancroft, A. (2001). *The pocket Buddha reader*. Boston: Shambhala Publications.

Barks, C. & Moyne, J.(1995). *The essential Rumi*. Harper San Francisco.

Bartletts Quotations (n.d.) Retrieved from www. BartlettsQuotations.com

Baruch Bush, R. A. & Folger, J.P. (1994). *The promise of mediation*. San Francisco: Jossey-Bass Publishing, Inc.

Beattie, M. (1987). *Codependent no more: How to stop controlling others and start caring for yourself*. New York: HarperCollins Publishers.

Beattie, M. (1989). *Gratitude: Affirming the good things in life*. New York: MJF Books.

Begley, S. (2007). Train your mind chamge your brain: How a new science reveals our extraordinary potential to transform ourselves. New York: Ballantine Books.

Bellah, R. N. & Madsen, R. (1985). *Habits of the heart*. New York: Harper & Row.

Blum,A. (2005). *Breaking trail: A climbing life*. Orlando, FL: Harcourt Books

Birnbaum, P. Translator. (1977). *Daily prayer book: Ha-Siddur Ha-Shalem*. NewYork: Hebrew Publishing Co.

Bodo, M. (1995). *The way of St. Francis: The challenge of Franciscan spirituality for everyone*. New York: Doubleday Publishers.

Booth, L. (1999). *The wisdom of letting go*. Long Beach. CA: Spiritual Concepts Publishing.

Borysenko, J. (1987). *Minding the body, mending the soul*. New York: Bantam Books.

Borysenko. J. (1996). *A woman's journey to God*. New York: Riverhead Books.

Bowling, D. (2005). Who am I as a mediator: Mindfulness, reflection and presence. *ACResolution Magazine*, 5, 3-15.

Bowling, D & Curtis, D. (2005). The reflective practitioner: Advanced mediator development. *ACR Spirituality Section Teleconference*. Washington, DC June 2005.

Bowling, D. & Hoffman, D. (2003). *Bringing peace into the room: How the personal qualities of a mediator impact the process of conflict resolution*. San Francisco: Jossey-Bass Publishing Inc.

Bradshaw, J. (1996). *The family*. Deerfield Beach, FL: Health Communications, Inc.

Brokaw, T. (1998). *The greatest generation*. New York: Random House.

Brussat, F. & Brussat, M.A. (1996). *Spiritual literacy*. New York: Scribner & Sons.

Bryan, M. & Cameron, J. (1998). *The artist's way at work*. New York: William Morrow & Co.

Cameron, J. (1998). *The artist's way*. New York: William Morrow & Co.

Cameron, J. (2000). *God is no laughing matter*. New York: Penguin-Putnam.

Campbell, J. (1949). *The hero with a thousand faces*. Princeton, NJ: Princeton University Press.

Campbell, J & Moyers, B. (1991). *The power of myth*. New York: Anchor Books.

Capra, F. (2002). *The hidden connections*. New York: Doubleday Publishers.

Catford, L. & Ray, M. (1991). *The path of the everyday hero*. New York: St. Martin's Press.

Center for Mindfulness in Medicine (n.d.). *Healthcare and Society*. Retrieved on September, 2006, from http://www.umassmed.edu/cfm/

Chappell, D. (1999). *Buddhist peacework: Creating cultures of peace*. Somerville, ME: Wisdom Books.

Chopra, D., M.D. (1997). *The path to love.* New York: Harmony Books.

Chopra, D., M.D. (1989). *Quantum healing.* New York: Bantam Doubleday Publishers.

Chopra, D., M.D. (1993). *Ageless body, timeless mind.* New York: Harmony Books.

Cloke, K. (2006). *The crossroads of conflict: A journey to the heart of dispute resolution.* Canada: Janis Publications.

Cloke, K. (2001). *Mediating dangerously.* San Francisco: Jossey Bass Publishing, Inc.

Cloke, K. (2005, Fall). Why every conflict breaks your heart: Conflict as a spiritual crisis. *ACResolution Magazine,* 5, 16-21.

Cloke, K. & Goldsmith, J. (2003). *The art of waking people up: Cultivating awareness and authenticity at work.* San Francisco: Jossey-Bass Publishing.

Cloud, H. & Townsend, J. (2000). *Boundaries in marriage.* Grand Rapids, MI.: Zondervan Press.

Cole-Whitaker, T. (1979). *What you think of me is none of my business.* New York: Jove Books.

Covey, S. R. (1989). *The 7 habits of highly effective people.* New York: Simon & Schuster, Inc.

Crum, T.F. (1987). *The magic of conflict.* New York: Touchstone Books.

Dante, A. (Translation Musa, M.) (1995). *The inferno.* Bloomington, IN: Indiana University Press.

Dalai Lama, HH, & Cutler, H.(1998). *The art of happiness.* New York: Riverhead Books.

Dalai Lama, HH, & Chan, V. (2004). *The wisdom of forgiveness.* New York: Riverhead Books.

Dalai Lama, HH, (1999). *Ethics for the new millennium.* New York: Riverhead Books.

Dalai Lama, HH, (1997). *Healing anger.* New York: Riverhead Books.

Das, L. S. (1998). *Awakening the Buddha within: Tibetan wisdom for the Western world.* New York: Bantam Books.

Davidson, R., et. al. (2003). Alterations in brain and immune function produced by mindfulness meditation. *Psychosomatic Medicine,* 65, 564-570.

Dayton, T., PhD. (1994) *The drama within.* Deerfield Beach, FL: Health Communications, Inc.

Dayton, T., PhD. (1995). *The quiet voice of soul.* Deerfield Beach, FL: Health Communications Inc.

de Shazer, S. (1988). *Clues investigating solutions in brief therapy.* New York: W.W. Norton & Co.

Deutsch, M., & Coleman, P.T. (Eds.). (2000). *The handbook of conflict resolution.* San Francisco : Jossey-Bass Publishing, Inc.

Deutsch, M. (1973). *The resolution of conflict: Constructive and destructive processes.* Binghamton, NY: Vail-Ballow Press, Inc.

DeMello, A. (1998). *Awakening: Conversations with the masters.* New York: Doubleday.

DeMello, A. (1990). *Awareness.* New York: Doubleday Publishers.

Dyer, W.W., PhD. (2006). *Inspiration: Your ultimate calling.* Carlsbad, CA: Hay House, Inc.

Dyer, W.W., PhD. (2004). *The power of intention: Learning to co-create your world your way.* Carlsbad, CA: Hay House, Inc.

Gilman, W. (Ed.). (1965). *Selected writings of Ralph Waldo Emerson.* New York: New American Library Publishers.

Emerson, R.W. (1864). *Nature: Addresses and lectures.* Philadelphia: David McKay.

Emery, R.E., Ph.D. (2004). *The truth about children and divorce.* London: Viking Penguin Group.

Estes-Pinkola, C. (1992). Women who run with the wolves. New York: Ballantine Books.

Fisher, R. & Ury, W. (1981). *Getting to yes.* New York: Penguin Books.

Fox, E. & Gafni, M. (2004). Negotiating wisely: The third eye of decision making. *Dispute Resolution Magazine,* 3 18-22.

Forester, M. (2000). *The spiritual teachings of Marcus Aurelius.* New York: HarperCollins Publishers.

Frankl, V. (1959). *Man's search for meaning.* Boston: Beacon Press

Gibran, K. (1923). *The prophet.* New York: Alfred Knopf.

Gafni, M. (2003). *The mystery of love.* New York: Atria Books.

Gardner, H. (1993). *Multiple intelligences.* New York: BasicBooks.

Gladwell, M. (2005). *Blink.* New York: Little, Brown & Co.

Glazer, S. (Ed.). (1999). *The heart of learning.* New York, NY: Penguin Putnam.

Goldsmith, J. S. (1963, June 23). Princess Kaiulani Hotel Speech. Retrieved August 15, 2007 from Infinite Way Circle of Christhood web site: http://www.infiniteway.com/hawaiihoteltalk62363.htm

Goldsmith, J. S. (1998). *The infinite way.* Athens, GA: Acropolis Books.

Goleman, D. (2003). *Destructive emotions: Scientific dialogue with the Dalai Lama.* New York: Bantam Books.

Goleman, D. (1997). *Healing emotions: Conversations with the Dalai Lama.* Boston: Shambhala Publications.

Goleman, D. (1995). *Emotional intelligence: Why it can matter more than IQ.* New York: Bantam Books.

Guber, P., Isenberg, C., Jones, Q., Kennedy, K., Marshall, F., Peters, J., et al. (Producers) & Steven Spielberg (Director). (1985). *The color purple* [Motion Picture]. United States: Warner Bros.

Hanh, T.N. (2002). *Peacemaking.* Boulder, CO: Sounds True, CD.

Hanh, T. N. (2006). *The present moment.* Boulder, CO SoundsTrue, CD.

Hanh, T. N. (1998). *Teaching on Love.* Berkeley, CA: Paralax Press.

Hanh,T. N. (1992). *Touching peace: Practicing the art of mindful living.* Parallax Press.

Hanh, T.N. (1993). *Love in action: Writings on non-violent social change.* Parallax Press.

Hanh, T.N. (1991). *Peace is Every Step.* New York: Bantam Books.

Harp, D. (1996). *The three-minute meditator.* New York: New Harbinger Publications, Inc.

Harris, Rachel (Ed.), (2000). *20 minute retreats: Revive your spirits in just minutes a day with simple self-led exercises.* Henry Holt & Co, LLC. New, York, NY.

Hawking, S. W. (1988). *A brief history of time.* New York: Bantam Books.

Hawkins, D. (1995). *Power vs.force: The hidden determinants of human behavior.* Carlsbad, CA: Hay House.

Hendrix, H. (1988). *Getting the love you want.* New York: Henry Holt and Co.

Hillman, J. (1996). *The soul's code.* New York: Random House.

Hillman, J. (1995). *Kinds of power.* New York: Bantam Books.

Hocker, J. L. & Wilmot, W. W. (2005). *Interpersonal conflict* (7th Edition). New York: McGraw-Hill.

Hoeller, S. (1982). *The Gnostic jung and the seven sermons to the dead.* Wheaton, Il.: The Theosophical Publishing House.

Holmes, E. (1938). *The science of mind.* Los Angeles: Dodd, Mead, and Company.

Homer. (1950).*The Iliad* (Rouse, R. Trans.). New York: Mentor/New American Library

Il Divo. (2005). Rejoice. On *Il Divo: The christmas collection* [CD]. Sony BMG Music Entertainment.

Isenhart, M. & Spangle, M. (2000). *Collaborative approaches to resolving conflict.* Thousand Oaks, CA: Sage Publications.

James, W. (2003). *The varieties of religious experience.* New York: Penguin Putnam.

James, W. & Fechner, G. (1943). *Life after dark.* New York: Pantheon Books.

Jampolsky, G. G., Cirincione, D.V. (1993). *Change your mind, change your life.* New York, NY: MJF Books.

Jennings, J. (2006, April). The way it works. *Science of the Mind,* v4, 79, 104 -105.

Johnson, S. (1985). *One minute for myself.* New York: Avon Books.

Johnston, W. (Ed.), (1973). *The cloud of unknowing & the book of privy counseling.* NewYork: Doubleday Publishing.

Josselson, R. & Lieblich, A. (1993). *The narrative study of lives.* Thousand Oaks, CA: Sage Publications.

Jung, C.G. (1974). *Dreams.* New York: Barnes & Noble Books

Kabat-Zinn, J. (2005). *Coming to our senses: Healing ourselves and the world through mindfulness.* New York: Hyperion Books.

Kabat-Zinn, J. (1994). *Wherever you go there you are.* New York: Hyperion Books.

Kabat-Zinn, J. (1990). *Full catastrophe living.* New York: Delacorte Press.

Keating, T. (2005). *Contemplative journey.* Boulder, CO: SoundsTrue, Inc.

Keating, T. & Reininger, G. (1998). *Centering prayer in the daily life and ministry.* New York: The Continuum International Publishing Group Inc

Keating, T. (1995). *Intimacy with God.* New York: Crossroads Publishing.

Keating, T. (1986). *Open mind, open heart: The contemplative dimension of the gospel.* New York: The Continuum International Publishing Group, Inc.

Keen, S. (1991). *Fire in the belly.* New York: Bantam Books.

Kornfield, J. (1993). *A path with heart: A guide through the perils and promises of spiritual life.* New York: Bantam Books..

Kramer, J. (Ed.). (1997). *Roots of healing.* Carlsbad, CA: Hay House.

Kushner, H. S. (1983) *When bad things happen to good people.* New York: Avon Publishing.

Kyokai, Bukkyo Dendo. (1966). *The teaching of Buddha.* Kosaido Printing Co., LTD. Tokyo, Japan.

Larsen, S. & Larsen, R. (2000). *The fashioning of angels.* West Chester, PA. Swedenborg Foundation.

Lappe, F. & Perkins, J. (2004). *You have the power: Choosing courage in a culture of fear.* New York: Penguin Group.

LeBaron, M. (2002). *Bridging troubled waters: Conflict resolution from the heart.* San Fransisco: Jossey-Bass Publishing, Inc.

Lederach, J. P. (2005). *The moral imagination: The art and soul of peacebuilding.* New York: Oxford University Press.

Lederach, J.P. (2003). *The little book of conflict transformation.* Intercourse, PA: Good Books.

Lederach, J.P. (1999). *The journey toward reconciliation.* Scottsdale, PA: Herald Press.

Lederach, J. P. (1997). *Building peace: Sustainable reconciliation in divided societies.* Washington: The United States Institution of Peace Press.

Lederach, J. P. & Jenner, J. M. (Eds.). (2002). *A handbook of international peacebuilding: Into the eye of the storm.* San Francisco: Jossey-Bass Publishers.

Levy, N. (2002). *Talking to God: Personal prayers for times of joy, sadness, struggle, and celebration.* New York: Alfred A. Knopf.

Leven, J. (Director). (1995). *Don Juan de Marco.* [Motion picture] New Line Cinema.

Lindbergh , A. (1955) *Gift from the sea.* New York: Random House, Inc.

Lipton, B. (2005). *Biology of belief: Unleashing the power of consciousness matter and miracles.* Santa Rosa, CA: Mountain of Love / Elite Books.

Mac Kenna, S. (1952*). Plotinus.* Chicago, IL: Encyclopedia Britannica, Inc.

Martin, M. (1987). *The Jesuits: The society of Jesus and the betrayal of the Roman Catholic church.* New York: Simon & Schuster, Inc..

May, R.(1983). *The discovery of being: Writings in existential psychology.* New York: WW Norton & Co.

Mayer, B. S. (2004.) *Beyond neutrality:Confronting the crisis in conflict resolution.* San Francisco: Jossey-Bass Publications, Inc.

McQuaid, J.R. & Carmona, P.E. (2004). Peaceful mind: Using mindfulness and cognitive behavioral psychology to overcome depression. Oakland, CA: New Harbinger Publications.

Merton, T. (1955). *No man is an island.* New York: Barnes & Noble.

Merton, T. (1968). *Conjectures of a guilty bystander.* New York: Doubleday Publishers Publishing.

Millman, D. (1993). *The life you were born to live.* Tiburon, CA: H.J. Kramer.

Miller, S. D., Hubble, M.A., & Duncan, Barry L. (1996). *Handbook of solution-focused brief therapy.* San Francisco: Jossey-Bass Publishers.

Miriam-Webster Inc. (1992). *Webster's dictionary of quotations.* New York: Smith Mark Publishers.

Moore, T. (2004). *Dark nights of the soul.* New York: Bantham Books.

Moore, T. (2002). *The soul's religion: Cultivating a profoundly spiritual way of life.* New York: HarperCollins.

Moore, T. (1996). *The education of the heart: Readings and sources of care of the soul.* New York: HarperCollins.

Moore, T. (1994) *Soul mates: Honoring the mysteries of love and relationship*. New York: Harper Collins Publishers.

Moyers, B. (1993). *Healing and the mind*. New York: Doubleday Publishers Publishers.

Mulligan, R. (Producer), & Pakula, A. (Director) (1961). *To kill a mocking bird*. [Motion Picture]. Mira Max.

Myss, C. (2001). *Sacred contracts: awakening your divine potential*. New York: Random House.

Myss, C. (1996) *Anatomy of the spirit*. New York, NY. Three Rivers Press.

Myss, C. & Occhiogrosso, P. (2004). *Sacred contracts: The journey-an interactive tool for guidance*. Carlsbad, CA.: Hayhouse, Inc.

Oliver, M. (2000). *Thirst: Poems*. Boston: Beacon Press.

Ornish, D., M.D. (1998). *Love and survival*. New York: HarperCollins Publishing.

Partington, A. (Ed.). (1996). The oxford dictionary of quotations. New York: Oxford University Press USA.

Palmer, H. (1995). *The enneagram*. Boulder, CO: Sounds True, Inc.

Patterson, K., Grenny, J., McMillan, R. & Switzler, Al. (2002). *Crucial conversations tools for talking when stakes are high*. New York: McGraw-Hill.

Paull, C. (1998) *The art of abundance*. Tulsa, OK. Honor Books.

Pearson, C.S. (1991). *Awakening the heroes within*. New York: HarperCollins Publishers.

Pearson, C. S. (1989). *The hero within: Six archetypes we live by*. New York: HarperCollins Publishers.

Peck, M.S. (1978). *The road less traveled*. New York: Touchstone Books.

Peers, E. A. (2003). *St. John of the cross: Dark night of the soul*. Mineola, NY: Dover Publications.

Perry, R. (1987) *Introduction to a course in miracles*. Glen Ellen, CA Foundations for Inner Peace.

Pollack, R. (2000). *The power of ritual*. New York: Dell Publishing.

Plato. (1955). *The republic* (D. Lee, Trans.). London: Penguin Books

Quinn, G. (2005). *Living in the spiritual zone: 10 steps to change your life and discover your truth*. Deerfield Beach, FL: Health Communications, Inc.

Remen, R.N. (1996). *Kitchen table wisdom: Stories that heal*. New York: Riverhead Books.

Reynolds, B. (2004). *Embracing reality: The integral vision of Ken Wilber*. New York: Penguin Group.

Rogers, C. (1961). *On becoming a person: A therapist's view of psychotherapy*. New York: Houghton Mifflin Co.

Rogers, Carl Quotes. (n.d.). Retrieved on August 7, 2006, from www.brainyquote.com/quotes/quotes/c/carlrogers385131.html

Rilke, R.M. (2000). *Letters to a young poet*. (Burnham, J.M., Trans.). Novato, CA: New World Library.

Rilke, R. M. Quotes (n.d.). Retrieved on September 2, 2006, from www.brainyquote.com/quotes/quotes/r/rainermari147752.html

Rubenstein, R. E. (2003). *Aristotle's children*. Orlando, FL: Harcourt Inc.

Ruiz, D.M. (1997). *The four agreements*. San Rafael, CA: Amber-Allen Publishing.

Sagan, C. (1997). *Billions and billions*. New York: Random House.

Samenow, S.E. (2002). *In the best interest of the child*. New York: Crown Publishing.

Satir, V. (1985). *Meditations & inspirations*. Berkeley, CA: Celestial Arts.

Steindl-Rast, D., O.S.B. (1995). *The music of silence* [CD]. Audio Renaissance Tapes.

Smith, H. (1958). *The world's religions*. San Francisco: HarperSanFrancisco.

Stoddard, A. (1994). *Making choices: The joy of a courageous life*. New York: Avon Books.

Teasdale, W. (2002). *A monk in the world*. Novato, CA: New World Library.

Teasdale, W. (2001). *The mystic heart: Discovering a universal spirituality in the world's religions*. Novato, CA: New World Library.

Thoreau, H. (2000). *Walden*. New York: Harper Collins Publishing.

Thornton, M.. (2004). *Meditation in a New York minute: Super calm for the super busy*. Boulder, CO: Sounds True, Inc.

Tillich, P.(1948). *The shaking of foundations*. New York: Charles Scribners, & Sons.

Tillich, P. (2003) *Eternal now*. New York: SCM Press.

Tipping, C. C. (2002). *Radical forgiveness, making room for the miracle*. Marietta, GA: Global 13 Publications, Inc.

Tolle, E. (2003). *Gateway to the now*. Audio Book. Inner Life Series.

Tolle, E. (2003). *Stillness speaks*. Novato, CA: New World Library.

Tolle, E. (1999). *The power of now*. Novato, CA: New World Library Publishers.

Tzu, Lao, (1990) *Tao te ching*. Boston: Shambhala Publications.

Ueshiba, M. (1992). The art of peace. Boston: Shambhala.

Vanzant, I. (1999). *One day my soul just opened up*. New York: Simon & Schuster.

Vaughn, F. & Walsh, R. (Eds.) (1986). *A gift of peace: Selections from the course in miracles*. New York, NY: Putnam Publishing Co.

Vickers, J. (2002). *Spiritual paths: Peace*. Kansas City, MO: Andrews McMeel Publishing.

Von Oech, R. (2001). *Expect the unexpected*. New York: The Free Press.

Walker, A. (1982). *The color purple*. New York: Harcourt Brace Jovanovich.

Walsch, N.D. (1999). *Friendship with god*. New York: Penguin Putnam Publishing.

Warren, R. (2002). *The purpose driven life: What on earth am I here for*. Grand Rapids, Mi.: Zondervan

Websters Dictionary (n.d.) Retrieved from www.Websters-online-dictionary.com

Weil, A., M.D. (1997). *Eight weeks to optimum health: Your body's natural healing power*. New York: Random House.

Weil, A., M.D. Quotes (n.d.) Retrieved on September, 2006, from www.changeforthegood.com/articles/aginggracefully.asp

Wiener-Davis, M. (2002). *The divorce remedy*. New York: Fireside Books.

Wheatly, M. (2005). *Finding our way: Leadership in uncertain times*. San Francisco: Berrett-Koehler Publishers, Inc.

Wilber, K. (2001). *Grace and grit: Spirituality and healing in the life and death of Treya Killam Wilber*. Boston: Shambhala Publications

Wilber, K. (2000) *A brief history of everything*. Boston: Shambhala Publications.

Wilber, K. (2000) *Integral psychology*. Boston: Shambhala Publications.

Wilber, K. (1996) *What really matters*. New York: Bantam Books

Wilber, K. (1979) *No boundary*. Boston: Shambhala Publications.

Wilber, K. (1977) *The spectrum of consciousness*. Wheaton, II.: The Theosophical Publishing House.

Wilhelm, H. & Wilhelm, R. (1995). *Understanding the I Ching: The Wilhelm lectures on the book of changes*. Princeton, NJ. Princeton University Press.

Williamson, M. (2004) *The gift of change:spiritual guidance for living your best life*. New York: HarperCollins.

Williamson, M. (1997) *Spiritual principals: Lectures based on a course in miracles*. Audio tape. Carlsbad, CA: Hay House, Inc.

Williamson, M. (1994). *Illuminata*. New York: The Berkley Publishing Co.

Williamson, M. (1992). *A return to love: Reflections on the principals of a course in miracles*. New York: HarperCollins.

Winslade, J. & Monk, G. (2001) *Narrative mediation. A new approach to conflict resolution*. San Francisco: Jossey-Bass Publishers, Inc.

Wolfson, R. (1995). *Einsteln's relativity and the quantum revolution: Modern physics for non-scientists*. The Teaching Company. Middlebury College. Course number 152.

Zajonc, D. (2004). *The politics of hope: Reviving the dream of democracy*. Austin TX: Synergy Books.

Zohar, D. & Marshall, I. (2000). *Spiritual intelligence*. New York: Bloomsbury Publishing.

Zohar, D. (1990) *The quantum self*. New York: William Morrow & Co.

Zukav, G. & Francis, L. (2001) *The heart of the soul*. New York: Simon & Schuster.

Zukav, G. (1989) *The seat of the soul*. New York: Fireside - Simon & Schuster Inc.

Daily Readings (Alphabetical Order)

Artist's Statement

I am in love with the circle, the rectangle, triangle, and the line. I am enthralled and emotionally moved by textures. Through these shapes and textures I create the poetry of my life.

Visual art is the creation of visual poetry. Poetry resides in the heart and soul of every human being. It is the personality of the Creator that must shine through, so that a piece is not merely an object, but a personal statement.

I find me and I find God through my work. I am a conduit through which the universe flows. If I understood what my work was about, I would probably stop making it.

David Grojean, MFA
www.GrojeanStudio.com

After two years in the Marines, David Grojean attended the American University in Washington, D.C., where he received his Bachelor of Arts degree in Graphic Design. Deciding against a career in design, he attended graduate school in Boulder, CO. In the spring of 1977, he received his Master of Fine Arts degree from the University of Colorado and committed himself fully to the art of painting. David Grojean's work is presently shown in galleries throughout the western United States, Canada, and Europe.

About the Author

Nan Waller Burnett, MA, is a high-conflict mediator and partner in Dispute Resolution Professionals, Inc., in Denver, Colorado (www.disputepro.com). She is an Advanced Practitioner in the Association for Conflict Resolution's (ACR) Family, Training, and Workplace Sections, and has served as the co-chair of the national ACR Spirituality Section (www.acrnet.org). In addition to her mediation practice in employment and family law disputes, Nan is a conflict systems consultant and has facilitated and developed conflict management training programs in all levels of government and in small businesses. She is an experiential psychotherapist and, in her role as mediator, specializes in high-conflict marital mediation, divorce mediation, crisis management, post-traumatic stress disorder, and critical incident debriefings.

A dynamic facilitator, Nan has facilitated training nationally for many organizations and is an affiliate professor at Regis University in Denver. She is a founding member and on the board of directors of Mediators Without Borders International (www.mediatorswithoutborders.org) and has served on the Advisory Council of the Program on Negotiation Insight Initiative at the Harvard Law School. In 1997, Nan went to Russia and Poland as a Citizens' Ambassador for Mediation, and co-lectured at the Moscow State University School of Law.

In 2005, Nan developed the Rocky Mountain Retreat, teaching Holistic and Reflective Practice to conflict practitioners and peacebuilders. In 1998 and 2001 respectively, she co-developed the curricula for the co-parenting education programs In the Best Interests of the Children and Growing through Conflict. *Calm in the Face of the Storm: Spiritual Daily Practice for the Peacemaker* is her first book (www.calminthefaceofthestorm.com). Nan enjoys life in a very spiritual part of the earth...Golden, Colorado with her family and a wonderful family of friends.

Order additional copies of

Calm in the Face of the Storm

Spiritual Daily Practice for the Peacemaker

DRP Publishers
1746 Cole Boulevard
Building 21, Suite 295
Golden, CO 80401
303~273~0459
www.calminthefaceofthestorm.com

info@calminthefaceofthestorm.com

DRP Publishers

Devenio Restituo Pacis

Additional Endorsements for Nan Waller Burnett

"Sometimes in life we find ourselves blessed by the presence of angels, people who bring us wisdom, insight, direction, and great joy. Nan Waller Burnett is an angel in my life, and with this book, she offers her glorious vision and inspiration to us all. I can't encourage you strongly enough to let this fiery angel into your life. You will be so thankful for her guidance."

Erica Ariel Fox, JD Lecturer, Harvard Law School, Director, Harvard Negotiation Insight Initiative

"To work with Nan is exhilarating. Her work reveals the insight of a gifted counselor and the skills of a master mediator. She teaches with such passion. To work with her has been a true blessing."

Michael John Aloi, Esq. Lawyer-Mediator, Manchin & Aloi, PC, West Virginia Bar Association former President 2002-2003. Co-Chair Spirituality Section~ ACR

"Nan Waller Burnett is possessed of some kind of divine madness which drives her relentlessly forward with courage, confidence and joy while the rest of us are still bent over trying to tie our shoes. Though she is a brilliant theorist of the human condition armed with a sharp intellect, she has a heart as warm and enveloping as a home-made quilt. Nan loves a challenge. Nan is drawn to the fire of conflict as casually as the rest of us would dip our feet in a cool stream on a summer day. She is a fearless mediator whose passion for her work and the people she encounters in her work raises the bar for mediators everywhere. The words of this book are challenging and inspiring, but the person behind these words is a one-of-a-kind treasure. Her wisdom, zeal and passion have propelled her to the front of the pack. It's time for everyone to finish tightening their laces and catch-up."

Hon. Leland P. Anderson (Ret.) served for ten years as a District Court Judge in Colorado. He is now employed as an arbiter with Judicial Arbiter Group in Denver, Colorado. He is a past president of the Colorado Trial Lawyers Association and has received the nationally prestigious Trial Lawyer of the Year award from Trial Lawyers for Public Justice.

"Nan Waller Burnett is a remarkable woman and I'm elated that she is sharing her insights and knowledge with us. As someone who has worked with her as a mediator, trainer, and business partner, I cherish this publication."

Charles A Turnbo, MSW, Mediator and Author

"Nan brings her compassionate and spirit-filled essence to her work as a mediator and peacemaker, aiding her clients in finding their way out of chaos and conflict to peace and understanding. Excellence and caring epitomize all that she does."

Christine A. Coates, J.D., mediator and co-author of *Learning from Divorce: How to Take Responsibility, Stop the Blame, and Move On.*

Calm in the Face of the Storm

Spiritual Daily Practice for the Peacemaker

This book is meant to live on the bedside table and to be read only one topic at a time. It is a touchstone, a reminder to reflect, to invite stillness and mindfulness, to feel your feelings, to prompt you to schedule fun, to laugh, and to bolster your boundaries each and every day. When I first undertook the assignment of maintaining a daily path, I expected the task to be laborious. It proved to be the most important fifteen minutes I spent every day. Since then, I have been able to maintain sanity and strength. My hope is that it will provide the same for you. A few words about the term "spirituality": I welcome all people on their path to their source, the inner journey, whatever that means for each individual. My intention is to provide a welcoming dialogue for all seekers, with no exclusions. If your work is in human relationships, peace, conflict, or conciliation, with patients, employees, or citizens—or you simply want peace on the planet—this book is meant for you.

Endorsements for *Calm in the Face of the Storm* and Nan Burnett

"The ADR field has been waiting for a book such as this. Brilliantly and soulfully, Nan Waller Burnett personally invites every person dedicated to the work of conflict resolution and transformation to a daily practice of working for inner peace by nourishing our own souls, and she provides an elegant and simple method for doing so on a daily basis. This refreshing and very practical book is a must have for every mediator and change agent interested in true peace."

Louise Phipps Senft, Esq. Mediator and Conflict Transformation expert, Author, Associate at the Institute for the Study of Conflict Transformation; Faculty at Harvard Law School Program on Negotiation Insight Initiative and University of Maryland Law School, Principle-Baltimore Mediation

"Too often, conflict resolution is something we do -- a series of moves or a collection of words. Our moves and words may be good, but seeing through this constricted prism is paradoxically the source of all conflict. Nan offers a guide to remind us that true peacemaking belongs to a field of communication, and so do we. Committing ourselves daily to Nan's beautifully inviting, warmly engaging practices allows us to abide in that field. Abiding in that field, we are peace."

Daniel Bowling, JD, co-author/co-editor, *Bringing Peace into the Room*, and Mediator, US District Court, San Francisco